TEHRAN BLUES

Kaveh Basmenji

TEHRAN BLUES

How Iranian Youth Rebelled
Against Iran's Founding Fathers

SAQI

British Library Cataloguing-in-Publication Data
A catalogue record for this book is available from the British Library

ISBN 0-86356-582-4
EAN 9-780863-565823

This edition first published 2005

SAQI
26 Westbourne Grove
London W2 5RH
www.saqibooks.com

To the memory of
Babk Dakhili

and to my schoolmates at
Kharazmi highschool

Each in my fond affections claim'd a part,
But none discern'd the secret of my heart.
Mowlana Jalaloddin Balkhi (Rumi)
(Translated by Sir William Jones)

Yet Ah, that Spring should vanish with the Rose!
That Youth's sweet-scented manuscript should close!
The Nightingale that in the branches sang,
Ah whence, and whither flown again, who knows!
Rubaiyat of Omar Khayyam
(Translated by Edward Fitzgerald)

Acknowledgements

In writing a book on Iranian youth, I should first of all thank dozens of young men and women who shared with me their viewpoints and experiences of living in present-day Iran. I would also like to thank all the experts and analysts who gave me interviews, including Jamshid Arjomand, Dr Sadeq Zibakalam, Mohammad Qaed, Nima Rashedan and Sina Motallebi.

I am also deeply grateful to William A. Samii and Golnaz Esfandiari of Radio Free Europe/Radio Liberty, who provided me with valuable information. Furthermore, I have greatly benefited from the works of Homa Katouzian, Dr Ali Behzadi and Dariush Sajjadi, whom I would like to thank sincerely.

My gratitude goes also to Amir Mosaddeq Katouzian who has been a precious source of information and support, as well as to Mohammad Mehdi Khalaji and his colleagues at Radio Farda.

Farzaneh Rezaei has been a great help for me with statistical data, and Nima and Maryam have given me insight into the formative years of the 'children of the revolution'.

I deeply appreciate the encouragement and professional advice of my old friend Afshin Molavi.

And finally, I would like to extend my thanks to the editors at Saqi, who have worked closely with me to make this book a good read as well as a reliable work of reference.

Contents

Elephant in the Dark

My concern is that we might not be able to respond to the new demands of the younger generation, and might therefore be faced with a crisis of legitimacy ... Our country's population has suddenly become younger and this will undoubtedly give rise to new requirements, attitudes, and values. Our duty is to link up the demands of this generation with those of the previous one ... Unfortunately, because we do not know enough about our young people, we look upon this development in the composition of the population with suspicion and with an expectation that we will have to confront the values of this younger generation. In the midst of this, ideological and factional attachments are in the process of taking shape. One faction might accommodate these changes in values, and another group might not be able to keep up with them.

Ali Rabii, Presidential Advisor on Social Issues and former Deputy Intelligence Minister, 1999

Thank God that with the growth of liberalism and fun-loving and pansyism, and with the spreading of moral deviations and social corruptions, the present generation is corrupt and not terrorist ... Thank God that with the death of the reforms, people's remaining hopes of religious intellectuals have faded away, so that they are now seeking a personal religion, and a social life based on rational and human-rights principles, and are not willing to sacrifice their lives for their religion or country.

Ebrahim Nabavi, satirist and writer, 2004

> *The youth play a vital role in transforming the society into a dynamic nation ... The blessings of the Islamic Revolution have fostered pious relations between the faithful and almighty Allah ... and it is due to this sacred relation that the Islamic state has as its treasured asset a unique younger generation.*
>
> Ayatollah Ali Khamenei, Iran's Supreme Leader, 2000

> *On a daily basis, our youth are pushing the envelope in their quest for self-empowerment ... Indeed, no generation in our history has been as politically aware as is today's.*
>
> Prince Reza Pahlavi, *Winds of Change*

> *Today's youth are totally indifferent towards politics, culture and society. If I pour a gallon of petrol on myself and set myself on fire in the classroom, none of my pupils will even turn to look.*
>
> Sadeq Zibakalam, Professor of political science at Tehran University, 2004

A familiar scene for many residents of Tehran:

Every weekday, hundreds of worried parents and relatives swarm outside a building in one of the capital's streets to find out if their children are held in custody for breaking 'moral laws' of the Islamic state. Just in case, they come with ready cash and their own real estate deeds, or those borrowed from friends or relations, with which to bail out their children. A revolutionary guard in olive-green uniform and a five-day stubble comes out of the grey marble building, calling the name of one of the arrested youngsters. The parents are then admitted into the building, where they are taken to a courtroom presided over by a clergyman, who cites the charges against their child and the penalty or bail to be paid to have him or her released. He has already tried and convicted the detainee, as in Iran's judicial system, plaintiff, prosecutor and judge are one and the same.

Besides paying a fine or depositing bail, the convicted young men and women are usually asked to sign a letter of repentance, making an oath not to repeat the offence again, before being allowed to go.

And their offences?

'Moral crimes', ranging from wearing make-up for girls – with certain amounts of fine for nail varnish, lipstick, eye shadow and so on – to attending parties where loud music is played, or alcohol is drunk, or the opposite sexes mix.

The indicted are either arrested on the streets or parks while walking with a friend of the opposite sex, or in parties raided by members of the paramilitary Basij force – hard-line religious boys of roughly their own age, armed with handcuffs and AK-47 automatic rifles.

The arrested youngsters are often abused and humiliated by the Basijis on their way to overnight detention in prison. While in the building, they are put into collective 'cells', sometimes sharing them with other detainees, including prostitutes, drug peddlers or drug users.

Upon leaving the premises, however, most of the released youngsters are defiant and derisive; their parents openly swear at the authorities and at the same time blame their own kids for not having been cautious enough.

The so-called Special Court to Fight Social Vice is but one example of the dilemma surrounding Iran's religious establishment in dealing with a young population that is not willing to cope with dictated 'values'. After twenty-five years of indoctrination in schools and universities, and non-stop propaganda by state media, the number of people taken to the court has only multiplied each year.

Ironically, the location of the court also epitomises another dilemma that Iran's clerical rulers have been grappling with for a long time. The street in central-north Tehran on which the court is located has been at the centre of a political row between Iran and Egypt. Still called Vozara ('Minister's') Street – a name that predates the Islamic Revolution of 1979 – the official name of the street is Khaled Eslamboli, after the Islamist militant officer who assassinated Egyptian President Anwar Sadat in 1981. The name of the street, a relic of the days when revolutionary Iran was energetically undermining pro-American Middle East states, has ever since been a major obstacle in the way of a rapprochement between the two countries, even after President Mohammad Khatami announced a new foreign policy aimed at defusing tension in 1997. Even in early 2004, threats by hard-line militants – including Basij members – prevented Tehran's conservative-dominated City Council from changing the name of the street to Intifada (the Palestinians' uprising against Israel), a move aimed to better the country's ties with Egypt while showing it was still committed to 'revolutionary values'.

Nevertheless, for thousands of youngsters who every day stroll up and down this street, share a cappuccino with a friend in one of its numerous coffee shops, look for a potential partner in the peaceful shadows of the nearby Saei Park, or just happen to pass through the street on their way to work or study, it is still Vozara.

But like so many other social phenomena in Iran, and despite what casual observers may maintain, this does not reflect an overt political defiance. It is true that many of the streets and squares that were re-baptised after the 1979 Revolution, in a bout of anti-monarchical, anti-imperialist fever, are still called by their old names. But it is also true that several 'new' names have indeed caught on. Almost no one any more calls Azadi ('Freedom') Square by its old name Shahyad ('Shah's Memorial'), or Jomhuri ('Republic') Avenue by its old name Shah. There is not any single explanation as to why some names have been accepted by the general public while others have not, and therefore, there is always a danger of oversimplifying things and taking them at face value. This, in my view, applies to all the aspects of life in today's Iran, and this is a key point I have tried to examine in this book.

In autumn of 2001, sporadic riots broke out in Tehran and other major cities across Iran. The cause: the national football team's defeat by Bahrain in the 2002 Japan-Korea World Cup qualifying matches. Angry youths took to the streets after the match in the dead of night, breaking bank windows (an act reminiscent of the 1979 Revolution) and committing other acts of vandalism, chanting slogans against the ruling clergy (not excluding the supreme leader), and clashing with the police and security forces. Zealous football fans were enraged because they believed – through word of mouth – that the authorities had ordered the team to lose the match, fearing a repeat of nationwide celebrations that followed Iran's qualification for the 1998 France World Cup in the final match against Australia. Anti-regime radio and television channels stationed outside Iran – mostly in Los Angeles, where the largest Iranian exile community lives – were convinced that here was another revolution in the making. In heated live broadcasts, they incited the people to pour onto the streets and topple the regime. Some of them went so far as to instruct their listeners on how to make Molotov cocktails. What happened in reality was that after a couple of nights, the protests died out entirely.

As observers in general, and journalists in particular, we have a tendency to reduce sophisticated, multi-dimensional phenomena to understandable clichés. It is like touching an elephant in the dark: each of us gives an account of the situation and events that can only represent one point of view – just one of the myriad manifestations of the big picture.

But equally misleading, in my view, is applying modern-day socio-economic theories to developments in Iran without taking into account the complicated implications and influences of its long and tumultuous past. These historical influences may date back aeons, but they still print their mark on the Iranian subconscious. This attitude proved flawed more than at any other time in the predictions made by the so-called 'religious intellectuals' who were carried away by the 1997 landslide victory of President Mohammad Khatami (voted in on a platform of social and political reforms), and precariously predicted the downfall of the religious state that has ruled Iran for the past quarter century.

Is Iran a democracy? Is it a dictatorship or a police state? Are people fed up with religion altogether? Are the youth ready – or hoping – for another revolution? If so, what kind of state do they wish to have? And if so, then who are the thousands of people who fill the streets on the anniversary of the Islamic Republic Day?

Iranians were the great alchemists of medieval times. But Persian culture was also an elixir that dissolved and transmuted rulers and states, as happened after Alexander conquered Iran, after Muslim Arabs put an end to the Sassanid empire, and after Mongols set up an atrocious rule in the land, to name a few examples. To get an understanding of what is going on in the minds of Iranian youngsters in the present day, therefore, one has to grasp the chemistry of pre-Zoroastrian beliefs, Iran's special blend of Shi'i Islam culture, and the impact of cyber-technology on a country ruled by a system that has no parallel in the world.

There is no doubt that Iranian youth is craving for change more than ever before. These young people have particularly captured the attention of the world for a paradoxical reason: whereas in many Muslim countries, anti-West sentiments run high in the younger generation, young Iranians seem to be dying for Western values. Perhaps it was only in Iran that after the September 11 attacks in the United States, groups of young people held candle-lit vigils for the victims. At the same time, was it not the Iranian youth that overthrew the pro-American shah in 1979? Was it not they who seized the American embassy in Tehran back in 1980? And wasn't it they who fought a fierce and protracted war with

Iraq, a country supported at the time by the major Western powers?

But then Iran *is* a country full of contradictions and paradoxes. It boasts the oldest constitutional movement in the Middle East and the second oldest parliament in Asia after Japan. Yet it has toppled a constitutional monarchy to replace it with a theocratic autocracy. It has the highest ratio in female higher education despite the fact that females are confined within the boundaries of the Islamic dress code. It is proud of its internationally credited scientists and researchers, and yet it has one of the largest numbers of drug addicts per capita in the world.

'How could you *not* see that? Everybody saw his face on the moon last night!'

In the summer of 1978, as a seventeen-year-old high-school boy, my jaw dropped to hear this remark from a classmate who excelled in all the empirical sciences. He was talking about seeing on the moon the portrait of Ayatollah Ruhollah Khomeini, the shah's arch enemy, and a man who would shortly become the omnipotent leader of an Islamic Revolution that rocked Iran and the whole world, and laid the foundations of the first religious state in ages. To the present day, Iranian intellectuals still blame each other for having 'fallen in such a trap'. In those days, however, anyone who openly doubted having seen the great man's portrait on the moon would be at the receiving end of derisive looks and sarcastic remarks.

To paraphrase a contemporary historian, throughout history, Iranians have kept surprising everyone – most of all themselves. Unless and until one takes into consideration the complex Iranian psyche and the sophisticated undercurrents of Iranian society, which lie to a great extent in its historical legacy, big question marks will continue to hang over one, with no apparent answer in sight.

It is now more than a hundred years since young people in Iran began fighting for the ideals they have always longed for: justice, freedom, democracy, prosperity. There have been moments in history when it seemed they were about to achieve their goals, but every success has, after a short while, turned into a big frustration. The Constitutional Movement of the beginning of the 20th century briefly raised hopes of putting an end to the absolute despotic rule that had governed the country for centuries. But all that followed was chaos and a harsher autocracy.

The early 1950s witnessed another great movement by Iranians and particularly the youth, which rallied around the legendary Prime

Minister Mohammad Mosaddeq. Having succeeded in nationalising the oil industry and thus sending shock waves through the region, Mosaddeq sought to attain what no other politician had managed to achieve: limiting the powers of the shah within the bounds of a constitutional monarchy. All hopes for a democratic and free Iran, however, sank into nothingness with the CIA-tailored coup d'état, which toppled Mosaddeq in 1953 and returned the shah – who had fled the country – to the throne.

The 1970s began as an unprecedented and extraordinary time in Iran's history. Soaring oil prices made Iran a rich country overnight, and fuelled the shah's ambitions to return the glory of ancient Persia to Iran; to take Iran to the gates of 'great civilisation'. His attempts to quickly modernise the country were supplemented by a policy of iron glove, manifested more than anything in the dreaded secret police SAVAK and the single-party system he introduced in 1974. Iran had never before experienced such wealth and prosperity, yet its young generation had never before been so alienated from and frustrated with the state. Thus, popular revolt started to rock what the world saw as an 'island of stability' in a region governed by turmoil, and in a few months' time, the shah and his dreams were just a memory.

Again, however, the honeymoon turned out to be short. For the first time in its long history, a religious establishment quick to crush all opposition and propagate fiery rhetoric against the United States and the West in general now ruled Iran. The following years saw a devastating war with neighbouring Iraq, which sent hundreds of thousands of young Iranians to early graves, and plunged the country into poverty and isolation.

Iranians kept surprising everyone again, though. This time it was the baby-boomers of the Islamic Revolution, coming-of-age in waves of millions, who shocked the ruling conservatives by electing as president a smiling, reformist clergyman who promised to create a civil society, to bring democracy and freedom – and hope – to them. The air was filled with optimism again, as it seemed that this time there would be no turning back for the reform movement. Suddenly there were dozens of new publications, openly criticising past policies and dogmas. The reformists went from strength to strength as they conquered the city and village councils, and later the parliament. The much-dreaded

Intelligence Ministry suffered a severe blow when it was revealed that its agents had secretly murdered several intellectuals and dissidents.

Yet the tide was to turn one more time, as the conservatives, awakened from their initial shock, mobilized all their powers to undermine the reform movement. The judiciary closed down tens of pro-democracy newspapers. Dozens of political activists, many of them former officials of the Islamic Republic and the so-called 'children of the Revolution' were jailed. In 1998 student demonstrations were ruthlessly crushed. The powerful Guardian Council rejected all the reforming bills approved by parliament, and eventually reformist candidates were barred from running in the 2004 elections.

One more time, the shadow of frustration fell over Iran. The public showed its discontent by turning its back on the parliamentary elections in 2004. By then, even the most ardent advocates of the reformist movement were saying that reform was dead. Exiled anti-regime opposition figures who had, from the start, called the move a fake and a conspiracy of the regime, now took an 'I told you so' attitude.

Since then, all eyes have turned to Iranian youth once more. Many see this young generation as a dormant volcano smouldering with unfulfilled demands that will, in due course, erupt in yet another revolutionary rage and bury the religious oligarchy under its lava once and for all. Others, however, hold – or hope – that change in Iranian society will come in a gradual way, even at a glacial pace. In any case, however, there can be little doubt that these young Iranians will be the harbingers of great changes in the future, changes that will not be confined within Iran's geographical borders.

But one would go nowhere in explaining the state of present-day Iran, or the peculiar double-think of love-hate fantasies at the back of the mind of an average Iranian individual, or in their collective way of looking at the world, without taking into due consideration the deep-rooted, far-reaching effects of Iran's historic hangover – caused by an amazing cocktail of glory, tyranny, repression, class distinction, corruption, foreign invasion, coercion and manipulation, and conspiracy.

The doublethink engendered – if only partly – by this historic fatigue manifests itself in the way many of we Iranians react to the outside world. We believe, on the one hand, that we deserve to lead the world; yet at the same time we are fatalists devoid of any hope of progress. As fallen masters or dissident slaves, we feel betrayed and oppressed. This discrepancy is to a great extent instigated by the contradiction between our stagnant, history-ridden, 'poetical' beliefs and outlooks, and the overwhelming, storming and expanding 'third wave' of western civilisation. It is as if we have been all of a sudden catapulted from a remote, forgotten village, into the heart of a modern, bustling city. In this sudden change of situation, we long to attain progress, and at the same time we despise it. We want to guard our traditions (without revising them in the light of modern-day practicalities), and at the same time metamorphose them. We are neither willing to cope with the requirements of the modern world, nor ready to miss out on its advantages. In this way, we lose our traditional values and lag behind the train of progress.

In the following pages, I have tried to explore why Iranian youngsters are the way they are and why they act the way they act. As an Iranian who has spent the years of his own youth during one of the most tempestuous periods of his country's history, I have tried to shed light on the reasons behind some of the major trends and developments of that period. As the father of two young boys who have grown up in the Islamic Republic, I have tried to examine the motives, ideals, demands and concerns of one of the world's youngest peoples, living – so to speak – under God. As a journalist, I have tried to depict a factual, objective, impartial and fair picture of the youth movement in today's Iran, without jumping to any conclusion or making any prediction. And borrowing a term from astrophysics, I have tried to look at every historical development within its 'event horizon', avoiding hindsight, or superimposing the present on the future.

Having said that, I cannot entirely disengage myself from the issues discussed here, as I myself have spent all the past twenty-five years dealing with the Iranian youth in one way or another. My early years happened to coincide with the Revolution, my twenties with the Iran-Iraq war, my thirties in dealing with university students and young journalists, and now I have two teenage kids. I have lost quite a few friends over these years: some were killed in the course of the 1979 Revolution, some in the battlefronts of the war with Iraq, some executed by firing squads in Tehran's Evin prison, and one killed by agents of the Intelligence Ministry in the infamous killing spree of dissidents and intellectuals in 1997. The latter's body has not yet been found. Nevertheless, I have tried my best to keep my judgements to myself.

The present book is by no means intended to be a research work about, or a methodological study of, the situation of the Iranian youth. Nor is it a historical account of developments in contemporary Iran. Rather, it looks at the developments of each epoch through the eyes of actual people who lived then and were involved with it. Notwithstanding this, in writing it I have looked up many works of reference and interviewed dozens of individuals, including sociologists, political scientists, economists, historians, education experts, and of course, young women and men from different walks of life.

In his *Masnavi Ma'navi*, Jalaleddin Balkhi, the great thirteenth-century Persian poet and Sufi, better known to the world as Rumi, uses fables to illustrate deep philosophical points. One of his famous fables, probably borrowed from Indian literature, shows how viewing a phenomenon from a certain vantage point can be misleading. Here is A. J. Arberry's translation of Masnavi:

> Some Hindus had brought an elephant for exhibition and placed it in a dark house. Crowds of people were going into that dark place to see the beast. Finding that ocular inspection was impossible, each visitor felt it with his palm in the darkness.
> The palm of one fell on the trunk.
> 'This creature is like a water-spout,' he said.
> The hand of another lighted on the elephant's ear. To him the beast was evidently like a fan.
> Another rubbed against its leg.
> 'I found the elephant's shape is like a pillar,' he said.
> Another laid his hand on its back.
> 'Certainly this elephant was like a throne,' he said.
> [Had each of them had candle in hand
> Differences in their sayings would have disappeared.]
> The sensual eye is just like the palm of the hand. The palm has not the means of covering the whole of the beast.
> The eye of the Sea is one thing and the foam another. Let the foam go, and gaze with the eye of the Sea. Day and night foam-flecks are flung from the sea: amassing! You behold the foam but not the Sea. We are like boats dashing together; our eyes are darkened, yet we are in clear water.

Like many other phenomena, Iranian society and Iranian youth are like an elephant in the dark.

ONE

Dormant Volcano

Every generation imagines itself to be more intelligent than the one that went before it, and wiser than the one that comes after it.

George Orwell

Youth is a strange force that even ridicules folly and deceit.

Bahram Sadeqi, *Malakut*

Why should I care about posterity? What's posterity ever done for me?

Groucho Marx

They slice through traffic on their motorbikes, racing each other at breakneck speed while holding their mobile phones. They listen to heavy metal, read Günter Grass and admire Tom Cruise. They don't go to the mosque the way their parents did, and they have given up on politics.[1]

In upscale north Tehran last summer, young men and their girlfriends walked along the streets holding hands – a display of affection that could have cost them a beating and time in jail a few years ago. A very few women dared walk the five yards from their front door to their cars without a headscarf. And while headscarves, or the more conservative head-to-toe black chador, are still required by law outside the home, increasingly women let some of their hair escape, wear colourful scarves and don short manteau coats, allowing their bare feet in dainty slippers to be seen – often with bright nail polish.[2]

Increasingly, even young Iranians who care little about politics are rebelling against a society whose architect, the Ayatollah Ruhollah Ayatollah Khomeini, once proclaimed, 'There is no fun in Islam'. Instead, many Iranian youths are intent these days on having fun, and their increasing defiance may represent the most potent challenge to one of the world's strictest Islamic societies. Typically, they do not feel they have to turn from Islam to live their lives as they wish; many profess to pray and fast.

But two decades after their parents revolted against the excesses of the then-ruling shah's pageants and palaces, more young people in Iran are risking jail, fines and official beatings for things American youths take for granted: wearing make-up, slow dancing at a party and holding hands on a date.[3]

In the ski resorts, life is more free than the socially restricted cities, drawing criticism from conservative parts of the establishment. Shemshak, the main resort town a ninety-minute drive from Tehran, is known for illegal parties, where young men and women mix without supervision, drink alcohol and use drugs.[4]

'What are you going to do this year?' I asked Dariush, an eighteen-year-old boy from a middle-class family in Tehran.

'Just like last year, only more powerful,' he said. 'I have bought four kilos of explosives. You remember the one we did in the stadium? Twice as powerful! We're going to have real fun!'

He was referring to the handmade 'grenades' that explode with a loud bang, giving out a huge mushroom of orange-grey smoke. During a football match between Iran and North Korea in 2003 in Tehran's Azadi (Freedom) Stadium, spectators threw one such grenade into the pitch, which injured a Korean player, put an end to the match, and resulted in a penalty against Iran's national squad.

'Aren't you afraid it may explode in your hands?' I asked him.

'Give me a break,' Dariush said, pulling back his heavily gelled forelocks from his face. 'This is the one night we can enjoy ourselves.'

'But aren't you afraid of the Basijis?'

'Oh, to hell with them! They can't do a damn thing! In the worst case, they'll keep us for the night and release us the day after. I've been arrested a couple of times. All I got was a few slaps on the back of the neck, a lot of bad words and spending one night with no food with fifty other guys in a tiny room.' Having said this, Dariush vanished into the shadows of the concrete buildings of Ekbatan Apartments, a neighbourhood in West Tehran that is usually the scene of some of the wildest *Chaharshanbeh Suri*, or 'fire festival', celebrations in town. He was carrying a worrying payload of homemade grenades in a rucksack. He was heading towards a huge bonfire around which a hundred or so young girls and boys were cheering and dancing.

Every year, on a Tuesday evening that often falls in the third week of March, the streets of Tehran, a sprawling metropolis of ten million people, as well as other major cities across Iran, seem to turn into battlefields in a civil war. For weeks before, the youngsters prepare themselves for the *Chaharshanbeh Suri*. Traditionally, on the evening of the last Tuesday of the Iranian year (which ends 20 March), Iranians hold these celebrations, at the centre of which lies the veneration of fire, a central tenet of Zoroastrianism, which was the predominant religion in Iran before the invasion of the Arab Muslims and the conversion of Iranians to Islam some fourteen centuries ago.

The twelve Persian months, named after Zoroastrian angels, match the seasons and the signs of the zodiac. The first six months all have thirty-one days, the next five have thirty, and the last has twenty-nine days plus an extra one in leap years. These lengths actually correspond to the seasons, as spring and summer are about a week longer than autumn and winter, and so the equinoxes and solstices are accurately reflected in the Persian calendar. Omar Khayyam is said to have been one of the scholars who worked on perfecting this system in the eleventh century.

In the years following the Islamic Revolution, the youngsters have in practice transformed *Chaharshanbeh Suri* into a festival of explosions and a show of defiance. Most of them hardly pay any attention to their parents' advice, or to televised footage that shows people of their own age lying with severe burns in hospital, let alone to warnings issued by the authorities, unhappy to see celebrations of a pre-Islamic tradition in an Islamic country.

The warnings are issued from different viewpoints. Conservative clerics such as Ayatollah Safi Golpaigani, an elderly high-ranking clergyman in the holy city of Qom, fundamentally reject the occasion. 'Superstitious customs such as *Chaharshanbeh Suri* do not befit the dignity of the Muslim people of Iran', said the Ayatollah in a statement made in March 2004. 'Those who take part in such ceremonies are mostly ignorant people – although some of them seek to undermine the Islamic identity of the society', he added, exemplifying the traditionalist attitude towards customs and rituals that are pre-Islamic relics.

But those who have a closer contact with the everyday realities of life, and are therefore well aware that it would be futile to keep youngsters at home on *Chaharshanbeh Suri*, have taken a different position in recent years. Avoiding banning the festivities, as was done during the early years after the 1979 Revolution, security officials have chosen to announce that they recognise the occasion and the festivities, but issue strong warnings against any incidents of 'unrest'.

On the other hand, during the days preceding the festival, anti-regime opposition radio and television stations abroad incessantly call on the Iranian youth to turn *Chaharshanbeh Suri* into a struggle against the state.

Despite sporadic clashes with security forces, however, the youngsters do not seem to be interested in outright politics. Once the sun is down, loud sounds of explosions fill the city. Huge bonfires are lit, into which all sorts of hand-made firecrackers and other explosive devices are thrown, amid the cheerful screams of young girls and boys. When, and if, the Basijis or the police intervene to disperse the crowd, youngsters flee in several directions, booing them, some taking ambush and throwing 'grenades' at them. Some get caught and are subsequently taken into minibuses bound for Basij or police stations. But as Dariush said, most of them are freed the following day.

Dariush's parents told me that they were worried about what he and his friends did, but added that there was nothing parents could do to stop their kids.

'These horrifying sounds scare the daylights out of us, let alone the sick and elderly people', Dariush's father, an architect in his late forties said. 'But what can we do? There are no other real opportunities for the youth to be happy together. Almost all kinds of fun are banned for them in this country.'

Dr Davar Sheikhavandi, a sociologist in Tehran, agrees, saying that the reason behind the transformation of *Chaharshanbeh Suri* celebrations into the current form is that the government has failed to provide legal facilities to celebrate the event:

'When you don't provide facilities for a tradition that has been celebrated throughout centuries, when you try to hamper it, when – like in the early years after the (1979) Revolution – you try to cancel it altogether, you're provoking the youth to resist. Obviously when a large number of excited angry youngsters is involved, there will be grounds for violence and vandalism.'[5]

Meanwhile, many youngsters brazenly sing and dance to illicit Iranian or Western music on the streets, some of them openly drinking contraband liquor or smoking marijuana.

In a corner of the big square where the outdoor party was going on, I saw a member of the Basij paramilitary force lurking in the shadows, clad in khaki uniform and brandishing an automatic rifle. He looked about twenty years old, although it was difficult to tell his exact age because of his unshaven face that was covered by a layer of soft curly hair. Shaving the face is considered a sin for strict Shi'ites according to the teachings of traditionalist ayatollahs – which explains why all the officials of the Islamic Republic have beards or stubble.

'This is blasphemy,' Ahmad, the young Basiji, told me, 'singing, dancing and worshipping fire, particularly in Moharram.' He was referring to the most sacred month for Shi'ites in the lunar calendar. The mourning period of Moharram commemorates the massacre of Karbala, when on 10 October 680, Hossein, the prophet's grandson and Third Imam of the Shi'ites, was butchered with his seventy-two followers on the orders of the Caliph Yazid. The ten days leading up to Ashura, the actual anniversary, are marked by anguished, almost hysterical, wailing, and on the last two days, men parade through the streets flagellating themselves with chains and metal scourges as women look on.

The lunar months are shorter than those in the solar calendar, and therefore they rotate and coincide with a different solar period each year.

'What are you going to do about it?' I asked Ahmad.

'Nothing serious. They're sissies, mother's babies. We just scare them, and they run away.'

That seems to be the most that the police, the armed forces and the authorities can do about the Last Tuesday extravaganza.

By tradition, the festivities of *Chaharshanbeh Suri* include several different rituals, the historical or mythological origins of which are not quite clear today. The key ritual is lighting up bonfires (traditionally with thorn bushes) outdoors, over which family members, neighbours and passers-by jump, chanting, 'Let your rosy glow be mine/ Let my wan pallor be yours,' thus asking the fire for bliss in the coming new year.

I remember as a teenager how excited I was on the occasion. Before the evening fell, most people rushed to buy 'Ajil-e Moshkel Gosha', a special blend of nuts, which, legend has it, can solve one's problems. Many of my relatives came to our house, and my grandmother would prepare 'Reshteh Polo', a special dish of noodles and rice, for the dinner. After jumping over the fire and asking it for bliss, young boys would go for 'Qashoq Zani' or 'spoon-rattling'. This involved going to the neighbours' clad in the chador (a single-piece women's dress that covers them from top to toe), knocking on the doors and rattling spoons in a bowl. The owner would then open the door and place nuts, sweets, or other edible things in the bowl.

Another old custom was Falgoosh: to listen furtively to the conversations of people on the street at random and take it as a good or bad omen.

All such rituals have virtually disappeared.

On a bench in one corner of the square, which was filled with dense smoke, the smell of gunpowder and screams of joy, I came across three girls relaxing momentarily before rejoining the crowd. They were wearing loose headscarves that let lush locks of blonde-dyed hair freely protrude, tight blue jeans, and short, bright-coloured tight-fitting robes. This latter item was to cause a lot of controversy and even some street clashes later in summer, when the 'moral police', aided by hard-line vigilantes from the political organisation known as Hezbollah ('party of God') and Basij forces, raided boutiques and beat up girls wearing such outfits, considered un-Islamic by conservatives and hardliners.

'Do you know anything about *Chaharshanbeh Suri* customs such as Qashoq Zani or Falgoosh?' I asked them.

'Are you a stranger?' they giggled, looking bewildered. '*Chahar-*

shanbeh Suri is all about having fun, singing and dancing and being free,' one of them said.

The transformation of *Chaharshanbeh Suri* into its current form is one example of how Iranian youth, the so-called 'third force', has found outlets to vent its compressed energies and find temporary relief from the individual and social restrictions imposed on them by an ideological state. It is also an example of the rift between older and younger generations, as no matter how many people may be disturbed by the sound of the explosions, the youth do almost whatever they want to do.

I asked the girls what they thought about their lives.

'Oh, it's such a bore most of the time,' Anahita, apparently the more outgoing one, replied. 'We can see on satellite TV how free and happy the youth are in other countries. But look at us: we can't dress the way we like, can't listen to the music we like, can't talk to a boy without fear of being harassed or arrested. We're all the time told what's good and what's bad. And we do the opposite!' They laughed.

These girls, however, did not have any idea how much more boring, depressing and worrying life had been a couple of decades ago.

'Do you have any idea how things were before the Revolution?' I asked.

'Since *they* say it was so bad, it *must* have been so good!' Anahita said.

Our conversation was interrupted by a sudden stampede of people. A dozen young men were running away from Basijis who chased them, shouting, 'Go home you idiots! Disperse or we'll shoot!' And in fact a few rounds were shot in the air, but the shots were hardly heard amid the deafening sounds of grenades going off. I noticed Dariush among the running boys. Suddenly from a farther corner of the square, a larger group of youngsters began booing the Basijis and chanting, 'Guns, tanks and Basijis/ Can't do anything any more.' These chants echoed a popular slogan of the 1979 days, when millions marched against the shah in Tehran's streets every day, defying tanks and truckloads of soldiers – only the old revolutionary slogan said 'rifles' rather than 'Basijis'.

I was wondering how things had changed since the 1980s, when just the sight of Basijis or Hezbollah members on the street would send shivers down the spines of youngsters and send them packing. Being free from memories of the violent crackdowns of the early post-Revolution years, the youth were now equally free from fear. This is a characteristic of today's younger generations that the subversive opposition tries to cash in on. Excited radio and television broadcasts from Los Angeles frequently call on the youngsters to finish the regime in one decisive mass movement. However, the youth seem to react as indifferently towards such calls as they react to calls by the state media to take part in rallies against the United States and Israel.

It is not only fear that they are free from. In the words of Tehran University professor Sadeq Zibakalam, they are also unburdened by values and ideals.

'For today's youth, neither politics nor culture, nor even society, is important. There is a true crisis of values going on,' he said. 'As young revolutionaries, we used to have great hopes for the future. We were dreaming of the day when the Revolution triumphed and we were all free. We were longing for the future, but today's youngsters do not believe in the future, because they see no future.'[6]

This crisis of values and identity is not new to Iranian society. Ever since the country began to modernise in the 1920s, and particularly in the second half of the twentieth century, Iranians have been caught between tradition and modernity. With a major difference, though: in the 'old days', there were always ideologies, schools of thought, opinion leaders and intellectual mentors who would show a way out of the crisis, whether it be Marxism, nationalism, Islamic revival, 'return to self', mysticism, even Buddhism, or, most recently, 'religious democracy'.

Regardless of how credible they were, each offered a refuge from the crisis, and gave direction and meaning to the souls suspended between the opposite poles of strong tradition and dashing modernity.

The reform movement of 1997, hallmarked by the role young people and women played in the landslide victory of President Mohammad Khatami, had briefly offered a new breathing space for the youth with their thirst for change. Now, with the disillusionment of the public in general and the younger generations in particular, they look, in the words of a dissident writer, 'like sheep without a shepherd'.

Immediately after the Islamic Revolution, early marriage and childbirth were announced as valued social assets by the new Islamic government. This resulted in very high fertility rates and a drastic increase in population growth. The outcome of this baby boom in the early 1980s has now become the country's major social concern with repercussions in education, employment, housing and many other fields.

More than half of Iran's seventy million people are under twenty-five, including twenty-four million at schools and universities. At a time of economic hardship and political uncertainty, many of these young people raise demands for education, social freedom, jobs, housing and easy marriage.

The proportion of adolescents (ages ten to nineteen) to the total population was 23.4 percent in 1976, 22.4 percent in 1986, and 27 percent in 1996.

The results of the last national census, conducted in 1996, showed that the population aged ten to nineteen had increased by 46 percent from 1986 and nearly 105 percent from 1976. The overall population growth rates from 1986 to 1996 and 1976 to 1986 were 21.5 percent and 78 percent, respectively. At the same time, the urban adolescent population had increased by 72 percent and 147 percent, respectively. The corresponding increased rates for rural adolescents were 18.5 percent and 62.5 percent. The rural-urban adolescents' ratio shrank from 0.98 in 1976 to 0.65 in 1996. All these statistics reflect the population migration from rural to urban areas.[7]

Although adolescent growth rates were different in urban and rural areas, the overall age distribution in both sectors has remained constant over time. This indicates that migration trends over the last two decades show whole families moving to urban centres rather than adults merely seeking jobs.

The projected size of the adolescent population shows that it will eventually decrease in number and percentage by the year 2020. However, the sheer number of young people enduring fierce social restrictions poses a serious problem for any establishment. According to social scientist Abbas Mokhber, 'If a fundamental solution is not found for their needs, society could be seriously disrupted.'[8]

The generation born in the 1980s, when fertility rates hit unprecedented, worrying highs, began to ring alarm bells for the state in the mid-1990s, when Iran was grappling with the aftermath of its devastating war with Iraq, with world isolation, an ailing economy, and with widespread corruption. Nevertheless, it was a generation that had been growing up in a relatively more relaxed cultural atmosphere, and in a society with an emerging, technocratic, middle class. It comprised mostly urban, educated youngsters who knew nothing about the Islamic Revolution, but were getting well acquainted with the outside world. And this generation was coming to the forefront when stress fractures were appearing in the panoply of the Islamic state. By this time, changes in their dress and appearance clearly showed a trend distancing the young from an era that was fast becoming history.

Disregarding the social signals, the more traditional figures of the state laid stress on the continuation of the closed-circuit policies of the past and even suggested implementing more strict behavioural codes. However, a new breed of Muslim intellectuals, as well as some of the more realistic officials within the establishment, was already raising the alarm and looking for ways to appeal to this multi-million-strong wave of newcomers. Thus, as a potential threat or support, the baby-boomers have come to the attention of Iran's rivalrous political factions, as well as to opposition forces.

Suddenly, prominent figures from these rivalrous political factions have entered a race to win the hearts and minds of Iran's young people, praising them and promising to cater to their needs. Khatami has spoken repeatedly of the need to relax restrictions on Iranian youth if they are to be attracted to religion and safeguard the Islamic republic.

Conversely, official education and state media try to keep them in line with revolutionary values, as a defence against the western 'cultural invasion' that is transforming their lives. At the same time, those very media have undergone a huge transformation during the past twenty-five years. Once mostly broadcasting ideological propaganda, the state television, now augmented to five channels, airs various programmes aimed at entertaining Iran's youth while protecting them from that western invasion.

But many young people enjoy easy, albeit illegal, access to pirate videos of Hollywood's latest productions, tapes of pop and rock music, and western satellite television. Boys and girls who ardently follow and try to imitate heavy metal or rap music groups now stroll together in the capital's shopping malls and parks. Under Khatami, they became less afraid of being arrested for flouting the ban on contact between unmarried couples, or the Islamic dress code for women.

Students are still called on to join the Basij, which aims to safeguard the Revolution against 'enemies'. Repeating a quarter-century-old cliché, Ahmad the Basiji told me, 'We will continue the path of our imam [Ayatollah Khomeini]. We will not let the West's cultural onslaught take over and dilute our Islamic principles'. But the actual number of young people showing any interest in revolutionary activities is meagre. Despite relentless slandering propaganda, Iran was perhaps the only Muslim country in which no spontaneous demonstrations were held against the US-led war in Iraq after 2003. In June 2004, hardliners called on the people to register for suicidal attacks against US forces in the holy Shi'i cities of Karbala and Najaf in Iraq, as well as against Salman Rushdie, the British author of the book *Satanic Verses*. In Tehran, a city of ten million people, some two thousand registered.

Many of the 'modern' youngsters take active part in traditional religious rituals such as the Moharram processions commemorating the martyred Shi'i Imam Hosein. But these ceremonies have also undergone drastic changes in the past few years, turning mass mourning into an opportunity to have fun and flirt on days when the public mood is subdued and there is virtually nothing to do by way of recreation.

There are observers who maintain that the rebellion of Iran's youth is only a manifestation of sexual drive at the age of puberty. This theory has advocates at both ends of the political spectrum: at one end are the ultra-conservatives who despise and scorn the 'westoxification' of the younger generation, their attitudes and behaviour, and their alienation from the values of the Islamic Revolution. What they prescribe is tougher control and more thorough indoctrination. However, they seem to be in the minority, even among conservatives themselves, most of whom cannot overlook the youth as a potential political threat.

At the other end, there are analysts who hold that the clash in today's Iran is one between the natural outburst of testosterone and a system that interferes with every aspect of personal life and seeks to suppress the normal instincts of youth. This frustration, they say, manifests itself in more ways than hedonism, including political excitement, vandalism, and other antisocial attitudes.

Analyst Nima Rashedan, an ardent supporter of reforms until 2002, later came to revise his views, proclaiming that the youth movement was a function of globalisation, the impact of western culture, and the suppression of the natural instincts and interests of young people by the government:

'Ignoring the cultural policies of the government, young citizens have practically accepted the "global" cultural norms. It would suffice to compare the excitement among the youth on Valentine's Day with the mood on the Revolution's anniversary. Fundamentalists in Iran will realise that their time is over if they just take a look at the appearance of their own brothers, kids and nieces,' he said. 'Let me stress with no reservations that the main motive for the massive participation of the youth in the elections, and their part in Mr Khatami's victories, was the demand for social and sexual freedoms,' he adds.[9]

But is it true that Iranian youngsters have turned to 'fun' after, and because, they were disillusioned with the reform movement? This would be rather an oversimplification of sophisticated social undercurrents in a sophisticated society. Just as they have never given up on fun, so they have always strived for freedom and justice when there has been a minimum of breathing space.

Youngsters show signs of rebellion more or less anywhere in the world. But what essentially worries the religious establishment is that, unlike in industrialised countries, the outrage of the youth in Iran has in the past proved to be a danger to the totality of the ruling regime.

A short while after Khatami was elected president, Ali Rabii, his social advisor, and a former deputy intelligence minister who kept a close eye on the demographic and political trends of the decades post-1979, warned that 'implying conflict between modern values and sacred values will result in a social hazard'. His speech, printed in the *Kar va Karegar* daily, of which he is the publisher, pointed at important facts for the Islamic state, particularly since he was for years at the centre of Iran's intelligence apparatus:

> Today, I can testify with complete confidence ... that no one other than Mr Khatami has been as successful at representing the Revolution in such a way as to attract young people to Islam, the Revolution, and the regime. All this has created unity, harmony, and accord among the various social classes and groups.
>
> I see many similarities between the past two or three years, and the first few years of the Revolution. I am experiencing those

same sweet, joyful feelings that we had in the first days after the victory of the Revolution.

In those days, we were full of hope, and although we had to put up with many hardships, limitations, and deprivations, we advanced with indescribable passion and enthusiasm, crying out for freedom, independence, and justice. Today, it is just like the old days. We feel the same passion and fervour. At the start of the third decade of the Republic, we all want to look back over our past performance, and see what we have done. We have to see what we wanted to achieve, and what things we wanted to wipe out, and whether we have succeeded.

If we cannot answer these questions today, we have in fact become weak and incapable. One of the hazards that threaten our revolution is the inability to define our values, and say just which foundations we destroyed, and which new foundations we laid down. The older generation that was directly involved in the Revolution may have some answers, but what do we have to tell our new generation?

Are we sure that the huge sector of our population made up of fifteen to twenty-five-year-olds is satisfied, or that we have convincing, adequate answers to their questions?

Sadly, today's young people do not have any real idea of what things were like before the Revolution. They do not understand what a huge event took place in our country. They do not yet realise or appreciate the dimensions of the independence we have achieved. They are not even fully acquainted with his eminence the imam and the immense task he achieved for his nation and this country. They do not realise the degree of esteem and glory the Revolution brought to Iran. We have not told our young people how dependent this country once was on foreigners, and how it was run literally as a colony, with chunks being partitioned each day, given away to this and that country.

The memories of the Revolution must not be reduced to a few formal ceremonies, limited within the scope of a narrow-minded outlook. Those who say the revolution is over, and should be seen as a thing of the past, are betraying the 200,000 Iranians who were martyred in the Revolution. Today, we have to cry out for a revolution within the Revolution, and demand the continuation of the Revolution as a perpetual fountain for all generations in all eras. The late imam's genius was his ability to correctly, accurately, and openly address the needs of the young people of his time. Today, the Revolution has to be able to respond to the needs of our new younger generation just as accurately and openly.[10]

It was already clear that the demands of the younger generation, not born when the Revolution toppled the pro-western shah Mohammad Reza Pahlavi, were cause for major concern among the custodians of a system heralded by the late Ayatollah Ruhollah Ayatollah Khomeini by the slogan: 'Independence, freedom, Islamic republic.'

'There was a time when the West was far away, no matter how good or bad one supposed it to be,' Zibakalam said. 'It existed in books, in magazines and in films. But with the information-explosion, now the West is inside our homes. Even in the most remote provinces, our youth have access to satellite televisions and to the Internet. They are faced with innumerable questions and no answers. And unfortunately the government has failed to establish a dialogue with the West. All it has done in these years has been to blast the West.

'We are facing deep cultural changes. Many of our beliefs and values are cracked. Sometimes I think to myself that if I pour a gallon of petrol on myself and set myself on fire in the classroom, none of my pupils will even turn to look.'[11]

'The Islamic republic is trying to harness a tremendous energy. The youth cannot remember anything about the shah and do not care about the old days, but they carry the heritage of the unfulfilled dreams of previous generations,' said Mohammad Qaed, publisher of the educational monthly *Lowh* in Tehran.[12]

Reza Pahlavi, the shah's exiled son who leads part of the non-violent opposition to the Islamic Republic, believes that today's youth enjoys strong political awareness. In his manifesto, entitled *Winds of Change*, he writes:

> This generation, however, is different. It has suffered enormously and has had to pay dearly through war, political suppression, loss of economic opportunity and loss of respect from the

international community. They are well aware that there is a different world out there, and realise that things need not be the way they are. Today's youth openly questions the inadequacies of the government. Dissatisfaction has forced the new generation to think much more politically and to take charge of their fate. They have indeed become more responsible citizens.[13]

Although the demands of young people have political implications on Iran's tense factional battleground, many agree that their motivations are anything but political. While hundreds of thousands of youths poured onto the streets to celebrate the victory of Iran's soccer team over the United States in the World Cup in 1998, the most heated pro-Khatami rallies in the heyday of his presidency never drew more than just a few thousand people. After Khatami and his reformist allies were in effect disarmed and rendered defunct by the conservatives, more and more youngsters turned away from politics altogether. Also, in the aftermath of the brutal crackdown on the student protests of 1999, many youngsters found it better to think twice before making any move with political implications.

Ahmad Batebi has arguably been the most well-known figure of Iran's student movement in recent years. His picture, which appeared on the cover of *The Economist*, and in which he is seen holding a blood-stained T-shirt during the student protests of 1999 that rocked Iran, landed him in jail. In March 2000, in a letter from prison addressed to the judiciary chief, he gave an account of his ordeal:

> I, Ahmad Batebi, son of Mohammad Bagqer, born in 1978, and having the National ID card 448 issued in Shiraz, am a student of film production of the University Jihad, and reside in Fardis of Karaj, and was condemned by the respectful judiciary power following the tragedy of July 1999.
>
> My purpose in this missive is to tell you, Your Honour, about the circumstances of my arrest, interrogation and trial, and it is my hope that by doing so, we would intervene for the promotion of the truth and reconstruction of destruction.
>
> From the end of June 1999 until my day of arrest, with the authorization of the University Jihad Office, I was producing

a documentary about the dangers of drug addiction and social problems.

Hearing about the student dormitory, I went to cover this incident, and I conducted my work in the university dorm area ... until the Wednesday when I was arrested by plainclothesmen who were participating in the student demonstration. I have been imprisoned since then and sentenced to death ...

On the first day of my arrest by the plainclothesmen, I was brought inside the university where they confiscated all my documents and possessions. While taunting me with insults, they beat me about my testicles, my legs and abdominal area. When I protested, they answered that this is the land of the Velayat [the governance of clerics] and that I should be blinded and not be allowed to live here.

They then transferred me to the Law Enforcement Force ... where, after more interrogation and under pretext of having proof of my participation in the destruction of public property, they handcuffed me and beat me with batons.

Later they transferred me in a van along with other people arrested. They blindfolded us with our shirts and tied us around our necks in a twelve square-metre room. Police beat us with batons. I lowered the blindfold to clean my bleeding nose. When the soldiers saw me do this, they took me to another room where they bound my hands and handcuffed my right foot to my hands ... I was sentenced to lashes. They blindfolded me and carried out the sentence in the same room.

They transferred us ... to another location where I was separated from the others ... I was told I was part of the recent unrest. They even accused me of stealing from a bank. When I protested the charges, they handed me over to a couple of heavy-set soldiers wearing commando uniforms, saying that these people would 'make me talk.' The soldiers bound my hands and secured them to the plumbing. They beat me on the head and abdominal area with their boots. They insisted that I sign a confession of the accusations made against me. Next, they threw me onto the floor, stood on my neck and cropped my hair, causing parts of my scalp to bleed ... I lost consciousness. When I came round, they started again.

They gave me some A4 papers and ordered me to write and sign a 'confession' of their accusations. Upon my protesting, they took me to another room, blindfolded me and secured my bound hands to the window bars. Once again they insisted that I 'confess.' When I protested, they beat me with a car-jacking cable. Under extreme duress, I was forced to write what they wanted ...

I asked to go to the bathroom, but they would not let me close the door on the grounds that I might commit suicide. I said I needed to have the door closed, but they refused. Not wanting to expose my bodily functions to others, I told them I no longer wanted to go to the bathroom. They insisted I must go, and the door must be open. Then they began lashing me.

I resisted and punched one of them in the face. At this point, they took me to the lavatory and ducked my head into a cesspool full of human excrement. They held me down for so long that I was no more able to hold my breath, so that when I gasped, the excrement ran up my nose and seeped into my mouth. For several hours, I was not allowed to wash myself. An interrogator who wanted to question me told me to clean up, because he could not stand the stink.

During the interrogations, they threatened several times to execute me and to torture and rape my family members as well as imprison them for long terms ... I was forced to sign a 'confession', fearing that they would carry out their threats ...

Some time after being transferred to Evin prison, I was given a piece of paper to sign, blindfolded. When I asked about the content, they said, 'creating street unrest,' and 'inciting people to create unrest.' When I denied the charges, they kicked me in the face causing fractures to my right jaw and knocking out my teeth. Later I had no choice but to have the remaining roots extracted ... In solitary confinement, I was beaten about the head, causing an infection in my left ear, damaging my hearing ...

During the first days [of detention], they wrote my name on my hand with a green-ink ballpoint pen. When I asked why, all they said was that they were going to take me to be executed, and that it was better for me to confess before dying, so as to purify my soul and not suffer while dying. Then they sat me on a chair and put a rope around my neck, keeping me in that position for more than two hours ... I was asked to write down my will ... [Finally] someone came in and told them I had not been sufficiently debriefed to be executed.

[After I was tried] the secretary of the court gave a folded paper, covering the text, and told me to sign it. When I asked what it was, he said, 'This paper. It is your sentence that has been contested by your lawyer, and you need to sign it.' I tried everything to be able to see it and to understand its content but couldn't ... I had to resign myself to doing it without being able to see it, to read it or to understand it.

I was summoned to the court two months ago, and they told me that the Supreme Court had approved my sentence. When I asked what the sentence was, they refused to answer ... saying that my lawyers were America's spies and that I need to revoke them ...

On 16 March 2000 ... [my interrogators] told me that I was taking my last breaths, and that this was my last chance. They told me that they would release me if I were honest. They said that by 'released' they usually meant, 'get killed', but they would really free me to go back to my family if I was honest with them ... Then, they brought me my file and showed it to me with my death sentence and told me to go and think until Saturday, 18 March 2000, when I would be summoned to the court, but I was not summoned again until the end of the year ...[14]

In 2003, while Batebi was serving his fifteen-year jail term, a dozen young boys and girls posed for a photograph on the foothills of northern Tehran. They were holding, not blood-stained T-shirts, but portraits of Michael Jackson, and placards, saying that the American pop idol was innocent of child molestation charges levelled against him by a court in Los Angeles.

The 'turning away' of Iran's youth from politics, however, does not provide the ruling clergy with much relief. The baby-boomers of the Islamic Revolution seem to be apt to create serious problems for their founding fathers. Alarming unemployment figures and bleak economic prospects, frustration with social restrictions, a massive brain drain, and growing figures for crime, prostitution and drug abuse are serious threats to any state, let alone to a political system faced with a legitimacy crisis from within and international criticism from without.

According to a study published in 2004, about nine million people would be added to the army of jobless in five years' time. The study said that unemployment in recent years has been more than 12 percent.

The authorities have warned against the danger of drugs among the youth, and the state television continually broadcasts anti-drugs clips, soap operas and panel discussions. Officials put the number of drug addicts at two million, but an AIDS prevention group said recently the actual number was closer to 3.6 million, including 260,000 schoolchildren.

The literacy rate of the adolescent population jumped from merely 60 percent in 1976 to over 95 percent in 1996. This rise was greater among females, reflecting a significant reduction in gender disparities in education over recent years. The literacy rate increased from 47.8 percent in 1976 to 91.5 percent in 1996 among females, and from 71.2 percent to 97.8 percent among males. The rise in literacy rate was even more impressive in rural areas, from 43.8 percent to 93.9 percent during the same period. Most of these gains in literacy could be traced to the vastly expanded opportunities for formal education, especially for rural females.[15]

'Today virtually everyone can enter universities, but there are not enough jobs for graduates,' Qaed said. And since their conception in the 1920s, universities have always proved to be hotbeds of dissent and protest.[16]

Zibakalam believes that in recent years the youth have been pumped up with unreal expectations and demands, and that this is the main cause of their rebellion. 'Political factions of the state saw the large number of youngsters as a potent political lever, and started to draw a utopian picture for them. They did not want to realise that the explosion of the youth population was only a natural phenomenon caused by a social mistake in the 1980s, and that by late 2000s, this wave would subside of its own accord.'[17]

But will it? It is true that the baby-boomers of the 1980s will be over twenty-five by the end of this decade, but will their fervour not be transmitted to, and resonate with, the generations that are up and coming? And no matter how the Islamic Republic has transformed over the past quarter century to survive in the face of changing and increasing demands of the people in general, and youth in particular, will it be able to contain the drastic change that even the most reform-minded members of the ruling system are wary of?

Some seventy kilometres from Tehran, towering above and dwarfing any other object in the Iran Plateau, stands Mount Damavand, a permanently snow capped dormant volcano rising about 5,700 metres above sea level. As a symbol of the land of the Aryans, it has a special place in Shahnameh, or Book of Kings, the epic poetry book composed in the tenth century by the great poet Ferdowsi, regarded as the jewel in the crown of Persian literature, and cherished by all Iranians.

Shahnameh tells the story of Zahak, a tyrant who ruled for one thousand years, during which 'wisdom and truth disappeared while harm and fallacy became widespread. Art was admonished while superstition and spellbinding was condoned'. Zahak had two serpents on his shoulders that fed on men's brains. So, to provide food for the snakes, every night two young men were captured and slaughtered.

At length Kaveh, a blacksmith whose sixteen sons had been killed to feed the serpents, revolted. People gathered around Kaveh as he called for justice. On his spear he placed his blacksmith's leather apron as a standard. The nobleman Fereydoon, who, with the help of the people and Kaveh, overthrew Zahak and became king, led Zahak to Mount Damavand, bound him to the rock with mighty chains and nails driven into his hands, and left him to perish in agony in an endless cave.

On clear days, when the blanket of smog does not totally block the view, residents of Tehran can enjoy the sight of the magnificent Damavand. A poet friend of mine likens Iranian youth to the towering mountain. Damavand has been dormant for millions of years although it still gives out sulphur fumes frequently. It might one day erupt without warning. But then it might also remain silent for thousands of years to come, slowly shaped and polished by the elements and the passage of time.

TWO

Theocracy and Techno

Youth is a wonderful thing. What a crime to waste it on children.
George Bernard Shaw

It is an illusion that youth is happy, an illusion of those who have lost it; but the young know they are wretched for they are full of truthless ideals which have been instilled into them, and each time they come in contact with the real, they are bruised and wounded.

W. Somerset Maugham, *Of Human Bondage*

We thought that with the victory of the Islamic Republic, many of the vices would diminish. Unfortunately this has not happened. There is widespread corruption and vice among some youngsters, and if the trend continues, it will be too late.
Ayatollah Fazel Lankarani, 2004

In May 2004, more than 1500 youngsters had a meeting with President Muhammad Khatami on the occasion of National Youth Day. Omid Memarian of the reformist newspaper *Sharq* wrote that the meeting was an exception to the rule because for the first time it was the youth who spoke, and 'Khatami, whose desire to speak is diminishing these days', listened. 'He frequently moved. Several times he wiped the sweat from his face. A few times he had a clogged throat, and a few times his eyes sparkled.'

A student spoke of the [Tehran University] dormitory [raid in 1999] and of Khatami's silence. She spoke of the arrests of the students and Khatami's silence. She said how they had craved to hear and how Khatami's silence had tortured them ...

Then a young journalist came up ... After a few minutes of hesitation, she addressed Khatami, who was looking down. 'Mr Khatami! Look into my eyes!' A few years before, if she asked a clergyman to look into her eyes, she had to suffer much blame. But not now. 'You didn't keep your promise!' she said, and added that although Khatami's silence had at times tortured them, his words had sometimes enraged them too ... and her last sentence dropped a heavy silence on the arena: 'Mr Khatami! Do you go to sleep with a peaceful mind at nights?'

Another young journalist spoke of how Khatami's promises had dragged many young people into journalism. 'Many of them have now changed their jobs. Some of them have remained and are having a not so happy time. And some others have left the country. Mr Khatami! Do you happen to know what journalists do when they leave the country? Do you know what they do? They cry ...'

The meeting was a typical manifestation of the situation of the youth in Iran, Memarian reported.

Their explicitness and boldness was indicative of a change in the relationship between the youth and the holders of power ... a relationship, not of a master and a disciple, but one of the askers and the accountable ... a feature which many believe is the outcome of the relatively open atmosphere created after the second of Khordad ...

Iranian society has two different social environments, and therefore two kinds of different demands have shaped up in it. One, the true demands of the people, and particularly of the youth, that have formed under the skin of society and that surface when there is an opportunity ... The other is what can be termed as 'long-distance demands', advertised by official organs and referred to when there is any talk of popular demands. The fact that the president admits that some of the remarks made by the youth cannot be uttered outside the presidential palace, is a proof for this dual environment ...

The time for chanting slogans and giving hollow promises is passed. The youth ask for action. For them, beautiful, heavenly words are less sweeter than small, but earthly steps ...[1]

The fact that so many taboos have been broken in the past few years is indicative of a change that can hardly be reversed. Culture is of course the main field in which such change is primarily reflected. The controversial movie *Marmoolak* ('Lizard') which broke all box office records in Iran in April 2004 was a clear example of the shifting of the theocracy's 'red lines'.

The film tells the story of a convicted thief who escapes from jail by disguising as a clergyman. Ten years before, it would have been impossible to imagine that the clerical garb could be shown on the screen at all, let alone in a comical context. In fact, there still are ultra-traditionalist mullahs in Iran who consider making films and going to the cinema 'haraam', or prohibited by the Sharia.

Much to the anger of the hardliners – some of whom threatened to set on fire the cinemas screening it – *Marmoolak* received an unprecedented welcome by the public. Soon many youngsters were whispering or yelling 'Marmoolak!' at clerics walking on the street – the lizard is a symbol of cunning in Iranian folklore. The reformist-controlled Culture and Islamic Guidance Ministry had already censored parts of the film before screening, but that was not enough for the hardliners. After much pressure, the film had to be pulled off the screens. This, however, was hardly a solution, for it was already available to millions both on DVD and on the Internet.

Ironically, the director, Kamal Tabrizi, is a religious figure and a veteran of the Iran-Iraq war. In his film, in compliance with melodramatic clichés, the marmoolak undergoes a change in personality owing to the turban and robe he wears, comes to believe in God and by the end of the film, he is a reformed character. But Iranian moviegoers have long been accustomed to disregard the 'moral' injected into films to obtain screening permit.

Back in the 1980s, when censorship was much more intense and it was impossible for filmmakers to express even mild criticism of the most superficial aspects of the post-Revolution era, I went to watch *The Cheetah*, which was supposed to be an action-packed thriller. During the scenes in which the 'bad guy' – a robber and murderer – got involved in a physical fight with a policeman, the audience was cheering and clapping for the villain, who in the end brutally killed the officer of the law.

Several films made by Iranian filmmakers have won international acclaim and festival awards in the past decades. However, many of them have failed to make it to the screens in their homeland, for the contents have been deemed in violation of the Islamic Republic's values. Nevertheless, cinema has served as a source of inspiration and fascination with young Iranians. Samira Makhmalbaf, the daughter of Mohsen Makhmalbaf, the celebrated Iranian filmmaker, is an example of how the clerical rule has produced its antithesis. Here is an excerpt of the report by *The New York Times's* Elaine Sciolino on Makhmalbaf:

> In 1999, at the age of eighteen, she made *The Apple*, her first film about the real story of two retarded locked at home for years by their beggar father. The film took him all the way to the prestigious Cannes Festival. 'The film is about every society but about Iran too,' she said.
>
> 'People are not free to say what they want here. They think a woman is a second-class human being. They tell you from the time you're a child that you can't do certain jobs because you are a girl.'
>
> With her slim pants and T-shirt, three-inch platform sandals, heavy black eyeliner and long ponytail, Makhmalbaf doesn't look much like a female role model for the Islamic Republic. But when her film was shown during the Cannes film festival this year, she wore a head scarf – tied fashionably behind her neck.
>
> 'You get used to it,' Makhmalbaf told the *New York Times*. 'The headscarf is a law. Even when I am outside the country, I obey my Islamic law because I want to come back to Iran. There's another thing. It's sort of like my national dress.'
>
> Makhmalbaf cannot explain why she voted for Khatami. 'Why did I? Why did I?' she asks, flustered. 'I beg you not to ask me about political things. I'm only eighteen. How can I care about everything?' She has no feel for the revolution and despises

the propaganda films shown repeatedly on television about Iran's eight-year war with Iraq. 'Revolution is a kind of suicide,' she said. 'You just kill yourself.'

Asked what kind of film she would make about her own future, she replied, 'With *The Apple*, I drew these children out of their locked room. *The Apple* drew me out of the country too. Now I can see the world.'[2]

Not all the young women in Iran, however, are as lucky as Samira has been. Against the backdrop of an ailing economy and widespread unemployment, increasing numbers of young women have turned to prostitution to make ends meet. Apart from call girls and prostitutes working on the streets of large cities, there are women who go 'to work abroad to earn hard currency'. The destination for most of such prostitutes are the United Arab Emirates, where they can earn enough money to run their families.

Once a taboo topic in the Islamic Republic, the authorities have been forced to admit the existence of 'street walkers', and express concerns over the social implications of prostitution. Although the hardliners have tried hard to blame the phenomenon on 'liberal policies', hard facts such as the rule of supply and demand can no more be concealed. The difficulties on the way of getting married for young people largely contribute to the trend.

The age of marriage and the number of marriages has undergone a constant drop in the past decades. According to the results of the 1996 census, about half of men under 24 are not married. In parallel with this trend, after the Islamic Revolution, the average marriage age has fallen by 2 years and 2.6 years for men and women respectively, reaching 25.2 and 22 years of age.

Based on the 1996 census, the share of the unmarried people between the ages of 15 and 24 went up to 75 percent. Married youth comprised only 24 percent of the total married population in 1996, showing a drastic rise in the marriage age. Also, about 89 percent of the population in the 15–19-year-old group and 55 percent of the 20–24-year-old group were never married. In the 1986–96 period, unmarried population rose from 75 to 86 percent for men, and from 45 to 63 percent for women.[3]

The sphere of influence of Iranian women has long been confined to the family, but today any political force eyeing a hold on power needs to attend to their ever-increasing demands for greater rights.

Twenty-seven years after millions of women took part in nationwide demonstrations that overthrew the shah, a new breed of Iranian women are calling for improved civil rights as well as a larger say in politics and the economy under a president they helped elect. Together with the youth, women came to the forefront of Iran's political priorities since the 1997 election of President Khatami, whose platform included a promise to attend to women's demands. Although Khatami's election did not bring about any major improvement in women's status, it nevertheless struck a blow against dogmatic attitudes.

According to a women's rights activist in Iran, the experience of the past twenty-five years has showed that no one could come to power without the support of women. Some women's rights activists say the Revolution turned back the clock more than half a century for their sex, but others argue that it gave birth to a new generation of women who have come to play an active part in society.

the women's movement has in recent years flown in the face of the conservatives, some of whom say that feminism is part of a Western 'cultural invasion' and insist that a woman's duty is to cater to the needs of her husband and children.

Things have also been changing on the professional front. It is now two years since more girls than boys passed national university entrance exams. Some 28 percent of the country's general physicians and about 64 percent of people with high school diplomas working in the medical sector are women. Official figures put women's literacy rate at 74 percent, compared to 84 for men. Women's life expectancy is 60 years, one year more than that of men. A new epoch in the social life of Iranian women has begun. Their voice of protest can clearly be heard. They are no more what they were twenty-five years ago. They are demanding their rights particularly in fields which earlier were inconceivable, including the economy. But there is still a glass ceiling for female graduates. The pressure of traditions, and the economic crisis with its chronic unemployment, block women's way.

The law is another battleground for women's rights. It gives men an absolute right to divorce their wives without having to produce any justification and, in the vast majority of cases, custody of the children. But thanks to the activities of women like 2003 Nobel Peace Prize winner Shirin Ebadi, family laws are undergoing change as a result of joint efforts by a handful of intellectual activists and thousands of ordinary women who have appeared before family courts. Today men cannot divorce their wives without the ruling of a court in which a female legal observer is present to make sure the woman's rights have not been violated. Improvements in custody regulations are also underway, and raising the age at which girls can legally be married from the current nine years is on the agenda. Women's rights activists believe that there are innumerable obstacles in the way of Iranian women, but the fact is that their current social status, with their recent achievements, is irreversible.

In July 2002 moderate cleric Ali Zam ignited a gunpowder keg by saying that prostitution and drug abuse were widespread among Iran's predominantly young population. 'Five tons of narcotics are consumed in Tehran every day. According to official reports, there are at least two million drug addicts in the country, some 100,000 of them prison inmates. Addiction to narcotics has even reached school classes,' he reported.

Zam's report, read out at the Tehran City Council, added that the average age of prostitutes in Iran had dropped from twenty-seven to twenty in a few years'. According to a women's rights website, there are three districts in Tehran in which men make a living by each bringing three to four women from remote villages and poor families and forcing them to sell their bodies.

In his report, Zam said that some 90 percent of girls who ran away from home fell into prostitution. Zam warned that violence and theft among teenagers were on the rise, too.

Besides prostitution, selling girls as sex slaves has hit the headlines in the past few years. Although selling girls is a tradition in certain Iranian border provinces, the phenomenon of selling girls by their families or husbands in metropolitan cities seems to be on the rise.

According to official estimates, some 3.5 million working-age Iranians were unemployed in 2004. Authorities have been calling unemployment a national threat and one of the country's most pressing priorities.

The official unemployment rate was put at about 13 percent in 2003. But economists estimate the real figure is more than 20 percent. According to official estimates, unemployment is especially rife among Iran's youth and women, where jobless rates can soar as high as 30 percent.

The rise in unemployment comes as more and more young women are pursuing university degrees, despite the lack of jobs. The Planning and Policy Affairs Ministry said the female unemployment rate is twice that of men. Economists say Iran will have to create more than a million new jobs every year in order to accommodate its young population. But only about 300,000 new jobs are created each year, leaving the country's youth frustrated and disillusioned.

Many observers have said that the rising unemployment rate is the cause of various growing social maladies, including drug addiction. There are currently more than two million drug addicts in the country. Economist Ali Rashidi said the roots of Iran's unemployment crisis date back to the early 1980s and the country's policies following the start of the Iran-Iraq War.

'[Iran] wanted to have an army of twenty million. And as a result, they encouraged pregnancy and the rate of population increased from something like 1.7 to 4 or 4.5. As a result, the population of Iran has doubled during the last twenty-five years. So this increasing population is far from what the economy can absorb, and at the same time the policies that have been followed since the end of the war have nothing to propose in terms of absorbing this extra population,' Rashidi said.[4]

The share of young (under twenty-four) people in the total population has undergone fluctuations in the past four decades. As of the 1976 census, this share rose by 4 percent: despite the drop in total population growth from 3.1 percent in the 1956–66 period to 2.7 percent in 1966–76, the growth in the youth population soared, reaching from 3 to 5 percent. In 1980s the share of the young population jumped to an unprecedented 24.5 percent of the total population. According to official statistics, the ratio will remain more or less the same until 2006, and then start to decline.

In 1986, the share of the young population was larger in cities than in villages. However, the trend indicated a reversal in the 1996 national census. Also, population growth of the female youth in the past two decades has been larger than that of males.

The unemployed youth (15–24 years old) comprised about half of the total jobless population in both 1986 and 1996 censuses. In both cases, the share of literate unemployed was larger than that of the illiterate. Official statistics show that the ratio of unemployed young men to the total unemployed population decreased in 1996, although the total unemployment rate went up.

Rashidi blamed economic policies for soaring unemployment. Iran's investments in industry and agriculture, he said, have not been planned to produce the greatest number of jobs possible. 'In other words, the industrial policy has been concentrated in industries absorbing a lot of capital with little labour. For example, you spend a lot of money for steel production or the metallurgy industry and the rate of employment does not go as far as the capital concerned. So the policy in industry, agriculture has not been conducive to absorb this extra population.'

Most of the new jobs created are in the services sector or on the black market, and therefore do not contribute to reducing overall unemployment rates or raising production rates. Most of Iran's jobless population is classified as unskilled labour with a high school education or lower. But unemployment is also growing among university graduates, pushing many of them to seek opportunities abroad.

The share of the literate young people compared to the total literate population was highest in 1996 (29.5 percent) compared to 25.9 percent in 1966. The ratio of the literate young males also registered the highest mark in 1996 with 28.6 percent. Among females, the highest ratio was registered in 1966 (33.1 percent). The figure was 29.3 percent in 1996.

Statistics show a consistent growth in literacy rates among the young population. In 1986, some 84 percent of young males were literate, 32 percent of whom were studying at the time of the census. According to the same census, 65 percent of all young females were literate, 25 percent of whom were studying. By 1996, literacy rates for the young reached 95 and 90 percent for males and females respectively. The figures show a faster pace of literacy among women, one reason of which is the large gap between the two groups in previous years. A comparison of the results of the 1986 and 1996 clearly shows the impact of the high fertility rates in the 1980s.[5]

In 1996 some 59.6 percent of the population in the 20–24 year old group was in higher education, registering a 24.1 percent increase compared to a decade before. The share of males has been constantly dropping ever since. Young people comprised 67.68 percent of the students in higher education in 1996. In a report in 2004, the International Labour Organisation urged countries to tackle youth unemployment in order to avoid what it called 'the creation of a huge cadre of frustrated, uneducated or unemployable young people that could have a devastating impact on long-term development prospects.'

Frustration with the clerical rule and the constant anti-West propaganda, together with easy access to the outside world through video, satellite television and the Internet, has turned the West and the United States into irresistible magnets for thousands of Iranian youth.

According to the International Monetary Fund, Iran has the world's highest rate of brain drain. A study conducted in 2002 showed that about 70 percent of Iranian students who had won awards in international scientific Olympiads had later left the country.

Faced with a grim economic and political prospect, immigration has become an obsession with many youngsters. In 2000 Behrooz Afkhami, a filmmaker turned reformist Majles deputy, enraged the hardliners by quoting his son as praising America and asking him why they did not leave Iran for the United States.

The *New York Times*' Nicholas Christof echoed that widespread feeling in 2004.

> On my first day in Tehran, I dropped by the 'Den of Spies', as the old US Embassy is now called. It's covered with ferocious murals denouncing America as the 'Great Satan' and the 'arch villain of nations' and showing the Statue of Liberty as a skull (tour the 'Den of Spies' here).
>
> Then I stopped to chat with one of the Revolutionary Guards now based in the complex. He was a young man who quickly confessed that his favourite movie is *Titanic*. 'If I could manage it, I'd go to America tomorrow,' he said wistfully. He paused and added, 'To hell with the mullahs.'

An opinion poll in 2002 showed that 74 percent of Iranians wanted to see re-establishing of ties with the United States. Ironically, the firm that conducted the poll was chaired by no one other than Abbas Abdi, a leader of the students who stormed the US embassy in 1979. The conservatives were so agitated by the findings that a case was quickly opened in the court against Abdi and his colleagues. Abdi was arrested exactly on the 25th anniversary of the embassy takeover, and given an eight-year sentence. Christof observed:

> Partly because being pro-American is a way to take a swipe at the Iranian regime, anything American, from blue jeans to 'Baywatch,' is revered ...
>
> Young Iranians keep popping the question, 'So how can I get to the US?' I ask why they want to go to a nation denounced for its 'disgustingly sick promiscuous behaviour', but that turns out to be a main attraction. And many people don't believe a word of the Iranian propaganda.
>
> 'We've learned to interpret just the opposite of things on TV because it's all lies,' said Odan Sayyed Ashrafi, a 20-year-old university student. 'So if it said America is awful, maybe that means it's a great place to live.'
>
> Indeed, many Iranians seem convinced that the US military ventures in Afghanistan and Iraq are going great, and they say this with more conviction than your average White House spokesman.[6]

In 1989 the movie *Sarzamin-e Arezooha* (Dreamland) which was made a couple of years earlier, was shown on the state television. It told the story of a young engineer fascinated by the United States, but later, in the best tradition of Iranian movies, underwent a fundamental change of personality, and decided to stay in Iran. A few days later, the supreme leader granted audience to the director and praised him for his film. Realities of society were somewhat different, however.

The American Green Card Lottery has become an endemic fever in Iran. Newspaper stands offer photocopied lottery forms, and many firms have been set up that help the applicants fill out the forms for a fee. The online market is equally hot, with tens of Iranian websites rendering similar services on the internet.

In their efforts to get out of the country, Iranian youth go to far lengths that in cases seem unimaginable. In recent years, asylum seekers in Turkey, Holland and Britain have sewed their lips and eyelids, amputated their limbs or set themselves on fire to prevent local authorities from deporting them.

In 2000, when I was also running an Internet café in Tehran, many young clients sought help in finding information on education or job opportunities abroad. One day, a 20-year-old man came to me. 'Can you please find a web address for me?' he asked.

'Yes, but only if it's got nothing to do with opposition groups or pornography. You know that both are prohibited.'

'Rest assured. It's not such stuff.' He handed me a piece of paper on which there was an Internet address. Having logged on, I found that the website belonged to an association that supported Jews in Austria.'

'Are you sure you've got the address right?' I said, telling him about the website.

'Exactly. That's it. Please give me a print-out.' He then explained to me that since he could not leave the country legally (he had not done his military service) or obtain a visa, he planned to convert to Judaism, illegally get to Austria somehow, and seek asylum on the grounds that in Iran conversion from Islam was punishable by death.

With the enforcing of tighter immigration laws by Western countries, conversion has become one of the outlets for young Iranians desperate to get away from the Islamic Republic. In Persian language newspapers published in Europe, asylum-seekers frequently have advertisements printed, proclaiming their conversion to other faiths – mostly Christianity or Zoroastrianism – and deplore the clerical rule.

For those who cannot obtain immigration visas, a more conventional way of staying abroad, however, is to go abroad for black labour. In the early 1990s, a tidal wave of immigration to Japan began, as Tokyo and Tehran had a visa abolition agreement at that time. The demand for travelling to the land of the rising sun was so high that Iran Air tickets for Tokyo were booked several months in advance, and sold at tenfold price in the black market. In 1992, the government devised an ingenious and unprecedented solution: nearly a hundred thousand applicants gathered in Tehran's huge Azadi football stadium, where a lottery was held to choose the would-be travellers.

The overflow of Iranian labourers into Japan, and the involvement of a number of them in illicit activities, such as forgery, human trafficking and drug dealing, led by the notorious Yakuza gangsters, forced Japan to introduce difficult visa conditions in order to stem the tide.

In the mid-1990s, Cyprus became a new magnet for young job

seekers, for it still did not require Iranians to hold a visa to enter its territory. In the summer of 1995 I was on board an Iran Air Boeing 747 bound for Larnaca. Almost two-thirds of the seats were occupied by young men who were wearing business suits complete with neckties in that hot weather. Most of them were friends or relatives. As soon as we were airborne, they opened Persian-English dictionaries of colloquial phrases, writing down phrases such as 'I am a tourist', 'I will stay here for two weeks', or 'I have 1,000 dollars with me' on a piece of paper or on the palms of their hands. This was a dress rehearsal to fool Cypriot airport officers.

At the airport, however, most of the young job seekers easily gave themselves out, after which they were taken to the departures lounge to return home with the same flight they had arrived. I also saw a few young Iranian deportees, handcuffed and accompanied by police officers, also to be placed in the Iran Air jumbo.

'I was a construction worker in Nicosia,' one of them told me. 'I lived there for nine months with some six other Iranians in one room. No insurance, nothing. Last week, when I went to the disco with a few other Iranians, a fight broke out. Police were called in, and arrested all of us.'

Iranians are among the top asylum seekers in many countries, and there have been a number of embarrassing incidents. In April 1999, a wrestler refused to return to Iran after a tournament in Italy, and he sought asylum in an unnamed European country. That same month, the Swedish foreign ministry filed charges against its Tehran embassy for illegally issuing visas and residency permits in exchange for bribes. The official responsible for issuing visas at the French embassy in Tehran was suspended and sent back to France for improperly issuing more than 350 visas to middlemen. Information on how to apply for a US Resident Alien card – a Green Card – was downloaded from the Internet and sold in Tehran book stores, newspaper stands, and supermarkets. Moreover, emigration agents advertise openly in Iranian newspapers.

Immigrating abroad is not the only outlet to the outside world for Iranian youth struggling against imposed restrictions. Information has kept flowing, although at times intermittently, into the Islamic country through the print media, satellite technology and the Internet.

Blamed by conservative clerics for spreading 'decadent Western culture', satellite television has been banned in Iran for everyone except some state and media offices, since the technology arrived in the country around 1994. However, just like the VCR a decade earlier, the ban is widely ignored and thousands of people watch foreign and exile-Iranian television stations using dish antennae hidden on their rooftops.

Moves to ease off the ban have repeatedly been blocked. In 2003, the Guardian Council rejected a bill passed by the reformist-dominated Majles to legalize satellite dishes, citing discrepancies against the Constitution and the Sharia. Considering the fact that the use of satellite dishes was already widespread, the Majles bill aimed at compiling regulations for public use of satellite equipment through devising certain restrictions on what residents were permitted to watch.

Police frequently warn residents to dismantle satellite dishes. Such warnings are usually followed by raids of residential buildings, confiscation of satellite equipment and fining the owner. After the subsiding of each tide, though, dishes are put back in place. The Islamic Republic has particularly been irritated by the setting up in recent years of several subversive satellite televisions, operating mainly out of Los Angeles. Ranging in political leanings from monarchism to communism, some of the Los Angeles-based televisions relentlessly lash out at the Islamic Republic and incite the people to revolt against the 'lice-ridden mullahs'. Others entertain their viewers by the latest Iranian pop music as well as movies dating back to the 1960s and 1970s. 'Bankrupt elements abroad are trying to use the satellite network to launch a political challenge. This shows that we have failed to seriously confront cultural threats,' Defence Minister Ali Shamkhani said in 2001. Many reformists have said that the mass closure of pro-reform newspapers played a key part in more and more people tuning to such stations.

But as more than a hundred newspapers were closed down since April 2000, the Internet gradually became an efficient means of communications among the youth and a vehicle for journalists to propagate messages and call for more freedoms and reforms in the country. The state, consequently, moved to exert tougher control of the worldwide web. In a fresh surge of intimidation, after January 2003 several individuals operating websites were arrested, along with Internet users.

According to a report by Reporters Sans Frontiers, privately owned Internet Service Providers (ISPs) began operating timidly in 1994 in the shadow of the big government-controlled ISP, Data Communication

Company of Iran (DCI), run by the Intelligence Ministry. As of 1997 with Khatami's liberal cultural policies, cyber cafes began to mushroom in large cities. By law, privately owned ISPs are obliged to obtain permission to operate from the ministries of intelligence and culture, and use firewalls on website viewing and email messages. Each user has to sign a statement promising not to browse 'immoral and anti-revolutionary' websites.

'The regime stepped up its control of cyber cafés in May 2001, closing 400 of them in Tehran,' RSF reported in 2004. Some have since reopened, but in November that year, the Supreme Council of the Cultural Revolution, chaired by President Khatami but dominated by hardliners, ordered all privately owned ISPs to shut down or put themselves under government control.[7]

In January 2003 Intelligence Minister Ali Younessi denounced the 'underground war' he said was being waged through websites that 'put out rumours and disinformation about all government bodies and their officials.'

A commission of officials from the culture and intelligence ministries and the state-run radio and TV was set up that month to compile a list of news sites considered 'illegal.' It was to be handed to the posts and telecommunications ministry, which would pass it on to ISPs, who would block access to them. The list is thought to contain between 100 and 300 websites, most of them sources of news.

In early May the country's prosecutor-general, Abdolnabi Namazi, announced a new commission to deal with offences committed online. He said people who posted material on sites created in Iran 'must respect the constitution and the press law or else risk being prosecuted. Until we have a law about Internet offences,' he said, 'courts can use the press law,' which provides for heavy prison sentences. The commission's main job is to draft an Internet law.

Deputy Posts, Telegraph and Telephone Minister Massoud Davarinejad said in May that the ministry had moved to block access to 'immoral sites and political sites that insult the country's political and religious leaders.' So when people try to access an 'illegal' site, they are cautioned that 'on orders from the posts and telecommunications ministry, visiting this site is not permitted.'

Measures were also taken against ISPs. Five privately owned ones in the northern city of Tabriz were shut down in early May because they had not installed filters against banned sites. Most of the ISPs still operating there were government controlled. At least seven ISPs were also closed down in Tehran for the same reasons.

The hardliners were not the only ones trying to control the Internet. In May, two reformist figures, government spokesman Abdollah Ramezanzadeh and posts and telecommunications minister Ahmad Motamedi, warned ISPs to apply the new rules and said the filtering system was quite legal.

Nevertheless, potentials of the Internet soon caught the eyes of journalists whose publications were under ever-increasing threat of the conservative judiciary. Websites such as Emrooz, Rouydad and Alliran virtually replaced the banned reformist newspapers *Sobh-e Emrooz*, *Mosharekat* and *Golestan*.

In 2002 Iranians, especially young people and women, became enthusiastic about weblogs, personal sites where they can get round the censors by using pseudonyms. This passion for the Internet (with at least 1,500 cyber cafés in Tehran alone) quickly scared the regime, which took steps to control it.[8]

Thousands of Iranian blogs, or personal web journals, have cropped up since late 2001 when Hossein Derakhshan, an Iranian émigré in Canada who became known as the 'father of Persian blogging' devised an easy way to use the free blogging service Blogger.com in Persian. Though several English blogs outside Iran are read by Iranians, the most popular ones are in Persian and operated inside the country. Even vice-president Muhammad Ali Abtahi, a liberal clergyman, runs his own website, in which he shares his thoughts with thousands of people. However, he reminds the website's visitors that he is not in his political shoes while in the website: 'Let me be only Abtahi here'.

Javad Tavaf, editor of the hugely popular news website Rangin Kaman, which for a year had been criticising Ayatollah Khamenei, was arrested at his home on 16 January 2003 by justice ministry officials. He was freed two days later, RSF reported.

Mohamed Mohsen Sazgara, editor of the news site Alliran, was arrested on 18 February at his home by plainclothes state security agents and his house and office searched and a large amount of written material seized. A week earlier, he had posted an article on his website calling for a reform of the constitution. He also wrote that the wishes of Iranians had been 'hijacked by six religious figures on the Guardian Council', a body controlled by hardliners and appointed by Khamenei, which supervises elections and ratifies laws. He was freed a few days later.

Nearly 70 schoolchildren were arrested in Teheran in March 2003 for using the Internet to organise dates and forbidden sexual relations. They were freed a few days later.

Sina Motallebi, a journalist with the reformist daily *Hayat-e-No* and editor of the website Rooznegar, was arrested on 20 April after being summoned the previous day by the Tehran police's morality section, or *Edareh-ye Amaken*, which is close to the intelligence services. After the closure of the paper in January, he had revived the website and used it to defend one of the paper's journalists, Alireza Eshraqi, who had been arrested on 11 January. The site, which especially defends imprisoned journalists, had angered some legal officials and also a number of reformists by criticising them for their silence about the arrests of journalists. He was freed on 12 May.

Authorities allowed it to expand in the 1990s without any serious controls – even as they hunted for illegal satellite television dishes and Western movie videos. The huge online appetite has been fed by thousands of Internet cafes, low-cost computers from East Asia and a rush of entrepreneurs offering Internet accounts.

Other tightly run nations – such as Saudi Arabia and China – keep reins on the Internet. In Iran, almost anything is a click away. Beside blogging, Iranians spend time in chat rooms, download music, read poetry, visit any of the countless Farsi news sites or even surf the erotic offerings.

At its present course, Internet usage in Iran is expected to grow sevenfold to 15 million users by 2006, according to studies cited by the *Middle East Economic Digest*. More than half of Iran's 65 million are under 25 years old and hungry for the Internet.[9]

Pedram Moallemian, an Iranian who runs the English-language eyeranian.net from San Diego, reaching many of those Iranians with observations on everything from the Iranian elections to US news programmes, told the *Associated Press* in 2004: 'The blog in Iran is truly an amassing phenomenon. It shows that Iranians are saying, "Look, we're part of the world as well"'.

The Internet revolution has begun to hit the traditionally secluded seminary schools too. As thousands of young Iranians share their thoughts through their personal weblogs, many clerics have also taken advantage of the Internet to express thoughts and feelings that would otherwise remain deep inside. Mehdi, a clergyman from Qom, wrote in his weblog in June 2004:

> Where is the one who would be able to able to say, 'I love you' in the simplest form? Where is the one who would, without acting coyly, submit herself like a female cat to the claws of the male sex, so that I would devote all my love to her in a moment? With all my human reality and all my attachment to the earth, only and solely out of instinct – a pure animal instinct – I long for someone like me to unite with …

The hardliners' distrust of the Internet does not stop them using it to spread their own propaganda, with sites such as daricheh.org and jebhe. com. The religious city of Qom also turns out several thousand students each year trained in computers and the Internet who are supposed to use their knowledge to serve the country and further Islam.

However, the Internet remains mainly a tool in the hands of intellectuals, dissidents and youngsters to access uncensored news, to speak out about issues that cannot even be approached in the print media, and to exchange ideas. The house arrest of Ayatollah Montazeri, which was aimed at muffling the most prominent clerical critic of the Islamic Republic, was literally broken when he had his own website set up, in which he published his controversial memoirs, and in which he keeps lambasting the ruling establishment and communicating with his disciples.

A shocking videotape that showed how the defendants in the case of the serial killings were tortured by the Intelligence Ministry interrogators to make false confessions – ranging from receiving money from Israel to having sex with animals – was viewed by millions of Iranians through the web.

On his website, Amir Frashad Ebrahimi, a former member of the Ansar-e Hezbollah, disclosed that my schoolmate at Kharazmi and left-wing activist Pirooz Davani was murdered at orders by a high-ranking cleric, and that his body – missing since the summer of 1998 – was actually buried in the backyard of an Intelligence Ministry building in northern Tehran.

But the web serves far more than politics. Millions of young Iranians listen on the Internet to the 'underground' rock bands whose music have failed to obtain recording and distribution permit from the Ministry of Culture and Islamic Guidance. In 2003, even an online 'contest' was held for such bands.

Despite all restrictions, young musicians in Iran have never been out of tune with global trends in pop and rock music. Once only dancing to the tune of exile pop music smuggled in from Los Angeles, young Iranians' started to show an interest in the domestically produced 'revolutionary' pop music in mid-1990s, when the state radio and television, as well as the Ministry of Culture, hitherto preserving a hard line on anything sounding Western, began to ease off the rules in a bid to appeal to the youth and distract them from 'dangerous' political ideas. For nearly 15 years after the 1979 Islamic Revolution, the only legal music in Iran comprised war hymns, traditional songs or anodyne instrumentals.

During the first years of the Revolution, there was pressure from the traditionalist clergy to ban all music. The late revolutionary leader Ayatollah Khomeini turned it down. In one of his most famous rulings, Ayatollah Khomeini said that if a piece of music were not 'intoxicating,' there was nothing wrong with it. But even today the state television refuses to show musical instruments when airing a 'legitimate' concert: one can only see the faces of the musicians in close-up.

The 'new wave' music was immediately a big hit. According to Mohammed Zarghami, 'This trend was so successful that video and audiocassettes imported from LA experienced a 30 percent drop in sales and over 55 percent of people turned to domestically produced pop music.'

Khashayar Etemadi was one of a dozen singers who jumped to popularity on the tide of the new pop music. Some critics said his appeal was strong because he sounded like Dariush, an Iranian exile in Los Angeles whose records are smuggled into the country and snatched up by eager listeners – a charge Etemadi dismissed. His most popular song, ironically repeatedly aired by the state radio and television, drew much criticism from hardliners because its lyrics were written by Ahmad Shamloo, a veteran dissident poet who was frequently denounced by suspicious conservatives as a 'wayward Westernised lackey.'

Revolutionary pop songs were mostly created by mounting lyrics about divine love and admiration for nature on an offbeat, slow theme. Nonetheless, the new music drew part of its appeal from similarities in the vocal style to that of expatriate Iranian artists, officially banned inside Iran but widely available. This similarity has been multiplied since early 'Islamic pop songs' appeared.

Los Angeles music never backed off, however. In bust squares and crossroads of large cities, young men standing on the pavement whisper to passers-by: 'I have new tapes, I have new films,' mainly contraband music from Los Angeles. Pop music from the West – in particular from 'Iran-geles' – still dominates most private parties, including raucous weddings.

But the local bands and musicians have been drawing more and more youngsters to live concerts. Thousands of people who go to watch Aryan – a band of seven young men and women – perform live, are frequently reminded by the 'officials' in the concert hall to remain seated. The same happens in live concerts by Alireza Assar, whose powerful lyrics about widespread poverty in one of his songs, brings the audience to tears and screams. But they are reminded that they should behave themselves if they do not want the concert to be cancelled.

Meanwhile fascination with Western pop music has remained predominant. Techno and trance are a common feature of many youth parties in modern Iran, and hearing the loud thumping of percussion pouring out of the windows of luxury cars in uptown Tehran have become an ordinary experience for some time. To augment the effect of trance or techno, some young Iranians use narcotics, from Ecstasy and marijuana to heroin and crack. Drug addiction is a growing and alarming social problem in Iran. And in recent years, the problem has been aggravated by the increasing number of addicts contracting AIDS.

More than 40,000 Iranians died from narcotics abuse between 20 March 2004 and 20 March 2005, and just over 26,000 died in car crashes, a report issued by the Iranian state coroner said. The report categorized drug-related deaths as 'suspect,' while automobile-related deaths were the leading cause of 'unnatural' deaths and caused serious injury to an additional 250,000 Iranians. Most 'natural' deaths were due to cardiac and cardiovascular conditions, with heart attacks the leading cause of death in that category, the report stated. Medical centres run by the state coroner's office also treated 1.5 million Iranians injured in fights, while just over 1,400 Iranians drowned that year, the report stated.

Drugs have been found to be the main cause of AIDS in Iran. The number of people with HIV/AIDS in Iran has risen in recent years, and Iranian officials describe the disease as a 'time bomb.' Officially, Iran identifies about 5,000 people infected with HIV/AIDS. However, some experts and officials put the actual number at 20,000. Drug addicts are said to make up about 70 percent of AIDS patients in Iran. And experts warn that with the country's fast-growing population of drug addicts, the deadly virus could spread even further.

As of 1 July 1999 the official figure for people living with HIV/AIDS in Iran was 1,676, of which 1,063 were male and 73 female. Of this total 1,157 were injecting drug users, and 226 had AIDS.

The National AIDS Committee was set up in 1995. A concerted effort has been made by the Ministry of Health to educate, in main, the medical community, and all donated blood is tested for the virus. Awareness surveys carried out amongst the general public have indicated a poor understanding of the disease and its impact. The dissemination of public information leaflets and private counselling has been carried out to some extent.

The first case of AIDS in Iran was identified in 1987 in a 6-year-old boy who contracted it from HIV-contaminated blood brought in from abroad. So far, about 700 people are believed to have died from AIDS in Iran. AIDS figures in Iran are still low by international standards, but officials and experts say the number of people infected with HIV/AIDS is increasing.

It is feared that the situation regarding HIV/AIDS in Iran may be more serious than generally realised. The main concern of the government is the potential spread of infection from injecting drug users to the general population. The strategic geographic situation of Iran and its long common borders with the countries of the Golden Crescent (Afghanistan and Pakistan), which produce a substantial proportion of the world's heroin, have confronted Iran with the problems of drug trafficking and concomitant drug addiction within the country.

In 2004 Dr Muhammad Mehdi Gouya, head of the disease management department of the Iranian Health Ministry, said: 'The [patients on the] official registries have undergone three tests, after which we declare them as being infected. There is a big gap between the registered statistics and the estimated ones. [Sexually transmitted diseases] are considered hidden diseases because no one admits to their deeds. Hence, the estimated statistics are important. We estimate that in Iran, there are between 23,000 to 25,000 cases of people infected with HIV.'[10]

Some experts even estimate that up to 40,000 people may be HIV-positive in Iran. Officials say the majority of those Iranians infected with HIV are drug addicts. There are believed to be more than 2 million drug addicts in Iran. Of these, 300,000 are intravenous drug users. Iranian health officials estimate that only about 12 percent of those infected acquired HIV through sexual contact.

Along with his brother, Doctor Arash Alaei established the first counselling and care centre for HIV-positive patients in Iran a few years ago, in the city of Kermanshah in western Iran. Alaei was recognised by the World Health Organisation for his HIV/AIDS work and is credited with helping Iran become more open in addressing HIV/AIDS problems. Alaei believes the spread of HIV through sexual contact will become a more serious problem in Iran. 'We should not neglect this issue,' he said. 'For example, a drug addict who spent some time in jail and became infected after using a common dirty needle could have sex after being released. Therefore, I anticipate that, in the future, AIDS transmission through sexual contact will increase.'[11]

Officials in the country have only recently begun to openly speak about AIDS, however. Alaei said many doctors in Iran are still not comfortable treating AIDS patients: 'As a doctor, I would suggest to you that among my colleagues in the health system, as in a segment of society, there is fear about AIDS. There is fear about treating an infected patient. For example, we had a case who had a broken arm and while being transferred to the operating room for surgical treatment, the operation was cancelled because [it was learned] he was infected with AIDS.'

Alaei said the attitudes of doctors are also shared by many in the general public: 'In the other classes of society, AIDS awareness is also still limited. There is fear and maybe they consider it as a social stigma.'

In a new effort to limit the spread of the disease, Iran's Health Ministry is urging health workers not to turn away patients who are HIV-positive and to give them proper treatment. Doctor Muhammad Mehdi Gouya, an official in the Iranian Health Ministry, said more AIDS counselling centres have been created across the country: 'It is imperative that health centres and clinics across the country make it easier for those who acted recklessly to come forward and receive proper counselling and even undergo tests, if necessary. This can now be done in medical universities across the country.'

Experts maintain that if a serious awareness campaign is not launched, the spread of AIDS will be disastrous for the country. Iran's Education Ministry announced recently that information on sexually transmitted diseases, including HIV/AIDS, would be included in school textbooks

Despite a concerted effort by the government of Iran to combat the problem, the number of drug addicts has been placed at more than one million, affecting not only the drug users themselves, but also their families, especially women and children. According to the latest observations, many drug-using men return home from prison with HIV/AIDS. Due to the lack of awareness in society, the wives of such men are at very high risk of contracting HIV.

This concern has been built into the UNDP country office project, Assisting Women Victims of Illicit Drugs, being implemented by the Bureau of Women's Affairs, Office of the Advisor to the President. The project will provide support services to women and girls affected by drug addiction in their families. The anticipated outcomes of the project include heightened awareness of the medical dangers of drug use, including the transmission of HIV/AIDS, the empowerment of women, through education on how to protect themselves and prevent the spread of HIV/AIDS, and reduction of the spread of HIV/AIDS by drug users to their families. As part of the UNAIDS Theme Group in Iran, UNDP has been supportive of the government's awareness raising campaign.

In the UNDP Project on HIV and Development in south and southwest Asia, Iran will take the lead in initiatives related to HIV and injecting drug use.

Besides the predominant conservative standpoint that regards problems such as AIDS, drug addiction or prostitution as vices exported by the West, there are also many traditionalists who view such traumas purely as products of 'sinful acts' and maintain that the victims deserve what they have got. Nevertheless, as a result of changes in the structure of society, such viewpoints are rapidly losing ground. There is at least one good reason why the authorities have come to revisit their long-held dogmas: that 27 years of relentless propaganda and indoctrination by a religious state has ultimately produced a generation that has become more than ever distanced from both religion and politics.

Ayatollah Khomeini's mausoleum in the Behesht-e Zahra cemetery in southern Tehran is a telling example. Once the scene of a hysterical welfare to the architect of the Islamic Revolution, the mausoleum – which now, in the tradition of the holiest Shi'i sites, features a golden dome four minarets – has gradually developed into something totally different. On Thursday nights in particular, when thousands of people visit Behesht-e Zahra to pay respects to their lost ones, Ayatollah Khomeini's tomb and its surroundings look more like a Shi'i Islamic Disneyland than a holy religious site. There are dozens of shops offering everything from the latest Western-fashion clothes to hi-tech electronic gadgets. You can order lamb kebab or pizza in several busy restaurants, or have fast food or ice cream in a sandwich bar. You can measure your pulse or blood pressure or gauge the strength of your biceps on a state-of-the-art digital machine. You can play the latest computer games or surf the web in an Internet cafe. You can buy souvenirs, from clocks decked with the portrait of Ayatollahs Khomeini and Khamenei to key rings with the portraits of the 'martyrs'. You can spread out your picnic gear and enjoy a family dinner under the lush plane trees. And if you are curious enough, sometimes you can catch a glimpse of a young couple in the shadows of the falling dusk, enjoying a quiet moment at a quiet corner, without fear of being persecuted by the custodians of 'Islamic morals'.

THREE

Bullets, Carnations and Turbans

*My soldiers are at the moment either in cradles or playing in the
streets.*
Ayatollah Ruhollah Khomeini, 1963

*Tomorrow, when the spring comes
We will all be released and free ...*
Revolutionary song, 1978

*Who controls the past ... controls the future: who controls the
present, controls the past.*
George Orwell, *1984*

Since 1980, every year in February, the Iranian government holds
celebrations called 'Ten days of Dawn' to mark the anniversary of the
Islamic Revolution of 1979. The celebrations start on 1 February, the
day Ayatollah Ruhollah Khomeini returned to Iran after fourteen
years in exile. His triumphant return happened two weeks after the
embattled and agitated shah had left the country for good, amid
daily demonstrations by hundreds of thousands of angry protesters,
nationwide strikes that had paralysed the country, and pressure from
Western powers, particularly the United States – the key supporter of
his regime for decades. The 'Ten days of Dawn' ended on 11 February,
when in 1979, the revolutionaries took over the garrisons, the state
radio and television, and all major centres of the monarchy's authority,

which were already hanging by a thread after the armed forces declared neutrality and refused to stand against demonstrators. The 'dawn' metaphor, derived from the Qur'anic verse 'I swear by the dawn and the ten nights', draws a fitting analogy with the revolution that put an end to the shah's benighted thirty-seven year reign, although for Ayatollah Khomeini and other revolutionaries who coined it, its implications went all the way back to twenty-five centuries of monarchy in Iran.

The ten-day celebrations include decorating schools, government offices and streets with colourful ribbons and banners, flashing lights and flags, and portraits of Ayatollah Khomeini and the present leader Ayatollah Ali Khamenei; and holding photo exhibitions, concerts, sports competitions and other events. The state television also plays its part in commemorating the Revolution by airing special programmes, from soap operas that tell the story of the Revolution from different angles, to documentaries and chronologies explaining how the 'bad old days' were replaced by a 'sacred system' by means of the 'martyrdom' of thousands of Muslim people.

All the propaganda, as one should expect, is focused on how terrible everything was before the Revolution, and how happy people have become after it. For the generations that have actually lived the days of the Revolution, however, the scenes they see on television are somewhat different from what actually took place.

For one thing, not in any of the footage broadcast by the Islamic Republic about the million-strong demonstrations prior to the Islamic Revolution is there a single shot showing women clad in anything other than the Islamic dress code, or hejab. In reality, however, a large part of the women taking part in anti-shah protests in those days did not observe the hejab. Although this may be a relief for many people who would nowadays like to insist that they had nothing to do with the Islamic Republic's rise to power, the fact is that thousands of women without the hejab – from university and high-school students to teachers and housewives – were there, among others, shouting 'Death to the shah'. It was in those days that Ayatollah Khomeini said in an interview in his residence near Paris that in the new system 'even the communists would be free to express their opinion'.

Another spectacle missing from the Islamic television shows to commemorate the Revolution are the marchers holding banners in support of the militant political groups which, shortly after the collapse of the monarchy, stood against the new regime, and which were ultimately crushed in brutal conflicts. More prominent than others was the Mojahedin-e Khalq Organisation (MKO) that lived to become the Islamic Republic's most hated nemesis. Posters and pictures of Muhammad Mosaddeq, the leader of the 1950s oil nationalisation movement, are also among the items cut out of films recording events leading to the Revolution.

The third, and perhaps most striking disappearing act, concerns Ayatollah Khomeini's close allies who later fell from grace, and paid for it dearly. Sitting next to Ayatollah Khomeini on the Air France Boeing 747 that took him back to Tehran on 1 February was Sadeq Qotbzadeh, a member of the anti-shah Islamic Association of Iranian Students in Paris who, together with a handful of other Association compatriots, had become his advisor and spokesperson during the months before the Revolution. After the fall of the shah, Qotbzadeh became head of the State Radio and Television, and served briefly as foreign minister in the first post-Revolution government before the office was discarded following the seizure of the American embassy in Tehran on 4 November 1979. Frustrated with the subsequent turn of events, the pro-West Qotbzadeh later went into hiding, established a subversive group to topple Ayatollah Khomeini, and was eventually arrested and executed after giving a televised 'confession' that was to become a ritual for arrested dissidents in the coming years. Many still remember the television footage of the day of Kohmeini's return, in which the Ayatollah, seated by the aircraft window beside a smiling, clean-shaven Qotbzadeh, made one of his trademark comments. Asked by a reporter what his feelings were now that he was coming back to his country after fourteen years, the often stoney-faced revolutionary leader answered tersely: 'Nothing'.

Two other 'invisible' figures strike one by their absence: coming home aboard the same aircraft as his then-beloved imam (leader) was Abolhassan Bani Sadr, who later became Iran's first president, only to flee back to Paris in 1981, after he refused to get along with hardline members of the government, who were favoured by Ayatollah Khomeini; and Ebrahim Yazdi, also on board that Air France plane, a US educated, secular anti-shah activist of the Freedom Movement, who became a foreign minister and later a parliament deputy, before Ayatollah Khomeini ruled that the Movement members were 'apostates', and the Freedom Movement was banned.

This pattern of altering past events to fit the requirements of the ruling establishment was meaningfully articulated by George Orwell in his depiction of the totalitarian regime in *1984*:

'If the Party could thrust its hand into the past and say of this or that even, *it never happened* – that, surely, was more terrifying than mere torture and death.

'And if all others accepted the lie which the Party imposed – if all records told the same tale – then the lie passed into history and became truth. Day by day and almost minute by minute the past was brought up to date. In this way every prediction made by the Party could be shown by documentary evidence to have been correct; nor was any item of news, or any expression of opinion, which conflicted with the needs of the moment, ever allowed to remain on record. All history was a palimpsest, scraped clean and reinscribed exactly as often as was necessary.'

However, the Islamic Republic was not the inventor of the Orwellian approach. Typical of all closed, despotic political systems, and perhaps exemplified most aptly by the Soviet Union, the shah's monarchy also practiced it for a long time. In the version of contemporary Iranian history taught in schools, Mosaddeq was described as a power-hungry politician who aimed to overthrow the shah. The CIA-sponsored coup that toppled Mosaddeq's government in 1953 was described as a 'national uprising'. Paradoxically, among other similarities, the monarchy and the Islamic Republic shared the same hatred towards the nationalist icon.

No matter how hard each of the two regimes has tried to alter the past, younger generations with no living memory of historical events have hardly bought the version of history offered to them by a state they mistrusted. Just as the young Iranians today – who have no memories of the 1979 Revolution – do not adhere to the much-publicised notion that everything before the Revolution was wrong, neither are they convinced by some royalists' claims that the shah could have taken the country to 'the gates of great civilisation' had his efforts not been sabotaged by 'the powers that be' and 'an unholy coalition of red and black reactionaries', i.e. the secular opposition and the clergy.

In the years following the 1979 Islamic Revolution, there has been much speculation about its roots and causes, and whether it could have been avoided. There are still ardent royalists who say the whole episode was a plot, a conspiracy, or alternatively a blind turmoil with catastrophic results. Some of them blame the shah for lacking the resolve and determination to use force to crush the movement, and for abandoning the country.

Also there are analysts and political activists who say that if the shah had remained loyal to the constitution, if he had not overthrown Mosaddeq, there would have been no revolution. Hundreds of volumes have been published to analyse the 1979 Revolution, most of which view it as a natural result of the way the shah's regime ruled the country.

In the words of Ervand Abrahamian, the Pahlavi regime was structurally weak, socially isolated and politically alienated from the general population long before the Revolution began to unfold:

> It was a regime conspicuously lacking in social support, and was therefore perpetually unstable and susceptible to revolution. What kept it going was not an inherent mythical ingredient, as royalist ideologues liked to claim, but the increasing oil revenues which both created an aura of economic prosperity and financed the constant expansion of the state institutions, especially the machineries of repression.
>
> In short, the Pahlavi regime was not an indestructible regime based on solid foundations, as it portrayed itself; it was rather a Titan with feet of clay – feet that shattered and brought the whole structure tottering down as soon as they were struck by ... minor blows.[1]

Satya J. Gabriel holds that in reality, Iran was, to a significant extent, a social formation comprising two separate and unequal class communities: one capitalist and the other ancient:

> The capitalist Iran, with its internecine conflict between oligarchic capitalism and petty capitalism, was growing more and more powerful, but this power was highly concentrated in the relatively small oligarchy. Most of the Iranian people lived in a very different Iran, ancient Iran, where self-exploitation,

devotion to traditional religious ideals, and political processes founded upon consensus building were the norm. The clergy were of the latter. The regime was narrowly focused on the former. So long as the boundaries of these two Irans did not intersect, there was probably not sufficient tension in the society to generate a revolutionary crisis.

However, the monarchist regime not only created internecine strife within capitalist Iran by encouraging the growth of oligarchic capitalism, but it continually pushed the boundaries of capitalist Iran into ancient Iran, threatening the survival of ancientism. This was a critical catalyst in the 1979 Revolution. In the end, struggles over class processes were an important condition for the widespread discontent with the monarchist regime and the ability of the opponents of that regime to mobilize such large numbers of people. The monarchist regime's failure to fully consider the class effects of its actions proved fatal.[2]

One morning in the fall of 1976, a few friends and I got to the Kharazmi Boys' high school an hour earlier than our fellow students, to play football. The school was located near Tehran University, long a hotbed of dissent and demonstrations against the regime. As soon as we turned the corner into the street on which the school was located, we found out that something had been happening.

A squad of municipality garbage collectors was busy at work, hurriedly wiping something off the wall that faced the school gates. But not before we could get a glimpse of the graffiti: 'Death to the traitor shah and his blood-sucking regime'.

Almost everybody was talking about the graffiti by the time we got our first break, which was usually characterised by a ritual of blowing pyramidal milk cartons under our feet and throwing pistachio nuts or palm dates at each other. The foodstuff was given to all students throughout the country in accordance with the 'free nutrition scheme' introduced by the government. Yet the middle-class Tehrani students could easily afford to ridicule and squander an offer that would have seemed like a dream for previous generations. Apparently those were heady days for Iran, but for the teenagers of the 1970s, the writing was already, and literally, on the wall.

Students from more politicised families were talking about Jimmy Carter's election campaign and how the shah's regime would soon crumble. There were also vague allusions to one Ayatollah Khomeini, who resided in Najaf and said that the monarchy was essentially un-Islamic, and should be replaced by a true Islamic state, although such remarks were made by only a handful of students with strict religious backgrounds. Otherwise, the anti-regime talks centred on such issues as human rights violations, censorship, political prisoners and torture.

The early 1960s saw the beginnings of fundamental changes to Iran's social order. The shah's so-called White Revolution, the land reforms and economic prosperity, transformed the traditional class structure. Having weathered the upheavals of the 1960s, the shah's regime was on the path of consolidation. Universities and other higher education institutes underwent rapid expansion, and therefore the number of students multiplied. More importantly, higher education was no longer the monopoly of the privileged classes; gradually, talented youngsters from all walks of life were able to enter universities. This, in turn, prepared the ground for a new form of student dissent.

By late 1976 and early 1977 it was evident that the Iranian economy was in trouble. The shah's attempt to use Iran's vastly expanded oil revenues after 1973 for an unrealistically ambitious industrial and construction programme, and a massive military build-up, greatly strained Iran's human and institutional resources, and caused severe economic and social dislocation. Widespread official corruption, rapid inflation, and a growing gap in incomes between the wealthier and the poorer strata of society, fed public dissatisfaction.

In response, the government attempted to provide the working and middle classes with some immediate and tangible benefits of the country's new oil wealth. The government nationalised private secondary schools, declared that secondary education would be free for all Iranians, and started a free meal programme in schools. It took over private community colleges and extended financial support to university students. It lowered income taxes, inaugurated an ambitious health insurance plan, and speeded up implementation of a programme introduced in 1972, under which industrialists were required to sell 49 percent of the shares of their companies to their employees.[3]

The programmes were badly implemented, however, and did not

adequately compensate for the deteriorating economic position of the urban working class and those who, like civil servants, were on fixed salaries. To deal with the disruptive effects of excessive spending, the government adopted policies that appeared threatening to the propertied classes, and to bazaar, business, and industrial elements that had benefited from economic expansion and might have been expected to support the regime. For example, in an effort to bring down rents, municipalities were empowered to take over empty houses and apartments and to rent and administer them in place of their owners. In an effort to bring down prices in 1975 and 1976, the government declared war on profiteers, arrested and fined thousands of shopkeepers and petty merchants, and sent two prominent industrialists into exile.

Moreover, by 1978 there were 60,000 foreigners in Iran – 45,000 of them Americans – engaged in business, or in military training and advisory missions. Combined with a superficial westernisation of dress, lifestyles, music, films, and television programmes, this foreign presence tended to intensify the perception that the shah's modernisation programme was threatening society's Islamic and Iranian cultural values and identity. Increasing political repression and the establishment of a one-party state in 1975 further alienated the educated classes.

The shah was aware of the rising resentment and dissatisfaction in the country, and the increasing international concern about the suppression of basic freedoms in Iran. Organisations such as the International Council of Jurists and Amnesty International were drawing attention to mistreatment of political prisoners and violation of the rights of the accused in Iranian courts. More importantly, President Jimmy Carter, who took office in January 1977, was making an issue of human-rights violations in countries with which the United States was associated. The shah, who had been pressed into a programme of land reform and political liberalisation by the Kennedy administration in the early 1960s, was sensitive to possible new pressures from Washington, but ultimately had no choice but to give in.

Beginning in early 1977, the shah took certain steps to counter both domestic and foreign criticism of Iran's human-rights record. He released a number of political prisoners and announced new regulations to protect the legal rights of civilians brought before military courts. In July, the shah replaced Amir Abbas Hoveyda, his prime minister of twelve years, with Jamshid Amuzegar, who had served for over a decade in various cabinet posts. Unfortunately for the shah, however, Amuzegar also became unpopular, as he attempted to slow the overheated economy with measures that, although generally thought necessary, triggered a downturn in employment, and in private sector profits, that would later compound the government's problems.

Leaders of the moderate opposition, professional groups, and the intelligentsia took advantage of the shah's accommodations, and the more helpful attitude of the Carter administration, to organise and speak out. Many did so in the form of open letters, addressed to prominent officials, in which the writers demanded adherence to the constitution and the restoration of basic freedoms. Lawyers, judges, university professors, and writers formed professional associations to press home these demands. Mosaddeq-supporting National Front and other political groups resumed activity.

The protest movement took a new turn in January 1978, when a government-inspired article in *Ettela'at*, one of the country's leading newspapers, cast doubt on Ayatollah Khomeini's piety and suggested that he was a British agent. The article caused a scandal in the religious community. Senior clerics, including Ayatollah Kazem Shariatmadari, denounced the article. Seminary students took to the streets in Qom and clashed with police, and several demonstrators were killed.

Ruhollah Mousavi Khomeini was born on 24 September 1902 in the small town of Khomein, some 160 kilometres to the southwest of Qom. His family had a long tradition of religious scholarship. His ancestors, said to be descendants of the sixth Shi'i Imam, Mousa Kazem, had migrated towards the end of the eighteenth century from their original home in Neishabour, in Khorasan province, to the Lucknow region of northern India, where they settled and became involved in religious instruction, and guidance of the region's predominantly Shi'i population.

Ayatollah Khomeini's grandfather, Sayyed Ahmad, left Lucknow (although according to a statement of Ayatollah Khomeini's elder brother, Sayyed Morteza Pasandideh, his point of departure was Kashmir, not Lucknow) some time in the middle of the nineteenth century on pilgrimage to the tomb of the first Shi'i Imam, Ali, in Najaf. While in Najaf, Sayyed Ahmad met Yousef Khan, a well-known local figure in

Khomein, upon whose invitation he decided to settle in Khomein for religious guidance, and to marry Yousef Khan's daughter.

By the time of his undated death, Sayyed Ahmad had two children: a daughter by the name of Sahiba, and Sayyed Mostafa Hindi, born in 1885, the father of Ayatollah Khomeini. Sayyed Mostafa began his religious education in Isfahan and continued his advanced studies in Najaf and Samara, according to an established clerical tradition of completing preliminary studies in Iran followed by advanced studies in the holy Shi'i cities of Iraq. Ayatollah Khomeini became an exception to this rule: he was the first religious leader of prominence whose formative years were entirely passed in Iran. After accomplishing his advanced studies, Sayyed Mostafa returned to Khomein and married Hajar, who gave birth to Ruhollah Khomeini.[4]

By 1918, having lost both his parents, his eldest brother Sayyed Morteza – later to be known as Ayatollah Pasandideh – was running the family.

Ruhollah Khomeini began his education by memorising the Qur'an at a traditional religious school. In 1920–21, Sayyed Morteza sent Ruhollah to the city of Arak, at the time known as Soltanabad, to enjoy better education. In 1923 Khomeini arrived in Qom to complete the preliminary stage of seminary school education.

Khomeini did not engage in any political activities during the 1930s. Believing that any political move should follow the guidelines of the foremost religious scholars, he was forced to accept the decision of Grand Ayatollah Haeri, the founder of Qom seminary school, to remain relatively passive toward Reza shah's measures to modernise the country. In any event, as a still junior figure in the religious institution in Qom, he would have been in no position to mobilise popular opinion on a national scale.

In 1955, when a nationwide campaign against the Bahai faith was launched, Khomeini tried with little success to obtain the support of Grand Ayatollah Boroujerdi, the supreme religious leader in Qom after the death of Ayatollah Haeri, in purging the Bahais. Therefore, during Ayatollah Boroujerdi's religious leadership in Qom, Khomeini concentrated on teaching *fiqh*, or the laws of Islamic jurisprudence known also as Sharia, and gathering round him students who later became his associates in struggling against the Pahlavi regime. Among them were figures that would become Iran's leaders in 1979: Ayatollah Hosseinali Montazeri, Ayatollah Morteza Motahhari, Ali Akbar Hashemi Rafsanjani and Muhammad Javad Bahonar.

After the demise of Ayatollah Boroujerdi in 1961, religious leadership was fragmented, as none of his disciples had a following among believers. Without Boroujerdi's authority, the time was ripe for Ayatollah Khomeini to embark on his political activities against the shah. He also introduced himself as a source of emulation, or Marja-e Taqlid, by publishing the basic handbook of religious practice, or *Tozih ol-Masael*, which every grand ayatollah should have to his name.

In the autumn of 1962, the government promulgated new laws governing elections to local and provincial councils, in which the requirement for the elected representatives to be sworn into office by the Qur'an was eliminated. Instead, the representatives were required to take an oath on 'the divine book'. Considering this move as a plan to integrate the isolated Bahais into society, Ayatollah Khomeini sent telegraphs to the shah and the prime minister, warning them to desist from violating both the law of Islam and the Constitution.[5]

In January 1963, the shah announced a six-point reform scheme, entitled the 'White Revolution', which included land reforms and voting rights for women. Ayatollah Khomeini urged other clerics to join him in opposing the move and boycotting the referendum on the reform plan. About a month later he issued a manifesto that also bore the signatures of eight other senior scholars, listing various infringements of the constitution by the shah, deploring the spread of moral corruption in the country, and accusing the shah of comprehensive submission to America and Israel. He also decreed that the Nowruz celebrations for the new Iranian year 1342 (beginning on 21 March 1963) be cancelled as a sign of protest against government policies.

On the afternoon of Ashura (3 June 1963), Ayatollah Khomeini delivered a speech at the Fayziyeh seminary school in Qom, in which he drew parallels between the Umayyad caliph Yazid and the shah, and warned the shah that if he did not change his ways the day would come when people would offer up thanks for his departure from the country. The immediate effect of Ayatollah Khomeini's speech was, however, his arrest two days later, at three o'clock in the morning, by a group of commandos who hastily transferred him to the Qasr prison in Tehran.

As dawn broke on 3 June, the news of his arrest spread first through Qom, and then to other cities. In Qom, Tehran, Shiraz, Mashhad and Varamin, tanks and paratroopers confronted angry demonstrators. It was not until six days later that order was fully restored. This uprising of 15 Khordad 1342 in the Persian calendar marked a turning point in contemporary Iranian history.

After nineteen days in the Qasr prison, Ayatollah Khomeini was moved first to the Eshratabad military base and then to a house in the Davoudiyeh neighbourhood of Tehran where he was kept under surveillance. He was released on 7 April 1964, and returned to Qom.[6]

The same year, Iran's parliament, or Majles, approved an agreement with the United States that provided immunity from prosecution for American citizens and their dependents in Iran. Ayatollah Khomeini delivered a fiery speech against the shah, denouncing the agreement as surrendering Iranian independence and sovereignty in exchange for a 200 million-dollar loan that would be of benefit only to the shah and his associates, and describing as traitors all those in the Majles who voted in favour of it. He concluded by saying that the government lacked all legitimacy.

On 4 November 1964, shortly before dawn, soldiers surrounded Ayatollah Khomeini's house in Qom, arrested him, and this time took him directly to Mehrabad airport in Tehran for immediate exile to Turkey. As Turkish law forbade Ayatollah Khomeini from wearing the clergyman's cloak and turban, in 1965 Ayatollah Khomeini left Turkey for Najaf in Iraq, where he spent the next thirteen years mobilising his followers and planning the overthrow of the Pahlavi regime.[7]

In his memoirs, Asadollah Alam, the shah's prime minister of the time, notes that he told the shah in 1974 that with the suppression of the clerics and the exiling of Khomeini, 'the mullah trouble in Iran was finished forever'. He did not live long enough to see what a mistake he had made.[8]

Upon the publishing in *Ettela'at* of the article lambasting Ayatollah Khomeini in 1978, the Isfahan bazaar closed in protest. On 18 February, mosque services and demonstrations were held in several cities to honour those killed in the Qom demonstrations. In Tabriz the demonstrations turned violent, and it was two days before order could be restored. By the summer, riots and anti-government demonstrations had swept dozens of towns and cities. Shootings inevitably occurred, and deaths of protesters fuelled public feeling against the regime.

The cycle of protests that began in Qom and Tabriz differed in nature, composition, and intent from the protests of the preceding year. The 1977 protests were primarily the work of middle-class intellectuals, lawyers, and secular politicians. They took the form of letters, resolutions, and declarations, and were aimed at the restoration of constitutional rule.

The protests that rocked Iranian cities in the first half of 1978, by contrast, were led by religious elements and took place in mosques and at religious events. They drew on traditional groups in the bazaar and among the urban working class for support. The protesters used a form of calculated violence to achieve their ends, attacking and destroying carefully selected targets that represented objectionable features of the regime: nightclubs and cinemas as symbols of moral corruption and the influence of Western culture; banks as symbols of economic exploitation; offices of the Rastakhiz, or 'Resurgence' party, created by the shah in 1975 to run a one-party state; and police stations as symbols of political repression.[9]

The protests, moreover, aimed at more fundamental change: in slogans and leaflets, the protesters attacked the shah and demanded his removal, and they depicted Ayatollah Khomeini as their leader, and an Islamic state as their ideal. From his exile in Iraq, Ayatollah Khomeini continued to issue statements calling for further demonstrations, rejecting any form of compromise with the regime, and demanding the overthrow of the shah.

Twenty-five years after the Revolution and sixteen years after Ayatollah Khomeini's death, the debate has not subsided among Iranian intellectuals about how he became the de facto leader of the popular movement. In the winter of 1985, at a private party attended by two renowned journalists and translators of western literary works – both leftists – I was witness to one such heated discussion. The actual conversation differed somewhat from my version below, as the two parties were already well-watered on bootleg Armenian vodka, and therefore used a rather rough language, but I have not altered the essence.

We intellectuals should be ashamed of ourselves for the suffering of people today. We should have known better and seen that a bunch of people representing the most reactionary segments of society would lead us into this mess.

How could you possibly say so? There was nothing wrong with what we did. Millions of people were out there, calling for the ousting of a bloodthirsty regime that had tortured and killed so many of our fellows.

Yes, to replace it with another regime that would torture and kill thousands more ...

Oh, that's not fair. How could we have predicted what would happen in the future?

Then why are we called intellectuals in the first place? Aren't we supposed to be pioneers of society, opinion makers and opinion leaders? How could we not see what the mullahs would lead to?

It had nothing to do with the mullahs then. They hijacked our revolution. There was no mention of Ayatollah Khomeini until it was quite late. By then there was no turning back.

Nonsense! For months people were chanting his name on the streets. His pictures were everywhere.

Even so, he spoke differently at that time. He spoke of freedom and justice. He said that once the revolution triumphed, the mullahs would have to go back to their mosques.

And we fools believed him! Shame on us! I'll never forgive myself!

There are pros and cons of both arguments, of course. In fact, of all the intellectuals opposing the shah, it was only the writer and jurist Mostafa Rahimi, who, in an essay published shortly after the Revolution (a little too late, some would say), rejected the notion of an Islamic Republic. Even the Marxists did not separate their ranks from those who were calling for an Islamic state. However, one should admit that Ayatollah Khomeini's 'manifesto' was there for all to see long before the movement had dashed beyond the point of no return.

As early as 1970, while in exile in Najaf, Ayatollah Khomeini had formulated his vision of an ideal state in a book entitled *The Islamic State: Velayat-e Faqih* (The governance of the jurisprudent). Although banned by the regime, like many other books written by dissidents, it was being openly distributed in large numbers by 1977, when the government's machinery of censorship was losing its grip.[10]

In that book Ayatollah Khomeini wrote:

> Just as the Most Noble Messenger was entrusted with the implementation of divine ordinances and the establishment of the institution of Islam, and just as God Almighty set him up over Muslims as their leader and ruler, making obedience to him obligatory, so, too, the just fuqaha (jurisprudents) must be leaders and rulers, implementing divine ordinances and establishing the institution of Islam.
>
> Since Islamic government is a government of law, those acquainted with the law, or more precisely, with religion – i.e. the fuqaha – must supervise its functioning. It is they who supervise all executive and administrative affairs of the country, together with all planning.
>
> The foqaha (clerical scholars) are the trustees who implement the divine ordinances in levying taxes, guarding the frontiers, and executing the penal provisions of the law. They must not allow the laws of Islam to remain in abeyance, or their operation to be affected by either defect or excess.[11]

Against the backdrop of such explicit state-making theory, today it may seem only too easy for the critics of Islamic rule to blame the intellectuals of the time. However, one should not underestimate the overwhelming power of the masses: the huge wave of popular dissent and unrest that was sweeping over the country, overshadowing every move, and muffling every sound against the movement.

It was not only the pious and the religious-minded who were out on the streets, calling for an Islamic government, torching banks, cinemas and liquor stores, shoving carnations into the barrels of the soldiers' rifles, and opening their chests to bullets. The streets were also dominated by the presence of young, well-to-do boys and girls in tight blue jeans and *à la mode* hairdos who, not long before, listened to Abba and the Bee Gees, went to the movies to see *Grease*, danced to the tune of *Saturday Night Fever* in discos, and swam together in the Caspian Sea while the national radio played *Surfing USA*.

One evening, during a school holiday in the summer of 1978, in a central square of Tehran, I ran into Behzad, a schoolmate of mine famous for his fun-loving nature. As a matter of fact, at the age of seventeen, he was one of the few students in our class who could boast of frequently visiting shahr-e Now (New City), Tehran's red-light district, which was later burnt down by zealous mobs just before the Islamic Republic took over. Having exchanged the usual pleasantries and wisecracks, I asked him what he was up to.

'Fighting the bastards, of course!' he said. 'The bloody vampire's days are numbered. Oh, boy, we're going to bring him to his knees!'

I asked him if he was still visiting Shahr-e Now, and if yes, how could he reconcile that with calling for an Islamic society.

'Are you blind? Don't you know what he's done to the youth in his prisons? Don't you know that he's sold the country to the Americans? Don't you see that his mercenaries butcher the youth every day? Don't you see all those people in the slums while he and his family plunder the country? We just want to get rid of the bastard and his SAVAK. This is what's willy-nilly going to happen. No one who replaces him would be worse.'

Behzad was not alone in his choice. Every day I saw people joining the revolutionaries whom I could never bring myself to believe knew how to say their prayers. But that was irrelevant. They wanted the shah out, and the shortest way was what Ayatollah Khomeini offered. Some six months after the victory of the Revolution, Behzad left for the United States. He never came back. He is a successful lawyer now, and hardly speaks about the Revolution.

The atrocities of SAVAK were always at the top of the list of crimes attributed to the shah and his regime. One evening in the summer of 1978, one of my father's closest friends came to visit us with his family. The couple were both educated in the United States and at that time worked as English teachers at the Iran-America Society in Tehran. Their two sons had been good friends of mine since early childhood.

Once seated, the lady started sobbing. Suspecting a possible family row, my mother approached her, asking her what was the matter. Suddenly she burst into tears, swearing at the 'criminal shah' who 'butchered our kids'.

'What's happened?' asked my father.

'You should know better, Colonel,' she replied caustically. My father was an army officer. 'A friend of us lives near the SAVAK headquarters. The other night she can't get to sleep. She gets out of bed, goes to the kitchen, and opens the window for a breath of fresh air. And what does she see?' By this time she was really crying. 'There's this man coming out of the backdoor of the SAVAK, pushing a wheelbarrow full of human hearts and livers towards the garbage can.'

How close such stories were to truth was not of any relevance to the revolutionaries. The only fact that mattered was that they saw the shah as a brutal dictator, and a thief who should be done away with. To paraphrase a contemporary social scientist, at that moment, as at several similar moments in history, the Iranians knew what they didn't want, but they had little idea of what they actually did want.

The 'religious intellectuals', though, apparently *did* know what they were after: a 'modern' interpretation of Islam that would bring about 'independence and freedom', as reflected in the key slogan of the Revolution, which would harbour progress and prosperity without changing the traditional identity of the people – an idea most of them would sooner or later come to call a blunder.

Mohsen Sazgara, a prominent critic of the Islamic Republic today, was twenty-three in those days. As a member of the Islamic Association of Students in the United States, he rushed back to Iran in 1978, taking an active part in the Revolution and later serving in different government posts. His open criticism of the constitution and the supreme leader landed him in jail twice in recent years. In an interview in March 2004, he recalled the ideals he and his fellow thinkers subscribed to during the Revolution:

'When we said 'independence', we meant a kind of negative balance similar to Mosaddeq's policy   something that was translated into 'neither the East, nor the West' after the Revolution. By 'freedom', we meant a system elected by and relying on the People. And by 'Islamic Republic', we meant a system based on a just distribution [of political power], some sort of socialist-oriented system.'[12]

Sazgara and his fellow thinkers would come to rethink all those ideals after the Islamic Republic consolidated and threw compromise to the winds. 'In all three issues we were simple-minded ... Achieving a full-scale republic requires compliance with modern reason, and modern reason cannot be confined under a ceiling such as religion,' Sazgara said in 2004.[13] Realising such facts cost a huge amount in time, resources and human life for the religious thinkers who came to revisit the dogmas they once cherished.

The government's position deteriorated further in August 1978, when more than 400 people died in a fire at the Rex Cinema in Abadan. Although evidence available after the Revolution suggested that religiously inclined students deliberately started the fire, the opposition carefully cultivated a widespread conviction that the fire was the work of SAVAK agents. The revolutionaries dubbed the disaster 'the shah's kebab shop'. Following the Rex Cinema fire, the shah removed Amuzegar, and named Jafar Sharif-Emami prime minister.

Sharif-Emami, a former minister and prime minister and a trusted royalist, had for many years served as President of the Senate. The new prime minister adopted a policy of conciliation. He eased press controls and permitted more open debate in the Majles. He released a number of imprisoned clerics, revoked the imperial calendar, closed gambling casinos, and obtained from the shah the dismissal from court and public office of members of the Bahai religion, a faith to which the clerics strongly objected.[14]

These measures, however, did not quell public protests. On 4 September more than 100,000 took part in the public prayers to mark the end of Ramadan, the Muslim fasting month. The ceremony became an occasion for anti-government demonstrations that continued for the next two days, growing larger and more radical in composition, and in the slogans of the participants.

The government declared martial law in Tehran and eleven other cities on the night of 7 September 1978. The next day, troops fired into a crowd of demonstrators at Tehran's Jaleh Square. Tens of protesters were killed. The Jaleh Square shooting came to be known as 'Black Friday'. It considerably radicalised the opposition movement and made compromise with the regime, even by moderates, less likely. In October the Iraqi authorities, unable to persuade Ayatollah Khomeini to refrain from further political activity, expelled him from their country. Ayatollah Khomeini went to France and established his headquarters at Neauphle-le-Chateau, outside Paris.

Ayatollah Khomeini's arrival in France provided new impetus to the revolutionary movement. It gave Ayatollah Khomeini and his movement exposure in the world press . It made possible easy telephone communication with lieutenants in Tehran and other Iranian cities, thus permitting better coordination of the opposition movement. It allowed Iranian political and religious leaders, cut off from Ayatollah Khomeini while he was in Iraq, to visit him for direct consultations. One of these visitors was National Front leader Karim Sanjabi. After a meeting with Ayatollah Khomeini early in November 1978, Sanjabi issued a three-point statement that for the first time committed the National Front to the Ayatollah's demand for the deposition of the shah, and the establishment of a government that would be 'democratic and Islamic'.[15]

Back in Iran, for the poetry-loving Iranian, the carefully constructed, often two-line slogan played a crucial part in exciting the crowds, and frequently launched them into an orbit of mass hysteria. As the protests gathered momentum, the slogans the angry crowds chanted became more and more venomous and explicit. For instance, in the case of slogans addressing the military stationed on the streets, the pattern proceeded thus:

> The army is our brother/ Khomeini is our leader
> Soldier brother! / Why kill your brother?
> We gave you flowers/ You replied by bullets
> Rise, O, soldiers / Your brother is killed
> I will kill, I will kill / Those who killed my brother
> No nation has ever seen / Armed forces so mean

Scattered strikes had occurred in a few private sector and government industries between June and August 1978. Beginning in September, workers in the public sector began to strike on a large scale. When the Sharif-Emami government quickly met the demands of strikers for improved salary and working benefits, oil workers and civil servants made demands for changes in the political system. The unavailability of fuel oil and freight transport, and shortages of raw materials resulting from a customs strike, led to the shutting down of most private sector industries in November.

In October 1987 the new academic year began, but only theoretically.

At Kharazmi, where I was supposed to study for my last year in high school, each day fewer students would show up to classes. I would see some of my classmates before school telling me they were going to take part in demonstrations.

After a couple of weeks, the teachers who bothered to attend the classes gave up, and the school was virtually closed. The students would nevertheless gather in the school's courtyard in the morning, sometimes accompanied by revolutionary teachers, and start a march towards the gates of Tehran University. There was a girls' school just across the street from Kharazmi, the students of which would also pour onto the street, joining the boys amid much laughter and fun and flirting, but all the same resolute to go and protest against the shah's regime. Those students who chose to stay at school were frequently called SAVAKI by their schoolmates.

Protestors marched onto Shah Reza Avenue, where students of Tehran University held daily demonstrations. The universities had been closed even before the schools, and served solely as arenas for people to gather together, organise, and get ready for demonstrations. Soldiers gazed at the protestors from tanks and army trucks stationed alongside the avenue, while daring youngsters at times approached them and shoved carnations into the barrels of their guns.

On 4 November, which coincided with the anniversary of Ayatollah Khomeini's exile to Iraq, clashes broke out between the army and the students who were marching out of Tehran University gates. The soldiers used tear gas and shot into the air to disperse the crowd. The protestors backed into the university campus with the soldiers following them. Reports said that one high-school student had been shot dead. The same evening, the state television aired footage of the clashes, supplemented by an emotional, tearful report. The television programme, showing armed soldiers with gas masks and automatic rifles chasing young boys throwing stones, was the first manifestation of dissent within the state-run media, and made many hitherto neutral or silent viewers take sides against the shah.

By this time the parliament deputies, who for years on end had been seen as appointed lackeys of the establishment, also began to lash out against the state. Their attacks, however, mainly targeted former Prime Minister Amir Abbas Hoveyda, and the 'corrupt courtiers'

– falling short of criticising the shah. On 5 November 1978, after violent demonstrations in Tehran, the shah replaced Sharif-Emami with General Gholamreza Azhari as Commander of the Imperial Guard.

Ironically, it was the shah, addressing the nation for the first time in many months, who first used the term 'revolution'. Hitherto the demonstrators had always used the expression 'Movement', as in the famous slogan: 'Our Movement is inspired by Hossein/ Our leader is Khomeini.' The shah declared he had heard the people's 'revolutionary message', promised to correct past mistakes, and urged a period of quiet and order so that the government could undertake the necessary reforms. Presumably to placate public opinion, the shah allowed the arrest of 132 former leaders and government officials, including former Prime Minister Hoveyda, a former chief of SAVAK, and several former cabinet ministers. He also ordered the release of more than one thousand political prisoners, including Ayatollah Hosseinali Montazeri, a close confidant of Ayatollah Khomeini.

The appointment of a government dominated by the military brought about some short-lived abatement in the strike fever, and oil production improved. Ayatollah Khomeini dismissed the shah's promises as worthless, however, and called for continued protests. The Azhari government did not, as expected, use coercion to bring striking government workers back to work. The strikes resumed, virtually shutting down the government, and clashes between demonstrators and troops became a daily occurrence. On 9 and 10 December 1978, in the largest anti-government demonstrations in a year, several hundred thousand people participated in marches in Tehran and the provinces to mark the 9th and 10th of Moharram.

Also by this time the revolutionaries had adopted an innovative method of psychological warfare that proved lethal to the morale of the military government's forces. Every night, millions of people would go to the rooftops, chanting 'Allah-o Akbar' (God is Great). The effect of the deafening roar that echoed and resonated throughout the empty, blackened city (empty, because of the curfew, and blackened owing to the strike by Power Ministry employees) on the soldiers patrolling the streets was devastating, and made many of them decide to join the already mounting number of deserters.

In a futile attempt at undermining the new revolutionary tactic,

Azhari said in parliament, 'The other evening, I personally went to the rooftop and looked around with night-goggles. I could see no one. It is obvious that the whole noise comes out of tapes and loudspeakers'.

The very following day, with a typical Iranian quick-wittedness, the anti-shah protesters had already added yet another rhyming slogan to their inventory: 'Azhari, you cow/ You still say it's a tape, how? / You think tapes can march, now?'

Not a single day passed without clashes between angry crowds and soldiers of the martial law. The streets of Tehran were a constant scene of burning buildings, gunshots and tear gas. What fanned the fire of the revolutionary youth's rage even more widely were distributed pictures of 'martyrs'. Many people now visited hospitals, the city morgue, and the cemeteries, taking pictures of the remains of those killed in clashes. A grim technicality multiplied the impact such pictures had on the public: the standard rifle of the Iranian army in those days was the German-made HK G-3, whose massive 7.62 millimetre bullets, rather than leaving a small hole in the bodies of their victims, opened up horrific wounds, sometimes mutilating or totally deforming organs. Soon 'picture galleries of martyrs' became yet more proof of the regime's brutality, and yet another efficient weapon in the hands of revolutionaries.

In December 1978, the shah finally began exploratory talks with members of the moderate opposition. Discussions with Karim Sanjabi proved unfruitful: the National Front leader was bound by his agreement with Ayatollah Khomeini. At the end of December, Shapour Bakhtiar (another National Front leader), agreed to form a government, on the condition that the shah left the country. Bakhtiar secured a vote of confidence from the two houses of the Majles on 3 January 1979, and presented his cabinet to the shah three days later.

Already grappling with advancing cancer, the shah, announcing he was going abroad for a short holiday, left Iran on 16 January 1979. As his aircraft took off, celebrations broke out across the country. Millions of people were out on the streets, cheering, dancing and chanting: 'Until the death of the traitor shah/ The Movement shall go on', and 'Until the shah is in his shroud/ The country will not come to order'.

Once installed as prime minister, Bakhtiar took several measures designed to appeal to elements in the opposition movement. He lifted restrictions on the press; the newspapers, on strike since November, resumed publication. He set free remaining political prisoners and promised the dissolution of SAVAK, the lifting of martial law, and free elections. He announced Iran's withdrawal from CENTO, cancelled seven billion dollars' worth of arms orders from the United States, and announced Iran would no longer sell oil to South Africa or Israel. Although Bakhtiar won the qualified support of moderate clerics like Shariatmadari, his measures did not win him the support of Ayatollah Khomeini and the main opposition elements, who were now committed to the overthrow of the monarchy and the establishment of a new political order, something they hardly could have dreamed of three months before.

The National Front, with which Bakhtiar had been associated for nearly thirty years, expelled him from the movement. Ayatollah Khomeini declared Bakhtiar's government illegal. Bazargan, in Ayatollah Khomeini's name, persuaded the oil workers to pump enough oil to ease domestic hardship, however, and some normality returned to the bazaar in the wake of Bakhtiar's appointment. But strikes in both the public and the private sector and large-scale demonstrations against the government continued. When, on 29 January 1979, Ayatollah Khomeini called for a street 'referendum' on the monarchy and the Bakhtiar government, there was a massive turnout.[16]

Bakhtiar sought unsuccessfully to persuade Ayatollah Khomeini to postpone his return to Iran until conditions in the country were normalised. Ayatollah Khomeini refused to receive a member of the regency council Bakhtiar sent as an emissary to Paris, and after some hesitation rejected Bakhtiar's offer to come to Paris personally for consultations. Bakhtiar's attempt to prevent Ayatollah Khomeini's imminent return, by closing the Mehrabad Airport at Tehran on 26 January 1979, proved to be only a stopgap measure.

Explaining his attempts to find a solution to the crisis, Bakhtiar later said:

> One night, as I was tossing and turning in bed, I asked myself what would happen if I were to go in person and meet him unconditionally and ask him: 'Sir, let us explore what you really want. I am prepared to sit with you and discuss all the problems concerning my country. Bring anyone you wish. I shall not bring

anyone, but if you were to require that I should, whomever you suggest, I can convince him to accompany me.'

The next morning I telephoned Bazargan and informed him of my intention. Bazargan agreed with me, because he could see the difficulty of the situation. He said that it was a good idea and asked me to write down whatever I was going to put to Ayatollah Khomeini. I said that I would write it all down and would have it delivered to him so that he could add his own suggestions. What I wrote turned out to be a letter of about ten lines, which said:

'Your Eminence Grand Ayatollah Khomeini, may God increase your blessings. I have played my insignificant role in fighting despotism for many years, and have done this and that, and have suffered the consequences ... I share the people's enthusiasm in their great movement towards freedom.

'During the short time since I have accepted to take charge, I have helped the movement by doing various things. Now I am ready to sit with Your Eminence the Ayatollah, not as the prime minister but as an ordinary Iranian, to review the country's problems. If you were to declare readiness to receive me unconditionally as well, I would come to see you within twenty-four hours.

'I even went and arranged to receive some foreign currency from the bank. I organised my passport and prepared everything in a matter of two hours. We had a plane ready and Bazargan said that he wanted to accompany me. I told him: "Fine, you come with me in the plane, but do not come all the way to Paris. This plane will land in Nice and there one of us can disembark to take another plane to Paris. I am concerned that if we arrive together in Paris, some people may say that we have colluded with each other." Well, Bazargan had enemies too, and everything was possible.'

Anyway, he read the letter and we discussed it for two hours. Afterwards I said: 'there is only one problem. You and I, as two Iranians, have discussed our country's problems politely, but I think others should judge the letter too.' I signed the letter and instructed someone to deliver it to Mr Beheshti, who was the head of their [the revolutionaries'] committee. Beheshti said that the idea was very good. His exact words were: 'It is a very good idea, good thinking and I endorse it.' I know that in addition to Beheshti, two or three other people agreed with it. Mr Beheshti kept the letter to read it overnight.

We, Bazargan and I, were very excited about the next day and kept discussing the arrangements for our morning flight. We said: 'Well, we meet at the royal pavilion in the airport and fly together.' Let me summarise that we came to the conclusion that Ayatollah Khomeini would either say yes or not. If he were to agree to sit and talk to me, he would lose half of his charisma. And should he refuse to see me, then we would tell the Iranian people: 'Look what sort of a man he is; we are offering to see him and he is not prepared to discuss anything. This fellow does not understand anything.'[17]

Abolhassan Bani Sadr, one of Ayatollah Khomeini's close advisors and later Iran's first president, later said it was he who persuaded the ayatollah not to meet the Bakhtiar, and, instead, to forward another proposal:

My proposal said that if he were to resign from his post as prime minister of the shah, I would discuss with Mr Khomeini about him carrying on as the prime minister of the Revolution. Abbasqoli Bakhtiar said that it was a very good proposal. I asked him to go and talk to the other side and added that I could not make any promises, because Mr Khomeini had to make the decision.

We then went to see Mr Khomeini and I told him: 'Do you think it is in anyone's interest if the army collapses in Iran now and the whole thing leads to anarchy?' He said: 'No'. I said: 'In that case, if we could persuade Bakhtiar to resign as the shah's prime minister, would you be prepared to appoint him as the prime minister of the Revolution?' Mr Khomeini paused for a while and then said: Yes'. I said: 'Think carefully before you decide, and if you really agree, I shall work on it.' He said that he was definitely in agreement. I said: 'No, you must take an oath.'

He said: 'There is no need to take an oath.' I said; 'No, it is a political decision of paramount importance, for if something were to go wrong tomorrow, everyone would blame me for bringing Bakhtiar and imposing him on you. Furthermore, it would not be good if I go and talk to Bakhtiar and then you go back on your promise.'

At this point he took an oath. He swore on the Qur'an that if Bakhtiar were to resign as prime minister of the shah, he would endorse him as the new prime minister of the revolutionary government. I saw Abbasqoli the next day and passed on Mr Khomeini's message. Abbasqoli said: 'Yes, the prime minister would not mind doing so. However, he well knows that the army would not submit and would stage a coup d'etat.' I told him: 'Up until yesterday you were saying that the prime minister was not a tool in the hands of the army, but today you are warning us that the army would stage a coup d'état. No, my friend, I know the army better than you. It will not stage a coup d'état. Tell Prime Minister Bakhtiar not to be a fool and miss the last chance he is given.' But he refused.

I went home in the evening and I was watching television at 11.30 at night, when I saw Mr Qotbzadeh being interviewed by a lady presenter on France's Channel 3. During that interview he said that Dr Bakhtiar was coming to Paris as prime minister. I telephoned Neauphle-le-Chateau to speak to [Ayatollah Khomeini's son] Ahmad. This Ahmad is the master of disappearance when he is needed, but I eventually managed to reach him by phone after ten minutes. I told him: 'Go and tell your dad that the people have accepted him as a source of emulation, but not as a politician. If he were to agree to receive Bakhtiar as a prime minister, he could not go back on his word.' In my message to Ayatollah Khomeini, through his son Ahmad, I added: 'If you tell the whole world that you have received Bakhtiar as prime minister of Iran, you cannot turn around the next day and say that he is no longer the prime minister of Iran. He will remain as prime minister and then you would have to go. In this game you cannot both survive.'[18]

But even before Ayatollah Khomeini had rejected Bakhtiar's offer, angry demonstrators had taken to the streets in Tehran and all major cities, accusing Bakhtiar of being an opium addict and chanting fresh slogans: 'We say we don't want the shah, but they change the prime minister/ We say we don't want an ass, but they change its packsaddle.' The ayatollah must have thought that going against the stream would only backfire.

Ayatollah Khomeini arrived in Tehran from Paris on 1 February 1979. Millions of people lined the road to the airport to welcome him. In his short-lived days as prime minister, Bakhtiar kept his promise of allowing freedom of expression: the whole ceremony was broadcast live on Iranian television, which was still guarded by the army.

Years later, when Bani Sadr had become one of the Revolution's devoured children, he bitterly remembered the day he accompanied Ayatollah Khomeini in his triumphant return to Iran:

> When the plane landed and came to a halt, its door opened and two people, Ayatollah Khomeini's brother, Mr Pasandideh, and Mr Motahhari, came into the plane to welcome him. He was flanked by the two of them and was led towards the plane's exit, as if the intellectuals had fulfilled their duty of bringing back His Eminence and handing him over to the clerics. You saw that from that day he changed his tune. Up until that point he had kept talking about liberation and freedom of speech, but from that moment he was purely in pursuit of power.

It was at this same time that the 'silent' part of the society – called 'the silent majority' by opponents of the Revolution – tried its chances at raising a voice in support of Bakhtiar. Tens of thousands of secular, mostly middle class men and women gathered in Tehran's Amjadiyyeh football stadium, expressing their support for Bakhtiar and his plans. Hard-line revolutionaries, however, attacked the demonstrators with bricks, sticks and chains, calling them 'agents of SAVAK', beating them up, and smashing their cars. It was the first and last pro-Bakhtiar rally Iran ever saw.

I happened to meet a friend who had attended the rally the day before. 'This is crazy,' he shook his head in despair. 'This is what they mean by freedom. This is going to go nowhere, honestly.' A few days later, he boarded a plane for England. He is a university professor in London now.

Two decades later, one of the zealous children of the Islamic Revolution looked back at the events with regret. Akbar Ganji, the renowned reform-minded journalist who was jailed in 1999 and was still serving his term when this book was published, was nineteen when the Revolution was in the making. In 2002, he wrote from his cell in Tehran's Evin prison:

> All the opponents of the shah's autocratic regime were considered freedom-fighters. However, they were plighted to theoretical despotism themselves; and since it is impossible to fight political despotism with a weapon of theoretical despotism, a democratic system failed to take shape after the victory of the Revolution ...

As in several other instances, here Ganji shows his almost unique courage. No more than a handful of Iran's reformists have ever hinted that they might have made a mistake in their support of the Revolution, or that Ayatollah Khomeini might have been at fault in certain cases.

Ganji continues:

> Many theoreticians of the 1970s rejected the notions of democracy and freedom from an ideological viewpoint. They condemned democracy as an 'anti-revolutionary system that is in contradiction with the ideological leadership of the society." They maintained that "the fate of the Revolution should not be relegated to democracy and worthless votes ...'

He goes on to say:

> Since the Revolution was born in such an ideological background, it could not give birth to democracy. The ideologue of the Revolution intended to set up a society which was constantly under control and guidance, which was more similar to an iron cage, rather than releasing the society from the chains of the ancient despotism and monarchical regime.'[19]

He concludes:

No generation possesses the right to deprive future generations of their right to decide how they want to be ruled ... therefore, popular sovereignty is non-transferable.

Any model aiming to replace the status quo must be precise, transparent and expansive, otherwise the problem of the 1979 Revolution will be repeated.[20]

Having received a rapturous welcome from millions of Iranians, Ayatollah Khomeini paid a symbolic visit to Tehran's Behesht-e Zahra cemetery, where he announced he would 'smash in the mouth of the Bakhtiar government.' He labelled the government illegal, and called for the strikes and demonstrations to continue.

Refah girls' secondary school, at which Ayatollah Khomeini established his headquarters in central Tehran, near Jaleh Square, became the centre of opposition activity. A multitude of decisions, and the coordination of the opposition movement, were handled there by what came to be known as the Komiteh-ye Esteqbal az Emam, or the Committee for Welcoming the Imam. On 5 February Ayatollah Khomeini named Mehdi Bazargan as prime minister of a provisional government. Although Bazargan did not immediately announce a cabinet, the move reinforced the conditions of dual authority that increasingly came to characterize the closing days of the Pahlavi monarchy. In many large urban centres local Komitehs (revolutionary committees) had assumed responsibility for municipal functions, including neighbourhood security and the distribution of such basic necessities as fuel oil.[21]

Government ministries and such services as the customs and the posts remained largely paralysed. Bakhtiar's cabinet ministers proved unable to assert their authority or, in many instances, even to enter their offices. The loyalty of the armed forces was being seriously eroded by months of confrontation with the people on the streets. There were instances of troops who refused to fire on the crowds, and desertions were rising. In late January, air force technicians at the Khatami Air Base in Isfahan became involved in a confrontation with their officers.

In his statements, Ayatollah Khomeini had attempted to win the army rank and file over to the side of the opposition. Following Ayatollah Khomeini's arrival in Tehran, clandestine contacts took place between Ayatollah Khomeini's representatives and a number of military commanders. These contacts were encouraged by United States ambassador William Sullivan, who had no confidence in the Bakhtiar government, thought the triumph of the Ayatollah Khomeini forces inevitable, and believed future stability in Iran could be assured only if an accommodation could be reached between the armed forces and the Ayatollah Khomeini camp.

United States General Robert E. Huyser, who had arrived in Tehran on 4 January 1979 as President Carter's special emissary, was also encouraging contacts between the military chiefs and the Ayatollah Khomeini camp. Huyser's assignment was to keep the Iranian army intact, to encourage the military to maintain support for the Bakhtiar government, and to prepare the army for a takeover, should that become necessary. Huyser began a round of almost daily meetings with the service chiefs of the army, navy, and air force, plus heads of the National Police and the Gendarmerie who were sometimes joined by the chief of SAVAK. He dissuaded those so inclined from attempting a coup immediately upon Ayatollah Khomeini's return to Iran, but he failed to get the commanders to take any other concerted action. He left Iran on 3 February, before the final confrontation between the army and the revolutionary forces.

On 8 February uniformed airmen appeared at Ayatollah Khomeini's home and publicly pledged their allegiance to him. On 9 February, air force technicians at the Doshan Tappeh air base outside Tehran mutinied. Units of the Imperial Guard failed to put down the insurrection. The next day, the arsenal was opened, and weapons were distributed to crowds outside the air base.[22]

The government announced a curfew beginning in the afternoon, but the curfew was universally ignored. Over the next twenty-four hours, revolutionaries seized police barracks, prisons, and buildings. On 11 February, twenty-two senior military commanders met and announced that the armed forces would observe neutrality in the confrontation between the government and the people. The army's withdrawal from the streets was tantamount to a withdrawal of support for the Bakhtiar government, and acted as a trigger for a general uprising.

'The radio had received the news [of the army's neutrality] before I did,' Bakhtiar said later. 'I waited until 1.30 in the afternoon, before deciding that there was no alternative left to me. I could see that when the people realised that the military men had decided to withdraw, no one could stop the others.

'I ordered a helicopter to land in the grounds of the military college. The helicopter arrived at about two o'clock in the afternoon. I picked up a few of my personal belongings and went downstairs. As I went down my secretary, Ms Kalantari, asked me: "What time will you return sir?" I replied: "I do not know, but I will come back one day." As I came through the doorway, there was one captain, two NCOs and four soldiers. They stood to attention and saluted me. One of them said: "We are almost totally surrounded now." I shook hands with them individually and got into the car, which then drove to the military college only 100 metres down the road. When I arrived there, a similar procedure took place. I got into the helicopter and it took off.

'I said: "How amazing! We want to give these people freedom and democracy, and they do not want it." What could we possibly do? I do not know, but despite the sadness, I experienced relief. Believe me, it seemed as if a huge burden, as heavy as Damavand Mountain, had been lifted from my shoulders. I felt as if I were flying with my own wings.'[23]

It was around noon that we at home heard a persistent doorbell. When my mother opened the door, in came her two young brothers, panting. The older one, a graduate of the law faculty, was holding in his hand a ceremonial sword of the Imperial Guards; the younger one, a soldier's helmet.

'They are finished!' my older uncle exclaimed, 'People have taken over the barracks. We were late: they had already taken away all the guns. All we could get were these.'

By late afternoon on 11 February, key points throughout the capital were in rebel hands. On the same evening the revolutionary forces took over the radio and television stations. In an excited tone loaded with tears, the radio presenter said:

> This is Tehran, the true voice of the Iranian nation, the voice of the Revolution. Please pay attention. Please pay attention. We will now bring to your attention the latest message of His Eminence the Grand Ayatollah Imam Ayatollah Khomeini, leader of the Iranian nation's movement: 'In the name of God,

the Compassionate, the Merciful, to the Muslim, heroic and struggling nation of Iran.'

Dear listeners, the time is now three minutes past eleven [in the evening] and now we draw your attention to a message issued by His Eminence Ayatollah Shariatmadari: 'In the name of God, the Compassionate, the Merciful, to the zealous and noble people of Iran. Now that, in the shadow of divine succour, your selfless struggle has put paid to the tyrannical regime, and dictatorship has abandoned its last trench, I wish to offer my congratulations to the entire nation of Iran. We are grateful to Almighty God and wish to express our gratitude to the army for responding to the call of the eminent ulama [scholars] to join the nation. I plead with the rest of the army commanders, officers and NCOs, who have not yet taken the big decision of their lives, to join the people. I would also like to ask the people be vigilant and confront and crush any conspiracy. Please maintain law and order and safeguard state buildings together with all their files and documents, which belong to the nation.'

General Beiglari, the acting commander of the guards, and General Ali Neshat, commander of the Imperial Guard, in their telephone messages announced that the units under their command had not left their barracks since the declaration of the army's neutrality. Their messages read as follows: 'We declare total solidarity with the nation and fully obey the instructions that we have been given;' 'I wish to announce with pride that the Imperial Guard is part of the nation;' 'I wish to ask everyone to try to substantiate every report about the air force before believing them;' 'There are no disconcerting reports about Firouzeh Palace. No one has attacked it. Just a group of young men are around celebrating and firing into the air in joy. The sound of shooting has scared some families in the vicinity of the building.'[24]

Meanwhile, Ayatollah Khomeini sent a statement to the nation, read by Ayatollah Abdolkarim Moussavi Ardabili, on Tehran Radio:

Now that the armed forces have stepped back, have declared their neutrality in the face of political affairs and have expressed support for the nation, the dear and courageous nation is expected to maintain law and order when the troops return to barracks. You should stop saboteurs, who may try to create catastrophe, and instruct them of their religious and humanitarian obligations. Do not allow anyone to attack foreign embassies. If, God forbid, the army were to enter the arena again, you must defend yourselves with all your might. I hereby inform senior army officers that if they were to stop the army's aggression, and instruct them to join the nation and its legal Islamic government, we would regard the army as part of the nation and vice versa. [Signed Ruhollah al-Mousavi al-Ayatollah Khomeini].[25]

In-between urgent news bulletins, the radio incessantly aired revolutionary songs secretly recorded in private, makeshift studios over the previous year: 'The air is now pleasant, the flowers have blossomed/ The dove, upon return, sang a song of hope ... / Happy spring! Happy spring!'

The Pahlavi regime had collapsed, and with it was buried almost twenty-five centuries of monarchy in Iran, if not necessarily its underlying principle: absolute rule. The joyous children of the revolution would soon part ways, standing against each other, and going through times they could not have possibly thought of when they took to the streets, and bared their chests to bullets in their quest for 'Independence, Freedom, Islamic Republic'.

FOUR

Awakenings

Tulips have risen from the blood of the Motherland's children.
Cypress trees have bent from the sorrow of their cypress-like figures.
Aref Qazvini, 1912

Either death or modernity and reform,
There's no other way before the country;
Iran's become old from tip to toe;
Its remedy is nothing but becoming new.

Malek ul-Sho'ara Bahar, 1914

Howard Conklin Baskerville was a Presbyterian missionary who was assigned to the Boys' School in Tabriz, Iran, for a two-year period beginning in 1908. He was teaching in Tabriz, Iran, when the shah attempted to suppress the constitution, and his people rose up in protest. The church warned missionaries not to interfere in local politics, but Baskerville resigned his post and volunteered to fight as a member of the constitutional forces. He was fatally wounded on 19 April 1909, while leading a group of his students to break a siege of Tabriz. The local people felt that Baskerville's sacrifice was 'noble' and that he was truly their friend. When he died, merchants in Tabriz designed a woven rug featuring Baskerville's face and an inscription to send to his family.

During a ceremony fifty years later, Baskerville was remembered as a brave young man who disobeyed mission policy because of his belief in the people of Iran. After discussions with mission staff, the Iranian

Government agreed to name the assembly hall of the former mission school after Baskerville and hung a portrait of him there. Iranian dignitaries who were involved in the constitutional struggle in Tabriz, as well as the governor-general of Azerbaijan Province and the US ambassador, attended the memorial ceremony. Baskerville is sometimes referred to as 'the American Lafayette in Iran'.[1]

It is almost one century since the Iranians, and particularly the younger generations, began attempting to modernise their country; to break the deadlock of backwardness, and to attain freedom, democracy, justice and human rights. The quest began with the Constitutional Movement (also called the Constitutional Revolution). The Baskerville story clearly shows how much hope and faith Iranians had put in the Constitutional Movement.

During the early 1900s, the only way to save the country from government corruption and foreign manipulation was to make a written code of laws. The desire for this drove the Constitutional Movement. There had been a series of ongoing covert and overt activities against Nassereddin Shah's despotic rule, during which many had lost their lives. The efforts of those seeking to change the power structure finally bore fruit during the reign of Mozaffareddin Shah, who ascended to the throne in June 1896. As a result of the relentless efforts of these advocates of freedom and justice, Mozaffareddin Shah was forced to issue the Decree for the Constitution and the Creation of an Elected Parliament (or Majles) on 5 August 1906. The royal powers were to be limited and a parliamentary system established.

The Constitutional Movement borrowed its ideals from Europe. In Britain, in particular, a new concept of the nature of the political system had emerged, which considered the state as the protector of public interest. Political philosophers in Europe sought to restrict the powers of the crown to legislation that served the public interest. Thus, in the words of Javad Tabatabaei, an historian of political thought in Paris, just as a constitutional monarchy that observed the public interest emerged in Europe in the nineteenth century, 'so also in Iran's Constitutional Revolution was there a move to limit the authority of the monarch within the law.'[2]

Before the Constitutional Movement, uprisings and rebellions in Iran sought not to change the structure and the nature of monarchy, but to replace a tyrant king with a 'just' one. The Constitutional Movement, however, considered absolute power the origin of all vice. It sought to end autocratic rule, for under such rule, justice and injustice were essentially the same. Its aim was to make the monarch reign, not rule.

According to Ahmad Salamatian, a former parliament deputy in the Islamic Republic, after the victory of the Constitutional Movement, the deputies of the Majles took an oath, saying that they would be loyal to the shah, as long as he was loyal to the articles of the constitution, for otherwise he would have lost his legitimacy.[3]

Monarchical rule had been an almost uninterrupted feature of Iranian government for nearly 500 years. The tradition of monarchy itself is even older. In the sixth century BC, Iran's first empire, the Achaemenian Empire, was already established. It had an absolute monarch, centralised rule, a highly developed system of administration, aspirations to world rule, and a culture that was uniquely Iranian, even as it borrowed, absorbed, and transformed elements from other cultures and civilisations. Although Alexander the Great brought the Achaemenian Empire to an end in 330 BC, under the Sassanids (224– 642 AD) Iran once again became the centre of an empire and a great civilisation.

The impact of the Islamic conquest in the seventh century was profound. It introduced a new religion and a new social and legal system. The Iranian heartland became part of a world empire in which the centre was not in Iran. Nevertheless, historians have found striking continuities in Iranian social structure, administration, and culture. Iranians contributed significantly to all aspects of Islamic civilisation; in many ways they helped shape the new order. By the ninth century, there was a revival of the Persian language, and of a literature that was uniquely Iranian, but now enriched by Arabic and Islamic influences.

The break-up of the Islamic empire led, in Iran as in other parts of the Islamic world, to the establishment of local dynasties. Iran, like the rest of the Middle East, was affected by the rise to power of the Seljuk Turks, and then by the destruction wrought first by the Mongols and then by Timur, also called Tamerlane (Timur the Lame).

With the rise of the Safavids (1501–1732), Iran was reconstituted as a territorial state within borders not very different from those prevailing today. Shi'i Islam became the state religion, and monarchy once again became a central institution. Persian became the unquestioned language of administration and high culture. Although historians no longer assert that under the Safavids Iran emerged as a nation-state in the modern sense of the term, nevertheless, by the seventeenth century the sense of Iranian identity, and of Iran as a state within roughly demarcated borders, was pronounced.

The Qajars (1795–1925) attempted to revive the Safavid Empire, and in many ways modelled their administration on that of the Safavids. But the Qajars lacked the claims to religious legitimacy available to the Safavids. They failed to establish strong central control, and they faced an external threat from technically, militarily, and economically superior European powers, primarily Russia and Britain.

The Qajars were a Turkmen tribe that held ancestral lands in present-day Azerbaijan, which was then part of Iran. In 1779, following the death of Karim Khan Zand, the Zand ruler of southern Iran, Agha Muhammad Khan, a leader of the Qajar tribe, set out to reunify Iran. Agha Muhammad Khan defeated numerous rivals and brought all of Iran under his rule, establishing the Qajar dynasty. By 1794 he had eliminated all his rivals, including Lotfali Khan, the last of the Zand dynasty, and had reasserted Iranian sovereignty over the former Iranian territories in Georgia and the Caucasus. Agha Muhammad established his capital at Tehran, a village near the ruins of the ancient city of Ray (now Shahr-e Ray). In 1796 he was formally crowned as shah. Agha Muhammad was assassinated in 1797 and succeeded by his nephew, Fathali.

Under Fathali Shah (1797–1834), Iran went to war against Russia, which was expanding from the south into the Caucasus Mountains, an area of historic Iranian interest and influence. Iran suffered major military defeats during the war. Under the terms of the Treaty of Golestan in 1813, Iran recognised Russia's annexation of Georgia and ceded to Russia most of the North Caucasus region. A second war with Russia in the 1820s ended even more disastrously for Iran, which in 1828 was forced to sign the Treaty of Turkmanchai, acknowledging Russian sovereignty over the entire area north of the Aras River (a territory comprising present-day Armenia and the Republic of Azerbaijan).

Fathali Shah's reign saw increased diplomatic contact with the west, and the beginning of intense European diplomatic rivalries over Iran.

His grandson Muhammad Shah, who fell under the influence of Russia, and made two unsuccessful attempts to capture Herat, succeeded him in 1834. When Muhammad Shah died in 1848 the succession passed to his son Nassereddin.

During Nasereddin Shah's reign (1834–1896), western science, technology, and educational methods were introduced into Iran, and a tangible, albeit feeble, trend of modernisation began in the country. Nasereddin Shah tried to exploit the mutual distrust between Great Britain and Russia to preserve Iran's independence, but foreign interference, and territorial encroachment increased under his rule. He contracted huge foreign loans to finance expensive personal trips to Europe. He was unable to prevent Britain and Russia from encroaching regions of traditional Iranian influence. In 1856, Britain prevented Iran from reasserting control over Herat, which had been part of Iran in Safavid times, but had been under non-Iranian rule since the mid-eighteenth century. Britain supported the city's incorporation into Afghanistan – a country Britain helped create in order to extend eastward the buffer between its Indian territories and Russia's expanding empire. Britain also extended its control to other areas of the Persian Gulf during the nineteenth century. Meanwhile, by 1881 Russia had completed its conquest of present-day Turkmenistan and Uzbekistan, bringing Russia's frontier to Iran's north–eastern borders, and severing historic Iranian ties to the cities of Bukhara and Samarqand. Several trade concessions by the Iranian government put economic affairs largely under British control. By the late nineteenth century, many Iranians believed that their rulers were beholden to foreign interests.[4]

Mirza Taqi Khan, better known by his title Amir Kabir, was the young Prince Nassereddin's advisor and constable. With the death of Muhammad Shah in 1848, Mirza Taqi was largely responsible for ensuring the Crown Prince's succession to the throne. When Nassereddin succeeded to the throne, Mirza Taqi was awarded the position of prime minister and the title of Amir Kabir, the Great Ruler.

By this time Iran was virtually bankrupt, its central government was weak, and its provinces were almost autonomous. During the next two-and-a-half years, Amir Kabir initiated important reforms in virtually all sectors of society. Government expenditure was slashed, and a distinction was made between the privy and public purses. The instruments of central administration were overhauled, and Amir Kabir assumed responsibility for all areas of the bureaucracy. Foreign interference in Iran's domestic affairs was curtailed, and foreign trade was encouraged. Public works such as the building of the bazaar in Tehran were undertaken. Amir Kabir issued an edict banning ornate and excessively formal writing in government documents; the beginning of a modern Persian prose style dates from this time.

One of the greatest achievements of Amir Kabir was the building of Dar-ol-Fonoon, the first modern university in Iran. Dar-ol-Fonoon was established to train a new cadre of administrators, and acquaint them with western techniques. Amir Kabir ordered the school to be built on the edge of the city so that it could be expanded as needed. He hired French and Russian instructors, as well as Iranians, to teach subjects as diverse as languages, medicine, law, geography, history, economics, and engineering. Amir Kabir did not live long enough to see his greatest monument completed, but it still stands in Tehran as a symbol of his ideas for the future of his country.

These reforms antagonised various notables who had been excluded from the government. They regarded Amir Kabir as a social upstart and a threat to their interests, and they formed a coalition against him, in which the Queen Mother played a key role. She convinced the young shah that Amir Kabir wanted to usurp the throne. In October 1851 the shah dismissed him and exiled him to Kashan, where he was murdered on the shah's orders.

Then, in 1896, Mirza Reza Kermani assassinated Nassereddin Shah, and the crown passed to his son Mozaffareddin. Mozaffareddin Shah was an ailing, weak and ineffectual ruler. During his reign, royal extravagance and the absence of incoming revenues exacerbated financial problems. The shah quickly spent two large loans from Russia, partly on trips to Europe. Public anger fed on the shah's propensity to grant concessions to Europeans in return for generous payments to him and his officials. People began to demand a curb on royal authority, and the establishment of the rule of law, as their concern over foreign, and especially Russian, influence grew.

The shah's failure to respond to protests by the religious establishment, the merchants, and other classes, led the bazaaries and clerical leaders, in January 1906, to take sanctuary from probable arrest in mosques in Tehran and outside the capital. When the shah reneged on a promise to establish a 'house of justice', or consultative assembly, ten thousand people, led by the bazaaries, took sanctuary in June in the compound of the British legation in Tehran. In August the shah was forced to issue a decree promising a constitution. In October an elected assembly convened and drew up a constitution that provided for strict limitations on royal power, an elected parliament, or Majles, with wide powers to represent the people, and a government with a cabinet subject to confirmation by the Majles. The shah signed the constitution on 30 December 1906. He died five days later. The Supplementary Fundamental Laws approved in 1907 provided, within limits, for freedom of press, speech, and association, and for security of life and property. The Constitutional Movement marked the end of the medieval period in Iran. The hopes for constitutional rule were never realised, however.

Mozaffareddin Shah's son Muhammad Ali Shah (reigned 1907–1909), with Russian help, attempted to rescind the constitution and abolish parliamentary government. The rising tide of dissatisfaction and discontent caused Muhammad Mirza to summon his cabinet members on 17 December 1907, under the false pretence of soliciting advice. He immediately ordered their detention. Ambassador Zapolski of Russia and Ambassador Marling of Britain warned the Iranian government to submit to the shah's will. After several disputes with members of the Majles, in June 1908 the shah ordered his Russian-officered Persian Cossacks Brigade to bomb the Majles building, arrest many of the deputies, and close down the assembly.

Led by Sheikh Fazlollah Nouri, conservative clerics, who from the beginning had opposed the notion of modernism embedded in the Constitutional Movement, found the time ripe for launching a counter-charge against the Constitutionalists by supporting the shah. They resumed warning of the grave dangers to Islam posed by 'western-style government'. Among the accusations they hurled at the Constitutionalists was that they promoted prostitution.

Resistance to the shah, however, coalesced in Tabriz, Isfahan, Rasht, and elsewhere. In July 1909, constitutional forces marched from Rasht and Isfahan to Tehran, deposed the shah, and re-established the constitution. The deposed shah went into exile in Russia. Sheikh

Fazlollah Nouri's opposition met with mixed results. Though the cleric and the shah's supporters (including Russia) managed to beat back the Constitutionalists in the early stages of the struggle, Nouri paid a dear price later. In the summer of 1909, in a moment of Constitutionalist ascendancy, Nouri was hanged by a cheering crowd.

Not surprisingly, some seventy years later, the Islamic Republic revived Nouri's ideas. He was hailed as a champion who had fought against corrupt Western values, and a major expressway in Tehran was named after him, on one point of which is a huge mural commemorating him. It includes his portrait, as well as a symbolic design distilling the idea of the conservative clerics, who have taken up his cause in the early twenty-first century: a tight noose strangling a rose.

But even in the 1970s, Nouri's ideas were revived as an antidote to Shah Muhammad Reza's rapid modernising. Even some intellectuals, notably the breakaway Marxist Jalal Al-e Ahmad, embraced his anti-western attitude, calling him a 'martyr', and calling on the Iranian nation to 'return to self'. He was also duly awarded the name of a main street in Tehran after the Revolution of 1979.

Although the constitutional forces had triumphed, they faced serious difficulties. The upheavals of the Constitutional Movement and civil war had undermined stability and trade. In addition, the ex-shah, with Russian support, attempted to regain his throne, landing troops in July 1910. Most serious of all, the hope that the Constitutional Movement would inaugurate a new era of independence from the great powers ended when, under the Anglo-Russian Agreement of 1907, Britain and Russia agreed to divide Iran into spheres of influence. The Russians were to enjoy exclusive rights to pursue their interests in the northern sphere, the British in the south and east; both powers being free to compete for economic and political advantage in a neutral sphere in the centre. Matters came to a head when Morgan Shuster, a United States administrator hired as treasurer-general by the Persian Government to reform its finances, sought to collect taxes from powerful officials who were Russian protégés, and to send members of the treasury gendarmerie, a tax department police force, into the Russian zone. When, in December 1911, the Majles unanimously refused a Russian ultimatum demanding Shuster's dismissal, Russian troops, already in the country, moved to occupy the capital. To prevent this, on 20 December,

Bakhtiari tribal chiefs and their troops surrounded the Majles building, forced acceptance of the Russian ultimatum, and shut down the assembly, once again suspending the constitution. There followed a period of government by Bakhtiari chiefs and other powerful notables.

Despite lofty ideals, in practice, however, the Constitutional Movement failed to uproot despotism in Iran and replace it with a long-lasting, law-abiding state, instead ending up in chaos and anarchy.

Homa Katouzian says that, in Iran, the other side of the coin of tyranny and despotism was always chaos. 'When the central government collapsed or was weakened for any reason, there was no alternative to it except another autocracy. Therefore the country sank into chaos and disarray, with rival political powers fighting each other, until one of them finally conquered and established a new tyrannical rule.'[5]

There are many historians who maintain that the Constitutional Movement was in fact idealistic in nature. Shojaeddin Shafa believes that in a backward country lacking minimum literacy, security, hygiene and welfare, attempts to emulate nineteenth-century Europe were but a daydream. 'Iran was basically not ready for a true democratic change. People rightly felt that they did not want the terrible Qajar despotism. What happened (and there was no other choice) was that the intellectuals decided to assimilate the best European constitutional system of those times, which belonged to Belgium, for Iran.' Useful in theory as it might have seemed, he says, it was not manageable in practical terms, as the basic standards of society did not even meet the minimum to cater for a democratic project.[6]

According to Mashallah Adjudani, even the nature of the demands of the Constitutionalists has been subject to exaggeration. 'What they meant by concepts such as law, freedom and democracy, was fundamentally different from similar concepts in Europe at the time.

'The majority of the people were illiterate. The intellectuals, in turn, had a limited understanding of the rule of law, and could not even speak openly about this limited understanding in a backward society. To be fair, in a situation in which the predominant superpowers of the time – Russia and Britain – exerted increasing influence on the day-to-day lives of the people, the priority for the nation was independence, and not democracy. The feeble democratic drive of the Constitutional Movement was actually sacrificed as the price for independence, and this was the outcome of the so-called deep historical, intellectual, structural and cultural changes in Iran.[7]

Ahmad Shah, who was born in 1898 in Tabriz and succeeded to the throne at the age of eleven, proved to be pleasure-loving, effete, and incompetent, and was unable to preserve the integrity of Iran or the fate of his dynasty. The occupation of Iran during World War I (1914–18) by Russian, British, and Ottoman troops was a blow from which Ahmad Shah never effectively recovered. On 21 February 1921, Reza Khan, an officer in Iran's only military force (Cossack Brigade), used his troops to support a coup d'état against the government, and consequently became the pre-eminent political personality in Iran.

Colonel Kazem Khan Sayyah, one of the commanders involved in Reza Khan's coup, gave an account of the hours before dawn on 21 February, when the leaders of the coup had ordered the arrest of Tehran police authorities:

> The room in which the coup leaders were sitting was spectacular and interesting ... Hands locked behind him and head down, Reza Khan was pacing the room in long steps. Sayyed Zia was lying on his side on a broken bench, resting his chin in his hand with his cloak wrapped around him. None of the two had the appearance of conquerors. They looked like people waiting for the dawn to see what would happen.[8]

In the words of Shojaeddin Shafa:

> None of the objectives of the Constitutional Movement were realized during the eighteen years that followed its conception and Reza Khan's coming-to-power. During the course of the fourteen years following the Constitutional Revolution, and again in the four years after its revival, the country was immersed in chaos, disorder and an absolute lack of progress ... This was a result of pressures from the big landowners, the aristocracy, and particularly the clerics. In the first fourteen years, twenty-seven cabinets were formed and dissolved – i.e. almost one cabinet per four months. The ministers were more or less the same figures; they only changed posts.[9]

Within four years, by suppressing rebellions and establishing order, Reza Khan had established himself as the most powerful person in the country. In 1925 a specially convened assembly deposed Ahmad Shah while he was absent in Europe, and named Reza Khan, who earlier had adopted the surname Pahlavi, as the new shah. Ahmad Shah died later, on 21 February 1930, in Neuilly-sur-Seine, France. Thus, with the ideals of the Constitutional Movement blown away, yet another period of absolute rule replaced a period of chaos.

FIVE

The Last Dynasty

O, Cyrus! Rest in peace, for we are awake, and will always stay awake to safeguard your heritage ...
Shah Muhammad Reza Pahlavi, 1976

I said, '... there is inflation, and people are suffering from high prices, most of the [government] services do not work properly either. People ask why these small problems are not solved when the Shahanshah has provided so much money and has so many plans ready.' [After a while the shah] said, 'Well, because of the people's indolence, I have called them corrupt. Don't they say anything in this regard?' I said, 'No! No one has any objection because it's a fact.' The Shahanshah said, 'When one is not awaiting people's votes (i.e. electing a president), one can utter whatever is in the interests of the country.'
Asadollah Alam, *Memoirs*, vol. 4., Ketabsara Publishers, 2001, p. 246

The rise of Reza Shah Pahlavi reflected the failure of the constitutional experiment. His early actions also reflected the aspirations of educated Iranians to create a state that was strong, centralised, free of foreign interference, economically developed, and which shared those characteristics thought to distinguish the more advanced states of Europe from the countries of the East.

This work of modernisation and industrialisation, expansion of education, and economic development, was continued by the second

Pahlavi monarch, Muhammad Reza Shah Pahlavi. He made impressive progress in expanding employment and economic and educational opportunities, in building up strong central government and a strong military, in limiting foreign influence, and in giving Iran an influential role in regional affairs.

Reza Shah had ambitious plans for modernising Iran. These plans included developing large-scale industries, implementing major infrastructure projects, building a cross-country railroad system, establishing a national public education system, reforming the judiciary, and improving health care. He believed a strong, centralised government, run by educated personnel, could carry out his plans.

He sent hundreds of Iranians, including his son, to Europe for education. During sixteen years between 1925 and 1941, Reza Shah's numerous development projects transformed Iran and set it on the path to modernisation. Public-education progressed rapidly, and new social classes – a professional middle class and an industrial working class – emerged.

'My grandfather was instrumental in preserving our territorial integrity and setting Iran on the path to modernity. During his short tenure, he managed to lead and transform Iran from a poor, disease-ridden, and chaotic country, into a secure, progressive nation,' said Prince Reza Pahlavi. But by the mid 1930s Reza Shah's dictatorial style of rule was causing dissatisfaction in Iran.[1]

Political analyst Ahmad Salamatian said, 'After a long time in Iran's history, Reza Khan was a ruler with no tribal alliances. From the formal point of view, too, his crowning was legitimate. A Constituents Assembly had been set up, 35 percent of whose members were clerics. It was those very clerics who opposed Reza Khan's proposal to establish a republic; it was the clerics who insisted that he become the shah. However, it was after he started infringing on the constitution, relying instead on military power, that he lost legitimacy, because he violated his oath of loyalty to the constitution.'[2]

Reza Shah tried to avoid involvement with Britain and the Soviet Union. But many of his development projects required foreign technical expertise. He avoided awarding contracts to British and Soviet companies. Although Britain, through its ownership of the Anglo-Iranian Oil Company, controlled all of Iran's oil resources, Reza Shah preferred to obtain technical assistance from Germany, France, Italy and other European countries. This caused problems for Iran after 1939, when Germany and Britain became enemies in World War II. Reza Shah proclaimed Iran a neutral country, but Britain insisted that German engineers and technicians in Iran were spies with missions to sabotage British oil facilities in the southwestern regions of the country. Britain demanded that Iran expel all German citizens, but Reza Shah refused, claiming this would adversely impact his development projects. Along with Iranian cynicism towards Britain, Reza Shah's inclination towards Germany was reflected in the widespread rumour that Hitler was in truth a Muslim, and that the word Germany was only a variation of the name of his birthplace Kerman. There were even people who would name their male newborn Alman-Ali, a combination of the Persian word for Germany and the name of the most revered Shi'i Imam in Iran.

Following Germany's invasion of the Soviet Union in June 1941, Britain and the Soviet Union became allies. Both turned their attention to Iran. Both allied powers saw the newly opened Trans-Iranian Railroad as an attractive logistical route to transport reinforcements from the Persian Gulf to the Soviet region. In August 1941, on the grounds of Iran's refusal to expel German nationals, Britain and the Soviet Union invaded Iran, arrested Reza Shah, and sent him into exile, taking control of Iran's communications and the coveted railroad. In 1942 the United States, an ally of Britain and the Soviet Union during the war, sent a military force to Iran to help maintain and operate sections of the railroad. This happened after the three allied leaders, Churchill, Stalin and Roosevelt, met in Tehran. Later, three main streets in central Tehran were named after them. Ironically, after the 1979 Revolution, Churchill Street was renamed as Bobby Sands Street (after the famous IRA member who died in prison in 1980), and Stalin was changed to Mirza Kuchak Khan (after the social-democrat rebel who fought against Reza Shah in the Caspian region in the late 19th century – the Islamic Republic maintained that he was betrayed by the Bolsheviks). The British and Soviet authorities allowed Reza Shah's system of political rule to collapse, and in the absence of a viable alternative, permitted his son Muhammad Reza to assume the throne. The new shah's reign began against a backdrop of social and political disarray, economic problems, and food shortages.

Muhammad Reza Pahlavi was born in Tehran on 26 October 1919, the eldest son of Reza Shah. He completed his primary schooling in Switzerland. He returned to Iran in 1935, and enrolled in Tehran's military college, from which he graduated in 1938. In 1939 he married a sister of Faroq I, King of Egypt. The couple divorced in 1949 since they could not have a male offspring to continue the monarchy in Iran. The shah married twice more, in 1950 to Soraya Esfandiari, and in 1959 to Farah Diba.

He replaced his father on 16 September 1941, shortly before his twenty-second birthday. He intended to continue the policies of his father, but there was a predominantly anti-dictatorial atmosphere in the country.

In 1941 large areas of Iran were under the occupation of allied forces. Despite his vow to act as a constitutional monarch who would defer to the power of the parliamentary government, Muhammad Reza increasingly involved himself in governmental affairs and opposed or thwarted strong prime ministers. Prone to indecision, however, Muhammad Reza relied more on manipulation than on leadership. He concentrated on reviving the army, and ensuring that it would remain under royal control as the monarchy's main power base.

After the fall of Reza Shah, Iran's political system became increasingly open, and chaotic. Political parties mushroomed, and in 1944 Majles elections were the first genuinely competitive elections in more than twenty years. Foreign influence remained a very sensitive issue for all parties. The Anglo-Iranian Oil Company (AIOC), which was owned by the British Government, continued to produce and market Iranian oil. In the beginning of the 1930s some Iranians began to support the nationalisation of the country's oil fields. After 1946 this caused a major common movement.

From 1949 on, support for the nationalisation of Iran's oil industry grew. In 1949 the Majles approved the First Development Plan (1948–55), which called for comprehensive agricultural and industrial development of the country. The Plan Organisation was established to administer the programme, which was to be financed in large part from oil revenues. Politically conscious Iranians were aware, however, that the British Government derived more revenue from taxing the concessionaire, the Anglo-Iranian Oil Company, than the Iranian government derived from royalties. The oil issue figured prominently in elections for the Majles in 1949, and nationalists in the new Majles were determined to renegotiate the AIOC agreement. In November 1950, the Majles committee concerned with oil matters, headed by Mosaddeq, rejected a draft agreement in which the AIOC had offered the government slightly improved terms. These terms did not include the fifty-fifty profit-sharing provision that was part of other new Persian Gulf oil concessions. In 1949 an assassination attempt on the shah, attributed to the pro-Soviet Tudeh party, resulted in the banning of that party, and the expansion of the shah's constitutional powers.

Subsequent negotiations with the AIOC were unsuccessful, partly because General Haji Ali Razmara, who became Prime Minister in June 1950, failed to convince the oil company of the strength of nationalist feeling in the country and in the Majles. When the AIOC finally offered fifty-fifty profit-sharing in February 1951, sentiment for nationalisation of the oil industry had become widespread. Razmara, who advised against nationalisation on technical grounds, was assassinated in March 1951 by Khalil Tahmasbi, himself a member of the militant Fada'eeyan-e Islam. On 15 March the Majles voted to nationalise the oil industry. In April, the shah yielded to Majles pressure and demonstrations on the streets, by naming Mosaddeq prime minister.[3]

Oil production came to a virtual standstill as British technicians left the country, and Britain imposed a worldwide embargo on the purchase of Iranian oil. In September 1951, Britain froze Iran's sterling assets and banned the export of goods to Iran. It challenged the legality of the oil nationalisation, and took its case against Iran to the International Court of Justice at The Hague. The court found in Iran's favour, but the dispute between Iran and the AIOC remained unsettled. Under United States pressure, the AIOC improved its offer to Iran. But the excitement generated by the nationalisation issue, anti-British feeling, agitation by radical elements, and the conviction among Mosaddeq's advisers that Iran's maximum demands would, in the end, be met, led the government to reject all offers. The economy began to suffer from the loss of foreign exchange and oil revenues.

Meanwhile, Mosaddeq's growing popularity and power led to political chaos and eventual intervention by the United States, which feared a leftist takeover. Mosaddeq had come to office on the strength of support from the National Front and other parties in the Majles, and as a result of his great popularity. His popularity, growing power, and intransigence on the oil issue were creating friction between the prime minister and the shah. In the summer of 1952, the shah refused the Prime Minister's demand for the power to appoint the minister of war (and, by implication, to control the armed forces). Mosaddeq resigned. But three days of pro-Mosaddeq rioting followed, with demonstrators chanting 'either death or Mosaddeq'. The shah was finally forced to reappoint Mosaddeq to head the government.

At the height of his political activities, Mosaddeq attained such popularity that tens of thousands of people would pour into the streets upon his call. If he protested a bill, objected to a government, or resigned, thousands of students would close university classes in support of him, gather at his house or at the Majles, and lift him above their heads.[4]

Some analysts believe that as domestic conditions deteriorated, Mosaddeq's populist style grew more autocratic. In August 1952, the Majles acceded to his demand for full powers in all affairs of government for a six-month period. These special powers were subsequently extended for a further six-month term. He also obtained approval for a law to reduce, from six years to two years, the term of the senate (established in 1950 as the upper house of the Majles), and thus brought about the dissolution of that body. However, Mosaddeq's support in the lower house of the Majles was dwindling, so on 3 August 1953 the prime minister organised a plebiscite for the dissolution of the Majles, claimed a massive vote in favour of the proposal, and then dissolved the legislative body.

Iran's nationalist aspirations had initially attracted the sympathy of the administration of President Harry Truman. Under the administration of President Dwight D. Eisenhower, however, the United States came to accept the view of the British Government that no reasonable compromise with Mosaddeq was possible and that, by working with the Tudeh Party, Mosaddeq was making probable a communist-inspired takeover. Mosaddeq's intransigence and inclination to accept Tudeh support, the Cold War atmosphere, and the fear of Soviet influence in Iran, also shaped United States thinking. In June 1953 the Eisenhower administration approved a British proposal for a joint Anglo-American operation, code-named Operation Ajax, to overthrow Mosaddeq.

Kermit Roosevelt of the United States Central Intelligence Agency (CIA) travelled secretly to Iran to coordinate plans with the shah and the Iranian military, which was led by General Fazlollah Zahedi.

In accord with the plan, on 13 August the shah appointed Zahedi Prime Minister to replace Mosaddeq. Mosaddeq refused to step down and arrested the shah's emissary. This triggered the second stage of Operation Ajax, which called for a military coup. The plan initially seemed to have failed, the shah fled the country, and Zahedi went into hiding. In the four days leading to the coup d'état, several ministers and Majles deputies made speeches against the shah. Many journalists attacked him in newspapers. However, according to Dr Ali Behzadi, it was Mosaddeq's Foreign Minister Hossein Fatemi, who went to the extreme:

> Later, some of the cabinet members blamed the events [of August 1953] on Dr Fatemi's excesses, and the Tudeh party's greed. During those few days, Dr Fatemi launched the harshest attacks against the shah. The Tudeh party wanted a democratic republic. This slogan scared the bazaaries and the religious ones. These excesses caused the neutrals to panic too. On Monday 16 August Dr Fatemi went to the [royal] court and sealed the rooms so as to prevent the plundering of royal properties which he said now belonged to the people.

A well-known picture of the time showed Fatemi sitting on a chair, taking Queen Soraya's clothes out of trunks with his walking stick, to be registered by the police. The picture was taken at the moment when a piece of lingerie dangled from his stick.[5]

After four days of rioting, however, the tide turned. On 19 August pro-shah army units and street crowds defeated Mosaddeq's forces. The shah returned to the country. Mosaddeq was sentenced to three years' imprisonment for trying to overthrow the monarchy, but he was subsequently allowed to remain under house arrest in his village Ahmad Abad, outside Tehran, until his death in 1967. Hossein Fatemi was sentenced to death and executed. Hundreds of National Front leaders, Tudeh party officers, and political activists were arrested. Several Tudeh army officers were also sentenced to death.[6]

The oil nationalisation movement became a legend for many Iranians, and the fall of Mosaddeq was the breaking of the dreams of millions. Mosaddeq almost gained the status of a saint for many Iranians. But his policies have come under a more objective analysis in recent years. Homa Katouzian believes that oil nationalisation was only one strategy in a war for sovereignty and democracy:

> For this reason, Mosaddeq should have obtained the best *possible* terms from a position of strength, and settled the question, disregarding the reaction of romantic idealists, Stalinist slanderers, and the spineless demagogues in his own entourage, all of whom by their very nature would have come into line with the socio-political success which would have followed such a settlement: the British Government would at least temporarily have suspended its operations against Mosaddeq; the shah and the conservatives would have been rendered defenceless; the inflow of oil revenues, used by an incorruptible and democratic government, would have increased the level *and* the spread of socio-economic prosperity; major social and economic reforms would have become both possible and irresistible; and, finally, all these developments would have made it easy to move towards a complete, even ideal, rectification of Iran's oil interests within a few years.[7]

The 1953 coup was a turning point in Iran's history, setting the scene for a series of developments that eventually culminated in the 1979 Revolution and the end of monarchy. It left a deep scar on the psyche of Iranian intellectuals hoping for a democratic, prosperous country, who dubbed the coup 'the big defeat'. Mehdi Akhavan Saless, a prominent contemporary poet, and an outstanding example of the 'defeat generation', symbolised the atmosphere of the post-coup period in a famous poem two years later:

> It's dastardly cold, ah ...
> No one is willing to answer your greeting
> The air is choked, doors closed, heads ducked, hands hidden
> Breaths are clouds, hearts weary and sad

Trees are crystallised skeletons
The earth is depressed, the ceiling of the sky low
The sun and the moon are hazy
It's winter.

A declassified memorandum from the US State Department to the President, circa 1953, reads: 'It appears that with some assistance from us, the present leaders of Iran may be able to capitalize on the wave of public opinion that could cause a virtual renaissance in the country.'[8]

Malcolm Byrne, director of the project on US-Iran Relations, examined the questions that have ever since weighed heavily on the minds of Iranians. He wrote in 1999:

> Prior to the 1979 hostage-taking episode, the most contentious issue in US-Iran relations was the 1953 coup against Iranian Prime Minister Muhammad Mosaddeq, which the CIA and British intelligence helped to instigate. Numerous questions remain about the coup itself, its impact, and the circumstances that brought it about. To what extent was Mosaddeq leading his country down the path toward communist subversion? Could the coup have succeeded without substantial Iranian public dissatisfaction with Mosaddeq's policies? Did key Iranian political and religious figures, wittingly or not, receive CIA payments in return for stirring up the population? What effects did the coup have on the future development of internal Iranian politics, including possibly radicalising anti-shah and anti-American opposition elements with consequences that would not be foreseen until the revolution itself?
>
> The search for answers will have to wait at least until more of the documentary record is available in both Iran and the United States. Unfortunately, a portion of the record on the American side will never be recovered because CIA operatives, according to former Director of Central Intelligence James Woolsey, destroyed them in the 1960s. The surviving files remain locked away from public view on the grounds that their declassification, even forty-six years later, would damage national security. Because of the obvious public interest value and historical significance of these

materials, the National Security Archive in May 1999 filed suit against the CIA to demand their release. The suit is still pending.[9]

James Bill recounts the repercussions of the 1953 coup thus:

> In April 1967, my wife Ann and I were invited to an elegant party at the home of a member of the shah's inner circle. Among those present were the British ambassador and several Iranian cabinet ministers. At one point during the evening Ann found herself standing near a short, ruddy-faced gentleman who struck up a conversation with her. He asked about her business in Iran. She explained that she was accompanying her husband who was a PhD candidate at Princeton. After some further questioning, Ann told him that her husband was studying the role of the alienated middle and lower classes in Iran. 'And what does your husband conclude?' the stranger queried. Ann indicated that increasing numbers of Iranians had a low opinion of the shah and his method of rule. Opposition was serious and it was increasing.
>
> Shaking the ice cubes in his cocktail glass, the gentleman, clearly annoyed, launched into a defence of the Pahlavi system. At the end of his outburst, he pointed out that he had been coming to Iran since the early 1950s. How could two young Americans recently arrived believe that they knew best? Having already grown weary of American visitors' superficial conclusions about Iran, Ann quietly asked her new acquaintance about his credentials. 'Do you speak Persian? Have you travelled into the villages and provinces? Have you studied Shi'i Islam and visited the mosques in Qom and Mashhad?' When he answered in the negative, Ann politely responded, 'I thought so.'
>
> Shortly afterwards, Ann joined me and the host of the party. 'Who is that annoying little man standing there in the corner,' she asked our host. 'Oh, that is our good friend Kermit Roosevelt. We call him "Kim". Let me introduce you.' Ann responded, 'No thank you. We have already met.'

There are two positions concerning the 1953 restoration of the shah. The first position argues that the overthrow of

Mosaddeq artificially bottled up the forces of nationalism. As time passed, the opposition to the shah deepened and became more extreme. This explosive mixture finally burst forth in the revolution of 1978–79, which gave birth to a virulent form of political extremism rooted in religion. The second argument postulates that by overthrowing Mosaddeq and supporting the shah, the US defeated the communist Tudeh party and gained access to tewenty-four billion barrels of oil at the deflated price of 1.25 dollars per barrel.[10]

The United States arranged for immediate economic assistance of forty-five million dollars to help the Zahedi government through a difficult period. The Iranian government restored diplomatic relations with Britain in December 1953, and a new oil agreement was concluded in the following year. The shah, fearing both Soviet influence and internal opposition, sought to bolster his regime by edging closer to Britain and the United States. In October 1955, Iran joined the Baghdad Pact, which brought together the 'northern tier' countries of Iraq, Turkey, and Pakistan in an alliance that included Britain, with the United States serving as a supporter of the pact but not a full member. (The pact was renamed the Central Treaty Organisation – CENTO – after Iraq's withdrawal in 1958). In March 1959, Iran signed a bilateral defence agreement with the United States. In the Cold War atmosphere, relations with the Soviet Union were correct but not cordial. The shah visited the Soviet Union in 1956, but Soviet propaganda attacks and Iran's alliance with the West continued. Internally, a period of political repression followed the overthrow of Mosaddeq, as the shah concentrated power in his own hands. He banned or suppressed the Tudeh, the National Front, and other parties, muzzled the press, and strengthened the secret police, or SAVAK (Sazman-e Ettela'at va Amniyyat-e Keshvar). Elections to the Majles in 1954 and 1956 were closely controlled. The shah appointed Hossein Ala to replace Zahedi as prime minister in April 1955, and thereafter named a succession of prime ministers who were willing to do his bidding.

The shah focused his attention on economic development. Rising oil revenues allowed the government to launch the Second Development Plan (1955–62) in 1956. A number of large-scale industrial and agricultural projects were initiated, but economic recovery from the disruptions of the oil nationalisation period was slow. The infusion of oil money led to rapid inflation and spreading discontent, while strict controls provided no outlets for political unrest. When martial law, which had been instituted in August 1953 after the coup, ended in 1957, the shah ordered two of his senior officials to form a majority party and a loyal opposition as the basis for a two-party system. These became known as the Melliyoun and the Mardom parties. These officially sanctioned parties did not satisfy demands for wider political representation, however. During Majles elections in 1960, contested primarily by the Melliyoun and the Mardom parties, charges of widespread fraud could not be suppressed, and the shah was forced to cancel the elections. Jafar Sharif-Emami, a staunch loyalist, became prime minister. After renewed and more strictly controlled elections, the Majles convened in February 1961. But as economic conditions worsened and political unrest grew, the Sharif-Emami government fell in May 1961.[11]

By this time, President John F. Kennedy's administration was pressing the shah for economic reforms. Yielding both to these pressures and the domestic demands for change, the shah named Ali Amini, a wealthy landlord and senior civil servant, as prime minister. Amini was known as an advocate of reform. He received a mandate from the shah to dissolve parliament and rule for six months by cabinet decree. Amini loosened controls on the press, permitted the National Front and other political parties to resume activity, and ordered the arrest of a number of former senior officials on charges of corruption. Under Amini, the cabinet approved the Third Development Plan (1962–68) and undertook a programme to reorganise the civil service. In January 1962, in the single most important measure of the fourteen-month Amini government, the cabinet approved a law for land distribution.

Numerous problems, however, bedevilled the Amini government. 'Belt-tightening' measures ordered by the prime minister were necessary, but in the short-term they intensified recession and unemployment. This recession caused discontent in the bazaar and business communities. In addition, the prime minister acted in an independent manner, and the shah and senior military and civilian officials close to the court resented this challenge to royal authority. Moreover, although enjoying limited freedom of activity for the first time in many years, the National Front and other opposition groups pressed the prime minister for elections, and withheld their cooperation. Amini was unable to meet a large budget deficit, the shah refused to cut the military budget, and the United States, which had previously supported Amini, refused further aid. As a result, Amini resigned in July 1962.

He was replaced by Amir Asadollah Alam, one of the big landowners and a confidant of Muhammad Reza Shah. Building on the credit earned in the countryside and in urban areas by the land distribution programme, the shah in January 1963 submitted six measures to a national referendum. In addition to land reform, these measures included profit-sharing for industrial workers in private sector enterprises, nationalisation of forests and pastureland, sale of government factories to finance land reform, amendment of the electoral law to give more representation on supervisory councils to workers and farmers, and the establishment of a Literacy Corps to allow young men to satisfy their military service requirement by working as village literacy teachers. The shah described the package as his White Revolution, and when the referendum votes were counted, the government announced a 99 percent majority in favour of the programme. In addition to these other reforms, the shah announced in February that he was extending the right to vote to women.

Certain sectors of the population expressed support for the government's new measures, but these measures did not deal immediately with sources of unrest. Economic conditions were still difficult for the poorer classes. Many clerical leaders opposed land reform and the extension of suffrage to women. These leaders were also concerned about the extension of government and royal authority that the reforms implied. In June 1963, Ayatollah Khomeini, by this time the most outspoken opponent of the shah's policies, was arrested after a fiery speech in which he directly attacked the shah. The arrest sparked three days of the most violent riots the country had witnessed since the overthrow of Mosaddeq, a decade earlier. The government ordered a severe suppression of these riots on 15 Khordad, or 5 June. Hundreds of protesters were killed throughout the country. Some historians have said that on that day, Alam had the shah's telephone lines disconnected, since the latter was against a violent crackdown. After the victory of the Islamic Revolution, Ayatollah Khomeini announced 15 Khordad a public holiday and 'a public mourning day forever'. In any case, for the moment, the Alam government appeared to have triumphed over its opponents.[12]

Such explosions of unrest as occurred during the 1951–53 oil nationalisation crisis and the 1963 riots indicated that there were major unresolved tensions in Iranian society, however. These stemmed from inequities in wealth distribution; the concentration of power in the hands of the crown, and bureaucratic, military, and entrepreneurial elites; the demands for political participation by a growing middle class and members of upwardly mobile lower classes; a belief that westernisation posed a threat to Iran's national and Islamic identity; and a growing polarisation between the religious classes and the State.

In September 1963, elections to the twenty-first Majles led to the formation of a new political party, the Iran Novin (Modern Iran) party, committed to a programme of economic and administrative reform and renewal. The Alam government had opened talks with National Front leaders earlier in the year, but no accommodation had been reached, and the talks had broken down over such issues as freedom of activity for the Front. As a result, the Front was not represented in the elections, which were limited to the officially sanctioned parties, and the only candidates on the slate were those presented by the Union of National Forces, an organisation of senior civil servants and officials, and of workers' and farmers' representatives, put together with government support. After the elections, the largest bloc in the new Majles, with forty seats, was a group called the Progressive Centre. Hassanali Mansour had established the Centre, an exclusive club of senior civil servants, in 1961 to study and make policy recommendations on major economic and social issues. In June 1963, the shah had designated the Centre as his personal research bureau. When the new Majles convened in October, 100 more deputies joined the Centre, giving Mansour a majority. In December, Mansour converted the Progressive Centre into a political party, the Iran Novin. In March 1964, Alam resigned and the shah appointed Mansour prime minister, at the head of an Iran Novin-led government.

The establishment of the Iran Novin and the appointment of Mansour as prime minister represented a renewed attempt by the shah and his advisers to create a political organisation that would be loyal to the crown, attract the support of the educated classes and the technocratic elite, and strengthen the administration and the economy. The Iran Novin drew its membership almost exclusively from a younger generation of senior civil servants, western-educated technocrats, and business leaders. Initially, membership was limited to 500 hand-picked individuals, and it was allowed to grow only very slowly. In time it came to include leading members of the provincial elite and its bureaucratic, professional, and business classes. Even in the late 1960s and early 1970s, when trade unions and professional organisations affiliated themselves with the party, full membership was reserved for a limited group.

In a bid to implement economic and administrative reforms, Mansour created four new ministries and transferred the authority for drawing up the budget from the Ministry of Finance to the newly created Budget Bureau. The Bureau was attached to the Plan Organisation and was responsible directly to the prime minister. In subsequent years it introduced greater rationality in planning and budgeting. Mansour appointed younger technocrats to senior civil service posts, a policy continued by his successor. He also created the Health Corps, modelled after the Literacy Corps, to provide primary health care to rural areas.[13]

The government enjoyed a comfortable majority in the Majles, and the nominal opposition, the Mardom party, generally voted with the government party. An exception, however, was the general response to the Status of Forces bill, known in Iran as Capitulation Law – a measure that granted diplomatic immunity to United States military personnel serving in Iran, and to their staffs and families. In effect, the bill would allow these Americans to be tried by United States rather than Iranian courts for crimes committed on Iranian soil. For Iranians the bill recalled the humiliating capitulatory concessions extracted from Iran by the imperial powers in the nineteenth century. Hostile feeling towards the bill was sufficiently strong that sixty-five deputies absented themselves from the legislature, and sixty-one opposed the bill when it was put to a vote in October 1964.

The move also aroused strong feeling outside the Majles. Ayatollah Khomeini, who had been released from house arrest in April 1964, denounced the measure in a public sermon before a huge congregation in Qom. Tapes of the sermon, and a leaflet based on it, were widely circulated, and attracted considerable attention. Ayatollah Khomeini was arrested again in November, within days of the sermon, and sent into exile in Turkey. In October 1965, he was permitted to take up residence in the city of Najaf, the site of the shrine of the first Shi'i Imam Ali, where he was to remain for the next thirteen years.

Economic conditions were soon to improve dramatically. The country, however, had not yet fully recovered from the recession of 1959–63, which had imposed hardships on the poorer classes. Mansour attempted to make up a budget deficit of an estimated 300 million dollars (at then prevalent rates of exchange) by imposing heavy new taxes on gasoline and kerosene and on exit permits for Iranians leaving the country. Because kerosene was the primary heating fuel for the working classes, the new taxes proved highly unpopular. Taxi drivers in Tehran went on strike, and Mansour was forced to rescind the fuel taxes in January, six weeks after they had been imposed. An infusion of 200 million dollars in new revenues (185 million dollars from a cash bonus for five offshore oil concessions granted to United States and West European firms, and 15 million dollars from a supplementary oil agreement concluded with the Consortium, a group of foreign oil companies), helped the government through its immediate financial difficulties.

With this assistance, Muhammad Reza Shah was able to maintain political stability despite the assassination of his prime minister and an attempt on his own life. On 21 January 1965 members of a radical Islamic group assassinated Mansour. Evidence made available after the Islamic Revolution revealed that the group had affiliations with clerics close to Ayatollah Khomeini. A military tribunal sentenced six of those charged to death, and the others to long prison terms. In April there was also an attempt on the shah's life, organised by a group of Iranian graduates of British universities. To replace Mansour as prime minister, the shah appointed Amir Abbas Hoveyda, a former diplomat and an executive of the National Iranian Oil Company (NIOC). Hoveyda had helped Mansour found the Progressive Centre and the Iran Novin, and had served as his minister of finance.

The appointment of Hoveyda as prime minister marked the beginning of nearly a decade of impressive economic growth and relative political stability at home. During this period, the shah also used Iran's enhanced economic and military strength to secure for the country a more influential role in the Persian Gulf region, and he improved relations with Iran's immediate neighbours, and the Soviet Union and its allies. Hoveyda remained in office for the next twelve years, the longest term of any of Iran's modern prime ministers. During this decade, the Iran Novin dominated the government and the Majles. It won large majorities in both the 1967 and the 1971 elections. The authorities carefully controlled these elections. Only the Mardom party and, later, the Pan-Iranist party – an extreme nationalist group – were allowed to participate in them. Neither party was able to secure more than a handful of Majles seats, and neither engaged in serious criticism of government programmes.

In 1969 and again in 1972 the shah appeared ready to permit the Mardom Party, under new leadership, to function as a genuine opposition, i.e., to criticise the government openly and to contest elections more energetically, but these developments did not occur. The Iran Novin's domination of the administrative machinery was further made evident during municipal council elections held in 136 towns throughout the country in 1968. The Iran Novin won control of a large majority of the councils and every seat in 115 of them. Only 10 percent of eligible voters cast ballots in Tehran, however, a demonstration of public indifference that was not confined to the capital.

Hoveyda's government improved its administrative machinery and launched what was dubbed 'the education revolution'. It adopted a new civil service code, and a new tax law, and appointed better-qualified personnel to key posts. Hoveyda also created several additional ministries in 1967, including the Ministry of Science and Higher Education, which was intended to help meet expanded and more specialised manpower needs. In mid-1968 the government began a programme that, although it did not resolve problems of overcrowding and uneven standards, increased the number of institutions of higher education substantially, brought students from provincial and lower middle-class backgrounds into the new community colleges, and created a number of institutions of high academic standing, such as Tehran's Arya Mehr Technical University.

The shah had remarried in 1959, and the new queen, Farah Diba Pahlavi, had given birth to a male heir, Reza, in 1960. In 1967, because the Crown Prince was still very young, steps were taken to regularize the procedure for the succession. Under the constitution, if the shah were to die before the Crown Prince had come of age, the Majles would meet to appoint a regent. There might be a delay in the appointment of a regent, especially if the Majles was not in session. A constituent assembly, convened in September 1967, amended the constitution, providing for the queen automatically to act as regent unless the shah in his lifetime designated another individual. In October 1967, believing his achievements finally justified such a step, the shah celebrated his long-postponed coronation. Like his father, he placed the crown on his own head. To mark the occasion, the Majles conferred on the shah the title of Arya-Mehr, or 'Light of the Aryans', which was added to his previous title Shahanshah, or 'King of Kings'. This glorification of the monarchy and the monarch, however, was not universally popular with the Iranians. In 1971 celebrations were held to mark what was presented as 2,500 years of uninterrupted monarchy (there were actually gaps in the chronological record), and the twenty-fifth centennial of the founding of the Iranian empire by Cyrus the Great. The ceremonies were designed primarily to celebrate the institution of monarchy, and to affirm the position of the shah as the country's absolute and unchallenged ruler. The lavish ceremonies (which many compared to a Hollywood-style extravaganza), the virtual exclusion of Iranians from celebrations in which the honoured guests were foreign heads of state, and the excessive adulation of the person of the shah in official propaganda, generated much adverse domestic comment. A declaration by Ayatollah Khomeini, condemning the celebrations and the regime, received wide circulation.[14]

At the same time, the seeds of struggle were furtively being sown. Having experienced the defeat of the Tudeh party and the National Front during the Mosaddeq era, and inspired by such events as the revolution in Algeria, the Vietnam War, and leftist movements in Latin America, dissident students, who believed that the regime had lost the last drop of its legitimacy, were examining the armed-struggle solution to create a better, more just world. This spirit was best illustrated in the hugely popular book, *The Little Black Fish*, written by Marxist schoolteacher and activist Samad Behrangi. Ostensibly a children's book, it told the story of a little black fish that did not want to live in its little pond forever. On the way to the sea, a kingfisher hunts the fish. Before dying, however, the little black fish rips apart the predator's stomach with a little sword given to him by a salamander, killing the evil bird.

Two major radical student movements emerged out of such an outlook. The first, led chiefly by the Fada'eeyan-e Khalq (People's Devotees), pursued the teachings of Marxism-Leninism. The second, heralded by the Mojahedin Khalq (People's Holy Warriors), adopted a revolutionary, ideological interpretation of Shi'i Islam to topple the shah and establish a 'classless, monotheistic society'. Mehdi Bazargan, at that time head of Tehran University's technical faculty, was originally the Mojahedin's intellectual father and mentor. But the young radicals soon deviated from the 'old-fashioned', 'non-revolutionary' methods he advocated. The lack of grassroots political parties meant the universities assumed a partisan political role, a function they continued after the Islamic Revolution.

Arguably, the religious ideology that eventually led to the Islamic Revolution of 1979 had little to do with traditional notions of Islam, represented by anti-shah clergy, most notably Ayatollah Khomeini. Rather, it was the 'Muslim intellectuals' who were busy formulating an ideological version of the faith to prepare and equip the masses for their struggle against the regime.

Political Islam, a term widely used in recent decades to describe the theoretical foundations of Iran's Revolution, is a vague and rather misleading expression. Islamologists maintain that unlike Christianity, Islam has never been an apolitical faith. In fact, the Prophet of Islam commanded wars against his enemies, and established the first city-state once he took over the town of Yathrib, significantly changing its name to Medina (City). What was new was the invention of a new version of Islam that claimed to be in compliance with all modern 'scientific' findings – which, in the discourse of the 1960s and in the political context, meant the sociological theories of Marxism.

In that sense, it was Ali Shariati, more than anyone else, who contributed to the development of this version of Shi'ism. It is therefore not without reason that he was called 'the teacher of the Revolution'. While Bazargan and some clerics, notably Morteza Motahhari, tried to show in their works that Islam was as against Marxism as capitalism, Shariati and the Mojahedin borrowed heavily from Marxism to prove that the Shi'i faith was essentially about class struggle.

Ali Shariati was born in 1933, and was a Mosaddeq supporter in the early 1950s. His father was an Islamic scholar in Khorasan, where he completed his studies before winning a scholarship to study philology in France. As of 1969, he started delivering speeches at Tehran's Hosseiniyyeh Ershad, a stronghold of religious dissidents. His speeches were taped and distributed in hundreds of thousands of copies. He was arrested and imprisoned in 1972. After his release in 1975, he was banned from lecturing or publishing. In 1997, after arriving in London, he died of a heart attack. The opposition quickly claimed that he had actually been murdered by SAVAK, although there was no evidence to prove this. Nevertheless, he soon acquired the title of 'our martyred teacher'.

As Abrahamian has said, in Shariati's view, the course of human development was governed by 'historical dialectic', or in another expression of his, 'historical determinism'. The motors of human development were God's will, man's innate desire to reach a higher stage of consciousness, and the class struggle symbolised by the Biblical story of Cain and Abel (where Cain represented the oppressor, the rulers and the elite, and Abel represented the oppressed, the ruled and the masses).

In the dialectical unfolding of human history, Shariati argued, Islam – especially Shi'ism – played a vital role. For God had sent the Prophet to establish an umma (people joined by a common belief) that would be in 'permanent revolution', striving for social justice, Islamic brotherhood, and eventually a classless society with public ownership of the means of production. Despite the true message of Islam, he continued, the Prophet's unlawful successors, the caliphs, had created a new imperial ruling class thus transforming the religion of liberation into a religion of oppression. This had prompted the Prophet's rightful heirs, the Shi'i Imams, to raise the banner of revolt and show the world that the caliphs had betrayed the revolutionary message of Islam.[15]

Shariati also asserted that despite its revolutionary beginnings, Shi'ism had met the same fate as early Islam. The upper class, including the official clergy, had expropriated, institutionalised and misused it as a public pacifier, as a rigid dogma, and as a dead scriptural text.[16]

Shariati's interpretation of Islam was indispensable, and allowed him to transform the faith into an ideology for social and political struggle, an arena in which the main player had hitherto been Marxism. In order to enable Islam to promise both earthly and heavenly utopias, and to put such a utopia in a loftier place than its Western rivals, many traditional and modern concepts had to be manipulated. Thus, in the hands of Shariati, and in the context of his interpretation of the holy texts, terms such as *towhid* (monotheism), *imamat* (religious leadership), *shahadat* (martyrdom), *qist* (justice), and *mostazafan* (the meek), became 'abolishing class structure', 'revolutionary leadership', 'dying for ideology', 'equal distribution of means of production', and 'the proletariat'.

For a few years after the Revolution, when 'commitment' was given priority over 'expertise' in appointing individuals to government posts, this method of interpretation prevailed. In 1984, when I was a staff writer for *Transport Industry* monthly magazine, I interviewed an urban transport expert. To prove his points in explaining the causes of Tehran's traffic problem, the learned engineer frequently referred to certain Qur'anic verses, and the concept of 'order and chaos' embedded in them.

Saeed Hanaee Kashani, a philosophy professor in Tehran, said that such tampering with traditional texts was one of Shariati's outstanding skills. 'He changed concepts such as "ideology" and "intellectual" in such a way that they assumed humanistic, epical meanings,' he said. 'In fact, perhaps at that time no one was as familiar with hermeneutics as Shariati. His interpretations might have contradicted scientific criteria, but they were not in contradiction with artistic standards. Shariati was the model of a religious, romantic, idealist thinker, the foundations of whose thought was to stir passion.'[17]

Although, or perhaps because, the traditional clergy attacked Shariati's ideas as eclectic and even blasphemous, the passion that he stirred infected the younger generation like an epidemic. Ironically, revolutionary clerics also came to adopt Shariati's concepts and jargon as an efficient tool to fight the shah's regime.

Iran, meantime, experienced a period of unprecedented and sustained economic growth. The land distribution programme launched in 1962, along with steadily expanding job opportunities, improved living standards, and moderate inflation between 1964 and 1973, help to explain the relative lack of serious political unrest during this period. But the increasing arbitrariness of the shah's rule provoked both religious leaders, who feared losing their traditional authority, and students and intellectuals seeking democratic reforms. These opponents criticised the shah for violation of the constitution, which placed limits on royal power and provided for a representative government, and for subservience to the United States. The cracks were already there for all to see, but the image of Iran as an 'island of stability' in a troubled region, and the lure of the petrodollar, blinded the eyes of outsiders.

In the words of James Bill, the United States never understood Iran. A 1977 State Department report stated that:

'The shah rules Iran free from serious domestic threat. At age 57, in fine health, and protected by an elaborate security apparatus, the shah has an excellent chance to rule for a dozen or more years.

'The embassy in Tehran was one of the largest US diplomatic facilities in the world. The US ambassadors to Iran during the 1960s and 1970s were mediocre. In fairness to them, however, they had to pursue the party line promoted back in Washington, where the shah was considered a close friend and one whose leadership was not to be questioned. Imposing figures such as Kermit Roosevelt, Richard Helms, Henry Kissinger, John J. McCloy, and David Rockefeller served as the shah's public relations men in the United States. Embassy officials posted to Iran were often out of touch and ill informed. The CIA failed to probe deeply into Iranian society. There were usually ten case-officers in Iran, and of these ten, at least six of them were occupied with the Soviet Union and China. The others who followed Iranian domestic affairs relied heavily upon the shah's secret police (SAVAK) for information. In general, American officials lacked contacts with the Shi'i religious leaders, the Persian-speaking intelligentsia, and the peoples in the villages. Briefly, they lacked what one might call "mosque time".'[18]

In 1974, the shah dissolved the two existing parties and announced the launch of his 'Resurgence party', declaring that anyone not loyal to it could receive a passport and leave the country.

In 1976, when the Majles, at government instigation, voted to alter the Iranian calendar so that year one of the calendar coincided with the first year of the reign of Cyrus rather than with the beginning of the Islamic era, many Iranians viewed the move as an unnecessary insult to religious sensibilities. Overnight, Iranians were living in the Imperial year of 2535 rather than the solar year of 1355. Government officials were at pains to convert the dates to the new system.

By the mid-1970s, the shah reigned amidst widespread discontent caused by the continuing repressiveness of his regime, socio-economic changes that benefited some classes at the expense of others, and an ever-widening gap between the ruling elite and the disaffected populace. Religious intellectuals and clerics, particularly Ayatollah Khomeini, were able to provide focus for this discontent, with a populist ideology tied to Islamic principles, and calls for the overthrow of the shah.

Against such a sociological background, Shafa sees the 1979 Revolution and the fall of the monarchy inevitable. 'From an academic and intellectual point of view, it was a twentieth-century revolution against despotic conditions that did not comply with the developments and advances in society. The continuation of despotism was not tolerable after literacy rates had multiplied, after the economy had improved, after security was provided and health conditions had advanced.'[19] Asadollah Alam, the shah's confidant and minister of the court in 1974, writes in his memoirs about a conversation he had with the shah one day:

> I said, 'there is inflation, and people are suffering from high prices, most of the [government] services do not work properly either. People ask why these small problems are not solved when the Shahanshah has provided so much money and has so many plans ready.' [After a while the shah] said, 'Well, because of the people's indolence, I have called them corrupt. Don't they say anything in this regard?' I said, 'No! No one has any objection because it's a fact.' The Shahanshah said, 'When one is not awaiting people's votes (i.e. electing a president), one can utter whatever is in the interests of the country.'

In *Winds of Change*, his manifesto about the future of Iran after the Islamic Republic, Prince Reza Pahlavi implicitly admits that his father's policies were flawed:

> At an early age, my father took responsibility of an Iran occupied by foreign forces. Under his leadership, the country rid itself of the occupiers and, in a relatively short time, transformed Iran into a unified, prospering nation. Ironically, some have argued that the crisis of the late seventies was due, in part, to an

excessively rapid rate of growth and modernisation. During the same period, unfortunately, the democratic process was curtailed and did not keep pace. This contributed greatly to the political crisis that preceded the 1979 upheaval.[20]

Beset by advanced cancer, the shah left Iran in January 1979 to begin a life in exile. He lived in Egypt, Morocco, the Bahamas, and Mexico before going to the United States for the treatment of lymphatic cancer. His arrival in New York City led to the Iranian takeover of the American embassy in Tehran by 'students of the Imam's Line', and the taking hostage of more than fifty Americans for 444 days.

The shah died in Cairo, Egypt, on 27 July 1980.

SIX

Liberals and Angry Young Men

*The Iranian Nation shed its blood at the foot of a tree whose fruit
was Velayat-e Faqih.*
Muhammad Ali Rajaei, 1980

I saw a train that was carrying fiqh, and how heavy was it moving,
I saw a train that was carrying politics, and how empty was it
moving ...
Sohrab Sepehri, 1974

The revolutionary ideals, however ambiguous they might have been,
were instantly mirrored in the changes that occurred across the surface
of the cities, from giving new names to streets and squares, to radical
changes in the appearance of young people.

Among others, Shah Street was renamed Islamic Republic Street;
Shah Reza Street was changed to Revolution Street; Eisenhower to
Freedom; Elizabeth II to Farmer; 6th of Bahman (the date of the shah's
White Revolution) to Worker; Kennedy to Monotheism; Koorosh-e
Kabir (Cyrus the Great) to Dr Shariati; Takht-e Jamshid (Persepolis) to
Taleqani; and Kakh (Palace) to Palestine. There were other changes that
would only last until the clerical rulers swept aside rivals and crushed the
opposition: Pahlavi Avenue, Tehran's main north-south thoroughfare,
became Mosaddeq, only to be renamed Vali-e Asr, after the title of
the twelfth Shi'i Imam, by a clerical establishment that loathed the
nationalist leader Mosaddeq, and the idea of secularism. Several streets

and squares named after Mojahedin-e Khalq members killed under the shah's rule were renamed a short while later.

The youngsters displayed revolutionary fervour in their appearance and attitudes. It seemed that in accordance with Hegelian theory, the middle class had actually produced its antithesis. Generally, boys got rid of their hippie-style long hair, instead wearing beards (for those who adhered to traditional religious values) or thick, Stalinesque moustaches (for the Mojahedin and the Marxists). Girls did away with flamboyant hairdos, many of them taking up the headscarf or chador, and others sporting simple, laid-back styles. Fashion took a trend towards the shabby and the working class, and smart was rejected as a symbol of the ousted regime; tight jeans and bright colours gave way to loose pants, khaki shirts, and military-style overcoats with Chinese sneakers or army boots. Neckties were particularly denounced as a token of 'westoxication'. This last point was rather bizarre, since the western-style suit became the official uniform of the Islamic Republic's non-clerical statesmen. These changes represented developments in the socio-economic undercurrents of the society.

Morteza Avini is a clear example of how the chemistry of revolutionary Islam changed the minds of the young and formed their world-view. Praised as the 'Lord of all pen-holding martyrs' by the Islamic Republic after his death, Avini made documentary films of the battlegrounds with Iraq for Iranian state television in the 1980s.

'I studied architecture at Tehran University's faculty of fine arts. I used to attend poetry-reciting evenings and visit art galleries,' Avini wrote. 'I spent hours of my time on futile discussions about things I did not know anything about. For years I lived pretending to be a very knowledgeable person. I had a professor's beard and Nietzsche-style moustache ... But fortunately life led me to a different path.

'Whatever I have learned I have learned it outside the university,' he wrote. 'I say with utmost certainty that true expertise can only be achieved through commitment to Islam ... With the beginning of the Revolution, I put all my writings – philosophical reflections, short stories, poems, etc – in a few sacks and burned them all. I decided not to write anything about myself any more. Unfortunately today's art is expressing the self ... so I tried to destroy myself so that only God remained. When the Construction Jihad was set up in 1979, we set out for villages to plough for God ... My fate was to put the shovel aside and pick up the camera ...'[1]

Avini died when a landmine from the Iran-Iraq war exploded while he was shooting pictures in 1994. He exemplified the angry young men that came to rule the country after the fall of the monarchy.

With sharp rises in oil prices and the ensuing economic boom, and particularly after the shah's land reforms, large cities began to emerge in Iran in the 1960s, with huge waves of village-dwellers, having abandoned their centuries-old professions, migrating to cities, particularly to Tehran, as the 'land of opportunities'. However, as sociologists have observed, the government of the time was not prepared to organise modern cities with inherent institutions and orderly relations. Therefore, in practice the cities of Iran became large, chaotic villages. As a result of unbalanced economic policies and the distorted distribution of wealth, newcomers failed to be integrated into the social structure, ending up as poor, disinherited and alienated masses dwelling in slums and shantytowns on the outskirts of large cities.

The traditional religious background of these classes, and particularly their youngsters, who had been brought up to despise society, made them an ideal audience for the revolutionary, ideological version of Islam advocated by Ali Shariati, Morteza Motahhari, the Mojahedin-e Khalq, and the likes. Thus, the Islamic Revolution provided them with a unique opportunity to vent their anger against the system, to claim their suppressed rights, and ultimately to merge and form the ranks of the new regime's leadership. The shantytowns of southern Tehran were hotbeds of revolutionary fervour. By the mid-seventies, the lines were drawn quite clearly. The materialistic, flamboyant city was the epitome of vice, rife with greed, consumerism, inequality, promiscuity, economic and moral corruption, and, in a word, westernisation. In direct contrast, the children of the slums longed for the 'just rule of Imam Ali', a rule in which, according to a *hadith* attributed to the Prophet, the individual can 'take honour in poverty'. They were burning with revolutionary anger, waiting for the day when they could level the uptown skyscrapers, palaces and villas, and cut them to the size of the slums in which they lived. But fate had something different in store for them.

The date of 11 February 1979 marked not only the end of the Pahlavi monarchy, but also the beginning of a period of dual power: on one side, Premier Bazargan, the provincial government, and the formal state institutions; on the other, Ayatollah Khomeini's disciples, the Revolutionary Council, and the shadow clerical state that had emerged during the course of the revolution. Bazargan headed a government that controlled neither the country nor even its own bureaucratic apparatus. Central authority had broken down. Hundreds of semi-independent revolutionary committees, not answerable to central authority, were performing a variety of functions in major cities and towns across the country. Factory workers, civil servants, white-collar employees, and students were often in control, demanding a say in running their organisations and choosing their chiefs. The lower ranks or local inhabitants frequently rejected governors, military commanders, and other officials appointed by the prime minister. A range of political groups, from the far left to the far right, from secular to ultra-Islamic, were vying for political power, pushing rival agendas, and demanding immediate action from the prime minister. Clerics led by Ayatollah Muhammad Beheshti established the Islamic Republican party (IRP). The IRP emerged as the organ of those clerics surrounding Ayatollah Khomeini, and the major political force in the country. Not to be outdone, followers of more moderate senior cleric Shariatmadari established the Islamic People's Republican party (IPRP) in 1979, which had a base in Azerbaijan, Shariatmadari's home province.

In the meantime, multiple centres of authority emerged within the government. As the supreme leader, Ayatollah Khomeini did not consider himself bound by the government. He made policy pronouncements, named personal representatives to key government organisations, established new institutions, and announced decisions without consulting his prime minister. The prime minister found he had to share power with the Revolutionary Council, which Ayatollah Khomeini had established in January 1979, and which was initially composed of clerics close to Ayatollah Khomeini; Secular political leaders sided with Bazargan.

With the establishment of the provisional government, Bazargan and his colleagues left the Revolutionary Council to form the cabinet. They were replaced by Ayatollah Khomeini's aides from the Paris period, including Abolhassan Banisadr and Sadeq Qotbzadeh, and by protégés of Ayatollah Khomeini's clerical associates. The cabinet was to serve as the executive authority, but the Revolutionary Council was to wield supreme decision-making and legislative authority.

Ayatollah Khomeini had charged the provisional government with the task of drawing up a draft constitution. A step in this direction was taken on 30 and 31 March 1979, when a national referendum was held to determine the kind of political system to be established. Ayatollah Khomeini rejected demands by various political groups, and by Ayatollah Shariatmadari, that voters be given a wide choice. The only form of government to appear on the ballot was an Islamic republic, and voting was not by secret ballot. The government reported an overwhelming majority of over 98 percent in favour of an Islamic republic. Ayatollah Khomeini proclaimed the establishment of the Islamic Republic of Iran on 1 April 1979.

Meanwhile, differences quickly emerged between the cabinet and the Revolutionary Council over appointments, the role of the revolutionary courts and other revolutionary organisations, foreign policy, and the general direction of the Revolution. Bazargan and his cabinet ministers were eager for a return to normalcy, and the rapid reassertion of central authority. Clerics of the Revolutionary Council, more responsive to the Islamic and popular temper of the mass of their followers, generally favoured more radical economic and social measures. They also proved more willing and able to mobilise the street crowds and the revolutionary organisations to achieve their ends.

In July 1979, Bazargan obtained Ayatollah Khomeini's approval for an arrangement he hoped would permit closer cooperation between the Revolutionary Council and the cabinet. Four clerical members of the Council joined the government, one as minister of interior and three others as undersecretaries of interior, education, and defence, while Bazargan and three cabinet members joined the Council. All eight continued in their original positions as well. Nevertheless, tensions persisted.

In parallel with their attempts to put in place the institutions of the new order, the revolutionaries turned their attention to bringing to trial and punishing members of the former regime they considered responsible for carrying out political repression, plundering the country's wealth, implementing damaging economic policies, and allowing foreign exploitation of Iran. A revolutionary court set to work

almost immediately in the school building in Tehran where Ayatollah
Khomeini had set up his headquarters. Revolutionary courts were
established in provincial centres shortly thereafter. The Tehran court,
led by Ayatollah Sadeq Khalkhali, later to be nicknamed 'the hanging
judge', passed death sentences on four of the shah's generals on 16
February 1979; all four were executed by firing squad on the roof of the
building housing Ayatollah Khomeini's headquarters. More executions,
of military and police officers, SAVAK agents, cabinet ministers, Majles
deputies, and officials of the shah's regime, followed on an almost daily
basis. In response to criticism concerning summary trials, Ayatollah
Khalkhali was quoted as saying that if someone got executed mistakenly,
he would go to heaven.

The activities of the revolutionary courts became a focus of intense
controversy. On the one hand, left-wing political groups and populist
clerics pressed hard for 'revolutionary justice' for miscreants of the
former regime. On the other hand, lawyers and human-rights groups
protested the arbitrary nature of the revolutionary courts, the vagueness
of charges, and the absence of defence lawyers. Bazargan, too, was
critical of the courts' activities. At the prime minister's insistence, the
revolutionary courts suspended their activities on 14 March 1979. On
5 April, new regulations governing the courts were promulgated. The
courts were to be established at the discretion of the Revolutionary
Council, and with Ayatollah Khomeini's permission. They were
authorised to try a variety of broadly defined crimes, such as 'sowing
corruption on earth', 'crimes against the people', and 'crimes against
the Revolution'. The courts resumed their work on 6 April. On the
following day, despite international pleas for clemency, Hoveyda, the
shah's prime minister for twelve years, was put to death. Attempts by
Bazargan to have the revolutionary courts placed under the judiciary,
and to secure protection for potential victims through amnesties issued
by Ayatollah Khomeini also failed. Beginning in August 1979, the
courts tried and passed death sentences on members of ethnic minorities
involved in anti-government movements. Some 550 persons had been
executed by the time Bazargan resigned in November 1979. Bazargan
had also attempted, but failed, to bring the revolutionary committees
under his control. The committees, whose members were armed,
performed a variety of duties. They policed neighbourhoods in urban

areas, guarded prisons and government buildings, made arrests, and served as the execution squads of the revolutionary tribunals. However, the committees often served the interests of powerful individual clerics, revolutionary personalities, and political groups. They made unauthorised arrests, intervened in labour-management disputes, and seized property. Despite these abuses, members of the Revolutionary Council wanted to bring the committees under their own control, rather than eliminate them. With this in mind, in February 1979 they appointed Ayatollah Muhammad Reza Mahdavi-Kani head of the Tehran revolutionary committee and charged him with supervising the committees countrywide. Mahdavi-Kani dissolved many committees, consolidated others, and sent thousands of committee men home. But the committees, like the revolutionary courts, endured, serving as one of the coercive arms of the revolutionary government.[2]

In May 1979 Ayatollah Khomeini authorised the establishment of the Islamic Revolutionary Guards Corps (IRGC). The IRGC was conceived by the men around Ayatollah Khomeini as a military force loyal to the Revolution and the clerical leaders, as a counterbalance to the regular army, and as a force to use against the guerrilla organisations of the left, which were also rapidly arming. Disturbances among the ethnic minorities accelerated the expansion of the IRGC.

On Ayatollah Khomeini's orders, two other important organisations were established in this formative period. In March he ordered the establishment of the Foundation for the Disinherited (Bonyad-e Mostazafan). The organisation was to take charge of the assets of the Pahlavi Foundation and to use the proceeds to assist low-income groups. The new foundation in time came to be one of the largest conglomerates in the country, controlling hundreds of expropriated and nationalised factories, trading firms, farms, and apartment and office buildings, as well as two large newspaper chains. In later years, the name of the Bonyad became associated with widespread corruption and profiteering. The Construction Jihad (Jahad-e Sazandegi), established in June, recruited young people for the construction of clinics, local roads, schools, and similar facilities in villages and rural areas. This organisation also grew rapidly, assuming functions in rural areas that had previously been handled by the Planning and Budget Organisation (which replaced the Plan Organisation in 1973), and the Ministry of Agriculture.

In March 1979 trouble broke out among the Turkmen, the Kurds, and the Arabic-speaking population of Khuzestan. The disputes in the Turkmen region of Gorgan were over land rather than claims for Turkmen cultural identity or autonomy. Representatives of left-wing movements, active in the region, were encouraging agricultural workers to seize land from the large landlords. These disturbances were put down, but not without violence. Meanwhile, in Khuzestan, the centre of Iran's oil industry, members of the Arabic-speaking population organised and demanded a larger share of oil revenues for the region, more jobs for local inhabitants, the use of Arabic as a semi-official language, and a larger degree of local autonomy. Because Arab states, including Iraq, had in the past laid claim to Khuzestan as part of the 'Arab homeland', the government was bound to regard an indigenous movement among the Arabic-speaking population with suspicion. The government also suspected that scattered instances of sabotage in the oil fields were occurring with Iraqi connivance. In May 1979, government forces responded to these disturbances by firing on Arab demonstrators in Khorramshahr. Several demonstrators were killed; others were shot on orders of the local revolutionary court. The government subsequently quietly transferred the religious leader of the Khuzestan Arabs, Ayatollah Muhammad Taher Shobair Khaqani, to Qom, where he was kept under house arrest. These measures ended further protests.

The uprising in Kordestan turned out to be more deeply rooted, serious, and durable. The Kurdish leaders were disappointed that the Revolution had not brought them the local autonomy they had long desired. Scattered fighting began in March 1979 between government and Kurdish forces, and continued after a brief cease-fire; attempts at negotiation proved abortive. One faction, led by Ahmad Moftizadeh, the Friday prayer leader in Sanandaj, was ready to accept the limited concessions offered by the government, but the Kurdish Democratic party, led by Abdolrahman Qassemlu, and a more radical group led by Sheikh Ezzeddin Hosseini, issued demands that the authorities in Tehran did not feel they could accept. These included the enlargement of the Kordestan region to include all Kurdish-speaking areas in Iran, a specified share of the national revenue for expenditure in the province, and complete autonomy in provincial administration. Kurdish was demanded to be recognised as an official language for local use, and for correspondence with the central government. Kurds were to fill all local government posts and to be in charge of local security forces. The central government would remain responsible for national defence, foreign affairs, and central banking functions. Similar autonomy would be granted other ethnic minorities in the country. With the rejection of these demands, serious fighting broke out in August 1979. Ayatollah Khomeini, invoking his powers as commander-in-chief, used the army against other Iranians for the first time since the Revolution. No settlement was reached with the Kurds during Bazargan's prime ministership.

Meanwhile, since the Bazargan government lacked the necessary security forces to control the streets, such control passed gradually into the hands of clerics in the Revolutionary Council and the IRP, who ran the revolutionary courts and had influence over the Revolutionary Guards, the revolutionary committees, and the hard-line vigilantes or Hezbollahis (members of the Party of God). The clerics deployed these forces to curb rival political organisations. In June, the Revolutionary Council promulgated a new press law, and began a crackdown against the proliferating political press. On 8 August 1979, the Revolutionary Prosecutor banned the mass-circulation, left-leaning newspaper *Ayandegan*. Ayatollah Khomeini supported the move by saying 'I will no more read *Ayandegan*'. Five days later Hezbollahis broke up a Tehran rally called by the National Democratic Front – a newly organised left-of-centre political movement – to protest the *Ayandegan* closure. The Revolutionary Council then proscribed the National Democratic Front itself, and issued a warrant for the arrest of its leader. Hezbollahis also attacked the headquarters of the Fada'eeyan organisation and forced the Mojahedin to evacuate their headquarters. On 20 August forty-one opposition papers were proscribed. On 8 September the two largest newspaper chains in the country, *Kayhan* and *Ettela'at*, were expropriated and transferred to the Foundation for the Disinherited.[3]

In June and July 1979, the Revolutionary Council also passed a number of major economic measures, the effect of which was to transfer considerable private sector assets to the state. It nationalised banks, insurance companies, major industries, and certain categories of urban land; expropriated the wealth of leading business and industrial families; and appointed state managers to many private industries and companies.

The clerical establishment unveiled a draft constitution on 18 June. Aside from substituting a strong president, on the Gaullist model, for the monarchy, the constitution did not differ markedly from the 1906 constitution and did not give the clerics an important role in the new state structure. Ayatollah Khomeini was prepared to submit this draft, virtually unmodified, to a national referendum or, barring that, to an appointed council of forty representatives who could advise on, but not revise, the document. Ironically, as it turned out, it was the parties of the left who most vehemently rejected this procedure and demanded that the constitution be submitted for full-scale review by a constituent assembly. Shariatmadari supported these demands.

A newly created seventy-three-member Assembly of Experts convened on 18 August 1979 to consider the draft constitution. Clerics, members and supporters of the IRP dominated the assembly, which revamped the constitution to establish the basis for a state dominated by the Shi'i clergy. Ayatollah Hosseinali Montazeri was instrumental in introducing the concept of Velayat-e Faqih as the backbone of the new constitution. The Assembly of Experts completed its work on 15 November and the constitution was approved in a national referendum on 2 and 3 December 1979, once again, according to government figures, by over 98 percent of the vote.

In October 1979, when it had become clear that the draft constitution would institutionalize clerical domination of the state, Bazargan and a number of his cabinet ministers attempted to persuade Ayatollah Khomeini to dissolve the Assembly of Experts. Ayatollah Khomeini refused to do so. Now opposition parties attempted to articulate their objections to the constitution through protests led by the IPRP. Following approval of the constitution, Shariatmadari's followers in Tabriz organised demonstrations and seized control of the radio station. A potentially serious challenge to the dominant clerical hierarchy fizzled out, however, when Ayatollah Shariatmadari wavered in his support for the protesters, and the pro-Ayatollah Khomeini forces organised massive counter-demonstrations in the city in 1979. In fear of condemnation by Ayatollah Khomeini and of IRP reprisals, the IPRP in December 1979 announced the dissolution of the party.

Amid fiery anti-imperialist rhetoric, few foreign initiatives were possible in the early months of the Revolution. The Bazargan government attempted to maintain correct relations with the Persian Gulf states, despite harsh denunciations of the Gulf rulers by senior clerics and revolutionary leaders. Anti-American feeling was widespread and was fanned by Ayatollah Khomeini himself, populist preachers, and the left-wing parties. Bazargan, however, continued to seek military spare parts from Washington, and asked for intelligence information on Soviet and Iraqi activities in Iran. On 1 November 1979 Bazargan met with President Carter's national security adviser, Zbigniew K. Brzezinski, in Algiers, where the two men were attending Independence Day celebrations. Meanwhile, the shah, who was seriously ill, was admitted to the United States for medical treatment. Iranians feared that the shah would use this visit to the United States to secure its support for an attempt to overthrow the Islamic Republic.[4]

By this time, the angry young men of the shantytowns were already frustrated with the moderate policies of Bazargan's government, and with the ageing, well-dressed, western-minded – albeit religious – liberal politicians who ran it. They despised Bazargan and his men for their nationalistic leanings, their upper-middle-class backgrounds, their pro-West attitude and their neckties – a symbol of western decadence. They were virtually ready to bulldoze the fancy palaces and fill the rich-poor gap with their debris. They sought to export the Islamic Revolution to the farthest corners of the world, and liberate the oppressed masses from the chains of corrupt, pro-American regimes. But at the same time, they loathed the revolutionary Marxists for their materialistic ideology and for their liberal personal lifestyles. Something had to be done, they thought. And that something turned out to be the seizure of the US embassy in Tehran.

On 1 November 1979, hundreds of thousands marched in Tehran to demand the shah's extradition, while the press denounced Bazargan for meeting with Brzezinski. On 4 November, some three thousand militants overran the US embassy in Tehran and captured fifty-two embassy staff members. Religious extremists and Ayatollah Khomeini praised their actions. 'We have control', Abbas Abdi, a leader of the students, recalled announcing to the world. The echo of that statement traumatised a superpower – as fifty-two American diplomats were held hostage for 444 days – and poisoned Iran-US ties for two decades.

The militants made several demands: that the shah, who ruled Iran for decades and was now seeking medical treatment in the West, be turned over to them for trial; that the United States apologise for crimes against the Iranian people; and that the shah's assets be paid to them. Bazargan resigned two days later; no prime minister was named to replace him. Robert C. Ode, one of the fifty-two American citizens taken hostage and held for a total of 444 days, recalled the event thus:

> 4 November 1979: Since I wasn't sure whether we were expected to work at the consular Section, in view of what the chargé had told me last evening, I went to the office just the same at 7.30 as I had quite a bit of work to do anyway. When I got there, however, I found that everyone was coming to work as usual but we were not open to the general public. About 9.00 I was in my office when a young American woman, apparently the wife of an Iranian, was shown into my office as she wanted to obtain her mother-in-law's Iranian passport that had been left at the consular section a day or so before for a non-immigrant visa. Just as I was talking to her in an attempt to find out to whom the passport had been issued, when it was left with us, etc, we were told by the consul general to drop everything and get up to the second floor of the consular section. I really didn't know what was happening but was told that a mob had managed to get into the embassy compound and, for our own protection, everyone had to go upstairs immediately.
>
> I noticed that the consul general was removing the visa plates and locking the visa stamping machines. I went upstairs with the American woman and could see a number of young men in the area between the rear of the consular section and the embassy COOP store. We were told to sit on the floor in the outer hallway offices. A Marine security guard was present and was in contact with the main embassy building (Chancery) by walkie-talkie. After an hour or so we could hear that the mob, which turned out to be student revolutionaries, were also on the walkie-talkie. The Marine guard then advised that we were going to evacuate the consular section.
>
> There were some visitors on the second floor in the Immigrant

Visa Unit and the American Services Unit. I was asked to assist an elderly gentleman – either an American of Iranian origin or an Iranian citizen, I don't know, since he was almost blind and was completely terrified – and to be the first one out of the building. When we got outside he was met by a relative who took him away in his car. The students outside the consular section appeared to be somewhat confused at that point, and the consul general and about four other American members of the consular section, of which I was one, started up the street with the intention of going to his residence. When we were about 1½ blocks from the consular section we were surrounded by a group of the students, who were armed, and told to return to the compound. When we protested a shot was fired into the air above our heads.

It was raining moderately at the time. We were taken back to the compound, being pushed and hurried along the way and forced to put our hands above our heads and then marched to the embassy residence. After arriving at the residence I had my hands tied behind my back so tightly with nylon cord that circulation was cut off. I was taken upstairs and put alone in a rear bedroom and after a short time was blindfolded. After protesting strongly that the cord was too tight the cord was removed and the blindfold taken off – when they tried to feed me some dates and I refused to eat anything I couldn't see. I strongly protested the violation of my diplomatic immunity, but these protests were ignored. I then was required to sit in a chair facing the bedroom wall. Then another older student came in and when I again protested the violation of my diplomatic immunity he confiscated my US Mission Tehran ID card. My hands were again tied and I was taken to the Embassy living room on the ground floor where a number of other hostages were gathered. Some students attempted to talk with us, stating how they didn't hate Americans – only our US Government, President Carter, etc. We were given sandwiches and that night I slept on the living room floor. We were not permitted to talk to our fellow hostages and from then on our hands were tied day and night and only removed while we were eating or had to go to the bathroom.

5 November 1979: After remaining in the living room the

next morning, I was taken into the embassy dining room and forced to sit on a dining room chair around the table with about twelve or so other hostages. Our hands were tied to each side of the chair. We could only rest by leaning on to the dining table and resting our heads on a small cushion. The drapes were drawn and we were not permitted to talk with the other hostages. At one point my captors also tried to make me face the wall but I objected since I had no way to rest my head and after considerable objections I was permitted to continue facing the table. Our captors always conversed in stage whispers. We were untied and taken to the toilet as necessary, as well as into a small dining room adjacent for meals, then returned to our chairs and again tied to the chair. I slept that night on the floor under the dining table with a piece of drapery for a cover.[5]

Zealous militant students from Mashhad, Shiraz, Isfahan and Tabriz took part in seizing the American embassy and thereby toppling Bazargan's government. However, the inner circle of the self-styled 'Muslim Students Following the Imam's Line' mostly included those who came from Tehran's southernmost districts.

Abbas Abdi was born in 1956 in central Tehran. Two years later his family moved to Nazzi Abad, a poor district in the southern border of the capital, where, after he grew up to be a teenager, he met a host of like-minded young revolutionaries, most of whom were to take government posts in the Islamic Republic. They studied Shariati and listened to fiery anti-shah sermons in the local mosque.

As Muhammad Quchani wrote, 'Their intellectual world was confined to the same tight geographical borders that distinguished Nazzi Abad, Ali Abad and other southern neighbourhoods of Tehran. They lived on the borders; not merely geographical borders, but the borders between tradition and modernity, between religious and revolutionary thought. Following the guidelines of the clerics' treatise was as important for them as analysing facts through modern scientific theories ...' Abbas Abdi was soon to become a central figure of the students, and one of their speakers.

Abdi was 'a rather small young man whose face was garnished with Islamic appearance [i.e. bearded], and if it was necessary to have a conversation with women, in compliance with the fiqh rules, he would stare at the horizon or the ground while speaking with them'. The provisional government of Bazargan was the students' primary target. Abbas Abdi later said, 'The first six months after the Revolution, the situation was very strained. Clashes in Gonbad, Kordestan, Azerbaijan, Khuzestan and other regions, particularly in the schools and universities, did not provide a promising perspective. Therefore, a number of students who were active in the framework of the Office of Unity Consolidation planned the takeover of the American embassy ... The seizure of the Spies' Den totally transformed the country's atmosphere'.[6]

But at the same time, the students eyed the rival political groups that were trying hard to win the hearts and minds of the young generation, particularly the Mojahedin and the Marxist organisations. The takeover of the embassy, so to speak, practically out-lefted the most extreme left, and ideologically disarmed the competition, albeit temporarily. But to embark on a venture so bold and raucous, without the consent of the charismatic leader of the Revolution – and moreso to bypass his possible opposition – the students needed a high-ranking clergyman to legitimise their plans. It was their mentor, Ayatollah Muhammad Mousavi Khoeiniha, who did the job and gave the go-ahead for the storming of the US embassy – yet another revolutionary figure who later changed from revolutionary extremist to moderate reformist, and consequently fell from grace.

In an interview with *Time* online magazine in 2000, Khoeiniha coolly admitted to his role in the hostage drama. 'Khoeiniha now said that he sanctioned the hostage-taking as part of a nascent reform movement against the shah's repressive regime. When student militants first came to Khoeiniha – who was the student liaison for the Ayatollah Khomeini – with their scheme, he recalls telling them to go ahead and capture the 'Nest of Spies'.' Khoeiniha was the Revolution's earliest spin-doctor, using his clerical stature to turn the rogue act of 300 radicals into the Iranian Revolution's version of the Boston Tea Party.

As the stakes mounted during the 444 day siege, Khoeiniha stayed on as the students' counsellor, tempering their more extreme decisions, and serving as a direct conduit to Ayatollah Khomeini. But after the hostages were freed, and the Revolution matured into a way of life, Khoeiniha said an ideological rift divided the Revolution's supporters, pitting founding fathers like himself against hard-line conservatives who closed ranks after Ayatollah Khomeini's death.

Khoeiniha has had a hand in both of the violent convulsions that frame the last twenty years of Iranian history. When students rioted last July in the worst street unrest since 1979, it was in response to the shutdown of Khoeiniha's daily newspaper *Salam*. As editor of *Salam*, Khoeiniha advocated freedom of thought and expression, and was a pioneer of the pro-reform press that became the heart and soul of President Mohammed Khatami's modernisation movement. Khoeiniha transformed *Salam* into the campaign headquarters for the Khatami presidency, and started the investigation into a series of political killings linked to high officials that eventually brought down former president Ali Akbar Hashemi Rafsanjani. Hard-liners tried to silence Khoeiniha by shutting down his newspaper, but the cleric's outspoken views were still too threatening. In 1999, the judiciary banned him from working as an editor or journalist for five years.

How did the man behind the 1979 hostage crisis become a guru of Iran's modern pro-democracy reform movement? In the throes of a fiercely ideological revolution, 'Democracy was considered a symbol of a movement against Islam', Khoeiniha explains. But twenty years of clerical authoritarianism have led to a convergence of sorts between Islamic and democratic values. 'You think that what I subscribe to today is in contradiction to what I advocated then,' he said. 'Not at all. My standpoint today is completely coherent with that of that time.'

The goals Khoeiniha sought then – political freedom and independence – motivate his current reformist push as well. In 1979, it seemed that an Islamic Revolution could deliver these goals. But by 2000, Khoeiniha believed that a democratic Islamic Republic was a better route to this destination. The idea of Iranian democracy is new, and has brought around Islamic radicals who once assumed that democracy and western neo-imperialism were inseparable.

Khoeiniha stops short of advocating diplomatic ties with the US, but his attitude is still forward-looking. 'One can feel a change of discourse and attitude among the Americans compared to previous times,' he said. 'And each of these comments automatically affects public opinion in Iran.' He points out that both countries are home to powerful lobbies that oppose renewed relations. But with Khoeiniha fighting on the side of dialogue and democracy, the prospects for positive change are encouraging.[7]

Khoeiniha later came to be known as the legendary figure behind the takeover of the US embassy in Tehran. He was, however, a shadowy figure at the time. The actual hostage takers were introduced to the world by images of Abdi and a fellow female militant student nicknamed 'Sister Mary', whose presence on the television news became synonymous with the hostage crisis. As its primary spokesperson, hers became the public face of the fledgling Iranian Revolution.

Massoumeh Ebtekar, the real name behind the alias, disappeared from the public scene once the hostage crisis had subsided. She re-emerged years later, ironically – but not surprisingly for Iranian politics – as a close ally of the reformist president Muhammad Khatami. She was the first woman in a post-Revolution cabinet, chosen to head the Environment Protection Organisation. In a book she published in 2000, Ebtekar gave the first-ever insider account of the American embassy takeover, aiming to correct 'twenty years of misrepresentation by the western media of what the aims of the Iranian students and the populist revolution they personified were.'

Since the embassy takeover, she became the mother of two children; the editorial director of *Farzaneh*, a journal of women's studies and research; received her PhD in immunology; became an outspoken advocate of women's rights, particularly in Islamic societies; and in 1997, was appointed by President Khatami as the first woman ever to hold a cabinet portfolio in Iran.

But where was Abdi all this time? Having seen his primary goal attained, a few months after the takeover of the US embassy he took part in the takeover of Tehran University, which ultimately led to the closing down of all higher education institutes, and was branded a 'cultural revolution' by the custodians of the Islamic Republic. Soon afterwards, he went to Shiraz to supervise a revolutionary land redistribution committee. Upon his return to Tehran, he was employed at the Prime Minister's Office, which, to the present day, is considered as the birthplace of the Islamic Republic's intelligence apparatus. There he once again joined his old friend, inspiration and fellow hostage-taker Saeed Hajjarian, who became the de facto theoretician and founder of the Intelligence Ministry, long before he became to be known as the 'theoretician of the reform movement' in the late 1990s, a title that would cost him a bullet in the mouth and a lifelong handicap. Abdi did not stay at the Intelligence Ministry for long. He chose to join his guru Ayatollah Khoeiniha when the latter was appointed as prosecutor general.

Abdi's next stop was the presidency's Strategic Research Centre, which turned out to be the stronghold of old Nazzi Abad friends, gathered once again around Khoeiniha, who had left the judiciary after the Islamic Republic turned to the right in the late 1980s. The 'political development project' (which eventually played a key role in opening up the political arena, and later provided a context for the face-off of rivalling factions), was the brainchild of the Strategic Research Centre, and was set up with the purpose of guaranteeing the survival of the Islamic Republic in the face of growing public frustration with clerical rule, and the imminent threat of the baby-boomers of the 1980s, who would soon be reaching their teen years.

In 1990, he helped Khoeiniha establish the newspaper *Salam*, the mouthpiece of the 'traditional Islamic left', to herald social justice and (to a lesser extent at the beginning) political tolerance. His harsh criticism of the economic policies of Rafsanjani's government cost him one year in jail in 1993.

By the mid-1990s, Abdi and his compatriots had undergone drastic changes. Inspired by what they had learned in universities and by researching sociological developments in the West, they were now the harbingers of a new middle-class bourgeoisie, something they had loathed and fought for years. Observing the thirst for freedom among the young generations, they replaced their original cause of social justice with democracy. The angry young men of 1979, who rejected democracy as a corrupt western idea, and who opposed classical definitions of statesmanship as hypocritical conservatism, now became full-time politicians, rallying around Muhammad Khatami and, after he was elected as president, together with other veteran 'Students Following the Imam's Line', set up the Islamic Iran Participation Front with the motto 'Iran for all Iranians'.

As celebrations were underway for the twenty-year anniversary of the Islamic Revolution, Abdi told *The Christian Science Monitor* that he was 'older and wiser' now.

'Everything has changed,' said Abdi, who was at that time an editor of the pro-reform moderate *Salam* newspaper. 'The world has changed, our regime has changed, our social environment has changed ... For sure I've changed too.'[8]

And later, the master hostage-captor even met his former captive, at the UNESCO headquarters in Paris. Abbas Abdi took part in the public meeting with former US hostage and embassy press attaché Barry Rosen, at a gathering organised by the Centre for World Dialogue based in Nicosia, Cyprus. Abdi apologised to Mr Rosen's family for their suffering but said that he did not regret his actions.

The takeover was meant to last ten days at most, he said, and its initial purpose was to force the US to deport the shah back to Iran. 'We thought we were doing something good,' he said. 'You don't see so many changes in your country, but I have seen many, many changes in twenty years in my country. I don't think we should reach the conclusion that what we do today is right, or what we did in the past was wrong.'

On 4 November 2002 – ironically, exactly the same date he climbed over the wall of the US embassy in Tehran twenty-three years before – Abdi was arrested. Even more ironic was the charge levelled against him: promoting America through fabricating lies. A poll conducted by a firm chaired by Abdi, found that more than 70 percent of Iranians supported dialogue with the United States.

And in June 2005, one of his former comrades became Iran's first non-cleric president, beating on his way to victory one of the 'pillars of the Islamic Republic'.

SEVEN

A Utopia of Ideas

An Islamic government does not resemble states where the people are deprived of all security and everyone sits at home trembling for fear of a sudden raid or attacks by the agents of the state. It was that way under [the Caliph] Mu'awiyah and similar rulers: people had no security, and they were killed or banished, or imprisoned for lengthy periods, on the strength of an accusation or a mere suspicion, because the government was not Islamic. When an Islamic government is established, all will live under complete security ...

Ayatollah Khomeini, *The Islamic State: Velayat-e Faqih*

God knows that whenever I look at these youngsters who are leaving for the battlefronts, I feel ashamed of myself ... In more than eighty years of my life, I have not served Islam as much as they will in a few days.

Ayatollah Khomeini, 1983

In every cry of every Man,
In every Infant's cry of fear,
In every voice, in every ban,
The mind-forg'd manacles I hear.

How the Chimney-sweeper's cry
Every black'ning Church appals;
And the hapless Soldier's sigh
Runs in blood down Palace walls.

William Blake, *London*, in *Songs of Experience*, 1791

In 1997, after Muhammad Khatami was elected president in a landslide victory that shocked the ruling conservatives, dozens of newly born reformist publications started brazenly criticising the Islamic establishment's past policies. The most critical and outspoken reformist commentators were former Islamic Republic officials affiliated with the 'left' faction that had fallen from grace following Ayatollah Khomeini's death in 1989. In their polemics, they accused the conservatives of being responsible for all the maladies the country was suffering from – from economic dire straits, to suppression of the press and freedom of expression. All criticism, however, stopped short of spilling over into the period when the imam was alive and ruling. On the contrary, the reformists spoke of those days with a certain sense of nostalgia. In every effort to advocate democracy, political pluralism, human rights and social justice they would rely on the remarks made by the late founder of the Islamic Republic, giving the impression that Iran had been a utopian state in Khomeini's days. As late as 2004, when the reform movement was declared 'dead', Saeed Hajjarian, the prominent reformist figure whose attempted assassination by hardliners resulted in terminal handicap, published an article in which he tried to justify why the imam had labelled Mosaddeq as 'non-Muslim'. Except for a handful of reformists, Ayatollah Khomeini remained one of the infallible ones, and his reign represented a 'paradise lost'.

There is little doubt that in the course of his struggle against the shah's regime, Ayatollah Khomeini had never actually dreamed that the clergy would one day rule the country. In fact, he had explicitly said that once victory was attained, the clergy would go back to mosques and resume guiding people in religious matters.

In the early 1980s I was invited to the wedding ceremony of a remote relative. The man who was conducting the wedding was a typical lower middle-class cleric who earned a living by attending funeral services and wedding ceremonies and speaking at small mosques during Ramadan and Moharram. Before the ceremony started, he asked the names of the couple-to-be. When he learned that the bridegroom's surname was Taj (Crown), he said sardonically, 'Son, you better change your name. The days of the crown are over; now it's the time of the turban!' He later complained to me in private how he was unhappy that all the respect he once enjoyed was largely replaced by derision, contempt and sometimes outright hatred. 'People don't see that I'm just an ordinary man like them; I don't ride in a bullet-proof car – in fact I don't even have a car,' he said. Notwithstanding the fact that Iran is under clerical rule, such ordinary men still make up the majority of clergymen.

Before the 1970s, villages produced the bulk of students for seminary schools, partly because education in rural communities was chiefly based on the traditional *maktabs*, or schools, run by clergymen. With the accelerating developments of the ensuing years, the number of applicants from urban households rose, and after the 1979 Revolution, gained the upper hand.

There is no accurate information on the number of clergymen in Iran. Some sources put the number between forty and fifty thousand, the majority of whom still preach in mosques, conduct weddings, and practice other traditional functions. According to journalist and former cleric Mehdi Khalaji, the early post-Revolution years saw an influx of volunteers, about five thousand people a year, into seminary schools, a trend that began to reverse towards the end of the war with Iraq. A significant fact is that for two decades after the Revolution, it was highly unlikely for someone to leave seminary school and doff his clerical garb, whereas in recent years many clerics have done so in frustration. Khalaji himself is one such dropout.

For more than 1,500 years before the introduction of Islam in the seventh century, several indigenous religions flourished in Iran. The most important of these were Zoroastrianism, Mithraism, Manichaeism, and Mazdakism. Only Zoroastrianism has persisted to the modern era, but all made an impact on Judaism, Christianity, and Islam that can still be seen. These religions developed out of ancient folk beliefs and practices that were polytheistic and consisted mainly of the worship of deified natural forces and elements, such as fire, water, earth, and air. Worship centred mainly on sacrificial rites conducted by magi (priests) but rituals were formed. Apparently, there was already present in these early religions a concept of good and evil, which later came to play a central part in the more highly developed Iranian religions.

Zoroaster (also known as Zarathustra) taught that a totally good universe, including man, was created by Ahura Mazda, the supreme god of pure goodness and wisdom, but countering his influence was that of Ahriman, the archdemon, who served to corrupt the universe by creating all things that are evil, such as death, disease, natural calamities, destructive creatures and forces, and moral vices. In the eternal mortal conflict between good and evil, man is an ally of Ahura Mazda but is free to yield to, or resist the temptations of, Ahriman, and can thus, through his moral choices, speed or retard the ultimate victory of good. This intimation of free will and good works was joined by a postulation of a Day of Judgment, a life after death, and heaven and hell. Despite the struggle of dual and opposing forces, the religion was basically monotheistic. From early times archangels named for the virtues of righteousness, good mind, dominion, integrity, immortality, and devotion were ranked on the side of Ahura Mazda, whereas falsehood, wrath, greed, and impurity were on the side of Ahriman. Gradually, these and other forces began to be worshipped as gods. Fire was considered holy, as an attribute of Ahura Mazda, and the maintenance of the fire temples became a primary function of the magi.

Zoroastrianism was established as the state religion of the Sassanid Empire. The organised priesthood had considerable influence in both spiritual and temporal matters between the third and seventh centuries AD, when the Sassanids were overthrown by the Islamic invaders. Persecuted by the Muslims, most Zoroastrians fled to India, where over 100,000 followers, known as Parsees, or Persians, still adhere to the ancient religion.[1]

The Islamic conquest was aided by the material and social bankruptcy of the Sassanids; the native populations had little to lose by cooperating with the conquering power. Moreover, the Muslims offered relative religious tolerance and fair treatment to populations that accepted Islamic rule without resistance. It was not until around 650, however, that resistance in Iran was quelled. Conversion to Islam, which offered certain advantages, was fairly rapid among the urban population but slower among the peasantry and the dihqans. The majority of Iranians did not become Muslim until the ninth century.

Although the conquerors, especially the Umayyads (the Muslim rulers who succeeded Muhammad from 661–750), tended to stress the primacy of Arabs among Muslims, the Iranians were gradually integrated into the new community. The Muslim conquerors adopted the Sassanid coinage system and many Sassanid administrative practices, including the office of vizier, or minister, and the divan, a bureau or register for controlling state revenue and expenditure that became a characteristic of administration throughout Muslim lands. Later caliphs adopted Iranian court ceremonial practices and the trappings of Sassanid monarchy. Men of Iranian origin served as administrators after the conquest, and Iranians contributed significantly to all branches of Islamic learning, including philology, literature, history, geography, jurisprudence, philosophy, medicine, and the sciences.

The Shi'i faith originated from the great schism of Islam after Muhammad's death. One group among the community of believers maintained that leadership of the community following the death of Muhammad rightfully belonged to Muhammad's cousin and son-in-law, Ali, and to his descendants. This group came to be known as the Shi'at-i Ali, the partisans of Ali, or the Shi'ites. Another group, supporters of Mu'awiyah (a rival contender for the caliphate following the murder of Uthman), challenged Ali's election to the caliphate in 656. After Ali was assassinated while praying in a mosque in Kufa in 661, Mu'awiyah was declared caliph by the majority of the Islamic community. He became the first caliph of the Umayyad dynasty, which had its capital at Damascus.

The Abbasids, who overthrew the Umayyads in 750, while sympathetic to the Iranian Shi'ites, were clearly an Arab dynasty. They revolted in the name of descendants of Muhammad's uncle, Abbas, and the House of Hashem. Hashem was an ancestor of both the Shi'ites and the Abbas, or Sunni, line, and the Abbasid movement enjoyed the support of both Sunni and Shi'i Muslims. The Abbasid army consisted primarily of Khorasanians and was led by an Iranian general, Abu Muslim. It contained both Iranian and Arab elements, and the Abbasids enjoyed both Iranian and Arab support.

Nevertheless, the Abbasids, although sympathetic to the Shi'ites, whose support they wished to retain, did not encourage the more extremist Shi'i aspirations. The Abbasids established their capital at Baghdad. Al-Ma'mun, who seized power from his brother, Amin, and proclaimed himself caliph in 811, had an Iranian mother and thus had a base of support in Khorasan. The Abbasids continued the centralising policies of their predecessors. Under their rule, the Islamic world experienced a cultural efflorescence and the expansion of trade and economic prosperity. These were developments in which Iran shared.

Iran's next ruling dynasties descended from nomadic, Turkic-speaking warriors who had been moving out of Central Asia into Transoxiana for more than a millennium. The Abbasid caliphs began enlisting these people as slave warriors as early as the ninth century. Shortly thereafter, the real power of the Abbasid caliphs began to wane; eventually they became religious figureheads while the warrior slaves ruled. As the power of the Abbasid caliphs diminished, a series of independent and indigenous dynasties rose in various parts of Iran, some with considerable influence and power.

Between the seventh and fifteenth centuries Iran was dominated first by the Arabs and then by the Islamised Seljuk Turks and the Islamised Mongols. Most of these foreign rulers were adherents of the Sunni branch of Islam. When a native Iranian dynasty, the Safavid, was able at last to assert its control over all Iran at the beginning of the sixteenth century, it declared the Shi'i form of Islam to be the official religion of the country, and it has since remained the official religion. The move was largely dictated by intense rivalry between Iran and the neighbouring Ottoman Empire, which, spanning across the largest part of the Muslim world, represented the Islamic State. The Safavid kings, it was claimed, were the rightful successors of the Shi'i imams, safeguarding the faith against the onslaught of the Sunni usurpers. With the advent of the Safavid era, Shi'i clergy came to prominence as the people's spiritual guide as well as the supporter of the ruling Shi'i king of the time. The tie between the royal court and the clergy was now a strategic alliance.

Thus, the rift over political heredity in early Islam resulted in a theological split, and the formation of Shi'ism as predominantly an ideology of the Iranian elite in opposition to the caliphate. According to Henry Corbin, the theoretical tenets of Shi'ism are largely derived from concepts of ancient Iran combined with a special interpretation of Islam. Among the Shi'ites, popular belief includes a doctrine of predestination that does not exclude the possibility of merciful intercession by the Prophet and the imams at the Last Judgement. They believe that the Messiah will be the last imam, who will return to re-establish a world of truth, peace, and justice. This notion bears a close resemblance to that of Soshians, the saviour Messiah of Mithraism and Zoroastrianism.

As Shi'i legends have it, a wife of the third imam Hossein was one Shahrbanu, the captured daughter of the last Sassanid king Yazdgerd

III. And since she gave birth to the fourth Shiʻi imam, it follows that there was some Iranian blood in the veins of the following imams. Also, according to Imami Shiʻites, after the passing down of the imamate from Ali to ten other infallible imams, and upon the murder of the eleventh imam, Hassan Askari in the ninth century, the imamate passed to Muhammad al-Muntazar, more widely known as Mahdi or Mehdi, his five-year-old son, who occupies an extraordinary position in Shiʻi doctrine. According to traditional accounts, the twelfth imam, who has several titles but is best known by the title Imam-e Zaman (the Imam of All Time), learned of plans of the caliph on his life. He went into hiding in the late ninth century and is expected to return to abolish all religions, slay the infidels, take revenge on the wicked, and fill the world with equity and justice. The twelfth or hidden imam, who is believed to be spiritually alive but invisible, continues to be the imam until the day of his return. The constitution takes cognisance of this doctrine and, accordingly, rulers rule in his name.[2]

Under the rule of the Baghdad caliphs and up to the Safavid era, when Shiʻism became the official religion, Shiʻi scholars were chiefly custodians of the Iranian minority. Before the Safavid era, therefore, the clergy did not represent a social class; clerics were religious teachers who studied and interpreted the holy texts and passed them on.

With Shiʻism proclaimed as the official religion, however, the clergy became a major lever of controlling political power; the shah exercised absolute rule, but only apparently – in reality his powers were limited by those of the clergy. Because of their financial independence of the court and at the same time its influence on it, the clergy gradually evolved as a kind of aristocratic class.

The notion of *marjaʻiyyat* (emulation) in its modern form was formed during the reign of Fathali Shah Qajar, who obtained the blessings of Mullah Ahmad Naraqi, the highest-ranking Marja, or source of emulation of the time, who was based in Najaf. Reza Shah's reign witnessed the creation of a parallel clerical core in Qom, where the activities of the clerics could be directly monitored and controlled by the political power more than in Najaf. The relationship between the monarchy and the clergy during the Pahlavi era was one of love and hate: the clerics could never have dreamed of toppling the regime and establishing a theocracy; their major concern was that the trend for modernisation would sever the ties between the two institutions. The death of Grand Ayatollah Boroujerdi, however, resulted in the fragmentation of *marja'iyyat*, and the creation of different camps within the clerical establishment. Ayatollah Khomeini eventually emerged as the leader of the most radical anti-regime faction.

As mentioned in chapter six, in the 1970s, Muslim intellectuals and most notably Shariati, embarked on turning Shi'ism into a revolutionary ideology against all forms of oppression, including monarchy. In *Tashayyo-e Safavi*, *Tashayyo-e Alavi* (Safavid Shi'ism, Alavid Shi'ism), Shariati claimed that the version of Shi'ism adopted as the official religion since the Safavid time had been but a distortion of the faith to serve the purposes of tyrant rulers, and that the mission of all true Shi'ites was to fight that false version and replace it with the true variant that supported the oppressed classes. This coincided with Ayatollah Khomeini's denouncement of monarchy and the advent of the theory of *Velayat-e Faqih*. An amalgam of these two unorthodox interpretations of Shi'ism ultimately served as the ideological background for the 1979 Revolution, and was presented by the revolutionaries as the solution to Iran's, if not humanity's, problems.

The dream of all revolutionaries, and the objective of the new rulers, was to create an Islamic, Shi'i utopia. But there had never been a theocratic rule in Iran before, and the conflicting interpretations of revolutionary Shi'ism, particularly when it came to govern the country in modern times, proved to be a major challenge to the new rulers.

Many analysts believe that to say that the clergy inspired the Islamic Revolution would be putting the cart before the horse. The Revolution brought the clergy within the framework of a modern social movement; this was an age-old tradition in which revolution took the form of a new ideology. As a matter of fact, the Revolution did not have a religious nature; rather, it had a religious façade. Although Ali Shariati called Shi'ism a 'complete party', the lack of structural integrity soon led to splits within the clerical institution once it came to power. It still does.

In late 1979, while the hostage crisis was in full force, the domestic political arena was undergoing fundamental changes. The Revolutionary Council took over the prime minister's functions, pending presidential and Majles elections. The elections for the new president were held in January 1980; Bazargan, fearing further personal attacks, did not run.

The three leading candidates were Jalaleddin Farsi, representing the IRP, the dominant clerical party; Abolhassan Banisadr, an independent associated with Ayatollah Khomeini who had written widely on the relationship of Islam to politics and economics; and Admiral Ahmad Madani, a naval officer who had served as governor of Khuzestan Province and commander of the navy after the Revolution. Farsi, however, was disqualified because of his Afghan origin, leaving Banisadr and Madani as the primary challengers. Banisadr was elected by 75 percent of the vote.

Banisadr's agenda as president was to re-establish central authority, gradually to phase out the Revolutionary Guards and the revolutionary courts and committees and to absorb them into other government organisations, to reduce the influence of the clerical hierarchy, and to launch a programme for economic reform and development. Against the wishes of the Islamic Republic party (IRP), Ayatollah Khomeini allowed Banisadr to be sworn in as president in January 1980, before the convening of the Majles. Ayatollah Khomeini further bolstered Banisadr's position by appointing him chairman of the Revolutionary Council and delegating to the president his own powers as commander-in-chief of the armed forces. On the eve of the Iranian New Year, on 20 March, Ayatollah Khomeini issued a message to the nation designating the coming year as 'the year of order and security' and outlining a programme reflecting Banisadr's own priorities.

Nevertheless, the problem of multiple centres of power, and of revolutionary organisations not subject to central control, persisted to plague Banisadr. Like Bazargan, Banisadr found he was competing for primacy with the clerics and activists of the IRP. The struggle between the president and the IRP dominated the political life of the country during Banisadr's presidency. Banisadr failed to secure the dissolution of the Revolutionary Guards and the revolutionary courts and committees. He also failed to establish control over the judiciary or the radio and television networks. Ayatollah Khomeini himself appointed IRP members Ayatollah Muhammad Beheshti as chief justice and Ayatollah Abdolkarim Mousavi Ardabili as prosecutor general (also seen as attorney general). Banisadr's appointees to head the state broadcasting services and the Revolutionary Guards were forced to resign within weeks of their appointments.

Amid growing tensions between Banisadr and the IRP, the hardline clerics and their supporters, in consolidating their position and infiltrating all institutions of the country, had not forgotten a potential danger that loomed on the horizon: the universities were already becoming boiling pots of dissent, with the Mojahedin and Marxist groups gaining ever-increasing popularity among the students, who, in turn, spread their message to families, friends and the public.[3]

In the early morning of 20 April 1979, as I got off the bus and started walking down the street towards Tehran's University of Science and Technology, I noticed a remarkable change. The metal fences that encompassed the large campus were fitted with numerous sheets of 100 x 70 cm cardboard. On each sheet there were a few pictures and captions. Some of the pictures had been taken from a book on the history of the university. One showed the dean of the university in the 1960s, bowing before Empress Farah Pahlavi and kissing her hand during the inauguration ceremony. The caption ran along the lines, 'Do you expect such a university to train students who would serve Islam?'

Another sheet included a picture of a student taking a nap on a turf in the campus with some books under his head as a pillow. The sarcastic caption read, 'Yes, go ahead and sleep! This university has got nothing to do with the awakening of the Muslim people'. In yet another one of the endless chain of sheets, there were two pictures: one of the students waiting in line to get their lunch at the university's mess hall; the other of an elderly Baluchi peasant in tattered clothes, biting on a loaf of bread. The caption read, 'Go ahead and enjoy your kebabs while your Muslim brothers are starving!' Other banners displayed sayings by Ayatollah Khomeini lambasting higher education: 'The universities should be human-building factories'; 'We do not need universities that produce the likes of Sharif-Emami'.

Going past the gates and into the campus, I instantly realised that the situation was far from ordinary. 'All the classes are closed,' said Shervin, a friend of mine who was a supporter of the Mojahedin. 'They are going to attack the university today. Yesterday they invaded the Tabriz University. There was a big fight. Several people have been killed or injured. Today they're going to do the same in Tehran. We shouldn't let them.' By 'they', Shervin meant the Hezbollahi gangs, aided and abetted by Komiteh forces, and supported by students of the Islamic Association.

Hundreds of Mojahedin and leftist students had made a human chain around the 15 Khordad building – a building that housed the headquarters of all the opposition groups. Loudspeakers were playing those groups' revolutionary hymns, with the students stamping on the ground to the beat. They chanted slogans such as 'Revolution will triumph/ reactionaries will be defeated' and 'Students will conquer/ Club-wielders will be destroyed'.

But it took less than two days for the revolutionary forces to conquer all the universities. Several hundred students were injured and dozens arrested during the raid.

The official version of the events of April 1979 as published by the Islamic Republic is that:

> The pre-Revolution academic structure of the universities, the educational system, and also the contents of the textbooks, particularly in human sciences, were not in compliance with the Islamic culture. Many of our universities were managed by foreigners; their form and content followed the will of foreigners; and their policies aimed to preserve and reinforce the politico-economic hegemony of America and other imperialist states.
>
> Therefore, after the Islamic Revolution triumphed, the committed students and professors of universities decided to create a Cultural Revolution so as to guarantee the survival and continuity of the Revolution, as well as providing a powerful vehicle for the export and expansion of the revolutionary culture.
>
> This required purifying universities of the elements affiliated with colonialists, superpowers, and in general anti-revolutionary elements; Revising the structure and the educational system so as to adapt them to the requirements of the Islamic Republic and rescue the country out of cultural and other dependencies; and introducing certain lessons into the syllabuses in order to familiarise students with the goals of the revolution and the viewpoints of Islam.

There are other versions of that story, though. In 2004, in a letter to Ayatollah Ali Khamenei, Muhammad Maleki, the head of Tehran

University at the time of the 'cultural revolution', accused Iran's top leadership of planning the attacks on universities in 1979, pointing his finger at Akbar Hashemi Rafsanjani:

'You must not have forgotten that the political secretary to the party of which you were a founder and leader [IRP],' he wrote, 'plotted the political invasion of universities in the name of "cultural revolution" and "Islamicising universities", whereas it was clear to everybody, including you, what were the [real] objectives in closing down universities.

'The [Islamic] Republic Party and their friends and fellow-thinkers in the Organisation of the Mojahedin of the Islamic Revolution ... did it only with the aim of unifying power, destroying critics, dissidents, and a generation that had fought the shah's regime with knowledge and awareness ... a generation that could not tolerate oppression and injustice by any dictator in any appearance. The price paid for the invasion that took place under the beautiful name of "cultural revolution" and taking pens and books and classes away from students was that thousands of students and professors were stood before firing squads, tens of thousands of them could never return to universities, and thousands of learned, renowned lecturers emigrated ... and the country's culture suffered such a loss the effects can still be seen after twenty-four years.'[4]

In praise of storming the universities and closing them down, Ayatollah Khomeini said, 'It is necessary to create a fundamental revolution in all Iran's universities so that lecturers who have ties with the East and the West would be put aside, the universities becoming a healthy environment for teaching the sublime Islamic sciences. It is imperative to seriously prevent the former regime's evil teachings ...'

Twenty-four years on, in his letter to the supreme leader, Maleki assessed the outcome of the 'cultural revolution' thus:

'Remember whom you and your fellow-thinkers trusted with the refining and selecting of students and lecturers ... What was the result of that invasion, the setting up of the Supreme Council of Cultural Revolution, and sending representatives of the Vali-e Faqih to all universities under the pretext of Islamicising them?

'Why have you failed to create Islamic universities after twenty-four years? Why is it that despite suppressing dissident students and professors and giving predominance to your protégés in higher education institutes, today hopelessness and frustration has dragged students to indifference and even addiction and corruption?'[5]

Two decades later many of the founders of the 'cultural revolution' came to admit that they had made a mistake. It had soon turned out that it was impossible to Islamicise natural and exact sciences, and even in the case of humanities, efforts proved ill-fated. After the universities were reopened in 1984, they were ruled by something approaching a police state. There were representatives of the supreme leader who kept a close eye on everything. There was Qur'an reciting at the beginning of every lesson. There were Hezbollahi students who reported any un-Islamic move to the authorities. And to the swallowed fury of the students, there were new entrants: bearded shabby men from the fronts (or so they were said to be) who had entered universities without taking any exams. They came and left whenever they willed, talked back to the lecturers, fought with them and spied on them, as well as on other students.

In March and May 1980, parliamentary elections were held in two stages, amid charges of fraud. The official results gave the IRP and its supporters 130 of 241 seats decided (elections were not completed in all 270 constituencies). Candidates associated with Banisadr and with Bazargan's IFM each won a handful of seats; other left-of-centre secular parties fared no better. Candidates of the radical left-wing parties, including the Mojahedin, the Fada'eeyan, and the Tudeh, won no seats at all. IRP dominance of the Majles was reinforced when the credentials of a number of deputies representing the National Front and the Kurdish-speaking areas, or standing as independents, were rejected. The consequences of this distribution of voting power soon became evident. The Majles began its deliberations in June 1980. Akbar Hashemi Rafsanjani, a cleric and founding member of the IRP, was elected Majles speaker. After a two-month deadlock between the president and the Majles over the selection of the prime minister, Banisadr was forced to accept the IRP candidate, Muhammad Ali Rajaei. Rajaei, a former street peddler and schoolteacher, was a Beheshti protégé. The designation of cabinet ministers was delayed because Banisadr refused to confirm cabinet lists submitted by Rajaei. In September 1980, Banisadr finally confirmed fourteen of a list of twenty-one ministers proposed by the prime minister. Some key cabinet posts, including the ministries of foreign affairs, labour, commerce, and finance, were filled only gradually over the next six months. The differences between president and prime minister over cabinet appointments remained unresolved until May 1981, when the Majles passed a law allowing the prime minister to appoint caretakers to ministries still lacking a minister.

Banisadr's inability to control the revolutionary courts and the persistence of revolutionary temper were demonstrated in May 1980, when executions, which had become rare in the previous few months, began again on a large scale. Some 900 executions were carried out, most of them between May and September 1980, before Banisadr left office in June 1981. In September the chief justice finally restricted the authority of the courts to impose death sentences. Meanwhile, a remark by Ayatollah Khomeini in June 1980 that 'royalists' were still to be found in government offices led to a resumption of widespread purges. Within days of Ayatollah Khomeini's remarks some 130 unofficial purge committees were operating in government offices. Before the wave of purges could be stopped, some four thousand civil servants and between two and four thousand military officers lost their jobs. Around eight thousand military officers had been dismissed or retired in previous purges.

The shah had meantime made his home in Panama. Banisadr and Foreign Minister Qotbzadeh attempted to arrange for the shah to be arrested by the Panamanian authorities and extradited to Iran. But the shah abruptly left Panama for Egypt on 23 March 1980, before any summons could be served.

In April the Carter administration attempted to rescue the hostages by secretly landing aircraft and troops near Tabas, along the Dasht-e Kavir desert in eastern Iran. Two helicopters on the mission failed, however, and when the mission commander decided to abort the mission, a helicopter and a C-130 transport aircraft collided, killing eight United States servicemen. The clerical establishment announced that the sandstorm that led to the failure of the operation was 'divine intervention'.

The failed rescue attempt had negative consequences for the Iranian military. Radical factions in the IRP and left-wing groups charged that Iranian officers opposed to the Revolution had secretly assisted the United States aircraft to escape radar detection. They renewed their demand for a purge of the military command. Banisadr was able to prevent such a purge, but he was forced to reshuffle the top military command. In June 1980, the chief judge of the Army Military Revolutionary Tribunal announced the discovery of an antigovernment plot centered on the military base in Piranshahr in Kordestan. Twenty-seven junior and warrant officers were arrested. In July the authorities announced they had uncovered a plot centered on the Shahrokhi Air Base in Hamadan. Six hundred officers and men were implicated. Ten of the alleged plotters were killed when members of the Revolutionary Guards broke into their headquarters. Approximately 300 officers, including two generals, were arrested, and warrants were issued for three hundred others. The government charged the accused with plotting to overthrow the state and seize power in the name of exiled leader Bakhtiar. Ayatollah Khomeini ignored Banisadr's plea for clemency and said those involved must be executed. As many as 140 officers were shot on the orders of the military tribunal; wider purges of the armed forces followed.

Some ten months after the hostage taking, perhaps believing the hostage crisis could serve no further diplomatic or political end, the Rajaei government indicated to Washington through a diplomat of the Federal Republic of Germany (West Germany) that it was ready to negotiate in earnest for the release of the hostages. Talks opened on 14 September in West Germany and continued for the next four months, with the Algerians acting as intermediaries. The hostages were released on 20 January 1981, concurrently with President Ronald Reagan's taking the oath of office. The United States in return released eleven-to-twelve billion dollars in Iranian funds that had been frozen by presidential order. Iran, however, agreed to repay one billion dollars in syndicated and nonsyndicated loans owed to United States and foreign banks and to place another one billion in an escrow account, pending the settlement of claims filed against Iran by United States firms and citizens. These claims, and Iranian claims against United States firms, were adjudicated by a special tribunal of the International Court of Justice at The Hague, established under the terms of the Algiers Agreement. As of 1987, the court was still reviewing outstanding cases, of which there were several thousand.

The hostage settlement served as a further cause of friction between the Rajaei government, which negotiated the terms, and Banisadr.

The president and the governor of the Central Bank, a presidential appointee, charged the Iranian negotiators with accepting terms highly disadvantageous to Iran. One major incentive that precipitated the settling of the hostage crisis was that in September 1980 Iran became engaged in full-scale hostilities with Iraq. The conflict stemmed from Iraqi anxieties over possible spillover effects of the Iranian Revolution. Iranian propagandists were spreading the message of the Islamic Revolution throughout the Persian Gulf, and the Iraqis feared this propaganda would infect the Shi'i Muslims who constituted a majority of Iraq's population.[6]

The confrontation between Iran and Iraq led to border incidents, beginning in April 1980. The Iraqi government feared the disruption in Iran would undo the 1975 Algiers Agreement concluded with the shah (not to be confused with the 1980 United States-Iran negotiations). There is also evidence the Iraqis hoped to bring about the overthrow of the Ayatollah Khomeini regime and to establish a more moderate government in Iran. On 17 September President Saddam Hussein of Iraq abrogated the Algiers Agreement. Five days later Iraqi troops and aircraft began a massive invasion of Iran.

The war did nothing to moderate the rift between Banisadr and the Rajaei government with its clerical and IRP backers. Banisadr championed the cause of the army; his IRP rivals championed the cause of the Revolutionary Guards, for which they demanded heavy equipment and favourable treatment. Banisadr accused the Rajaei government of hampering the war effort; the prime minister and his backers accused the president of planning to use the army to seize power. The prime minister also fought the president over the control of foreign and domestic economic policy. In late October 1980, in a private letter to Ayatollah Khomeini, Banisadr asked Ayatollah Khomeini to dismiss the Rajaei government and to give him, as president, wide powers to run the country during the war emergency. He subsequently also urged Ayatollah Khomeini to dissolve the Majles, the Supreme Judicial Council, and the Guardian Council so that a new beginning could be made in structuring the government. In November Banisadr charged that torture was taking place in Iranian prisons and that individuals were executed 'as easily as one takes a drink of water'. A commission appointed by Ayatollah Khomeini to investigate the torture charges, however, claimed it found no evidence of mistreatment of prisoners.

There were others critical of the activities of the IRP, the revolutionary courts and committees, and the Hezbollahis who broke up meetings of opposition groups. In November and December, a series of rallies critical of the government was organised by Banisadr supporters in Mashhad, Isfahan, Tehran, and Guilan. In December, merchants of the Tehran bazaar who were associated with the National Front called for the resignation of the Rajaei government. In February 1981, Bazargan denounced the government at a mass rally. A group of 133 writers, journalists, and academics issued a letter protesting the suppression of basic freedoms. Senior clerics questioned the legitimacy of the revolutionary courts, widespread property confiscations, and the power exercised by Ayatollah Khomeini as faqih. Even Ayatollah Khomeini's son, Ahmad Ayatollah Khomeini, initially spoke on the president's behalf. The IRP retaliated by using Hezbollah gangs to break up Banisadr rallies in various cities and to harass opposition organisations. In November it arrested Qotbzadeh, the former foreign minister, for an attack on the IRP. Two weeks later, the offices of Bazargan's paper, *Mizan*, were smashed.

Ayatollah Khomeini initially sought to mediate the differences between Banisadr and the IRP to prevent action that would irreparably weaken the president, the army, or the other institutions of the state. He ordered the cancellation of a demonstration called for 19 December 1980, to demand the dismissal of Banisadr as commander in chief. In January 1981, he urged non-experts to leave the conduct of the war to the military. The next month he warned clerics in the revolutionary organisations not to interfere in areas outside their competence. On 16 March, after meeting with and failing to persuade Banisadr, Rajaei, and clerical leaders to resolve their differences, he issued a ten-point declaration confirming the president in his post as commander in chief and banning further speeches, newspaper articles, and remarks contributing to factionalism. He established a three-man committee to resolve differences between Banisadr and his critics and to ensure that both parties adhered to Ayatollah Khomeini's guidelines. This arrangement soon broke down. Banisadr, lacking other means, once again took his case to the public in speeches and newspaper articles. The adherents of the IRP used the revolutionary organisations, the courts, and the Hezbollahi gangs to undermine the president.

The three-man committee appointed by Ayatollah Khomeini returned a finding against the president. In May, the Majles passed measures to permit the prime minister to appoint caretakers to ministries still lacking a minister, to deprive the president of his veto power, and to allow the prime minister rather than the president to appoint the governor of the Central Bank. Within days the Central Bank governor was replaced by a Rajaei appointee.

By the end of May, Banisadr appeared also to be losing Ayatollah Khomeini's support. On 27 May Ayatollah Khomeini denounced Banisadr, without mentioning him by name, for placing himself above the law and ignoring the dictates of the Majles. On 7 June *Mizan* and Banisadr's newspaper, *Enqelab-e Eslami*, were banned. Three days later, Ayatollah Khomeini removed Banisadr from his post as the acting commander-in-chief of the military. Meanwhile, gangs roamed the streets calling for Banisadr's ouster and death, and they clashed with Banisadr supporters. On 10 June participants in a Mojahedin rally at Revolution Square in Tehran clashed with Hezbollahis. On 12 June a motion for the impeachment of the president was presented by 120 deputies. On 13 or 14 June Banisadr, fearing for his life, went into hiding. On 15 June the Freedom Movement called on its supporters to gather in Tehran's Ferdowsi Square to protest against a bill by the government to enact Qisas, a type of reprisal punishment advocated by the Sharia. From early morning, the state media started attacking the Freedom Movement leaders, while Hezbollahis mobilised in different parts of the city. Following attacks on the Movement's supporters and the disruption of the meeting by the vigilantes, Ayatollah Khomeini announced in a radio message that the Movement was 'apostate'. Several clashes occurred in Tehran, with tens of individuals wounded by the Hezbollahis.

Majles speaker Rafsanjani, after initially blocking the motion to impeach Banisadr, allowed it to go forward on 17 June. The next day, the Mojahedin issued a call for 'revolutionary resistance in all its forms'. The government treated this as a call for rebellion and moved to confront the opposition on the streets. On 19 June, on the fourth anniversary of the death of Ali Shariati, the Hezbollahis attacked a memorial service held at his house, destroying property and injuring several participants.

On the same day, the Mojahedin and Banisadr called upon the whole nation to take over the streets the next day to express their opposition to the IRP 'monopolists' who they claimed had carried out a secret coup d'état. According to Abrahamian, their real intention – never made explicit – was to duplicate the Islamic Revolution.[7]

On 20 June vast crowds appeared in many cities. In Tehran the demonstration drew as many as 500,000 determined participants. Meanwhile, warnings against demonstrations were broadcast over the radio-television network. Prominent clerics declared that demonstrators, irrespective of their age, would be treated as 'enemies of God' and as such would be executed on the spot. Hezbollahis were armed and trucked in to block off the major streets. Revolutionary guards were ordered to shoot. 50 were killed, 200 injured and 1,000 arrested in the vicinity of Tehran University alone. The march was resolutely crushed.[8] On the late afternoon of that day, in Tehran's Firouzgar hospital, I saw dozens of young men and women shot by bullets or wounded by knives and other weapons. Being moved on a stretcher from an ambulance, a teenage girl with a bullet in her back was showing the victory sign with her hands and chanting, 'long live the Mojahedin'.

Twenty-three protesters were executed on 20 and 21 June, as the Majles debated the motion for impeachment. In the debate, several speakers denounced Banisadr; only five spoke in his favour. On 21 June, with thirty deputies absenting themselves from the House or abstaining, the Majles decided for impeachment on a vote of 177 to 1.

Rafsanjani, Majles speaker at the time, recalled the events of 21 June in his memoirs:

> I went to the Majles. The bill of 'political incompetence' of Banisadr was on the agenda ... The pros and cons spoke. The cons did not have anything to say. They pretended to be both against Banisadr and against his dismissal. The pros did not speak well although they had a lot to say. A huge crowd of the Hezbollahis had gathered outside the Majles and urged the speedy passing of the bill. During the break and in the afternoon I talked with them.
>
> Mojahedin Khalq, Paykar, Ranjbaran [a Maoist group], Fada'eeyan and other small groups had made extensive preparations to cause turmoil and sabotage the work of the Majles;

they had, in a way, declared armed struggle. At 4pm they poured into the streets, thus began the destruction, murdering, looting and disruption of Tehran and many other cities ... Gradually the forces of the Revolutionary Guards and the Komitehs and the Hezbollahis rose to counter them. I was in the Majles. Gunshots could be heard from several parts of the city. In the early evening the insurgents were defeated and dispersed, without having accomplished much more than the destruction of a few cars and the death and injury of a few people on both sides ...

The minor disturbances created by these small groups in several cities was suppressed by the people's intervention. Reports say that in yesterday's incidents in Tehran sixteen people were killed and 156 others injured. Despite threats made by the groups that they would set the city on fire if Banisadr was dismissed, there was not the slightest sign of this; perhaps owing to the Revolutionary Court's resolve that morning which resulted in the prompt trying and execution of fifteen of the instigators, as well as to the presence of Hezbollah.[9]

Following the fall of Banisadr, opposition elements attempted to reorganise and to overthrow the government by force. The government responded with a policy of repression and terror. The government also took steps to impose its version of an Islamic legal system and an Islamic code of social and moral behaviour. This marked the beginning of a reign of terror. Scores of young boys and girls who had supported opposition groups – and chiefly the Mojahedin – were arrested, tortured and summarily executed on a daily basis. Many of them were underage boys and girls who had been spotted and given away by the Hezbollahis while distributing opposition newspapers and pamphlets on the streets. To intimidate the opposition and discourage any further disturbance, the state radio and television regularly broadcast the names of the executed. Meanwhile, Hezbollahis armed with guns, machetes, clubs, chains and brass knuckles patrolled the streets and beat up passers-by at will.

Banisadr remained in hiding for several weeks. Believing he was illegally ousted, he maintained his claim to the presidency, formed an alliance with Mojahedin leader Massoud Rajavi, and in July 1981 escaped with Rajavi from Iran to France. In Paris, Banisadr and Rajavi announced the establishment of the National Council of Resistance (NCR) and committed themselves to work for the overthrow of Ayatollah Khomeini's regime. They announced a programme that emphasised a form of democracy based on elected popular councils; protection for the rights of the ethnic minorities; special attention to the interests of shopkeepers, small landowners, and civil servants; limited land reform; and protection for private property in keeping with the national interest. The Kurdish Democratic Party, the National Democratic Front, and a number of other small groups and individuals subsequently announced their adherence to the NCR.

Meanwhile, violent opposition to the regime in Iran continued. On 28 June 1981 a powerful bomb exploded at the headquarters of the IRP while a meeting of party leaders was in progress. Seventy-three persons were killed, including the chief justice and party secretary general Muhammad Beheshti, four cabinet ministers, twenty-seven Majles deputies, and several other government officials. Elections for a new president were held on 24 July and Rajaei, the prime minister, was elected to the post. On 5 August 1981 the Majles approved Rajaei's choice of Muhammad Javad Bahonar as prime minister.

Less than a month later, however, Rajaei and Bahonar, along with the chief of the Tehran police, lost their lives when a bomb went off during a meeting at the office of the prime minister. The Majles named another cleric, Mahdavi-Kani, as interim prime minister. In a new round of elections on 2 October Ali Khamenei was elected president. Division within the leadership became apparent, however, when the Majles rejected Khamenei's nominee, Ali Akbar Velayati, as prime minister. On 28 October the Majles elected Mir-Hossein Mousavi, a protégé of the late Muhammad Beheshti, as prime minister. Although no group claimed responsibility for the bombings that had killed Iran's political leadership, the government blamed the Mojahedin for both. The Mojahedin did, however, claim responsibility for a spate of other assassinations that followed the overthrow of Banisadr. Among those killed in the space of a few months were the Friday prayer leaders in Tabriz, Kerman, Shiraz, Yazd, and Kerman Shah; a provincial governor; the warden of Evin Prison, the chief ideologue of the IRP; and several revolutionary court judges, Majles deputies, minor government officials, and members of revolutionary organisations.

Street clashes continued. In September 1981, expecting to spark a general uprising, the Mojahedin sent their young followers into the streets to demonstrate against the government and to confront the authorities with their own armed contingents. On 27 September the Mojahedin used machine guns and rocket-propelled grenade launchers against units of the Revolutionary Guards. Smaller left-wing opposition groups, including the Fada'eeyan, attempted similar guerrilla activities. In July 1981, members of the Union of Communists tried to seize control of the Caspian town of Amol. At least seventy guerrillas and Revolutionary Guards members were killed before the uprising was put down. The government responded to the armed challenge of the guerrilla groups by expanded use of the Revolutionary Guards in counterintelligence activities and by widespread arrests, imprisonment, and executions. The executions were facilitated by a September 1981 Supreme Judicial Council circular to the revolutionary courts, permitting death sentences for 'active members' of guerrilla groups. Fifty executions a day became routine; there were days when more than 100 persons were executed. Amnesty International documented 2,946 executions in the twelve months following Banisadr's impeachment, a conservative figure because the authorities did not report all executions. Several youngsters of my neighbourhood were among those who were imprisoned or executed. So were several of my fellow students at the university, including Shervin.

The pace of executions slackened considerably at the end of 1982, partly as a result of a deliberate government decision but primarily because, by then, the back of the armed resistance movement had largely been broken. The radical opposition had, however, eliminated several key clerical leaders, exposed vulnerabilities in the state's security apparatus, and posed the threat, never realised, of sparking a wider opposition movement.[10]

In his letter to Ayatollah Khamenei in 2004, Muhammad Maleki recounted that the Ayatollah, on the eve of the Iranian year beginning on 21 March 1981, had named the coming year 'the year of law', and yet, 'in that unforgettable year, the most unprecedented violations of the law took place everywhere, particularly in prisons. In that year, by stamping on various articles of the constitution ... storming private homes, unlawful arrests, summary trials without any attorney, torture and executions – particularly of women and girls – the violation of people's rights expanded so much that it can be called an unrivalled year with respect to law-breaking ...'[11]

By moving quickly to hold new elections and to fill vacant posts, the government managed to maintain its authority, however, and by repression and terror it was able to crush the guerrilla movements. By the end of 1983, key leaders of the Fada'eeyan, Paykar (a Marxist-oriented splinter group of the Mojahedin), the Union of Communists, and the Mojahedin in Iran had been killed, thousands of the rank and file had been executed or were in prison, and the organisational structure of these movements was gravely weakened. Only the Mojahedin managed to survive, and even it had to transfer its main base of operations to Kordestan, and later to Kurdistan in Iraq, and its headquarters to Paris.

The clerical establishment also moved against other active and potential opponents. In April 1982 the authorities arrested former Ayatollah Khomeini aide and foreign minister Qotbzadeh and charged him with plotting with military officers and clerics to kill Ayatollah Khomeini and to overthrow the state. Approximately 170 others, including seventy military men, were also arrested. The government implicated the respected religious leader Shariatmadari, whose son-in-law had allegedly served as the intermediary between Qotbzadeh and Shariatmadari. At his trial, Qotbzadeh denied any design on Ayatollah Khomeini's life and claimed he had wanted only to change the government, not to overthrow the Islamic Republic. Shariatmadari, in a television interview, said he had been told of the plot but did not actively support it. Qotbzadeh and the military men were executed, and Shariatmadari's son-in-law was jailed. In an unprecedented move, members of the Association of the Seminary Teachers of Qom voted to strip Shariatmadari of his title of *Marja-e Taqlid* (source of emulation). Shariatmadari's Centre for Islamic Study and Publications was closed, and Shariatmadari was placed under virtual house arrest.[12]

All these moves to crush opposition to the Republic gave freer rein to the Revolutionary Guards and revolutionary committees. Members of these organisations entered homes, made arrests, conducted searches, and confiscated goods at will. The government organised *Gasht-e Sarallah* (God's Blood Patrol) to patrol the streets and to impose Islamic dress and Islamic codes of behaviour. Instructions issued by Ayatollah

Khomeini in December 1981 and in August 1982 admonishing the revolutionary organisations to exercise proper care in entering homes and making arrests were ignored. 'Manpower renewal' and 'placement' committees in government ministries and offices resumed wide-scale purges in 1982, examining officeholders and job applicants on their beliefs and political inclinations. Applicants to universities and military academies were subjected to similar examinations. With the priority given to commitment over expertise, job seekers applying to government organisations and ministries had to pass 'ideological tests' which included questions involving the number of pieces a winding sheet was made of, or how to step in and out of the lavatory according to *fiqh*.

Having dealt harshly with the armed opposition, the Islamic Republic turned its attention to political groups that had so far supported it vis-à-vis the opposition as supporting petit-bourgeoisie against liberal bourgeoisie. In February 1983 the government arrested Tudeh leader Noureddin Kianouri, other members of the party Central Committee, and more than 1,000 party members. The party was proscribed, and Kianouri confessed on television to spying for the Soviet Union and to 'espionage, deceit, and treason'. Possibly because of Soviet intervention, none of the leading members of the party was brought to trial or executed, although the leaders remained in prison. Many rank and file members, however, were put to death. By 1983 Bazargan's IFM was the only political group outside the factions of the ruling hierarchy that was permitted any freedom of activity. Even this group was barely tolerated. For example, the party headquarters was attacked in 1983 and two party members were assaulted on the floor of the Majles.

A review of the evolution of the main slogans manufactured by the government's propaganda machine, and chanted at Friday prayer gatherings and other occasions during the first few years following the Revolution, signifies the political trend leading to the consolidation of the theocracy. This evolution had begun even before the fall of the shah and as early as February 1979, when Ayatollah Khomeini delivered his landmark speech at the *Behesht-e Zahra* cemetery. Whenever he paused and the crowd wanted to show its support for him by clapping, those close to the imam started yelling *Allah-o Akbar* (God is great). Thus clapping disappeared as a means of approval, and in later years, together with whistling, it became an evil symbol of the West. In fact, in the late 1990s Khatami was heavily criticised by conservative clerics and hardliners because his supporters committed the un-Islamic acts of clapping and whistling. Next came the addition of *Khomeini Rahbar* (Khomeini is the leader), which neatly dovetailed with *Allah-o Akbar*. The slogan kept growing in length as time passed:

> *Allah-o Akbar* (God is great);
> *Khomeini Rahbar* (Khomeini is the leader);
> *Marg bar Zedd-e Velayat-e Faqih* (Death to the opponents of Velayat-e Faqih);
> *Marg bar Amrica* (Death to America);
> *Marg bar Shuravi* (Death to the Soviet Union);
> *Marg bar Monafeqin-o Saddam* (Death to hypocrites [*Mojahedin Khalq*] and Saddam);
> *Marg bar Esrail* (Death to Israel).

And as certain occasions required, the tail end of the slogan varied from 'death to England' and at times 'death to the liberals'.

Also, at the end of any speech by Ayatollah Khomeini or other officials of the Islamic Republic, a few verses of 'prayers' by the audience would follow. In the final stage of their evolution, these included:

> *Khodaya, Khodaya, ta Enqelab-e Mahdi, Khomeini ra negah dar* (O God, O God, keep Khomeini alive until the revolution of Mahdi [the twelfth Shi'i Imam]);
> *Az omr-e ma bekah-o beh omr-e u biyafza* (Shorten our lives and add to his life);
> *Razmandegan-e Eslam, nosrat ata befarma* (Grant victory to the combatants of Islam);
> *Majroohin-o maloolin, shafa enayat farma* (Grant cure to the wounded and disabled);
> *Qaem maqam-e Rahbar, mohafezat befarma* (Protect the designate successor of the imam [Ayatollah Montazeri]).

By the mid-1980s the personality cult of Ayatollah Khomeini was firmly established. A slogan published in millions of copies in the form of banners and posters said, 'One cannot love Mahdi without loving Khomeini'. Reports said that one of Ayatollah Khomeini's famous disciples had even asked him to drop the cover and publicly announce that he was indeed the imam of all times, another reference to the twelfth Shi'i imam.

Thus, not only was there now one, and only one, government ruling Iran and representing Islam, but also there was only one specific, ideological version of Islam that was considered legitimate; a reading that was supposed eventually to create an Islamic utopia. And the Iran-Iraq war proved to be instrumental to that end.

> Saeed was born in 1968 in Tehran. His father was one of the champions of Varzesh-e Bastani [traditional martial sports], so he followed suit, and by the age of seven, he was already a famous athlete. With the beginning of the war with Iraq, despite his young age, he insisted on going to the front. He could not rest in peace while his older brothers Ali, Muhammad and Hamid were all fighting the enemy.
>
> When Ali was injured and Muhammad went missing in action in 1984, Saeed's determination to fill the empty places of his brothers in the front redoubled. Finally, after much persistence, he managed to go to the front with his father and a group of Varzesh-e Bastani athletes for a sports performance. However, this was only an excuse to join the Combatants of Islam.
>
> When he came back, while his body was apparently in the classroom, his spirit remained on the battlefront. At length, in 1985 he succeeded in getting to the front after he altered the date of his birth on his identification card.
>
> In the winter of that year, taking part in Operation Badr, a heavy machine-gun shell ripped his stomach apart ... Ten years after his martyrdom, his bones were found and brought back home to be buried.

The story of Saeed Towqani is the story of how a war between two Muslim neighbours was presented by the Islamic Republic as a war between Islam and *Kufr* (infidelity); how that war became an end in itself; how 'martyrdom' overshadowed victory; how young men at the prime of life competed in rushing to the minefields; and how Iran's 'human wave' strategy succeeded in repelling Saddam Hussein's modern, highly organised army.

His story, however, is not the story of all Iranian youth. Many of those who fought Iraq were conscripts; many resorted to all kinds of acts – including having a finger cut off or a kidney removed – to be exempted from military service; many deserted the armed forces; many went into hiding and refused to be drafted. Also, many young men fled the country. And many others were in jail.

But the 'Battlefront Culture', or the synonymous 'Basiji Culture', as it came to be known, was the official culture promoted by the state, and the 'Sacred Defence' cast a heavy shadow on all aspects of life in Iran. Martyrdom was promoted as the greatest virtue, and together with it, a belief in the worthlessness of earthly life and its pleasures. It has frequently been said, chiefly by the opposition to the Islamic Republic, that the clerics sent teenagers to the front by giving them 'Hong Kong-made plastic keys to Heaven'. The truth, however, is that the 'Battlefront Culture' had indeed transformed the mentality of many youngsters. One of those honest, devoted combatants was a friend of mine. Whenever he came back from the front, he would read the Qur'an or listen to an Ashura mourning audiotape for hours on end. He would wake up in the dead of night to pray and weep. His aspiration was not to defeat the Iraqis – that was something that would evidently happen – he wanted to join his martyred comrades. Mentalities such as my friend's greatly helped the state to tighten its ideological grip on the country.

When I was undergoing basic military training in the Revolutionary Guards' Corps, my teacher at the explosives' course – a man who had lost three fingers in the war – told a story that was supposed to set an example for us conscripts drafted unwillingly into the armed forces and considered ideologically 'impure'. 'During a lesson with the Basijis once,' he said, 'I dropped in the classroom a mock hand grenade I had painted as a real one, and quickly ran outside. I was waiting for the grenade to be thrown out of the window or kicked out of the door. When nothing happened after a couple of minutes, I went back in and saw that each of the Basijis was trying to grab the grenade out of the others' hands, pressing it to his stomachs and begging of God to grant martyrdom to him.'

Such was the effect of the 'Battlefront Culture' on the zealous, that the war came to represent a kind of ideal world to them. For them, the battlefront stood for devotion, honesty, purity and brotherly love, while the 'normal life' of the cities signified corruption, greed and lies. Mohsen Makhmalbaf, who later became an internationally acclaimed filmmaker, was an ardent advocate of this view. Before he underwent an ideological metamorphosis in the late 1980s, he depicted, in *Marriage of the Blessed,* a confrontation between the utopia of the battlefield with the 'sinful' world of the city.

On the other hand, during the same period, one of the best-selling books in Iran was the Persian translation of Czech writer Jaroslav Hasek's *The Good Soldier Svejk,* a parody of Austro-Hungarian militarism during World War I. The book was avidly read by those who believed that the Islamic Republic should have agreed to end the war after Iraq retreated to international borders in 1982, and that the war no more served any national interest.

Iran and Iraq fought one of the longest wars of the twentieth-century, a war that lasted more than eight years, during which time both countries suffered millions of casualties and billions of dollars in damage. The collateral damage to the economies of other nations was also immense. In geopolitical terms, the war was one of the most strategically important conflicts of modern times because it involved two major oil producers and took place in a region where more than half the world's reserves are located.

After the Islamic Revolution of 1979, the essentially secular Iraqi leadership became more of an issue when Ayatollah Khomeini, who had spent part of his exile in Iraq, began encouraging his former fellow clergymen to overthrow Saddam Hussein in Iraq because of the anti-Islamic nature of his regime. Some considered this as a part of Ayatollah Khomeini's broader strategy of spreading the Islamic Revolution throughout the Middle East. Saddam responded as he did to any challenge with a ruthless crackdown on Shi'i leaders and activists, and by sending aid to Arab separatists in Iran.

On the hot summer afternoon of 22 September 1980, residents in several Iranian cities were startled by the sound of explosions. Formations of Iraqi MiG-23s and MiG-21s attacked Iran's air bases at Mehrabad International Airport and Doshan Tappeh near Tehran, as well as airfields and bases in Tabriz, Bakhtaran, Ahvaz, Dezful, Urmiyeh, Hamadan, Sanandaj, and Abadan. The aim of these pre-emptive strikes was to destroy the Iranian air-force on the ground – a lesson learned from the Arab-Israeli war in June 1967. The Iraqis succeeded in destroying runways and fuel and ammunition depots, but much of Iran's aircraft inventory was left intact. Iranian defences were caught by surprise, but the Iraqi raids failed because Iranian jets were protected in specially strengthened hangars and because bombs designed to destroy runways did not totally incapacitate Iran's very large airfields. Within hours, Iranian F-4 Phantoms took off from these same bases, successfully attacked strategically important targets close to major Iraqi cities, and returned home with very few losses.

Simultaneously, six Iraqi army divisions entered Iran on three fronts in an initially successful surprise attack, where they drove as far as eight kilometres inland and occupied 1,000 square kilometres of Iranian territory.

The blitz-like assaults by Saddam's forces against scattered Iranian troops led many observers to think that Baghdad would win the war within a matter of weeks. Indeed, Iraqi troops did capture the Shatt al Arab and did seize a 48-kilometre-wide strip of Iranian territory. Iraqi troops, however, faced untiring resistance in Khuzestan. Saddam may have thought that the approximately three million Arabs of Khuzestan would join the Iraqis against Tehran. Instead, they joined Iran's regular and irregular armed forces and fought in the battles at Dezful, Khorramshahr, and Abadan. Soon after capturing Khorramshahr, the Iraqi troops lost their initiative and began to dig in along their line of advance.

Iran turned down a settlement offer and held the line against the militarily superior Iraqi force. It refused to accept defeat, and slowly began a series of counteroffensives in January 1981. Despite political confrontations and the crackdown on opposition, nationalist feelings were running high. Both the Basij volunteers and the regular armed forces were eager to fight back. Armed forces were seeing an opportunity to regain prestige lost because of their association with the shah's regime.

Iran's first major counterattack failed, however, for political and military reasons. President Banisadr was engaged in a power struggle with key religious figures. Although many experienced and well-trained officers had been purged, in addition to enlisting the Iranian pilots, the Islamic Republic also recalled veterans of the old imperial army. Furthermore, the Revolutionary Guard and Basij (what Ayatollah Khomeini called the 'Army of Twenty Million') recruited at least 100,000 volunteers. Approximately 200,000 soldiers were sent to the front by the end of November 1980. They were ideologically committed troops (some members even carried their own shrouds to the front in the expectation of martyrdom). Iran stopped Iraqi forces on the Karoon River and, with limited military stocks, unveiled its 'human wave' assaults, which used thousands of Basiji volunteers, a large part of them underage boys. After Banisadr was ousted as president and commander-in-chief, Iran gained its first major victory, when the army and Revolutionary Guard forced Baghdad to lift its long siege of Abadan in September 1981. Iranian forces also defeated Iraq in the Qasr-e Shirin area in December 1981 and January 1982. The Iraqi armed forces were hampered by their unwillingness to sustain a high casualty rate and thus their refusal to initiate a new offensive.

The tide of the war began to turn in mid-1981, when Iran broke the siege of Abadan and later recaptured Khorramshahr. The Iranian high command passed from regular military leaders to clergy in mid-1982. In March of the same year, Tehran launched its Operation Fath-ol-Mobin, which marked a major turning point, as Iran penetrated Iraq's 'impenetrable' lines, split Iraq's forces, and forced the Iraqis to retreat. Operation Beit ul-Moqaddas in May 1982 saw Iranian units finally regain Khorramshahr, albeit with high casualties. After this victory, the Iranians maintained the pressure on the remaining Iraqi forces, and Saddam Hussein announced that the Iraqi units would withdraw from Iranian territory. The conquest of Khorramshahr was marked by mass celebrations across the country. Like the day when the shah left Iran, streets were clogged by cheering, dancing people, and honking cars. There was hope that the war would soon be over, and that there would be a prestigious victory.

Believing Iran would agree to end the war, Saddam ordered a withdrawal to the international borders. Iranian authorities, however, did not accept this withdrawal as the end of the conflict, and continued the war into Iraq.

Years after the end of the war, the issue still remained a controversial one. In an article in *Sobh-e Emrooz*, a daily published in 1998, Akbar Ganji called on Rafsanjani to account for the decision to continue the war after the retaking of Khorramshahr, when Iran was in its strongest position. In his Friday prayers sermon, Rafsanjani slandered Ganji as someone who 'questions the greatest honours of the country'.

But while the Islamic Republic continued the war amid heated anti-American rhetoric, it turned out that the United States changed its position and unexpectedly helped the Iranians. In 1985, to win support for the freeing of American hostages being held by Islamist militant groups in Lebanon, the Reagan Administration secretly agreed to sell weapons to Iran. The principal negotiator for the United States was Lieutenant Colonel Oliver North, a military aide to the National Security Council, who reported his activities to the National Security Adviser Robert McFarlane and then his successor John Poindexter. The broker on the Iranian side was Majles Speaker Rafsanjani. Shortly after the disclosure of the dealings, Mehdi Hashemi, the son-in-law of Ayatollah Montazeri, was arrested. He was tried for the alleged murder of a clergyman in the years preceding the 1979 Revolution, as well as for storing arms. Shortly afterwards Hashemi was executed. It was widely believed, however, that he actually paid the price for letting the Iran-Contra affair leak to the Lebanon-based daily newspaper *al-Shira*.

In 1987 and 1988, Ayatollah Khomeini continued to threaten a 'final' offensive against Iraq, but none of these changed the situation on the battlefield. Then came the 'War of the Cities' which ultimately played a major role in ending the eight-year war. Iraqis had modified their Scud-B missiles, adding more fuel and reducing the payload, so that they could now reach targets in Iran's heartland. They fired some 190 missiles over a six-week period at Iranian cities in 1988. These caused little destruction, but created havoc and panic in cities.

Several times a day, the ordinary broadcasts of state radio and television were interrupted. A sombre, rather harsh, male voice announced: 'What you hear is the announcing of red alert, meaning that the enemy will attack. Leave your work and go to a shelter.' The wailing siren that followed the recorded message caused turmoil. Apart from some high-rise housing complexes, there was literally no public shelter in Iranian cities. Some rushed to cellars; others stayed together and prayed in anguish; while the braver ones went to the rooftops to watch the Scud-Bs striking. Soon residents of large cities were leaving for remote towns and villages by the thousands. Although Rafsanjani played down the missile attacks on cities and ridiculed 'those who get diarrhoea as soon as they hear a loud bang', there were times when almost 30 percent of Tehran's population fled the capital. What intensified the panic was the fear that Iraq might hit Tehran with missiles capable of carrying chemical warheads. The fateful event happened. On 3 July 1988 the USS Vincennes was patrolling the northern portion of the Straits of Hormoz. A group of Iranian gunboats had been threatening a Pakistani merchant vessel and one fired on the Vincennes. During the confrontation with the gunboats, the Vincennes picked up an aircraft on radar moving in its direction. The plane did not respond to the ship's warnings, so the Vincennes fired a missile, bringing the plane down. It turned out to be an Iran Air commercial jet carrying 290 people, who all died in the crash. President Ronald Reagan said it was a terrible accident, apologised and offered to pay compensation to the victims. The Iranian government insisted that it was an intentional act of aggression. The incident was instrumental in Iran's ultimate decision to accept ceasefire.

Finally, in August 1988, a grim statement by Ayatollah Khomeini declared Iran's acceptance of UN Resolution 598 and an end to the war. He likened his decision to 'drinking a goblet of poison' in the interests of Islam and the nation.

> As to the acceptance of the Resolution, which was really a bitter and unwholesome issue for all, especially for me, until a few days ago, I was of the opinion that the same defence method and position that was maintained during the war be held. I regarded its implementation as beneficial and expedient to the System, the country and the Revolution. Because of events that I will not divulge now but which, God willing, will become clear in due time, and considering the views of all the country's high-ranking political and military experts in whose devotion and truthfulness I have full faith, I have agreed to accept the Resolution and the ceasefire. And, at the present stage, I regard it as expedient to the Revolution and the System, and, had it not been for our shared motivation that our honour and credibility must be sacrificed

in the path of all that is expedient to Islam and the Muslims, I
would not have consented to it, and death or martyrdom would
be much more enjoyable for me. But what is there to do? All
must submit to the consent of Almighty God, and, surely, that is
how the brave nation of Iran has been and will be ...[13]

The official justification of the Islamic Republic in calling an end to a
war which, in the words of its spiritual leader, should have continued
not only until victory over Iraq but until 'the world became devoid of
evil', is reflected in the state radio and television's commentary:

As Imam Khomeini had often warned, Saddam's claim to peace-
seeking was to deceive public opinions. After acceptance of
the ceasefire by Iran, he resumed aggression, and in the south,
he occupied further land sites. The publication of the exciting
and sentimental message of the imam once more caused general
mobilisation all over the country. Fighters and Revolutionary
forces from everywhere hurried to the war fronts and by imposing
another defeat on the Ba'athist elements made them flee. No
road was open to Saddam except to admit defeat. And now, God
willing, as the imam had promised, the nation, on whom an
unwanted war had been imposed, was, by offering innumerable
sacrifices of many of its dear ones, and by creating epic events – of
the kind which can be cited only in Islam's wars of the early days
– is in a position to impose peace on its formerly vainglorious
and presently miserable enemy. By the US's nod, Saddam had
come to divide Iran and put an end to the Revolution, but now,
to save his own life and rule over the innocent people of Iraq,
Saddam has no alternative but to accept the terms put forward by
the revolutionary nation of Iran. Of the marvellous happenings
notable during Iran's long holy defence period was that, in
the whole duration of war, the Iranian nation never desisted
from construction and repairing the ruins inherited from the
previous regime. Rather, they succeeded, in addition to efficient
management of the war fronts, to carry out enormous projects,
such as dam buildings, road constructions, oil exploration and
exploitation plans, development of power stations, improvement

of agricultural concerns, increasing the number of universities and research centres, as well as following up other national development activities.[14]

Analysts maintain that a major factor in the decision to end the war was the Iraqi use of poison gas. Both sides used chemical weapons, but the Iraqis had the capability to use them on a large scale, a factor that sapped the morale of the Iranian troops and the civilian population.

No one is sure of the total casualties during the Iran-Iraq war, but estimates range from 500,000 to one million dead, one-to-two million wounded, and more than 80,000 prisoners. There were approximately 2.5 million refugees, and whole cities were destroyed. The financial cost is estimated at a minimum of 200 billion dollars.

After Iran agreed to abide by UN Resolution 598 in July, Mojahedin Khalq's self-styled National Liberation Army, now transformed into a full-scale cult led by Rajavi, found the situation ideal to launch an attack across the border with Iraq, where many Mojahedin members had been based after being deported from France. The Iranian armed forces were so demoralised at the time that Mojahedin forces, using armoured vehicles and other equipment supplied by the Iraqis, advanced almost unopposed several hundred kilometres inside Iranian territory and seized the western city of Eslamabad Gharb, a few hundred kilometres from the capital. The operation was codenamed 'Eternal Light'. Soon, however, Iran's armed forces launched a counterattack, backed by fighter planes and helicopter gunships. Having hopelessly extended their lines of communication, the Mojahedin had run short of supplies, and the counterattack devastated them. Once the danger was over, the state television began showing footage of the destroyed equipment and lifeless bodies of Mojahedin fighters. According to some sources, some 2,000 Mojahedin fighters were killed.

Here again, both sides relied on ideological interpretations of Shi'ism. Mojahedin's leadership claimed that it followed the example of Imam Hossein, willing to sacrifice whatever it took to defy oppression and tyranny. The Islamic Republic said that it was only doing what Imam Ali had done: putting to the sword those who had deviated from the true path of Islam and chosen to fight the Islamic state.

Several Mojahedin members who later broke up from the

organisation accused Rajavi of having ordered the operation to enhance his own powers, at the cost of the lives and limbs of hundreds of people killed in the battlefront, as well as executed in prisons. According to A. Singleton, Rajavi 'sent many completely untrained and unarmed 'troops' into the battle. These were young Iranian men and women who were living in the West ... As many supporters as could be persuaded were hurriedly sent to Iraq, given a few days' basic training and then expected to go on a military operation to invade Iran; something the Iraqis had failed to do after eight years ... The people who were sent included old men and women (parents and grandparents of the combatants) and youths under eighteen years of age.'[15]

Shortly after the episode, thousands of Mojahedin prisoners, as well as a number of the members of other political groups, were executed in prisons inside Iran. Even many prisoners who had been released after serving their terms were re-arrested and handed over to firing squads. The execution of these prisoners began with Ayatollah Khomeini's *fatwa* in summer 1988, which read in part:

> Those who are in prisons throughout the country and remain committed to their support for the Monafeqin [Mojahedin], are waging war on God and are condemned to execution ... Destroy the enemies of Islam immediately. As regards the trials, use whichever criterion that speeds up the implementation of the [execution] verdict.[16]

The only official to raise his voice against the mass killings was Ayatollah Hosseinali Montazeri, Khomeini's designated successor. In 2002, Montazeri made public that about 3,800 prisoners had been killed by 31 July 1988. As he recalled in his memoirs, many of those executed had already been 'tried' and sentenced to lesser punishments in the past, or had even been found innocent of committing any crimes, and had not engaged in any new activities. This act 'shows total disregard for all judicial guidelines and the verdicts of judges', Ayatollah Montazeri noted.

None of those executed was accorded a public trial by an independent and impartial tribunal. Nor was any accorded legal counsel or the right to appeal the verdict. None was granted the 'right to an effective remedy by the competent national tribunals for acts violating the fundamental rights granted him by the constitution or by law'.

'At least order to spare women who have children ... the execution of several thousand prisoners in a few days will not reflect positively and will not be mistake-free,' Montazeri wrote in a letter to Ayatollah Khomeini. 'A large number of prisoners have been killed under torture by their interrogators ... in some prisons of the Islamic Republic young girls are being raped ... As a result of unruly torture, many prisoners have become deaf or paralysed or afflicted with chronic diseases.'[17]

The Islamic Republic leader's reply was resolute: 'Showing mercy for enemies is simple-mindedness. Islam's decisiveness against God's enemies is the fundamental and undoubted principle of Islamic discipline. We hope that with your revolutionary anger and hatred towards enemies of Islam, you earn the Almighty God's endorsement'[18]

Ayatollah Montazeri was to pay dearly for daring to question the orders of Ayatollah Khomeini. By that time, it was evident for the insiders that the rift between the two clergymen, which had begun on a theoretical basis, was heading for the point of no return.

Fourteen years after those events, it was still not clear how many people died during the six-month period from July 1988 to January 1989. Two years after the killings, Amnesty International reported the names of over two thousand political prisoners. One of the prisoners who survived the 1988 killings later gave an account of his time in Evin:

> Altogether, I have spent more than six years of my life in the political prisons of Iran's Islamic regime, all of it in Evin prison in Tehran. During that time, I suffered savage tortures by interrogators of the regime's Intelligence Agency. Later, I was able to leave Iran and was accepted as a political refugee by the United Nations High Commissioner for Refugees, through their office in Ankara/Turkey ...
>
> In 1981 when the Islamic regime of Iran executed my father, Mr Ali Mokhtar Zibaii, he was only forty years old, the same age that I am now. He was an officer of the air force in the First Fighter Base in Mehrabad, Tehran. At that time I was almost eighteen years old. From 1981, the date of my father's execution,

until 1986, the regime was searching for me, and in hiding I was unable to be with my family during that time.

In 1986 I was arrested, and was kept in prison until 1991. During those years I suffered the most savage tortures such that when they released me in 1991, the left side of my body was paralysed. When I came out I was alien to my family because while I was in prison, my family were rarely allowed to visit me. This was one of the common ways of torturing political prisoners by the Islamic regime.

I am one of about 900 survivors of the massacres of almost 30,000 helpless political prisoners, all executed by the Islamic regime. Most of these victims were killed in a time period of less than ten days in July and August of 1988. These killings were done by shooting, hanging or even by grenade and TNT explosives. The executions were done on the hills around Evin.

On 11 July 1988, they put all prisoners in locked rooms and allowed no more visits by their families. In fact, on the first days of July the speakers in prison announced to all prisoners 'we are not going to give this opportunity to people to save you from prison and treat you as their heroes ...

In each room (about twenty-four square metres, equivalent to about 220 square feet), there were more than forty-five prisoners. Finally on 29 or 30 July they started the massacre. Many of the victims had not eaten for days and were thirsty before their execution.

The massacre continued until October 1988, but they killed more than 90 percent of prisoners during the first ten days. So many times we heard the heavy machine guns, which were shooting the victims in the 'Shooting Execution Hall' of the prison. These were in addition to hanging on cranes and other hanging stands.[19]

Thousands of streets and alleys were named after the victims of the Iran-Iraq war. Victims of the mass killings in prison, however, were not even granted the right to be buried in Tehran's main cemetery. Nor were their relatives allowed to hold memorial services. The executed prisoners were buried in a piece of land in Khavaran, in eastern Tehran, a place dubbed La'nat Abad (Town of the Damned) by Hezbollahis, who frequently visit the graveyard, breaking tombstones. Many former

Mojahedin supporters have blamed Massoud Rajavi's ill-fated invasion of Iran as the major factor that led to the killings.

Not even the most prominent reformist figures that came to power years later, in the wake of Khatami's 1997 landslide victory, ever spoke out about the massacre. In 1998, when the hard-line judiciary started persecuting and prosecuting Tehran's district mayors in a bid to undermine the capital's maverick mayor Gholamhossein Karbaschi, I interviewed him on behalf of the news agency I used to work for. Karbaschi was furiously accusing the judiciary of torturing his colleagues in prison. I asked him what he thought about the thousands of political prisoners that had been tortured in Iran's jails over the previous years. Karbaschi replied, 'Do you mean to compare some of the Islamic system's most competent managers with traitors who spied for Iraq?' And in 1999, when Assadollah Lajevardi, the so-called 'Butcher of Evin' was assassinated in Tehran's bazaar by Mojahedin members, Khatami called him a martyr.

The general public, however, hardly took note of what had been going on in the prisons. By the winter of 1989, Iran was emerging from the grip of war. There was a tangible change in the mood of the people. Black clothes were gradually disappearing from the streets; new businesses were being opened; there was a meagre dash of colour in the grey atmosphere as youngsters ventured out looking much more jubilant and flamboyant; thousands of young men who had deserted the armed forces were coming out of hiding to register at the barracks: hitherto deprived of social rights as deserters, they now looked forward to a new future. For the first time in eight years, Iranian families were looking forward to celebrate *Nowruz* without a war, without having to run for shelter in fear of Iraqi bombs and missiles, without expecting the remains of a young man to arrive from the battlefields. And it was exactly at that time when Ayatollah Khomeini dropped another bombshell.

On 14 February the state radio and television announced that Ayatollah Khomeini had issued a death sentence against British author Salman Rushdie and his publishers over the book *Satanic Verses*, and declared that the rest of the day should be one of mourning:

> I inform the proud Muslim people of the world that the author of the *Satanic Verses* book, which is against Islam, the Prophet

and the Qur'an, and all those involved in its publication who are aware of its content, are sentenced to death.

The Iranian Prime Minister Mir Hossein Mousavi consequently sanctioned Hezbollah groups to 'take the necessary action' against the author. Rushdie, forty-two, responded hours later. 'I am very sad it should have happened,' he said. 'It is not true that this book is a blasphemy against Islam … I doubt very much Ayatollah Khomeini or anyone else in Iran has read this book or anything more than selected extracts taken out of context.'

Published in September, the *Satanic Verses* had sold 100,000 hardback copies in Britain and the US, and was runner-up for the Booker and Whitbread literary awards. However, it was already banned in five countries. The first demonstrations against the book took place in Bradford, West Yorkshire, where a copy was publicly burned. Then six people died in clashes that followed protests by angry Muslims in Pakistan.

Ayatollah Khomeini's *fatwa* was almost unequivocally supported by Iran's clerics and government officials, and led to the marring of Iran's relations with Britain for nearly a decade. In an attempt to resolve the crisis, the then President Ayatollah Ali Khamenei said during Friday prayers in Tehran that the sentence could be revoked if 'Rushdie repented'. Ayatollah Khomeini's reaction was, however, prompt and harsh. Much to Khamenei's humiliation, the leader said that the sentence would not be revoked 'even if Rushdie became the most zealous worshipper of the time'.

Hardliners marched on the streets and proclaimed their readiness to 'execute the apostate Rushdie or to be killed themselves', and the 15 Khordad Foundation set a one-million-dollar bounty on Rushdie's head. Over the next decade, several people associated with the book were killed or injured, although investigators never linked the Iranian government directly to the attacks.

Hitoshi Igarashi, a Japanese scholar who translated the book, was stabbed to death in July 1991. Italian translator Ettore Caprioli was wounded in a knife attack the same month.

In July 1993 Turkish author and publisher Aziz Nesin, who had printed extracts in a newspaper, was attacked by Islamist rioters in the central city of Sivas. They cornered him in a hotel and set it on fire, killing thirty-seven people, but Nesin escaped. And in October 1993, Norwegian translator William Nygaard was shot three times and seriously wounded.

Although the Rushdie affair was still hot, 28 March 1989 was a sleepy day in Tehran. Few suspected that yet another political earthquake was in the making. In the middle of the two-week *Nowruz* holidays, many people had gone on supposedly peaceful vacation after eight years of war. No newspaper was published. Everything seemed calm. But early risers passing by Tehran's Fatemi Square quickly noticed that something was wrong. On the façade of the high-rise building of the Ministry of Construction Jihad, something was missing. Until the night before, there had been two huge portraits on that wall, beaming at residents. One belonged to the imam, the other one to Ayatollah Montazeri. The second one was now missing, covered with a thick, hurriedly applied layer of paint. Soon the state radio and television broke the news in as tongue-in-cheek a tone as was possible: Ayatollah Montazeri was sacked from his position as designate-successor.

It was widely believed that this disavowal was a result of his repeated criticism of the Islamic Republic's excesses against the opposition, and their pursuit of the 1980–88 war against Iraq. In his last letter to Montazeri, accepting his resignation and removing him from the position of designated successor, Ayatollah Khomeini claimed that he had disagreed with Montazeri's appointment from the outset and had regarded him as 'lacking the stamina necessary for acceptance of this important, arduous and grave responsibility'. Ayatollah Khomeini had not publicly opposed the selection of Ayatollah Montazeri as his successor, he added in his letter, because he did not want to interfere in the lawful duties of the Assembly of Experts.[20]

Expressing his 'affection' for Montazeri, Ayatollah Khomeini wrote that he thought it expedient for Montazeri to 'avoid past errors and keep your homestead clear of incompetent individuals and the traffic of those opposed to the Islamic System, so that the people, the System and the theological assemblies may benefit from your jurisprudential views'.[21]

It was not just the men-on-the-street who were taken aback by Montazeri's abrupt fall from grace. After years of state propaganda endorsing him as Ayatollah Khomeini's successor, the dismissal shocked many authorities. For this reason, in a letter addressed to the Majles and the government, Ayatollah Khomeini explained: 'I have heard that you are not aware of the affair relating to His Excellency Mr Montazeri and do not know what it is all about. Know then, that "your old man" [Ayatollah Khomeini's reference to himself] has been trying for two years by messages or in statements, to no avail, to prevent the matter from reaching this stage … On the other hand, my religious duty called for a decision to be taken to protect the System and Islam. Therefore, with a bleeding heart, I have removed the fruit of my life from his position in order to safeguard Islam and the System …'[22]

In his letter, Ayatollah Khomeini went on to threaten other officials. 'The Revolution owes nothing to any group … I have often declared that I have entered into no brotherhood pact with anyone, regardless of his or her position or status … The framework for my friendship lies in the honesty and veracity of each individual.'

Years later, Ayatollah Montazeri said that in his view, and based on the personal relationship he used to have with Ayatollah Khomeini, he seriously doubted that most of the controversial letters and written orders attributed to him in the last years of his rule, 'when he was sick, depressed and out of touch with the realities' were written by him.

In his memoirs, Montazeri openly accused the 'trio' of Khamenei and Rafsanjani, the then president and Majles speaker respectively, as well as Ayatollah Khomeini's son Ahmad, of having manipulated the leader. 'A small but power-hungry group had imposed their own rule over the ruler … Knowing I might one day replace Ayatollah Khomeini, the same trio wanted also to have the upper hand on me and my office, and when they realised I was not yielding to their desire, that I was not going to dance to their tune, they started plotting, spreading rumours that my office is swamped by hypocrites.'[23]

Ayatollah Montazeri's removal set the scene for an apocalyptic farewell to the founder of the Islamic Republic – who was already suffering from advanced cancer – as well as to an era of religious charisma in Iran.

Early in June 1989, the state media broke the news that Ayatollah Khomeini was in a critical condition. Saying he was to undergo an abdominal operation, they called on the Muslim people to 'pray for the wellbeing of His Holiness'. But it turned out that the imam had already passed the point of no return. On the morning of 4 June the radio started airing mournful verses from the Qur'an for hours on end. Finally, at seven o'clock, a tearful presenter announced that 'the spirit of God has joined Him', making reference to a literal translation of Ayatollah Khomeini's first name – Ruhollah – which means 'the spirit of God'.

Soon there were long lines at bakeries and petrol stations, as fears of instability mounted. At the same time, thousands of the imam's followers were flowing from all corners of the country into Tehran. His funeral turned out to be a macabre show of zeal and frenzy. As a foreign correspondent observed:

> The death of Ayatollah Ruhollah Mousavi Ayatollah Khomeini on 4 June was mourned by millions of his followers with an extravagance that surprised even the Iranian authorities. Time and again, funeral plans were disrupted by gigantic mobs unwilling to give way either to schedules or politicians. The scene in Tehran was one of unrelieved chaos. In the traditional Shi'i manner, men pounded their chests and flagellated themselves with chains. Some sacrificed sheep, and some shouted, 'We wish we were dead, so as not to see our beloved imam dead'. Others ran twenty-five miles to the cemetery. The grave dug for Ayatollah Khomeini's body was occupied by mourners who refused to leave. The authorities appealed to citizens to stay away from Ayatollah Khomeini's house and the cemetery, but to no avail.
>
> Fire trucks sprayed water on mourners in an effort to keep them from fainting in the intensity of the June heat and the press of humanity. According to official sources, some 10,879 people were injured and received on-the-spot medical attention, 438 were taken to hospitals, and 8 died in the crush to view Ayatollah Khomeini's body. In the cemetery, mourners climbed on buses, to catch a better glimpse of the body, and in one case the roof of a bus collapsed, injuring those sitting inside. Ali Khamenei, the president of the republic, could not even reach the special stand set up for dignitaries. Indeed, the stand for state officials and foreign dignitaries almost collapsed under the weight of the crowd.

The height of frenzy occurred at the gravesite itself. Bringing the body by land vehicle was out of the question, so it arrived by helicopter. The first time the helicopter landed, the crowd swarmed in and grabbed pieces of the shroud, causing the corpse actually to fall to the ground. After fifteen frantic minutes, the coffin was put back on the helicopter, which then bore the body away. In an attempt to thin out the crowd, it was announced that the funeral had been postponed by a day. The trick worked, as many went home. Then, six hours after the first attempt, a second effort at a helicopter landing was made. This time more guards were on hand, and the body was placed in a metal casket. Still, it was not easy. As the Iranian news agency described it: 'The grave was only ten metres away but the pushing and shoving of thousands made it seem like kilometres. It took ten terrible minutes to be able to put the casket down near the grave.' Once the body was finally buried, concrete blocks were placed on top of it.[24]

In 1989, Ayatollah Khomeini had outlined a course of action for the authorities. In a letter to then President Khamenei less than a year before, he had also decreed the appointment of a body of authorities and experts to study and amend the constitution. The amendments chiefly included the elimination of the post of prime minister, as well as granting much wider authority to the supreme leader. The Assembly of Experts (an elected body of senior clerics) chose the outgoing president of the republic, Ali Khamenei, to be his successor as national religious leader in what proved to be a smooth transition. In August 1989, Majles speaker Rafsanjani was elected president by an overwhelming majority. Thus a chapter was closed in the history of post-Revolution Iran, and a new era began: an era marked by pragmatism trying to replace ideology.

During the years when the theocracy was waging its 'holy war' and relentlessly pumping ideology into society, the second generation was in the making. Maryam, born in 1979, recalls her childhood in the 1980s: 'What I clearly remember about my school is that before going to our classes in the morning, we had to chant 'death to America', 'death to Israel', and religious slogans; we also had to pray for the imam's wellbeing.

We had to memorise and recite a *hadith* (Prophet's saying) every week. We had special teachers called *Tarbiati* (Cultivation) teachers. They were mostly young girls from lower classes who wore black chadors and were very harsh on keeping us in line with Islamic principles. We had to wear black veils that covered our chins also. Wearing colourful stockings or perfume was prohibited. Most of us pretended to be zealous and revolutionary Muslims. We were afraid of spies among us.'

The world outside the school was not much more amusing, either. There were long queues for basic commodities that were all rationed. There were regular power shortages that left people desperate in summer and shivering in winter. Television – the major source of entertainment – was dominated by war propaganda and religious sermons. Most families were eagerly waiting for Friday afternoons, when a Japanese cartoon about the adventures of a beaver called 'the brave boy' was shown, albeit heavily censored. This was later followed by a Japanese soap opera that lasted three years and made a big hit. It told the story of a woman who managed to become a successful businessperson against all odds. Obviously, all mention of earthly love, let alone sexual relationship, was cut out. Interestingly, the person in charge of censoring television programmes at that time was a blind man.

Commercials, as a token of 'bloodsucking capitalism' and a means to deceive the masses, were non-existent after the Revolution. Besides, in a situation of rationed goods and economic sanctions, there was not much to advertise, either. The state media even censored sports news. There was neither any mention of women's competitions nor any news about 'un-Islamic' sports such as boxing, snooker, and the like. The only way to access such news was through Persian-speaking radio stations, such as the BBC and VOA, which, as sources of uncensored news, already had many listeners. One relief, although dangerous, was the video. If one could not afford a VCR, it was possible illegally to rent a video machine and some films for a few days, and thus 'video parties' became popular: friends or family members gathered together cautiously, watched pre-Revolution Iranian films, extinct Hollywood or Bollywood movies, and shared salted nuts or contraband Armenian vodka.

A prominent cultural feature of the 1980s was the ban on making or promoting heroes and stars by the media. This applied to every aspect of life, from cinema to sports, to books and television. The only 'true' heroes were, according to the state, the combatants of Islam who were sacrificing their lives in the battlefronts. As a result, there could be no posters or large pictures of famous footballers or movie stars. The *Tintin* books were banned because they propagated western values, with Tintin's heroic acts, and Captain Haddock's drinking. Cinemas showed either war, revolutionary, and 'moralised' domestically made films, or bland, boring, anti-American, censored foreign-made movies. In fighting Hollywood's influence, revolutionary cinema-policymakers of the time devised another measure: promoting hyper-intellectual films made by the likes of André Tarkovsky and Sergey Parajanov. In fact, straitjacketed by censors, many Iranian directors chose to make heavy philosophical films. There were exceptions, however. Dariush Mehrjuei's comedy *The Tenants* for a short while brought back what had been missing from cinema halls for a long time: the sound of joyous laughter. And Bahram Beizaei's *Bashu, the Little Stranger* painted a shocking portrait of the traumas of the war.

In 1984 I went to see a movie called *The Epic of the Warriors*, a Hungarian or Bulgarian production of the 1970s. For nearly an hour medieval warriors butchered each other, torched villages, or grappled with poverty and misery. I could not make head or tail of the film. Later, a friend of mine whose brother worked at the office in charge of reviewing films told me that the movie was originally called *For the Sake of Vera*, and that the whole story was about a fight between two villages because a young man had eloped with the pretty – and now, thanks to the censors, non-existent – girl of the rival tribe.

The press was also suffering. It was almost impossible to obtain a licence for a new publication unless the applicant was known to be in line with the state. There were exceptions however: *Adineh*, a literary and cultural weekly that tried to keep its readers abreast of world trends while indirectly criticising state politics; *Film Monthly Magazine*, which was a window to the world outside and a welcome relief from revolutionary propaganda; *San'at-e Haml-o Naghl* (Transport Industry) *Monthly*, which, despite its misleading title, was a leading intellectual publication that questioned the government in a very calculated way. But the most popular periodical was *Danestaniha*, a sort of large-size *Readers' Digest* that appealed to hundreds of thousands of readers. Its popularity rested to a great extent on its being the only full-colour publication in an otherwise grey world. Also, it published stories on science, technology, nature and culture: a pleasant break from the war propaganda.

The music market was dominated by smuggled Los Angeles productions, as local pop music was banned. Traditional Iranian music was permitted, chiefly serving, with its sad melodies and melancholic lyrics, as a tranquilliser for an escapist generation facing a bleak future. The youth, however, more or less kept pace with western pop music, again through smuggled cassettes. Michel Jackson, Modern Talking, Sandra, Kim Wilde, Alfaville and other 1980s performers had a strong presence at private parties. However, Pink Floyd, always a source of fascination for both the young and the older generations, was the most talked-about western band. In particular, *The Final Cut* album with its bitter anti-war lyrics was passed around and intently listened to.

Nima, a teenager at that time and a journalist later, said that the major social feature of the 1980s was that people learned to be two-faced and lead double lives: while superficially complying with the dictated norms of the theocracy, they were building a shadow-society in private. At school, the teenagers marched to the rhythm of revolutionary hymns and chanted 'death to the opponents of Velayat-e Faqih'. At home, they bopped to the tune of *Flash Dance* and performed the 'egg roll' they had picked up from contraband videotapes.

EIGHT

Looking to China

If there is anyone who believes that there will be another wave [of unrest] in Iran, I totally disagree. In Iran, an event will not take place easily. Because the clergy and the religious forces are the most rooted classes of this society ... There are a hundred thousand mosques and Hosseiyyehs, surrounded by a lot of good people, and the clergy has the leadership. Now that we are in power, the mosques must be accountable to the opposition. If someday a government takes over that is against these [religious classes], putting them in opposition, they will give such a government hell.

Akbar Hashemi Rafsanjani, 2004

Every revolution evaporates and leaves behind only the slime of a new bureaucracy.

Franz Kafka

Although Rafsanjani himself liked to be called 'the commander of construction' and 'Amir Kabir of modern times', many people half-jokingly called him 'Akbar Shah'; and a journalist called him 'Ayatollah Deng Xiao Ping'. And not totally without reason. During his tenure, flamboyance and extravaganza were reintroduced. After years of watching the imam sitting on a dilapidated chair, people now saw Rafsanjani in a huge golden-framed leather upholstered armchair, talking of a 'display of luxury'.

The first two years after Ayatollah Khomeini's death, in mid-1989, roughly coinciding with the presidency of Akbar Hashemi Rafsanjani were marked by the gradual liberalisation of social and economic controls. Hopes grew of a more tolerant society, reflecting Iran's multi-ethnic populace and traditions of diversity.

Ayatollah Khomeini's demise in 1989 more than anything else marked an end to the epoch of charismatic revolutionary leadership in Iran. In the absence of his authority, a new labour division, so to speak, was imperative if the system was to survive and consolidate itself. The unlikely successor to the imam was President Ali Khamenei, elected by the Assembly of Experts. While observers generally expected the Assembly to come up with a Leadership Council, the consensus among the ruling clergy was that the system based on Velayat-e Faqih indeed needed a single Vali-e Faqih. The lack of charisma, however, was later to be compensated for by extra powers given to the faqih when the constitution underwent changes a short while later.

Ali Khamenei was born in Mashhad in 1939. He began religious studies before completing the elementary education. He attended the classes of masters of 'Sat'h' (seminary lectures based on reading textbooks) and 'Kharej' (seminary lectures not based on reading textbooks) in Mashhad, such as Hajj Sheikh Hashem Qazvini, and Ayatollah Milani, and then went to Najaf in 1957.

After a short stay he left Najaf for Mashhad, and later he settled in Qom in 1958. Khamenei attended the classes of Ayatollahs Boroujerdi and Khomeini. Later he was involved in the Islamic activities of 1963 that led to his arrest in the city of Birjand in southern Khorasan province. After a short period he was released and continued his life by teaching in religious schools of Mashhad and teaching Islamic texts in different Mosques.

In December 1974 Khamenei was arrested at his home by SAVAK and dispatched to the joint committee prison of the police department in Tehran. He was released in autumn 1975, went back to Mashhad, but he was not allowed to hold his public classes.

In 1977, together with some clerics from Qom and Tehran, he established the Jamey-e-ye Rouhaniyat-e Mobarez (Militant Clergy Association) which became the basis of the Islamic Republic party.

In January 1979 Ayatollah Khomeini appointed Khamenei, by then a Hojjatol-Eslam, or mid-ranking cleric, as a member of the Revolutionary Council. And in March of the same year, in collaboration with his four brothers, established the Islamic Republic party. He likewise served in the Central Council of the party, and as deputy of the Ministry of Defence and representative of the Council in the Ministry, Commander of Islamic Revolution's Guards Corps.

Ayatollah Khomeini appointed him in 1980 to be the leader of the Friday congregational prayers in Tehran. He was also elected as a deputy of the Majles in the same year.

In the summer of 1981, after delivering a speech in the Majles that led to the dismissal of Bani Sadr, an attempt was made on his life by the Mojahedin Khalq organisation while making a speech in a mosque in Tehran, in which his chest and hand were badly injured and his right hand disabled for life.

Following President Rajaei's assassination in 1981, Khamenei was elected president of the Islamic Republic with 95 percent of the votes cast in his favour. He was president for another four years. During this time, he was chairman of the Supreme Defence Council as well as the Supreme Cultural Revolution Council. He was given the title of Ayatollah almost overnight when the Assembly of Experts chose him as the supreme leader after Ayatollah Khomeini. His title still remains a matter of debate in religious circles, particularly among clerics opposing conservatives. In addition to ayatollah, his supporters soon gave him new titles, including Vali-e Amr-e Muslimin-e Jahan (the governor of the affairs of the Muslims of the world) and Maqam-e Ozma-ye Velayat (the sublime holder of guardianship).

In August 1989, Akbar Hashemi-Rafsanjani, the Majles speaker and already considered by many as the most influential figure in the Islamic state's top echelons, was elected president by an overwhelming majority.

Unlike most Iranian clerics, who earn a living through religious posts and practice, Rafsanjani was born into a well-to-do rural family that gave him the opportunity to engage in politics without concern about having to make a living.

The first half of Hashemi Rafsanjani's political life was spent either in jail or in political campaigns against Muhammad Reza Shah's regime. After the culmination of Iran's Islamic Revolution, he was at the helm of top government positions, thanks to his close affinity with Ayatollah Ruhollah Ayatollah Khomeini.

Between the years 1979 to 1980, he was a member of the Council of the Revolution, deputy minister, and interior minister. He served as Majles speaker from July 1980 to August 1989.

Ayatollah Khomeini appointed him as one of Tehran's Friday prayer leaders in 1981 after an aborted assassination bid against Khamenei. In October 1981, he was appointed the leader's representative to the High Council of Security. In July 1983, he was appointed vice-president of the Experts Assembly, which is in charge of appointing and supervising the leader, a post he still holds. In July 1988, he was appointed commander-in-chief of Iran's armed forces, a position he had to give up a year later when he was elected president.

As a junior cleric, Rafsanjani had published a book on the life of Amir Kabir, the Qajar-era reformist prime minister who had tried to modernise Iran. Amir Kabir, or his impression of Amir Kabir, served as Rafsanjani's essential role model as an ideal statesman.

In 1989 there were obvious parallels to the time of Amir Kabir. Economic activity, severely disrupted by the revolution, was further depressed by the devastating war with Iraq and by the decline of oil prices beginning in late 1985. The country's industrial infrastructure had suffered heavy damages; the collapse of the price of oil on the world market had resulted in a drastic reduction in annual oil revenues, almost 42 percent; real GDP between 1984-85 and 1988-89 had dropped by an average two percent a year; the United States had imposed sanctions on Iran since 1984; many entrepreneurs had fled their homeland with their capital; inflation and unemployment were soaring; hundreds of thousands of people had been displaced as a result of the war; the population was growing at a relentless pace; government bureaucracy had grown into gargantuan proportions; and the parliament was dominated by the traditional left-wing Islamists whose top priority was a socialist style, centralised, 'rationised' economy, whereas Rafsanjani was apparently now looking to Japan for a model, although it turned out later that he had been eyeing the Chinese example.

In the words of Lars Haugom, the recognition of the need to change the direction of state policy was mostly due to the regime's inability to cope with the massive problems that it faced as a result of its isolation. In addition, the revolutionary elite began to lose its ideological cohesiveness and profound differences began to emerge.[1]

By 1988 the Iranian economy nearly collapsed and domestic production had decreased by fivefold. Iran continuously used up its resources during the war and at the same time the population increased around 40 percent. Iranian economy was not in good shape even shortly after the Revolution. A profound currency crisis, the loss of human life and material damages that resulted from the war, a severe budget deficit, and floating petroleum prices presented extremely grave problems for Tehran.

The 'second republic', according to Anoushiravan Ehteshami, began with Ayatollah Khamenei in a position of religious authority and the assumption of Rafsanjani to the presidency. In this era, the rights that accompanied religious leadership were extended by legal amendments and the office of the premier was merged with that of the presidency. The subsequent erosion of the legitimacy of the religious regime, the economic demands of the people, coupled with the collapse of the Soviet bloc led to a search for a new economic order in Iran. Rafsanjani's tenacious personality and his progressive ideas concerning economic development were central factors that led to an eventual restructuring of the economy. Economic reconstruction became the central goal of this era. Other government objectives included a gradual separation of the economic realm from ideological elements, large-scale privatisation, greater freedom with respect to foreign trade, and a restructuring of the legal framework in conformity with international laws and norms.[2]

Economic reform was at the top of Rafsanjani's agenda. In March 1989 Ayatollah Khomeini had approved Rafsanjani's five-year plan for economic development, which allowed Iran to seek foreign loans, and this was his trump card. Determined to open up the economy, and defiant of the pressure from the left, he embarked on an 'economic adjustment programme' that became to be known as 'Rafsanjani's perestroika'.

The programme included an orderly exchange-rate unification, increased fiscal and monetary disciplines, trade and business deregulation, streamlining of the state bureaucracy, privatisation of money-losing public enterprises, attraction of foreign private investments, and the establishment of budgetary control over the semi-independent, non-accountable, extra-governmental foundations, or Bonyads. Without these sorely needed economic reforms, and without the resolution of certain external disputes with the United States and

Europe, further inflation, slower growth, and larger unemployment were to be expected.

After the war with Iraq ended, the situation began to improve: Iran's GDP grew for two years running, partly from an oil windfall in 1990, and there was a substantial increase in imports. A decrease in oil revenues in 1991 and growing external debt, though, dampened optimism. The rift between factions of the ruling clergy had come to the fore in Ayatollah Khomeini's last years. Bills aimed at tightening state control economy, ratified by the predominantly leftist Majles, were frequently rejected by the Guardian Council. The Guardian Council comprises of six clergymen and six jurists, mostly appointed by the leader, to monitor bills passed by the Majles and check them against the Sharia and the constitution. The Council has almost always been dominated by the conservative clerics of the right faction, many of who had gathered under the name of Society of Militant Clergy during the shah's reign. To break the deadlock, Ayatollah Khomeini devised the Expediency Council, a congregation of figures from both factions as well as those endorsed by the imam himself, to arbitrate between the two conflicting bodies.

No matter how hard the imam tried to muzzle discontent through lectures and assigning arbitrators, and no matter how much the two factions swallowed their words in fear of the old man's wrath, by the end of the war the chasm could no longer be concealed. Having realised the fact, the imam authorised the leftist clerics to set up an outfit of their own, which eventually was named League of the Militant Clerics, counterweighing and challenging the authority and policies of the conservative, or right faction ever since. With the ousting of Ayatollah Montazeri, the death of Ayatollah Khomeini, the elimination of the prime minister's post – which had always been chaired by a member of the left faction – and finally the advent of President Rafsanjani, the decline of the left began. At the same time, in one of his first appointments as the new supreme leader, Ayatollah Khamenei replaced all the key officials of the judiciary with conservative figures.

There were also important amendments made in the constitution following Ayatollah Khomeini's death. Failing to find a suitable successor to Ayatollah Khomeini among the leading ayatollahs, the qualifications needed to become leader were downgraded so that the incumbent would no longer have to be a Marja. Consequently, the position of the faqih was reduced to little more than a political office, thereby separating supreme religious and political leadership in the Islamic state. At the same time, the presidency was upgraded to include the responsibilities of the prime minister, a position that was now abolished.

Rafsanjani was given a more open hand in implementing his economic policies when the last obstacle on his way was apparently removed with considerable help from the conservative Guardian Council. Prior to the Majles elections of 1992, the Council disqualified most of the prominent leftist candidates, and thus the Society of Militant Clerics and its affiliated groupings, backed by the bazaar, which was looking forward to the loosening of state control on economy as well as the unprecedented influx of imports, conquered the last trench of the radicals, effectively marginalising the left. The turnout of the election was low, but the outcome was a clear sign of frustration with the austerity policies of the past.

Encouraged by the seemingly unequivocal support of the bazaar and its allies, as well as by the proponents of 'brotherhood and equality', Rafsanjani hammered on his 'free-market policies'. For the first time after the Revolution, businesses were flourishing, imported goods were pouring into shops, and foreign-made cars were being seen on the streets.

These attempts at economic reconstruction and political liberalization created great excitement throughout the society, and the debate over passing from a religious to a more modern or secular administration dominated discussions in intellectual circles. Cornerstone premises of the revolution, such as the hegemony of religious values, came to be seen by many as obstacles to reconstruction.

Weary of a devastating, protracted war with Iraq, and fed up with the repressive policies of the period, the general public nevertheless showed relative satisfaction with the taking over of Rafsanjani, for, as there was no prospect of fundamental change on the horizon, he represented the 'milder' face of the Islamic Republic.

As early as August 1989 Ali Akbar Saeedi Sirjani, a dissident writer and a credited professor of Persian literature, published an article in *Ettela'at*, one of the two evening newspapers of the country, which was supposed to be the more moderate daily newspaper. In the essay titled

'Nokteh' ('Point'), praising Rafsanjani as a patriotic man as well as a realistic statesman, he went so far as to question the wisdom of continuing the war with Iraq for eight years as well as the seizure of the US embassy in Tehran back in 1979. Criticising the anti-American propaganda and slogans of Ayatollah Khomeini's days, he welcomed Rafsanjani's policy of 'trying to put our own house in order before reorganising the order of the firmament'.

By and large, Sirjani's essay reflected the general mood of the majority of the nation, as well as the conclusions that a part of the establishment had come to, for it could not have been published without a nod from Ettela'at manager Muhammad Doaei, a Majles deputy and a veteran leftist cleric. Many observers even regarded the essay as a subtle move by Rafsanjani himself to test the political waters, particularly in terms of defusing tensions with the United States.

The reaction of the conservatives was abrupt and harsh in coming. All the official and non-official mouthpieces of the right faction, including Friday prayer leaders, the press, the armed forces and state organisations, issued statements of denouncement and contempt, vowing to continue the path of the late imam in fighting 'criminal America to the last drop of our blood.'

At the time when Sirjani's essay appeared, I was a conscript with the Revolutionary Guards, and as I was a journalist, I served in the cultural unit. A couple of days after the essay was published, I saw the commander of the cultural unit giving orders to the calligraphers under his command to prepare several large banners. 'Write down,' he said, 'The Revolutionary Guards strongly condemn the despicable insults made against holy Islam and the Islamic Republic by the mercenary writer of the article Nokteh.' Having given relevant orders for other banners proclaiming the ongoing struggle with the Great Satan and readiness to obey the orders of the supreme leader to the last breath, he turned to me and said, 'Do you happen to know what was written in that article?'

Sirjani's name was not mentioned in the press until a few years later when he was arrested by the Intelligence Ministry and made a public 'confession'. The episode, in the words of one analyst, was a clear sign of the discord between Rafsanjani and Khamenei, who would keep the United States as a bugbear for years to come.

Rafsanjani, however, seemed adamant not to do away with his tongue-in-cheek policy of approaching the US. In May 1990 Ataollah Mohajerani, Rafsanjani's eloquent vice-president who would later become Khatami's controversial culture minister, published an article, again in *Ettela'at*, titled 'Direct Talks'. Expounding on the reasons why the imam had challenged the US and emphasising the point that the times had changed and with them the interests of the country, he explicitly advised direct Iran-US negotiations, reasoning that talks did not necessarily mean retreat or surrender, and that even the Prophet Muhammad held talks with his enemies. This time the supreme leader himself reacted, slandering those who thought about establishing ties with the Great Satan as simple-minded if not under the influence of the enemy, reiterating that according to the imam, the relations between the US and Iran were those between a wolf and a sheep. Mohajerani replied that he had only wished to act in the interests of the country and Islam, and that he would regard Ayatollah Khamenei's remarks as *fasl-ul-khitab* (the end of the talks).

Having failed in a possible thaw with the US, Rafsanjani carried on a more pragmatic line with respect to foreign policy, especially toward Europe and the Gulf Arab monarchies. In the words of Anoushiravan Ehteshami, 'In foreign policy, the doctrine of non-alignment and support for Islamic and other third-world liberation movements was more or less abandoned. Under Ayatollah Khomeini, Iranian foreign policy gave priority to Islamic countries and Islamic ethics in world affairs, while avoiding bilateral and multilateral co-operation in a system dominated by Western powers. In the 1990's, in contrast, Iran actively sought reintegration into the international system by promoting co-operation in the fields of economy, politics and culture, indicating that Iranian foreign policy was guided more by pragmatism than by any Islamist persuasion. Iran's approach to the Gulf crisis and war in 1990–91, the Arab-Israeli peace process, co-operation with secular states in the Middle East and the rapprochement with the United States were all examples of Tehran's 'new foreign policy line.'

The principal goal was to attract foreign investment and aid in order to overcome the massive damages caused by the war. He sought to find a place for Iran in the international political economy.

However, mismanagement and inefficient bureaucracy, as well as political and ideological infighting, hampered the formulation and execution of coherent economic policies. Iran's economy remained a mixture of central planning, state ownership of oil and other large enterprises, village agriculture, and small scale private trading and service ventures. Rafsanjani pursued diversification of Iran's oil-reliant economy, although he made little progress toward that goal.

According to Jahangir Amuzegar, a former finance minister of the shah, the doubts raised in the mid-term review regarding the fate of these reforms were later justified. The Majles, which was widely (and optimistically) expected to support the president's pragmatic economic policies, turned out to be resistant to his plans, partly because the traditional right was scared by efforts in modernising the economy, which would in practice loosen the grip of the bazaar on economy, and partly because the general public was alarmingly becoming wary of the elimination of state subsidies and the soaring inflation. 'Rafsanjani's own highly-praised economic team also badly miscalculated both its own professional prowess and the responses of ordinary people. The exchange-rate unification and foreign-currency management were badly botched. Bank credits to debt-ridden public enterprises were imprudently increased. Widening the tax base never came to pass. Price decontrol was partly reversed. Interest-rate rationalization proved impossible to achieve. Meaningful subsidy cuts on consumer goods were effectively resisted by the Majles, as were the privatisation efforts. Extremely low prices on public goods and services were increased later, but still remained low and, in many cases, still below cost. Bonyads continued their freewheeling exercises and pursued their unfettered control over some crucial aspects of the private economy. Imports were allowed to double within two years, paid for by short-term suppliers' credit, and favouring consumer goods. Public investments were stepped up in projects of questionable value. External debt, which had been skilfully kept low during the eight-year war, suddenly skyrocketed.'

> In other projections, also, the First Five-Year Plan showed significant shortfalls. Annual investment grew half as fast as planned. Budget balance was ultimately achieved for one year, but only by selling petrodollar earnings at the free-market rates and replacing subsidies to public enterprises with bank loans. Total

liquidity and inflation numbers rose at twice the planned rates. The jobless rate was reduced by increasing underemployment in the inefficient informal economy. Foreign exchange deficits were made up by obtaining short-term suppliers' credit. In short, the 1989–93 plan, which started with a detailed list of quantitative objectives, ended up with a different set of figures that bore little resemblance to the initial targets. Here, again, deviations from original objectives had nothing to do with the US sanctions and was the legacy of Iran's long-standing planning problems inherited from the past.

Despite the costly futility of such non-coordinated and non-enforceable planning, the vast (and vested) planning establishment within the Iranian government embarked on the preparation of the Second Five-Year Development Plan (1995–99) in roughly the same manner. But due to some confusion stemming from the reversal of several reform measures, and under the pretext of evaluating the performance of the First Five-Year Plan, the Majles postponed the finalization of the Second Five-Year Plan for a year until March 1995.[3]

By then Rafsanjani was already being widely accused of filling his family's pockets through economic corruption. In 2004, Ray Takeyh told Bloomberg that a dozen families with religious ties controlled much of Iran's 110 billion-dollar gross domestic product and shaped its politics, industries and finances. 'The Rafsanjanis – who have investments in pistachio farming, real estate, auto making and a private airline worth a total of 1 billion dollars – are among the best connected and most influential of the families,' he said.

'The whole Iranian economy is set up to benefit the privileged few. Rafsanjani is the most adept, the most notorious and the most privileged,' Takeyh added.[4]

Rafsanjani was re-elected in June 1993, with a more modest majority; some Western observers attributed the reduced voter turnout to disenchantment with the deteriorating economy. By this time, he was under pressure from his previous backers, who were as critical of his modernization plans as with the relative relaxation in cultural, social and personal restrictions. By this time, also, clearly he was no longer a member of the 'traditional right'; rather, as coined by insiders, he represented the 'modern right', technocrats who advocated, at least in theory, free-market economy, and relative social and cultural openness within the norms of Islam, but did not tolerate political dissent and opposition.

In parallel with his economic adjustment scheme, Rafsanjani had undertaken a policy of somewhat relaxing the restrictions imposed on individuals' freedoms. This could be attributed to several factors: First, the war had ended in a way far from desirable for the Islamic Republic, and particularly for Rafsanjani himself, who had supported its continuation; there was no more an enemy occupying parts of the territory of Iran, and it was therefore not easy any more to resort to the excuse of 'war conditions' to silence voices of dissent.

Second, Rafsanjani, or at least his Western-educated advisors, were well aware of the social implications of a bitter-pill approach to open up and industrialise the economy, knowing that it was next to impossible to modernize the economic infrastructure while preserving a traditional social framework.

Third, the Islamic Republic was thriving to break out of its international isolation and improve relations with the outside world, eyeing the much-needed foreign investment. Evidently, it was assumed, the potential foreign investors, particularly the Europeans, would first of all make sure that their capital was going to a safe and secure place.

And fourth, after successfully crushing the opposition, the last thing Rafsanjani and the Islamic establishment would want was the emergence of a fresh hoard of dissidents that could hamper their efforts in consolidating power and normalising the country. The baby-boomers of the early 1980s were already entering their teens, providing a lucrative target for the subversive opposition, now mainly in exile. Therefore, any move to depoliticize society required other outlets into which the energies of the general public, and particularly the younger generations, could be channelled into. Giving people more leeway in their personal affairs and in pursuing 'harmless' recreational and cultural activities seemed to be the answer.

The key minister in Rafsanjani's cabinet was Muhammad Khatami. A mid-ranking cleric, Khatami was an exception to the rule: in 1970 he was one of the few clergymen who entered the University of Tehran and graduated with an MA; and afterwards he served in the army for two years at a time when clerics could be exempted from military service. He later returned to Qom and resumed theological studies at the seminary school.

Khatami became involved in political activities and anti-shah campaigns. He began his political activities at the Association of Muslim Students of Isfahan University, and worked closely with Ayatollah Khomeini's son Ahmad, organising. After the 1979 Revolution he replaced Ayatollah Muhammad Beheshti as head of the Islamic centre in Hamburg, Germany.

Returning to Iran, he was elected as a Majles deputy from the province of Yazd in 1980. At the same time, Ayatollah Khomeini appointed him as his representative and head of *Kayhan* newspaper, the largest circulation daily of the time, a post from which he resigned after a short while.

In 1982 he was appointed as the minister of culture in Prime Minister Mousavi's cabinet. During the 1980–88 war with Iraq, he served in different capacities, including deputy and head of the Joint Command of the Armed Forces and chairman of the War Propaganda Headquarters.

In 1989 President Rafsanjani appointed Khatami as the minister of Culture and Islamic Guidance. The advent of Khatami very quickly manifested itself in the cultural environment of the country. Conditions for granting publishing licences eased off, book censorship was relaxed, and the film industry began a period of unprecedented flourishing. Traditionalists were furious at Khatami's liberal policies, at a time when Ayatollah Khamenei was already siding with the traditional right, warning of a Western 'cultural invasion' and calling the 'nation' to wage a war against 'social vice'.

After four intellectual publications were closed down by the judiciary on charges of spreading Western thoughts and diluting revolutionary values, Khatami was forced to resign under pressure from hardliners for his liberal policies on art and the press.

Another particularly outstanding figure in Rafsanjani's administration was Gholamhossein Karbaschi, whom he appointed mayor of Tehran in 1989. Karbaschi embarked on the Herculean venture of transforming the ramshackle capital after eight years of war with Iraq with an effective, but ruthless development policy. Along the way, Karbaschi developed the reputation of a competent manager who cut through Iran's notorious mountains of red tape. He promoted like-minded officials who together formed a crucial and powerful element of the bloc that later played a part in bringing Khatami to power.

A Reuters correspondent wrote that 'the no-nonsense moderate technocrat brought to life decades-old plans for landscaped freeways drawn up by US-educated urban planners, built housing and supermarkets for the masses and introduced the Internet to the well to do'.

Karbaschi brought art and concerts to teeming south Tehran districts and sponsored book and music shops around the city – all paid for through a 'tax' on development and informal sources of revenue that some residents dubbed 'the Karbaschi system.' Karbaschi's critics often accused him of using the municipality as a private political machine and enriching himself, his business associates and political cronies by looting city coffers.

Born to a religious family in the Shi'i Muslim holy city of Qom, Karbaschi combined a secular education with traditional religious learning in local seminaries before heading to Tehran University in 1972 to study mathematics.

He immediately took up with the growing anti-government student movement then sweeping the university. He gave speeches, wrote anti-government pamphlets, distributed forbidden taped lectures of the exiled Ayatollah Khomeini who was to become the father of the Islamic Revolution, and took part in student protests.

Karbaschi was soon arrested by the shah's security forces and in 1973 was sentenced to three years in prison. Upon his release he returned to both mathematics and political activism. By the time Ayatollah Khomeini returned to Iran in triumph in February 1979 to lead the Revolution, Karbaschi was recognised as an exemplary young leader.

He worked in Ayatollah Khomeini's office for six months before taking over as ideological head of the new Islamic republic's television. In 1982 Ayatollah Khomeini personally selected him to serve as governor of the central province of Isfahan. A successful stint there led to his promotion to mayor of Tehran in 1989, where he won plaudits from residents for beautifying the city and rebuilding its tired infrastructure.

Conservatives were enraged by Karbaschi's urban as well as cultural policies. Many traditional bazaar merchants were angered by his taxation policies, not to mention his policy of modernizing distribution and the retail chain. Introducing department stores and hypermarkets meant that the city economy would much less be formed in the labyrinthine vestibules of Tehran's old bazaar. As if that was not enough, he put on his agenda a daring – and politically dangerous – plan to demolish the whole Tehran bazaar district and rebuild it in a modern way. Karbaschi reasoned that the existing architectural texture of the bazaar – which is said to be the largest covered market in the world – with its narrow, meandering corridors and dungeon-like chambers, made it an inescapable inferno should a fire or an earthquake break out. The plan was a thorn in the side of the conservatives, and not even Karbaschi was in the end able to shake the foundations of the traditional stronghold of conservatives.

Feeling the pressure of increasing prices of goods and services, many Tehran residents, particularly government employees and other groups with fixed salaries, began to criticise Karbaschi, but it seemed that nothing could stop him. One of the first comments he made after becoming mayor was 'people should understand that for living in the capital there is a price to be paid.' In fact, some economists say his unorthodox methods contributed to the capital's high rate of inflation, while others accuse him of legitimizing any offence if only the proper fine was paid for it. His policies in developing cultural centres, promoting the press and advocating environment protection, however, made a huge impact among the younger generations.

As if the policies of Khatami and Karbaschi were not enough to cause concerns for the right wing, Rafsanjani's daughter Faezeh Hashemi opened a new front by advocating women's rights and calling on them to take an active part in social, political and cultural activities. As head of the women's Olympics committee as well as a number of non-governmental organisations, Faezeh was soon the epitome of 'Muslim feminism' and a popular figure among young women. She initiated the first Asian games for Muslim women in 1993.

The conservatives attacked her for being outspoken, wearing blue jeans and riding bicycles, acts that had been considered taboo for chaste woman in Iran. 'One of the main problems is that traditions have been mixed up with religion,' Hashemi told a newspaper in 1997. 'Women have been under strain for many centuries. There are many things – which we have witnessed during our activities – which are not mentioned explicitly in the Koran but are rather Islamic sayings which should be regarded as dubious. However, in our country they are implemented as self-evident facts.'[5]

By the early 1990s the face of the cities had considerably changed. Young boys and girls were much bolder. They wore brighter colours inspired by foreign – mostly Turkish – satellite televisions, openly listened to Western music, and went hiking with their opposite-sex friends. They had also become more aggressive: young boys defied the schools' orders to cut their hair very short, girls used make-up and perfume which was against the rules. To cater to the ever-increasing needs of the youth, the state television also took a number of measures. A third channel was launched, almost exclusively dedicated to sports news. In many cases, the grim, bearded and shabby presenters were replaced or supplemented by young, handsome and cleanly shaven men. New foreign-made serials – chiefly German detective films – were shown. The restriction on the contents of the domestic soap operas was relaxed: now there could be talk of earthly love if, of course, it led to marriage.

The same trend was adopted in the film industry. The films started to be made around the focal point of young, good-looking actors and actresses. Commercial filmmaking was no longer considered a sin. Directors turned to melodramatic clichés, and even when making films about the 'sacred defence', the heroes tended to look more like Rambo than the down-and-out characters of the 1980s films. More taboos had started to crack.

At the same time, after nearly a decade of silence, which could be attributed to the total silence enshrouding the whole country, the Hezbollah mobs appeared again during Rafsanjani's reign, this time renamed Ansar-e Hezbollah, or the supporters of the party of God. These hard-line fundamentalists were apparently manipulated by the traditional conservatives. They harassed government critics of all kinds, burned property, beat up individuals and disrupted gatherings with impunity. In May 1995, a Hezbollahi mob prevented philosopher Abdolkarim Soroush from delivering a lecture at Amir Kabir Technical University. In an open letter to President Rafsanjani, sparked by this incident, Soroush noted that he had turned down all previous invitations to speak, and cancelled his university classes for the interests of the country, but had not gained anything from this approach. He added, 'I have gradually lost my professional and personal security as the brazen have become more impudent.' Hezbollahi militants attacked two Tehran cinemas showing the film *Souvenir from India*, which they thought to be 'vulgar' even though it had been approved by government censors. They assaulted audiences and vandalised the cinemas.

Hezbollahi mobs also frequently demonstrated in the streets of Tehran against women cyclists, criticising Faezeh Rafsanjani. They even burned facilities at a new cycling track in western Tehran, a popular hangout of young girls and boys. The authorities ceded to Hezbollahi demands, limiting women to riding on segregated paths out of sight of men.[6]

Women received the worst share of the restrictions on personal liberty. In November 1995, the Basij, which had recently been assigned to fight 'vice', announced that it had detained 86,000 suspects in the previous twelve-month period. Most of them were thought to have been women detained for violating the dress code. The new penal code, which went into effect in July that year, substituted fines and prison terms for the penalty of lashes for violators of the dress code. One positive development for women, however, was the reform of the divorce law in November 1995, enabling women to obtain a divorce in certain circumstances even if their husbands did not consent.[7]

Although it was generally thought that the extremists of the right faction, particularly the judiciary officials and the Guardian Council, were pulling the strings of Hezbollah, some analysts pointed the finger at Rafsanjani himself. 'Hezbollahi hardliners, following the ideology of their older left-wing revolutionary brothers, were originally against social injustice and the materialist spirit brought about by Rafsanjani's policies,' a veteran journalist told me. 'However, Rafsanjani played a very subtle trick on them by turning their attention to "social corruption", "cultural invasion of the West" and "dilution of Islamic and revolutionary values", so that he could have a free hand in pursuing his economic priorities.'

By the time of the Majles elections in 1995, the gap between Rafsanjani and the traditional right was so wide that a split seemed inevitable and imminent. And perhaps for the first time after the imam's death, the schism was visible to the passive bystanders, i.e. the majority of the people who hitherto assumed the clerical establishment of being a more or less monolithic body.

Confident of backing by the supreme leader as well as the long arm of the Guardian Council in rejecting 'unfavourable' candidates, the Association of Militant Clerics was certain it would dominate the next Majles. Therefore, in pre-election lobbying, it brazenly refused Rafsanjani's proposal to include six of his associates in its slate of twenty-five candidates for Tehran. This proved to be the last straw for Rafsanjani and his modern right, and with a nod from him, they announced the formation of 'Servants of Construction', later to be renamed 'Executives of Construction', as the emerging rival of the traditional right, challenging its authority.

The conservative ideologues controlling the Majles urged a slower pace on reforms in order to retain popular support, regarding Westernisation and foreign liberal influence as the country's main threats. Rafsanjani's supporters, on the other hand, continued backing of his tough economic policies to counter what they saw as the main threat to Iran's future, which they believed was domestic economic difficulties rather than foreign pressures.

Despite low overall turnout, and notwithstanding the small number of the 'modern right' candidates, the outcome of the elections was a big humiliation for the traditionalists, and a token of the predominant trend in society. Faezeh Hashemi swept to a landslide victory as Tehran's number one deputy, outvoting Nateq-Nouri who enjoyed the backing of all key conservative groups, as well as the bazaar. The embarrassment was too much to bear: after a recount, which observers said was obviously vote tampering, it was announced that it was Nateq-Nouri who had gathered the largest number of votes.

It was also rumoured that elections officials had given Nateq-Nouri a substantial number of votes that had been cast for Abdollah Nouri, a former interior minister and a moderate cleric.

Overnight, there was a new joke circulating in town: Someone happens to ask Nateq-Nouri, 'Excuse me sir, what's your name?'

'Interesting question,' Nateq-Nouri replies, 'Well, my name's Nateq-Nouri; but my friends call me just Nouri; and at home I'm nicknamed Faezeh.'

The result of the elections showed that there was finally a jinx in the armour of the right. It encouraged the left, now for four years in reclusion, licking its wounds and reorganising its approach and strategy, to prepare itself to re-enter the political arena by harshly criticising the traditional right, but not targeting Rafsanjani for the time being. Dissidents also found a new atmosphere in which to raise their voices again. In general, interestingly the focus shifted from economics, which used to be the classic battleground of the rivalling factions, to the question of freedom, democracy and political pluralism. This ultimately set the scene for the shock of 1997.

Although his policies were hampered by pressure from the traditional right wing as well as by his preoccupation with becoming a 'hero of construction', Rafsanjani's two terms nevertheless brought about extensive changes to the Islamic Republic, changes that were to a large extent a result of developments in the socio-economic structure, and the coming of age of the baby-boomers. Dariush Sajjadi maintains that during Rafsanjani's tenure, 'the tragedy of the distorted economic development of the Pahlavi era was repeated, with the difference that unlike the shah, Rafsanjani, with his pragmatic caution, closed his eyes on political and cultural development. His skill is to erase the problems and not to solve them.

'Despite his awareness of the Iranian society's need for political and cultural development at the beginning of his reign, when he found himself under pressure from the traditional clergy, he did away with political and cultural development. He replaced Khatami with Mirsalim in the Culture Ministry, and Nouri with Besharati in the Interior Ministry, devoting all his resources practically to reconstruction and economic development.

'As a result, in this period, Iran witnessed a rapid growth in the number of universities and students, but in the universities the students were not allowed to express their opinion freely. Numerous publications were printed in different colours and sizes; however, with a few exceptions such as *Salam* and *Kian* – which had something to say – there was no opportunity for the growth of the enlightening press,' Sajjadi said.

By the end of its term, the First Five-Year Development Plan was successful in achieving some of its quantitative objectives, but not all. Output growth at an average real annual rate of 7.2 percent was not far from the 8.1 percent goal, and quite respectable for a country at Iran's income level. But, the annual real growth rate fell each year from 11.5 percent in 1990–91 to 4.8 percent in 1993–94. Sectoral performance was also rather erratic. Yearly increases in output in such areas as water, power, and services were slightly higher than the target rates. Results in the agriculture and petroleum sectors, on the other hand, fell short of the targets, but again not by much. Manufacturing and construction, however, showed annual growth rates of only about half and one-third, respectively, of planned goals. Total oil exports revenues, during the 1989-93 period, were only 90 percent of the projected level, and non-oil exports, only 65 percent. Industrial exports were less than one-third of their targets.[8]

But accusations of mismanagement and particularly financial corruption lasted much longer than Rafsanjani's tenure as president. According to the Bloomberg report published in 2004, one of Rafsanjani's close relatives currently controls 47 percent of an airline link between Iran and Saudi Arabia, 22 percent of the profits of which would go into his pocket. After one oil-and-gas deal in 1998, an investigation into internal corruption led to the arrest of several close friends of Rafsanjani's son Mehdi. They were forced to return up to five million dollars to state coffers.[9]

But the eight years that Rafsanjani proudly recalls as the 'golden era of reconstruction' were also marked by a rule of dark terror, albeit not making ripples on the surface until after the election of Khatami and the disclosure of the serial killings of dissidents and intellectuals. Some reformist journalists – most notably Akbar Ganji and Emadeddin Baqi – have said that more than 100 men and women, including writers, intellectuals and political activists were silently murdered by the agents of the intelligence ministry over that period

Upon his re-election as president in the summer of 1993, Hashemi Rafsanjani introduced his new cabinet members to the Parliament for a vote of confidence. When he got to his proposed minister of intelligence Ali Fallahian, who had already held the post for four years, Hashemi Rafsanjani sufficed by uttering only one sentence: 'Then there is Mr Fallahian, and no one dares to deny him the vote of confidence!'

Fallahian, who was present in the session, was apparently happy with this introduction and reacted by forcefully smiling at Hashemi

Rafsanjani. The fear that Hashemi Rafsanjani alluded to was very real: The Majles deputies were well aware that if they wanted to run again for Parliament, they had to get the Ministry of Intelligence's approval, which would be handed over to the Guardians Council that is in charge of vetting the candidates. And Fallahian headed the Intelligence Ministry.

The deputies present in the session well-remembered how the Intelligence Ministry had directly intervened to disqualify most left-wing candidates for the fourth Parliament elections. And these deputies did not want to have the same fate.[10]

In 1985 Iran's intelligence body was transformed into a ministry that was to be supervised by the parliament. Ironically, it was the would-be pioneers of the reform movement, including Saeed Hajjarian, who laid the foundations of the intelligence ministry. And ironically again, in the words of Dariush Sajjadi, this supervision ran the other way around, as the Intelligence Ministry actually supervised the Parliament by monitoring the deputies' public and private lives.

Since then the Intelligence Ministry was not bothered by parliamentary supervision over its performance. In fact, the Ministry's power was even redoubled in 1992 when it obtained license for economic activities. Such power increased and enhanced self-confidence and made corruption even more rampant among the Intelligence Ministry's power circle that acted on its own.

The first murder that hit the headlines was perhaps the brutal assassination of Dr Kazem Sami in 1988. Sami, health minister in Bazargan's transitional government, was murdered with knife stabs, similar to the way Dariush Forouhar and his wife were assassinated a decade later. Based on information released after Sami's murder, the Intelligence Ministry launched a nationwide manhunt for the assassin and finally found that he had committed suicide in a public bath in Ahvaz, the same fate that later befell Saeed Emami, a high-ranking Intelligence Ministry official who turned out to be the mastermind behind political killings.

Speaking at her husband's funeral in Tehran's Hojjat-ebn-al-Hasan Mosque, Sami's wife told Bazargan and others present that she 'knew who had killed her husband'. Sami's assassination was timed to concur with the then German Foreign Minister Hans Dietrich Genscher's visit to Iran. This visit was of paramount importance for Iran, which had pinned hope on improving relations with Europe for political and economic reasons, topped by the urge to offset the upshots of the Iran-Iraq war. The assassination of Sami prompted Genscher to announce, upon his return, that Iran was not still safe for foreign investment. This announcement dashed Iran's hope to benefit from the German official's visit.

Another suspicious murder took place three years after Sami's assassination, this time outside Iran. On Friday, 9 August 1991, the state television reported Shapour Bakhtiar's assassination in Paris by unidentified assailants. The assassination seemed strange, as Bakhtiar, last prime minister of the Pahlavi regime, who fled Iran and obtained political asylum from France after the Islamic Revolution's victory, did not pose a serious political threat to the Iranian establishment.

The morning after Bakhtiar's assassination, Dariush Sajjadi published a story in the Tehran-based Persian-language *Abrar* morning daily on the assassination. In the article, titled 'Global Symphony', he reasoned that as Bakhtiar's assassination caused the cancellation of the then French president Francois Mitterand's scheduled visit to Iran, the unidentified assailants must have opposed improved Iran-Europe relations. He concluded that as the United States did not favour improvement of Iran-Europe ties, it might have had a hand in the assassination.

The same day the article was published, the Ministry of Intelligence's public relations department sent a letter to Abrar daily, approving the contents of the article and calling on other papers to follow suit and use the same analysis for Bakhtiar's assassination. 'If the Ministry of Intelligence had not sent this letter,' Sajjadi said, 'I would have probably never doubted the correctness of my analysis.'

Ali Akbar Saeedi Sirjani, the author whose article 'Nokteh' had stirred much uproar among the hardliners back in 1989, published two open letters in 1992 and 1993 in which he scathingly attacked the country's cultural climate. The publishing of the letters coincided with the launching of the Intelligence Ministry's newly established Press Research Bureau that was housed in a four-story building in Gandhi Street in north Tehran. The Bureau was vested with the task of reviewing all Iranian newspapers every day, indexing the contents, and compiling bulletins to provide government officials with information on current issues.

In the spring of 1993, the Bureau was relocated to a luxurious building in Pasdaran Avenue, close to Saeed Emami's home and office. Directly supervised by the Intelligence Ministry's Social Department, the Bureau worked three shifts a day to prepare its classified bulletins.

Following Sirjani's correspondence, the Bureau prepared a special classified bulletin on Sirjani, and this marked the start of the scenario of the dissident writer's detention, repentance, confession, and suspicious death.

In 1993, in a letter to Rafsanjani, 134 Iranian writers, dissidents and activists objected to Sirjani's detention. Failing to be of any help to Sirjani, the letter was rather played into the hands of the Intelligence Ministry to pressure the signatories. One of the signatories Abbas Zaryab Khoei passed away after the Intelligence Ministry exerted heavy pressure on him. Another signatory, Ahmad Mir Alaei, died of heart arrest in 1995 after a suspicious intravenous injection.[11]

Faraj Sarkouhi, the editor of *Adineh* magazine, was arrested in February 1996 on charges of attempting to leave the country illegally. He was held for months without access to family members or his lawyer. Controversy surrounded his whereabouts during the six weeks preceding 13 December 1996, when Sarkouhi was showed at an unusual press conference at Tehran's Mehrabad airport in an apparent attempt by the authorities to refute accusations that they had been holding him in custody during this period. At the press conference, Sarkouhi declared that he had been in Germany during the six-week period. This version of events was undermined by the publication abroad of a letter smuggled out of Iran in which Sarkouhi claimed that he was the victim of an elaborate plot orchestrated by the authorities, who had held him in detention during the period in question. In the letter, he claimed that throughout this period he had been subjected to interrogation and torture. In June 1997 authorities announced that Sarkouhi was on trial for espionage, an offence that could be punished by the death penalty. They seemed at the time to be seeking to use Sarkouhi as a bargaining chip with Germany following the May verdict of a Berlin court that implicated the Iranian government in the killing of four of its political opponents in Berlin in 1992. The German authorities appeared to corroborate Sarkouhi's version of events by stating that he had not entered the country in late 1996 and that the German entry visa stamped in his passport appeared to be forged. In September, after the case had attracted concern internationally, it was reported that Sarkouhi had been sentenced to one year of imprisonment for circulating harmful propaganda, a charge that had not been mentioned prior to his trial.

Meanwhile, the suspicious deaths of dissidents and cultural figures continued. In October 1996 Ghaffar Hosseini died a suspicious death. Ahmad Taffazoli's body was found with his head smashed in by a crow bar in January 1997. Ebrahim Zalzadeh was reported missing in March 1996 and his body was recovered in April 1997 in Tehran's suburbs. Then came a plot to drive into a valley a bus carrying dissident writers to Armenia.

The European Union officially suspended its policy of 'critical dialogue' with the Iranian government in April, following the verdict of a German court holding 'the Iranian political leadership' responsible for the murder of Sadeq Sharafkandi, the leader of the Kurdish Democratic party of Iran, an armed opposition group, and three companions in Berlin's Mykonos restaurant in 1992. While EU member states, with the exception of Greece, withdrew their ambassadors from Tehran, European leaders showed no eagerness to recast their relations with Tehran over the Mykonos verdict or other human-rights issues.[12]

The move by the European Union enraged hardliners. Less than a week after the withdrawal of the European ambassador, Ansar-e Hezbollah gathered outside the German embassy in Tehran. They chanted slogans against Germany and called for the closure of the embassy, which they labelled 'the second den of spies'. I was covering the event for an international news agency at the time. After much chanting and threatening by the Hezbollah militants, a blind, wheelchair-bound member – who was said to be a university professor – gave a speech. He mentioned how after World War II, the Israelis had hunted down German Nazi fugitives. He then addressed German officials: 'How come you kept silent at that time? And how come you make such a fuss when we hunt down a handful of counter-revolutionary elements?'

An informed diplomat disclosed in the 1990s that after the assassination of Iran's Kurdish Democratic party leaders, Qassemlu and Sharafkandi, in Berlin's Mykonos restaurant, some of Iran's Intelligence Ministry agents, acting on their own, transferred medium and long range missiles to Germany on the grounds that the United States would react to the assassination by launching a direct military attack on Iran.

The missiles were confiscated in Hamburg upon the ship's arrival in Germany. The Germans, however, showed self-restraint. They did not disclose the event but dispatched a high-ranking envoy to Tehran to demand explanation from the Iranian government.

The same diplomatic source noted that the Germans informed Rafsanjani of this 'strange move'. Rafsanjani followed up the case and incidentally got to know the details from one of his old merchant friends who had assisted the Intelligence Ministry by procuring and transferring the missiles.

According to Sajjadi, the 'power circle's' influence kept the then president from bringing it to book for this remarkable disgrace. Rafsanjani sufficed with demoting Saeed Emami from deputy intelligence minister for security to an advisor after the missile scandal. After Muhammad Khatami took over as president in 1997, Fallahian was dismissed from the Intelligence Ministry, yet those loyal to him retained the ring inside and outside the Intelligence Ministry.[13]

According to Robert Fisk, Akbar Ganji reportedly asked ex-president Rafsanjani's influential daughter Faezeh if her father knew of the suspected judicial executions. She told Ganji that her father had 'no control' over the Intelligence Ministry and 'no information' on the murders. Ganji recalled their conversation with a smile. 'I told her that if we accepted this argument, then Mr Rafsanjani would be Cardinal Richelieu,' he said. 'I said it was unacceptable that Hashemi Rafsanjani had no control over the Intelligence Ministry. I wrote in my paper that if Rafsanjani really had no control, then how did he once manage to fire one of Fallahian's deputies – in a case that involved Rafsanjani's family?'

'In those days,' Fisk wrote, 'when Rafsanjani was the darling of our Western leaders – we thought he was fighting off the radical clergy, not collaborating with them – all talk of his personal wealth was banished from the headlines. Not a single Western reporter bothered to dig into the story of his friends and relatives. How come his son Yasser worked in the procurement office of the National Iranian Oil Company? Or his nephew Ali was deputy minister of oil? Or his son Mehdi was employed in the main Iranian gas company? Was it true, they are now asking in Tehran, that Rafsanjani had large business interests in Germany, that his family had residence cards in the West?'[14]

NINE

Playing Chess with an Ape

Blossoming of a single flower does not mean that spring has come.
Persian proverb

The current generation should be given the right to choose their own structure of government and constitution. The nation must say 'No' to the totalitarians with its passive resistance.
Hashem Aghajari, 2004

We then spoke of the great beauty and importance of Democracy, and were at much trouble in impressing the Count with a due sense of the advantages we enjoyed in living where there was suffrage ad libitum, and no king ... He said that, a great while ago, there had occurred something of a very similar sort ... The thing ended ... in the most odious and insupportable despotism that was ever heard of upon the face of the Earth.
Edgar Allan Poe, *Some Words with a Mummy*

In the early months of 1997, the political and social atmosphere in Iran could hardly be described as lively, although there was a sense of tension in the air. President Rafsanjani was approaching the end of his second term, which had been a constant balancing act between ongoing criticism by the influential conservative clerics and the mounting international pressure, particularly after the Mykonos Affair, which had led to the recalling of the ambassadors of the European Union countries

– Iran's largest trade partner – from Tehran.

The conservatives were obviously on the offensive: having dominated the Majles by help from the Guardian Council that had disqualified most of the left-wing candidates – not to mention the legal opposition – from running in the elections, they were now confidently eyeing to conquer the executive branch by winning the presidential elections set for 23 June. Rafsanjani's supporters had earlier tried to persuade the supreme leader to order a review of the constitution so that Rafsanjani could run for a third consecutive term, reasoning that the reconstruction of the country could be fully achieved only if a figure of his calibre headed the government. Ayatollah Khamenei, however, explicitly ruled out such a move.

The fears of Rafsanjani's supporters of a total conservative hegemony, which would possibly turn back the clocks on them for eight years, coincided with the left wing's renewed hopes of a gradual comeback after undergoing a thorough soul-searching that had resulted in drastic changes in its approach and equipped it with a fresh outlook towards society.

Frustrated with Rafsanjani's policies as different left-wing outfits and figures were, their priority now was to forestall an overall conservative supremacy. This brought the two long-lasting rivals together in an unlikely coalition. Chiefly through the newspaper *Salam*, the left had intensified criticism of the conservatives, temporarily and silently announcing a truce with Rafsanjani and his 'modern right'. The major problem of the anti-conservative camp was the want of a viable candidate to run against parliament speaker Nateq-Nouri, who, confident of support from the supreme leader, the Guardian Council, and the bazaar, already considered himself the next president of the Islamic Republic. In a relaxed mood, in his interviews and lectures he even called on the opposition to bring in as many contenders as they could, to 'heat up the furnace of the elections' and invigorate the political atmosphere.

The Islamic left, as a matter of fact, was not optimistic to have any practical success in the elections: as the first step of its resurrection, it was only hoping to gather enough votes to prove to the conservatives that they were facing a real challenge. Mir Hossein Mousavi, the prime minister of the war years, was the only figure the left believed could make a promising shake-up of the status quo. However, after lengthy talks, Mousavi declined to stand as a candidate. This eventually proved to be beneficial to the different groups opposing the conservatives' domination.

Though frustrated with Rafsanjani's failure to stop the Hezbollahis, the Basij and the security forces from harassing people and interfering with their personal lives, for the general public the mention of Mousavi's name invoked memories of economic hardship, long queues for meat and rice, and even harsher social restrictions. Thus public opinion was by and large acting as an indifferent bystander again, watching the proliferating factional dispute as 'another game of theirs' or 'their quarrel for more power'. The picture, however, was changed by the advent of an unlikely latecomer to the contest.

While the propaganda of the right faction was running on full throttle, various political groups bracing up for a face-off with the conservatives finally came up with the name of their candidate: Muhammad Khatami, the former minister of culture and Islamic guidance, who, after resigning under pressure from the conservatives who criticised his cultural policies as 'corrupt' and 'Westernised', had gone into seclusion in the recesses of the National Library.

As soon as Khatami's picture appeared on posters and billboards – largely thanks to Karbaschi and his allies – there was a remarkable excitement, particularly among the young and women. Arguably, Khatami's personal charm as a mild-mannered, smiling, learned and curt clergyman played as much a role in his victory as his election campaign, which radically differed from that of other candidates in being centred around social and political reform. On the other hand, his revolutionary credentials made it almost impossible for the Guardian Council to disqualify him. Nevertheless, the artillery fire of conservative propaganda was quick in coming. Hard-line and traditionalist newspapers, namely *Kayhan* and *Resalat*, began a relentless campaign, reminding their readers of how the policies Khatami had implemented as the culture minister had served the West's cultural invasion.

Morteza Haji, the head of Khatami's election campaign in 1997, recalled in 2004: 'There were tendencies in society which could be easily realised through polls and everyday conversation with people. These you could not find in the speeches and platforms of other candidates. Respecting people, dialogue instead of fight, tolerance towards your opponent, rejecting violence ... were among his slogans, which were in the first place intrinsic of his character ... He was very reluctant in becoming a candidate, though.[1]

Conservative figures and media also opened a new front, saying that although all the four 'respectable' candidates had been okayed as 'competent' by the Guardian Council, it was a religious duty for the people to choose 'the most competent', and in doing so, to look at the religious leadership.

Apart from Khatami and Nateq-Nouri, a third presidential hopeful was former intelligence minister Muhammad Muhammadi Rayshahri, who now, under the banner of the Society for Defence of the Values, promised to stop the free fall of the rial against the dollar, and to provide facilities for easy marriage of young people.

The only non-cleric to run in the race was deputy head of judiciary Reza Zavarei, but there was no questioning about the main contenders.

With the evident growing support for Khatami among political groups unhappy with the right wing – but mostly among the youth – worries of losing the battle of words were creeping deeper into the ranks of the conservatives. Consequently, apart from Hezbollahi gangs disrupting pro-Khatami meetings in different provinces, the conservatives went so far as to quote Ayatollah Ali Mahdavi Kani – the chairman of the Society of Militant Clergy – as saying that he 'guessed the supreme leader would vote for Mr Nateq-Nouri'. All this, however, only helped strengthen Khatami's position and increase his popularity even more.

'It was evident that supporters of some of the other candidates would not be glad about [Khatami's] presence,' Haji said. 'There were other candidates who, confident of their victory, felt that a closer competition would give them more legitimacy,' he adds, in an obvious reference to Nateq-Nouri.[2]

By June 1997, Iran was a fire bowl. Young girls and boys practically ran Khatami's election campaign, getting people to go to Khatami's lectures and to invite sympathetic parliament members to speak in local mosques, distributing leaflets and putting up Khatami posters until late into the night. His election headquarters in different parts of towns were reminiscent of the headquarters of students supporting opposition groups in 1979 before they were banned and suppressed. They mostly worked in rented down-at-heel offices surrounded by pots of glue and ladders needed to paste up posters of their candidate on walls. The liaison officer of one such office told me: 'Khatami's appeal to the young people has created a shockwave in society. The young are brighter and more up to date and have more demands.' No one seemed to care about the calls by the exile opposition to boycott the elections as another 'trick of the regime'.

'Trying to impose a certain candidate on people [by the conservatives] played a key role in mobilising the youth,' Haji said. 'We conducted regular opinion polls, which gave us peace of mind. The day we started the campaign, most of our friends did not believe that Khatami would win the elections. But as days passed, his popularity soared.'

Khatami's campaign focused on political pluralism, freedom, and a 'civil society'. Summing up his platform, the young liaison officers said, 'Freedom of expression is the common point between Islam and liberalism ... What we are looking for is a religious government, not a governmental religion,' echoing the punchline of the religious intellectuals who had by now come to the conclusion that the Islamic Republic had so far failed to make people more religious.

On the same day, I visited a Nateq-Nouri campaign office in western Tehran, based in a modern gym complete with bench-presses, weights and cycle machines. Davood Asghari, the manager of the gym who doubled as the office's director, handed me his business card, which showed a picture of him bare-chested in a kung fu high-kick. He emphasised that Nateq-Nouri's devotion for the supreme leader and his experience in politics obviously made him the 'most competent candidate'. Asghari said that one of Nateq-Nouri's top priorities would be to re-establish ties with the United States, although this was never mentioned in his official platform.

As more social freedom for young people and women became a central issue of the campaign, together with problems of rampant inflation and unemployment, clouds of uncertainty gathered over the conservative camp: their confidence was wearing away by the observation of what was happening on the streets. There was another blow on the way though: a few days after *Salam*, almost the sole newspaper that supported Khatami, warned about possible vote-rigging in the upcoming elections, Rafsanjani echoed the same worry at the podium of Tehran's Friday prayers, and said that tampering with the votes would be an 'unforgivable crime'. This encouraged Khatami's supporters even more.

Two days before the elections, the headline of *Akhbar* daily newspaper shocked the readers: according to an official opinion poll by an obscure polling institute, Nateq-Nouri stood a 75 percent chance of becoming president. The details of the polling covered a whole page of the daily, complete with an interview with the institute's director, who was as unknown as the firm he said he headed. This was all the more astonishing for the fact that so far only *Akhbar*, considered to be a moderate, pro-Khatami paper, had printed the story. Later, one of the paper's editors told me that the story had come directly from the supreme leader's office, and that there was no choice but to print it. *Salam* retorted by printing an opinion poll of its own, saying it was Khatami who had a considerable edge over Nateq-Nouri.

Conservative papers' move to have Nateq-Nouri endorsed by a number of famous movie actors and sportsmen also backfired: the youth thought it was all a sham, as Khatami was already enjoying the almost unanimous backing of intellectuals, writers, filmmakers, actors and actresses, not to mention opposition groups such as the Freedom Movement. His campaigners, however, were careful not to alienate Ayatollah Khamenei, ignoring the support from opposition, and accentuating his loyalty to the Islamic Republic, and exploiting the fact that he was a Sayyed, someone believed to be a direct descendant of the Prophet Muhammad. For instance, one of his campaign posters featured separate pictures of Ayatollah Khomeini, Ayatollah Khamenei and Khatami himself, each shedding tears in Ashura ceremonies. The caption, in the typical fashion of rhyming and rythming Persian verse, read: 'Hail to three descendants of Fatemeh (the Prophet's daughter)/ Khomeini, Khamenei, Khatami'.

23 June – or 2nd of Khordad in the Iranian calendar – was a hot day, both literally and metaphorically. Later, in a derogatory tone, some conservative figures called it a 'political picnic'. Surely there was a picnic spirit in Tehran and large cities: whole families, mostly in their best clothes, swarmed the voting stations set up in mosques, schools, shops and even buses. The most striking fact was the overwhelming presence of youngsters and women. In a busy queue outside a voting station in

central Tehran, I asked a well-dressed man in his fifties whom he was going to vote for. 'Mr Khatami,' he said. 'You know, I'm a merchant, and until a few days ago I was sure I was going to vote for Mr Nateq-Nouri. But my daughter made me change my mind. You know, the future belongs to the youth, and they say Mr Khatami will make a decent president.'

Mina, his eighteen-year-old daughter, was wearing a light-blue coat, a white-and-blue scarf that showed her hair, and the latest-fashion sunshades. 'Khatami is such a loveable man. He is different from all the others. He understands the modern world and the needs of the youth,' she said.

Mina was not alone. Hundreds of thousands of youngsters encouraged, persuaded and even forced their parents and grandparents who would otherwise have stayed home to come out and vote for Khatami.

Most voters said Khatami was committed to solving the country's problems, although they were sceptical about how much room for manoeuvre Khamenei would give him.

Meanwhile, the state media was clutching at the last remaining straws, if there were any left, that is. The radio continuously repeated parts of a sermon by Ayatollah Khamenei, calling on the nation to vote for the candidate who was most loyal to Islam and Islamic values, who would be loyal to the blood of the martyrs and who would fight the 'world arrogance'. The head of the state radio and television, Ali Larijani, went on air in person, lambasting 'Westoxicated intellectuals', a thinly veiled reference to Khatami's liberal cultural policies when he was a minister.

If there were any doubts about the outcome – besides concerns about possible fraud – they were blown away by early afternoon the following day, when the radio announced that Nateq-Nouri had sent a message of congratulation to Khatami. As the news spread that Khatami had clinched a stunning landslide victory, Khatami's supporters showed cautious jubilation, giving out sweets on the streets. Khatami gathered nearly twenty million votes, representing about 77 percent of the turnout.

Many young people whom I interviewed on that day summarised the shock victory as a big 'no' to Ayatollah Khamenei and the conservatives who had used all their power to promote Khatami's rival. 'The important thing is that people have voted for someone who values civil liberties which were non-existent before,' said Morad, a 21-year-old university student. 'We don't really expect democracy, but there's hope that people can be more relaxed.'

A foreign journalist aptly wrote about Khatami's victory:

> The story of elections, as usually told in the press, is the story of the leaders who rise and fall by them ... . Muhammad Khatami, three-to-one victor in Iran's presidential election, is already being touted as the man who will lead his nation into an era of Persian perestroika. Khatami's election means both less and more than that. Less, because although a moderate who has articulated a vision of Islam as 'a gentle religion,' Khatami is unlikely to challenge the country's ruling clerics, who in addition to religious authority maintain control of crucial state industries. More, because ... the country has in fact been swept by profound cultural and political change in the past decade. True, public behaviour and women's dress remain subject to clerical rule. True, the fatwa against Salman Rushdie still holds. Yet alongside this oppressive structure Iran has evolved a cultural and intellectual life as varied and scrappy as any in the Middle East: art galleries draw long lines for controversial exhibits; bookstores are filled with novels by Islamic feminists and translations of Western writers ... In recent years Iranians have been leading two different lives, one officially designated and the other private and cultural.[3]

'Khatami's election,' he continued, 'reflects a widespread desire – particularly though not exclusively among women and the young – to bridge this gap ... In other words, Iran's future is very much a contested field, in spite of theocratic rigidity.'

There has been much debate over the meaning of Khatami's surprising victory, particularly after the reform movement epitomised by that victory came to a cul-de-sac under increasing pressure of the conservatives a few years later. Some observers, mostly among the subversive opposition abroad, believe that the whole episode was a 'show' directed by the regime itself to distract people from fundamental issues and divert the youth from the basic question of the nature of the

Islamic Republic in order to buy more time. Some go further and say that Rafsanjani and his technocrats were the actual writers of the show's screenplay.

Muhammad Mohsen Sazgara, one of those same intellectuals who later came to reject the possibility of reforms within the framework of the existing constitution, does not agree. In an interview in 2004, he said that like any political system facing an inefficiency crisis, the Islamic Republic decided to reform itself

> because with the developing of such crisis, a gap opens up between the state and the people, and only reforms can bridge that gap.
>
> In 1997, we came to the conclusion that the system would increase its efficiency if it moved towards democracy, a civil society, political development, promotion of civil liberties and returning to the international community. I don't think that Mr Rafsanjani shared such an idea.
>
> People conveyed a clear message to the state through elections; they said you [the state] can remain in power providing that you reform yourself. They voted for Khatami within the framework of the existing system, which means they agreed with his slogans of political and cultural reforms.[4]

Proponents of the theory that the reform movement was engineered by left-wing Islamist intellectuals, also to guarantee the survival of the religious state, stress the movement's elitist nature. In the words of Mahan Abedin,

> The reform movement in Iran is less an outgrowth of popular disenchantment than a reconfiguration of factional politics in the Islamic Republic. While most informed observers are well aware that the most prominent leaders of reform in Iran are products of the Islamic system, it is generally overlooked that most hail from its most sensitive and secret branches – the security and intelligence community. This reformist elite has forged its overall strategy outside the realm of public scrutiny and is not directly influenced by the disenchanted masses.[5]

Many conservative strategists recognize the service rendered to the Islamic Republic by the reformist elite in channelling the public's disenchantment away from radical solutions to an evolutionary activism that operates within the confines of the Islamic Republic's constitution. As a result, fears that the rightwing backlash currently underway will morph into an assault on the reformist movement as a whole are exaggerated.[6]

There are other analysts who maintain that the voters did not have any idea of Khatami, and that their vote was just a negation of the past policies. In the words of Dariush Sajjadi,

> The Iranian peoples' demands over the past 200 years have alternated between security and freedom. But due to the absence of a genuine mission among the governments and non-existence of political parties, the peoples' choices have been unconsciously eliminative.
>
> The same feature prompted 98 percent of the Iranians to vote for the Islamic Republic on 1 April 1979 without having the slightest knowledge about such a government system and relying solely on their repulsion with a regime whose unfavourable strategies they had been exposed to for a quarter century.
>
> Actually, the overwhelming vote for the Islamic Republic stemmed from the peoples' aversion toward the Pahlavi regime. The votes cast in favour of the Islamic Republic were, in fact, a negation of the Pahlavi rule, as most of those who voted for the Islamic Republic did not have the slightest awareness of this system's legal and political shape and policies.
>
> The same mechanism was at work during the 23 May 1997 presidential elections when urban and rural masses turned out in millions to cast protest votes against policies that had dominated Iran for two decades following the revolution.
>
> As such, the votes cast in favour of Khatami carried a blunt message: they were a bold negation of the former policies, as the people had no idea whatsoever about the civil community which Khatami championed. The 20 million votes for Khatami thus served as the peoples' way to negate Iran's dominant social

and political policies rather than as their approval of – and submission to – Khatami's electoral promises.[7]

There are yet other observers who view the whole reform movement as a function of globalisation, an impact of the modern media – including the video, satellite television and the internet – on a young population grown up under and alienated by constant bombardment of ideological values. Nima Rashedan, an analyst and journalist who was himself previously an unequivocal supporter of Khatami and his allies, said:

> There is one undeniable trend in all the recent elections: wherever there is the video recorder, satellite television, and a tendency towards American and Western behaviour and fashion, there is also extraordinary turnout in favour of reforms. This is a fact we have neglected
>
> For a long time, we thought that the reform movement was born out of a democratic discourse; that it was an extension of the discourse of the Constitutional Revolution. But 80 percent of all such analyses were wrong: twenty million young boys and girls voted for reforms because of the impact of globalisation and the Western culture. Just like in other countries, they demand absolute freedom.[8]

This latter view was implicitly expressed in some of the inner circles of the conservatives and hardliners. A conservative journalist was reported as having said that '20 million punks voted for Khatami'. Later, member of Guardian Council Ayatollah Abolqassem Khazali said, 'If you do not believe in Velayat-e Faqih, not only twenty million, but even thirty million votes are worthless unless approved by the supreme leader.' Such remarks, however, were seldom made publicly, as even Supreme Leader Ayatollah Khamenei called the elections an 'epic' that one more time proved 'people's support for Islam and the system and gave the enemies a hard smack in the jaw'. Until much later, even the most daring reformists avoided stepping into the minefield of admitting that many voters may have meant to say 'no' to the entire system. In May 2004, reflecting on the reformists' early appeal among the young people, Ali Shakuri Rad, a leading member of the Islamic Iran Participation Front, said, 'We noticed that 80 percent of the youth followed their nature [fetrat]; 10 percent had virtues [fazilat] and 10 percent vices [razilat]. The key to our success was that we opened up to that 80 percent; we accepted them as they were.'[9]

Whatever the reasons, there was no denying that Khatami rode to victory on the waves of support from youth and women. There was no question either that no matter how brave a face the conservatives put on, the shock was nearly lethal. In a prompt reaction the day after Khatami's victory, Hossein Allahkaram, a leader of the Ansar-e Hezbollah, said: 'Nothing has changed.' Six years on, he may have proved to be right, but in the immediate months after Khatami's election, a lot changed.

For the first couple of months after Khatami's victory, the conservatives were in a state of shock, or as the reformists later said, 'in a coma'. However, they gradually came round. After all, they still controlled all the key levers of power. Not only did the president have no control over the Judiciary, the Guardian Council, the armed forces or even the radio and television, but neither had he a free hand in choosing all his cabinet members. The intelligence minister in particular could not be named without the supreme leader's consent. Besides, Khatami could well remember the fate of Bani Sadr, who had also come to power with the overwhelming vote of the public, only to be ousted and to escape to exile. Khatami did not want to scare or estrange the conservatives. And in the view of many of his critics, that very point turned out to be his Achilles' heel.

The summer of 1997 was overshadowed by the introduction of the new cabinet. Khatami's final list was clearly a compromise, and a disappointment to many reformists, as it included a conservative Majles deputy nominated for the post of intelligence minister, as well as several Rafsanjani allies as vice-presidents. After all, the Majles could easily reject his entire list. Appearing before the conservative dominated parliament, Khatami said his candidates were the 'most suitable of the suitables.'

Interest in that first crucial test for Khatami was intense: many shops in Tehran were shut and people stayed at home to watch two days of parliamentary debate broadcast live on state television. 'The most important principle is to create a lawful society in which the people can participate,' he told the Majles.

Two of Khatami's appointments came under particular fire from the majority faction of the Majles – Ataollah Mohajerani, tapped as culture minister, and Abdollah Nouri, as interior minister. But in the end, Khatami's opponents could not muster the votes to stop either nomination. Mohajerani's eloquence and articulation was the highlight of the session. In a speech to the Majles, Mohajerani said he wanted to reform the Culture Ministry and said more personal freedoms could be granted to Iranian citizens within the framework of Islam.

'We have to create an atmosphere where all citizens can express their ideas,' he said. 'Islam is not a narrow dark alley. Everybody can walk freely in the path of Islam.' He also called for more tolerance, saying he condemned 'the burning of book shops, the beating of university lecturers and attacks on magazine offices,' references to actions by hard-line groups against liberal and dissident intellectuals.

The main argument put forward by Khatami supporters was that it would be politically unwise for the Majles to thwart the reform mandate given to the new president, who was swept into office over his conservative challengers with 70 percent of the popular vote.

'We will continue our programme step by step,' said Khatami after the vote. 'We thank the Majles for its vote of confidence and look forward to close cooperation between the executive and the legislative powers.'

Reformists were generally pleased with the outcome: the 'reform cabinet' was finally on track, pressure from hardliners seemed to have somewhat eased off, and dozens of new publications were promoting concepts such as civil society and rule of law, taking to task more and more subjects hitherto considered taboo.

But a huge taboo was broken, albeit momentarily, on 28 November. Football-loving Iranians had been nervously glued to their radios and televisions for more than a month. What caused the excitement was the national squad's struggle to find a place in the 1998 World Cup in France. Iran's chances were hanging by a thread: the last play-off match to determine the last team from the Asia-Pacific region to make it to the World Cup was played between Iran and Australia, the latter admittedly being the more powerful side (the best Iran could achieve against it in Tehran a week earlier, was a 1–1 draw).

Last rays of hope were fading away as the soccerooes scored twice in the first half-time in Melbourne. However, in the last moments – perhaps analogous to Khatami's victory – Iran turned the tables and scored two goals, securing a place in the World Cup after twenty years. Within minutes, jubilant fans were ruling the streets, cheering, singing, dancing and defying all the rules and restrictions set by the religious states. The Christian Science Monitor correspondent reported that 'young and old alike poured onto the streets to wave Iranian flags, block traffic, and climb atop cars.' The soccer jubilation brought a brief but unstoppable disregard of tough Islamic restrictions on public behaviour – restrictions that are often flouted in private. Men and women openly danced in the streets, and some women removed their mandatory headscarves and let their hair down. 'If I was a conservative cleric, I'd be quaking in my shoes, because the security forces lost control of [the capital] Tehran for five hours,' said a senior Western diplomat.

On a busy junction in central Tehran, clogged by hundreds of honking cars waving their windscreen wipers and thousands of cheering people, young girls and boys were dancing on the car roofs, and on the sidewalk, several young men had surrounded a clergyman, clapping and inviting him to join in their dance. Police and security forces were totally taken aback.

> Even Iran's top Islamic rulers had shared in the victory with profuse praise ... Even in Qom – the centre of Islamic learning south of Tehran, and among the most conservative cities in Iran – security forces were nervous as rowdy celebrants banged buckets and pots in place of drums to make 'music.' Since the Islamic Revolution of 1979, nothing but the most traditional music has been allowed in Iran. Also since then, Iranians say there has never been such a display of people power on the streets. 'It was a revolution,' said one Iranian man, mindful of the special meaning of the word here. The raucous street scenes have coincided, however, with the dispute over the role of Velayat-e-faqih, which began to emerge last month. It underscores a growing rift between hard-line conservatives – led by Ayatollah Ali Khamenei, Iran's spiritual guide who is meant to represent the will of God – and moderates such as the recently elected President Mohamed Khatami.[10]

Ali Rabii, then a senior intelligence official, later said that the jubilations of football fans on 28 December 1998 indicated a common pattern throughout the country, which signified a drastic break between the demands of the 'second generation of the Revolution' with their predecessors. Not all the officials of the Islamic Republic were open to receive the signal transmitted by millions of people who apparently were just football fans. No political event after the Islamic Revolution had ever dragged so many people onto the public arena. It was, in the words of a political analyst, 'a referendum by joy'. The signs were out there for all to see.

Against all odds, Khatami now moved to play his foreign policy card. As promoted during his election campaign, he sought to diffuse tension with the outside world, end Iran's isolation, and replace the classical confrontational approach of the Islamic Republic with a 'dialogue between civilisations'. Earlier the European Union countries had sent back their ambassadors to Iran in a bid to demonstrate support for Khatami's moderate policies. Now it was a time to melt the ice with the archenemy, the United States. This, however, was a political minefield, as Ayatollah Khamenei had previously silenced any voice raised in support of a dialogue with the Great Satan. Khatami's approach, therefore, was extremely cautious and decidedly ambivalent.

In an interview with CNN's Christiane Amanpour, Khatami said that Iran and the United States should create a 'crack in the wall of mistrust' by exchanging writers, scholars, artists and thinkers. Although Khatami said that all doors should now be open for such dialogue and understanding and the possibility for contact between Iranian and American citizens, in order not to anger the supreme leader who might entirely quash the initiative in a single strike, he repeated the old formula that Iran felt 'no need for ties with the United States.'

In his interview, Khatami criticised the US government for a catalogue of cases where America's foreign policy had caused Iranians to feel 'humiliated and oppressed.' Most notable were the 1953 coup d'etat that toppled Mosaddeq's government, the shooting down of an Iranian airliner in 1988 with 290 people aboard by the USS Vincennes in the closing stages of the Iran-Iraq war, and the allocation of 20 million dollars by the US Congress to, in his words, 'overthrow' the Iranian government.

Khatami several times praised 'the great American people' and made it a point to separate them from American foreign policy, which he called a 'flawed policy of domination'.

'The feelings of our people were seriously hurt by US policies. And as you said, in the heat of the revolutionary fervour, things happen which cannot be fully contained or judged according to usual norms,' Khatami said. 'This was the crying out of the people against humiliations and inequities imposed upon them by the policies of the US and others, particularly in the early days of the revolution. With the grace of God, today our new society has been institutionalised and we have a popularly elected powerful government, and there is no need for unconventional methods of expression of concerns and anxieties. And I believe when there is logic, especially when there are receptive ears, there is no need other than discourse, debate and dialogue.'

Perhaps the highlight of his interview was the moment when Khatami said that he was sorry about the grievances caused by the storming of the US embassy in Tehran in 1979, although he added that events should be analysed within their proper context and with circumspection.

Khatami's overture was played down by American officials chiefly because he stopped short of supporting government-to-government talks. Inside Iran, although no opinion poll was conducted, his remarks made a hugely positive impact among the majority of people fed up with two decades of isolation marked by anti-American propaganda, judging by the comments made in reformist newspapers that now sold more than a million copies. The youth were particularly impressed, and hoped that things were more or less moving in the right direction.

Nevertheless, the hardliners immediately opened fire. Conservative clerics in the Majles and from Friday prayer podiums rejected any thaw with the Great Satan, reminding their audiences of the bitter remarks made about America by Ayatollah Khomeini and his successors. One hard-line newspaper printed a full list of 'errors' Khatami had committed in his interview, a list that included Amanpour's not observing proper Hejab, and extending to Khatami's 'silence about the massacre of Indian natives by American immigrants' some 300 years before.

Although direct talks between the two arch-foes seemed a far-fetched idea, Khatami's notion of dialogue between peoples found material reality very soon. In February 1998, the US national freestyle wrestling squad arrived in Tehran on an official invitation by Iran's wrestling federation to take part in the international Takhti Cup tournament.

This was the first such visit since 1979, and immediately drew analogies with the 'ping pong diplomacy' of the early 1970s when, as one of the first public hints of improved US-China relations, when the American Ping-Pong team, in Japan for the 31st World Table Tennis Championship in 1971, received a surprise invitation from their Chinese colleagues for an all-expense paid visit to the People's Republic. *Time* magazine called it 'The ping heard round the world.' On 10 April , nine players, four officials, and two spouses stepped across a bridge from Hong Kong to the Chinese mainland, ushering in an era of 'Ping-Pong diplomacy.' They were the first group of Americans allowed into China since the Communist takeover in 1949.

If sports were ever a scale to gauge socio-political trends, many lessons could have been learned from sports events in Iran. Just as the celebrations after the victory of Iran's football team against Australia were indicative of major tendencies in relation to domestic politics, the visit by the American wrestling squad was a prism reflecting how many Iranians, particularly young generations, felt about what they had been taught to be their number-one enemy.

For the first time in twenty years, the Stars and Stripes appeared not in a flag-burning rally outside the former 'den of spies', but hanging from the ceiling of Tehran's 12,000-seat Azadi sports hall. 'We had been told by Iranian friends that wrestling would be a good way to launch non-official exchanges between Iran and the US,' said John Marks, president of Search for Common Ground, an organisation that helped to arrange US participation in the tournament. The American team was met at Tehran airport by 200 reporters.

The five American athletes and their coaches received an unprecedented warm welcome by the spectators, second only to that shown to Iran's national team. Larry Sciacchetano, president of the governing body of US wrestling said, 'Everything has been really tremendous. The Iranians have been great hosts – I'm really happy we came and it is.' American wrestlers were cheered by the enthusiastic crowd even when they lost.

There were 13,000 cheering fans, all male and mostly young, in the Azadi arena at the finals. When former Olympic champion, Kevin

Jackson, hugged his Iranian opponent after winning his match, and patted him on the back of the head, the crowd burst into a deafening cheer, shouting 'Jackson, we love you' and showering him with thousands of small paper flags.

The climax of the evening was the final clash between 215-pound World Champion rivals, Melvin Douglas and Abbas Jadidi, a long-anticipated event. At the end of their match, winner Jadidi and his American rival embraced while still on their knees, and walked off the mat with arms around each other, amid thundering cheers as well as teardrops. And when US wrestler, Larry 'Zeke' Jones raised a small Iranian flag over his head from his corner of the arena at the end of his event, the crown went mad.

'Their interest in Americans,' said Marks, 'mirrored what we experienced elsewhere in Tehran: namely, that Iranians seemed overwhelmingly pro-American. Obviously, hard-line radicals, who are jockeying for power with more moderate elements, do not share such sentiments.'[11]

The finals, however, was marked by a couple of minor, but extremely meaningful incidents that went unmarked in the media. First, while the semi-final matches were in process, the announcer of the arena, in a typical resonating tone to excite the spectators and create suspense among them, said on the loudspeakers, 'In a few minutes, one of the most favourite officials of the Islamic Republic will appear in the hall.' In no time, the crowd was chanting 'Khatami, Khatami', only to see Nateq-Nouri enter the Special Pavilion after a few minutes. Upon his arrival, a chilling silence immediately fell over the arena. The conservative cleric managed to keep his smile unscathed and even wave a hand for a silent crowd.

The second incident involved an individual sitting among the crowd. While the wrestlers were busy at work down on the mats, the crowd started pointing fingers at a certain spot, and in a few seconds nearly everyone was chanting, 'Fardin, we love you! Fardin, we love you!' I looked in that direction, and finally recognised among the crowd Ali Fardin, a former wrestling champion, but renowned as a hugely popular cinema actor before the Revolution. Fardin, already in his middle age by then, had been banned from acting in movies after the Revolution because he was considered a symbol of the shah-era corruption in the eyes of the new regime's cultural officials. In most of his movies, he had epitomised what the Revolution had despised: a carefree, frivolous, singing and drinking kind of guy who was content with being poor but having fun.

The fact that a typical relic of the 'bad old times' was receiving such a wholehearted tribute from a crowd raised by revolutionary dogmas was not as interesting and astonishing for me as *who* was paying the tribute. Wrestling being the most popular sport after football in Iran, the 13,000 people who had filled the arena represented a roughly even, random sample of the Iranian society, coming from all walks of life and every sector of the society. They were mostly under the age of twenty-five, which meant they had hardly any living memories of the days when monarchy reigned, let alone of the black-and-white films of the 1960s and early 1970s in which Fardin had starred. The only possible answer to the dilemma was that pre-Revolution memories, habits, norms and culture had kept on living, albeit in hiding, and mostly on videotapes. They had been passed on to the young generation by parents and older relatives.

Enthusiastic cheers for the former B-movie star, set in stark contrast to the deadly silence that had greeted Nateq-Nouri – who was watching the whole episode from his pavilion – was enough for the officials of the arena to politely see off Fardin to the exit, but not before he bowed to a rapturous crowd. A couple of years later, thousands of people, old and young alike, took part in Fardin's funeral.

As early as 1998, it was clear that there was a dual government ruling Iran. With his typical tact and considerateness, Khatami reminded his rivals of the votes behind him: 'I do not consider this a serious conflict. Of course, there are various tendencies, which were present during the elections as well. The people have made their decision.'

'The rule of law should be paramount, and no one should consider himself above the law and try to impose his views on others. Some of these frictions are quite natural in a democratic society. Our objective is to bring everything within the framework of the law. There may be occasional irregularities and actions outside the legal framework. But we will spare no effort to institutionalise the rule of law,' Khatami said. But in a short while, his powerful opponents would utilize law as a weapon against Khatami and his allies.

Unlike the Prague Spring in 1968, which was abruptly quashed by

Warsaw Pact forces led by the Soviet Union, the conservatives' move to undermine Khatami's government came in successive stages. Since 'rule of law' ranked high in Khatami's mandate, his powerful opponents chose to beat him at his own game, choosing the law as the most efficient weapon in fighting him. They had an open hand in utilising the judicial system for their objective, for the head of judiciary is appointed by the supreme leader and is practically accountable to no one.

While the Ansar-e Hezbollah mobs were mobilized again to disrupt reformist and dissident gatherings, the hard-line judiciary targetted a key Khatami ally: Tehran mayor Gholamhossein Karbaschi, who had played a crucial role in his victory. Two months before Karbaschi was personally indicted, the counter-intelligence department of the police, led by hard-line General Alireza Naqdi, raided the offices of Tehran's district mayors, making arrests and confiscating documents. Naqdi was later tried for abuse of power, torture, misleading officials, illegal imprisonment of prisoners in secret places and spreading wrong information.

Under Naqdi's instructions, Karbaschi's close aids were put in solitary confinement and came out with 'confessions' to crimes ranging from corruption to un-Islamic conduct. Finally, the judiciary arrested Karbaschi in April 1998. His arrest sparked sporadic student protests throughout the capital and a furious reaction by Khatami's cabinet. But the judiciary showed no sign of faltering in taking him to task. His trial, broadcast live on the state radio and replayed by the television, transfixed the nation as the two sides – Karbaschi as the defendant and Judge Gholamhossein Mohseni Ejei who doubled as prosecutor as well as plaintiff – bombarded each other with unheard-of accusations.

During the hearings, Karbaschi repeatedly denied any wrongdoing, alleging that the case was based on evidence collected through torture of witnesses and other heavy-handed methods. Ejei rejected his claims, stressing that the judiciary was resolute to root out corruption anywhere it might exist. Finally, the judge said he had found Karbaschi guilty of embezzlement and sentenced him to five years in jail, banned him from holding public office for twenty years and gave him sixty lashes. The court suspended the flogging because of 'his social standing'. He was also fined 333,333 dollars. Karbaschi's conviction was a reassurance to the conservatives: that the arrest and imprisonment of reformists was a successful means in destroying Khatami's proposed reforms.

After Karbaschi, it was Interior Minister Abdollah Nouri's turn. First, the conservative-dominated parliament impeached and ousted Nouri in July 1998, after which Khatami appointed him to the spontaneously introduced post of vice-president for political development affairs. Having left the ministry, Nouri concentrated his energies on publishing the daily newspaper *Khordad*. But that was not the end of Nouri's story.

October 1998 saw the elections for the Assembly of Experts, the first election to follow Khatami's upset win in the 1997 presidential race. The assembly, which meets for one week every year, consists of 86 clerics that the public elects to eight-year terms. Its members, in turn, elect the supreme leader from within their own ranks and periodically reconfirm him. As the candidates for the Assembly are screened by the Guardian Council – whose members are appointed by the supreme leader – it is no wonder that it has never been known to challenge any of the supreme leader's decisions.

The Guardian Council once again cut down the list of candidates for the Assembly election. Of the 396 candidates, fewer than 150 made the final cut; none of the women or non-clerical candidates was approved. The supreme leader's younger brother, reformist cleric Hadi Khamenei, was among the disqualified candidates, as were several other pro-reform clergymen. Only half of the eligible voters showed up at the polls in October 1998, an unimpressive turnout by Iranian standards. Predictably, the conservative establishment won a majority of the seats on the assembly.

The reformists had never really any hopes of having a say in the ultra-conservative Assembly. However, their optimism remained intact as they pinned great hopes on the upcoming municipal elections scheduled for March 1999. However, in November something happened that rocked the Islamic Republic almost to its foundations: disclosure of the serial killings of dissidents and intellectuals.

First came the news that Dariush Forouhar and his wife Parvaneh had been stabbed to death at their residence in November in a manner that led many human-rights observers to believe that the couple were murdered for their political beliefs. The Forouhars were under continual monitoring by state security officials. Dariush Forouhar had been active in Iran's pre-Revolutionary National Front movement, and had served as labour minister in an early post-Revolution government. However, since that time, as the leader of the small Iranian Nation Party, he had spoken out frequently against the abuse of power of the revolutionary government, in particular with respect to human-rights abuses. Ayatollah Khamenei, President Khatami, and other senior officials condemned the murders.

A few days later, the body of writer and translator Majid Sharif, whose published political views included advocacy for the separation of state and religion, was discovered in a Tehran morgue several days after his mysterious disappearance.

Muhammad Jafar Pouyandeh, a translator and writer, disappeared on 9 December while on his way to a meeting of publishers at 2.00 pm in midtown Tehran. His body was found on 13 December. The family was contacted by the police who informed them that his body had been found in Shar-e Ray, a southern suburb of Tehran, and had been moved to a Tehran city morgue. According to the family, Pouyandeh was apparently strangled although no autopsy has yet been carried out.

The body of Muhammad Mokhtari, a writer and poet, was also found in a Tehran city morgue on 9 December. He was last seen alive on 3 December, going to a local shop. Marks on his head and neck made it appear that he had been murdered, possibly by strangulation. Pouyandeh and Mokhtari, with four other prominent writers, had been summoned by the authorities in October 1998 in connection with their attempt to establish an independent writers association. Sharif, Mokhtari and Pouyandeh were among 134 signatories of the 1994 Declaration of Iranian Writers; several signatories had been targets of regime harassment and violence since the release of the declaration.

Earlier, in September, Pirooz Davani, a former political prisoner and an independent Marxist publisher and critic of the Government, disappeared. Amnesty International said it received unconfirmed reports that Davani's mother was contacted by unnamed persons who told her that her son was killed. The spree of killings created a wave of fear and uncertainty among people in general and in intellectual circles in particular.

Popular reaction to these deaths was strong and immediate. Thousands of mourners marched in the funeral procession for Dariush and Parvaneh Forouhar in Tehran on 30 November. Different branches of the government, including the judiciary and the National Security Council (NSC), the latter headed by President Khatami, announced that enquiries would be established into the killings and the perpetrators brought to justice. Ayatollah Khamenei and President Khatami issued explicit orders that the case be investigated seriously. Khatami described the killings as 'disgusting acts' perpetrated with an aim of questioning the Islamic system.

Later, the supreme leader, in his Friday prayer sermon, expressed shock at the murders while downplaying the victims' political significance as dissidents. He pointed his finger at 'foreign conspiracies', urging the authorities to unveil the plot behind the crimes. Echoing Khamenei's remarks, the judiciary spoke of mysterious 'domestic and external hands' being behind the murders. Although it was widely believed that extremist elements within the system had committed the killings, the general expectation was that, in the case of Kazem Sami, a scapegoat would be found, probably a convict already sentenced to death. The turn of events' however, was different.[12]

Khatami assigned a three-member committee to investigate the case. The names of the committee members were not disclosed at that time for 'security reasons'. After conducting thorough investigations into the case, the committee reported the outcome of its probe to the Iranian officials concerned. On 6 January 1999 an extraordinary event happened which was unprecedented in Iran's history: State radio and television cited a terse statement by the Intelligence Ministry, in which a number of 'deviated, evil minded and rogue' members of that ministry were held responsible for the murders. The statement said that those elements had 'undoubtedly been deceived by aliens to serve their interests, in perpetrating such criminal acts ...'

Hardly ever before had any government body, let alone the secret service, come out criticising itself. Now, Iran's most dreaded security apparatus that had hitherto felt free to do whatever it had willed, was in broad daylight admitting to heinous crimes, albeit by 'rogue elements'. This was arguably Khatami's greatest ever accomplishment.

In the aftermath of the Intelligence Ministry statement, pressure was mounting on Intelligence Minister Qorbanali Dorri Najafabadi to resign or be dismissed. After much resistance, Khatami forced him to resign, promising that a drastic revamping of the ministry would entail.

The indications, however, pointed that the murderous 'circle' was alive and kicking.

In December, a statement was issued in Tehran by a group calling itself 'Mostafa Navvab's Devotees of Pure Muhammadian Islam'. The statement said in part:

> Now that domestic politicians, through negligence and leniency, and under the slogan of rule of law, support the masked poisonous vipers of the aliens, and brand the decisive approaches of the Islamic system ... as extremist and a threat to freedom, the brave and zealous children of the Iranian Muslim nation took action and by revolutionary execution of dirty and mercenary elements who were behind nationalistic movements and other poisonous moves in universities, took the second practical step in defending the great achievements of the Islamic Revolution ... The revolutionary execution of Dariush Forouhar, Parvaneh Eskandari, Muhammad Mokhtari and Muhammad Jafar Pouyandeh is a warning to all mercenary writers and their counter-value supporters who are cherishing the idea of spreading corruption and promiscuity in the country and bringing back foreign domination over Iran ...

This was the first time that anyone had claimed responsibility for the murders that all the state's top leadership had condemned. Such a group, however, was not known to have existed. About a month later, a number of the Intelligence Ministry agents were arrested, but their names were not disclosed due to 'security reasons'.

Meanwhile the second statement of Mostafa Navvab's Devotees of Pure Muhammadian Islam was issued. It claimed that the group had 'a well organised structure, following certain regulations in their missions.' The group, it said, 'through relentless efforts, has opened a file for each and every mercenary and hypocrite person taking advantage of the cultural atmosphere, regarding it as a safe haven to launch their endless attack on the principles of the system. In its recent operation, the judicial unit of the group consisting of three experienced and fair judges tried in absentia and condemned to death this group of people ... We believe that had these trials taken place in normal courts of law free from any political pressures, the results would have been the same, and all we did was to accelerate the procedure ...' The statement also claimed that preparations had been made to execute Salman Rushdie.

While total silence covered the case of the detained Intelligence Ministry agents, Ruhollah Hosseinian, a former Islamic judge in that ministry, took part in interviews with the hard-line *Kayhan* newspaper and the state television on the same day. In the television programme *Cheragh* ('Lamp') that was broadcast live, he termed the victims as *mortad* ('apostate') and *nasebi* ('those who had insulted the Prophet or the Shi'i imams'). Since by the law of Sharia, such offences were punishable by death, the obvious implication was that the victims had deserved to be killed. As for perpetrators, Hosseinian said that they were 'among religious left-wing forces and supporters of the president.' His remarks infuriated the reformists, who lashed out at Hosseinian. Ganji wrote that the former judge's claims were just a smoke screen to cover Fallahian from accounting for what had been going on in the Intelligence Ministry under his command.[13]

Shortly afterwards, the Judicial Organisation of the armed forces, which had the case in hand, announced that Mostafa Navvab's Devotees of Pure Muhammadian Islam was an imaginary group that had never existed. It also called on the press to remain silent for a while to let the investigations proceed under a calm atmosphere. On 20 June 1999 head of the organisation Muhammad Niazi disclosed the names of four detainees involved in the serial murders' case: Saeed Emami, a former deputy intelligence minister, Mostafa Kazemi, Mehrdad Alikhani and Khosrow Barati (all high-ranking ministry officials). But the really shocking news was that, according to Niazi, Emami – known also by the cover-name of Eslami – had died in prison. Niazi said that Emami, whom he introduced as the mastermind behind the killings, had attempted to commit suicide by drinking hair-removing lotion in the jail shower. He had immediately been taken to undergo treatment. However, he died of cardiac arrest and respiratory problems.

Just like so many officials of the clerical system, Saeed Emami was a child of the Islamic Revolution. Born in the town of Abadeh, near Shiraz in southern Iran, he was forty-one years old when he died. According to the English language daily *Tehran Times*, Emami was of Jewish origin. In 1978, at the age of nineteen, he went to the United

States with help from his uncle Soltan Muhammad Etemad, who was the military attaché at the Iranian embassy in Washington. After completing his higher education at an American university, he worked at the Iranian interest section in the United States for one year and at Iran's mission to the United Nations for another year. At that time he was recruited by security agents and after his return to Iran he went directly to the Intelligence Ministry. When Muhammad Rayshahri was minister, Saeed Hajjarian, then a director general of the Ministry, had opposed Emami's appointment at key posts on the grounds of his family records. In 1989, however, when Fallahian replaced Rayshahri, Emami immediately appointed Emami as his deputy for security affairs.

After Emami's death was made public, his family held a memorial service for him in a Tehran mosque. The memorial was attended by some 400 people, some of them from security and other state organisations. During the ceremony Hosseinian spoke highly of Emami, called him a 'martyr' and claimed that he had been murdered. In a speech some time later, Hosseinian praised Emami as someone who 'firmly believed that all those opposing the [Islamic Republic] system should be treated to swords,' and that 'he had vast experience in this field.'

Following Emami's death, reformist newspapers disclosed some of the acts committed by him or at his orders before his arrest. It turned out that he had planned the production of a video film to defame Khatami a short while before his election. He had also co-produced a series of televised programmes called *Hoviyyat* ('Identity') in which the notion of 'cultural invasion' was put forward and dissident intellectuals were introduced as the domestic agents of such invasion. The programme included footage of recorded 'confessions' by a number of detained intellectuals and political activists. In 1996, his agents had tried to throw a bus carrying a number of writers and intellectuals into a precipice. The intellectuals and writers had been invited to Yerevan by the Armenian Pen Association for lectures and recitals. The bus driver was Khosrow Barati, who had jumped out at a sharp bend, but one of the passengers managed to control the bus.

Akbar Ganji said that the activities of Saeed Emami and his circle had a much wider scope. In an interview with *Arya* daily, Ganji said that besides plotting the execution of the serial murders, in the past the circle used to receive transit fees from convoys of drug traffickers. But

Ganji's point that stirred a political storm and, as many believe, cost him a jail sentence, was that Emami and other detainees of the Intelligence Ministry were only cogs in a large machine of terror and repression. He termed the circle 'the dungeon of the ghosts', which was composed of different departments, including a judicial committee that issued the fatwas necessary to 'execute' the victims. He explicitly pointed a finger at Fallahian, calling him the 'Grey Eminence'. Fallahian never replied to the charges, and only said that if he was supposed to account for what had happened during his tenure as the intelligence minister, he should be accompanied by his chief, i.e. former President Rafsanjani.[14]

Besides Ganji, journalist Emadeddin Baqi was also persistently following the case of murders and mysterious deaths, a venture that cost him a year in jail. In one of his articles, he quoted an associate of Emami as saying that he had witnessed how Emami had murdered dissident writer Saeedi Sirjani while in detention in a ministry safe house. According to this source, Emami had inserted a potassium suppository into the rectum of Saeedi Sirjani, causing an immediate heart attack followed by death. The revelation gave rise to the speculation that many intellectuals and dissidents who had apparently died of 'heart attacks' over the past decade may in fact have been killed by the same method.

A court trying the remaining defendants of the serial murders' case in 2002 sentenced Kazemi, as the murderer, to life imprisonment, a decision that prompted objections from the relatives of the victims, who said they did not seek vengeance but wanted the whole truth to be unveiled. A short while later, Nasser Zarafshan, an outspoken lawyer of the relatives, was tried and sentenced to five years for 'disclosing secret documents' as well as 'keeping liquor in his office'.

In 2004, Hossein Ansari Rad, a reformist Majles deputy who headed the parliamentary commission that investigated the serial killings, summed up the picture in a meaningful way. 'For certain reasons', he said, 'we could not follow the case of the serial killings beyond a certain point.'

As part of its agenda of 'political development', Khatami's government moved quickly to hold nationwide elections for city and village councils, predicted by the constitution but never held after 1979. Reformists had high hopes on those elections as a key element of the democratisation project, in a bid that aimed at decentralising power and paving the way for grassroots movements, particularly because the Guardian Council was not authorised to screen the candidates for those elections.

Deputy interior minister Mostafa Tajzadeh said: 'The elections are a vehicle for transferring power from the Revolution's old generation to the new one.'

The eligibility of the candidates was checked, chiefly on the basis of criminal records, by the Interior Ministry. As a result, more than 334,000 individuals, including 5,000 women, registered as candidates to run for office. For the first time in nearly two decades, there were a large number of hopefuls, without any revolutionary credentials, from television actors to engineers to businessmen. Of particular interest was the fact that posters of some of the candidates featured their picture wearing neckties, a long-time symbol of 'Western corruption' and un-Islamicness. In perhaps the freest elections after 1979, the sifting mechanism had failed to separate expertise from commitment.

In the eyes of politicians and pundits, this appeared to be an insignificant development amid the political uproar and fierce rivalry surrounding the municipal elections. However, it contained a clear message to the rulers, accentuating the failure of the Islamic system to institutionalise its norms. For, the slogan of priority of 'commitment to Islam, the Revolution and Velayat-e faqih' over 'expertise' was one of the main dogmas, introduced by early revolutionaries, notably former president Muhammad Ali Rajaei. In the words of Dariush Sajjadi, this attitude exposed Iran's administrative system to group collectivism based on affinity, submission, and religious formalism. 'Only those close to the power poles could enter the system, while only those fully submissive to the power poles could remain in the system, features which led to the prevalence of ignobility, meanness, and short-sightedness in Iran's executive system.'

Nevertheless, Iran's political atmosphere was too polarised on the threshold of the municipal elections to afford such 'luxuries'. The lines of the battle were already drawn between the two major political camps. Both reformists and conservatives had complete slates of nominees for some 190,000 city and village council seats. Most notably, Abdollah Nouri, Khatami's key ally and former interior minister, who had been impeached and ousted by the Majles in June 1998, had resigned from his post as vice-president for development and social affairs to run as a candidate, and was now Tehran's major contender. The elections were held in February 1999 and, as expected, reformist candidates swept aside the competition, winning twelve out of the fifteen seats in Tehran alone. Nouri was the top winner, securing 589,000 out of a total 1.4 million votes cast in Tehran.

Officials estimated that about 25 million people, or 65 percent of the electorate, voted. That was less than the turnout for the presidential poll in May 1997, but much more than for the elections of Assembly of Experts. As with the presidential election, young people constituted the bulk of voters. Many independent candidates were elected in the provinces. Women also made a significant mark, even though heavily outnumbered by male candidates.

Other well-known reformists who won seats included Ebrahim Asqarzadeh, a former militant student who played an active part in storming the American embassy in Tehran twenty years before, and Saeed Hajjarian, a Khatami advisor and widely regarded as 'the brain behind the reformist movement'. The municipal councils were officially inaugurated after Nouri and other Tehran Council members were sworn in.

The 'Movement of the 2nd of Khordad' was now eyeing the Majles elections in 2000. The euphoria of the reformists, however, was short-lived. A thunderstorm was brewing as the conservatives pondered their next move.

The lack of institutionalised political parties in Iran has always been a major malady of its drive for democracy. Notwithstanding step-by-step advances by the reformists, the vacuum of organisation and leadership was a fact well realised by the conservatives who still controlled major levers of power. In the absence of parties, their role was played by reformist newspapers that had been mushrooming since Khatami's election. For instance, the press proved of crucial importance in exposing parts of the facts about the serial killings and not letting the case be fudged and brushed under the carpet. Every day that passed, they were becoming blunter in criticising the conservative establishment, questioning, albeit cautiously and in academic jargon, the very principles of Velayat-e faqih, and promoting democratic values. The task of dealing with the press was assigned to the judiciary, which embarked on a systematic approach to summon publishers and journalists to the court, or just summarily announce the suspension of a publication on charges such as 'fabricating lies', 'disturbing public minds' or 'insulting Islamic values'. Akbar Ganji argued that the spirit of Saeed Emami, the detained intelligence minister accused of masterminding the killings, was still alive, and that followers of his doctrine of suppressing dissent, having lost their base in the intelligence ministry, had now moved to the judiciary.

In summer of 1999, the conservative-dominated Majles decided to do something about the outspoken press. It prepared a bill that would make obtaining a publication licence very difficult and put the press under pre-emptive censorship. The bill caused a wave of uproar among reformists and their supporters. However, the conservatives were determined to go forward with it. In July, just one day before the bill was supposed to be discussed in the Majles, Salam, the oldest and one of the most popular pro-reform newspapers, published an internal memorandum said to have been written by Saeed Emami. In the memo, Emami set out a policy to harass and stifle the independent press through a variety of legal and extralegal measures, remarkably similar to the bill suggested by the Majles.

Salam was quickly closed down and charges of spreading false information brought against its publisher, Muhammad Mousavi Khoeiniha, in a Special Court for the Clergy. The closure triggered a peaceful protest by students at Tehran University on 8 July. During the early hours of 9 July, members of an unidentified uniformed militia force entered the university dormitories while the students slept and attacked them, throwing some of the students out of windows and taking some others away. The dormitory rooms were ransacked and furniture and equipment smashed. Witnesses said that the raiders beat up the students with clubs, metal rods and chains, and brass knuckles. Reformist student activist Fatemeh Haqiqatjoo, who became an outspoken Majles deputy in the 2000 elections, later reported that when the raiders threw students out of dormitory windows, they chanted slogans in praise of 'the glorious figure of the supreme leader'.

One resident of the dormitory – a relative of one of the students – was killed by a direct shot to the head. Three hundred people were wounded and 400 taken into detention.

The following day students took to the streets to protest the assault on the dormitories, to demand an inquiry, and to call for the release of their colleagues from detention. The demonstration was broken up by hard-line enforcers associated with conservative leaders within the government, the Ansar-e Hezbollah, wielding clubs and chains while members of the security forces stood by or joined in the assault on the demonstrators.

However, student protests continued in Tehran on 10 July and spread to other cities with calls for the dismissal of Tehran police chief, Hedayatollah Lotfian, and for the prosecution of those responsible for the raid. Outrage about the brutality of the initial night-time assault on the dormitories spread throughout Iranian society. Both President Khatami and Supreme Leader Ayatollah Khamenei condemned the raid and the minister of the interior, Abdullah Mousavi-Lari declared that it had taken place without any authorization from the ministry.[15]

The demonstrations initiated by the violent suppression of the students and the storming of their dormitory caught everybody by surprise. The wave of public disgust and fury at the way the students had been treated was so intense that even the hardliners retreated into defensive position for a short while. In fact, many people who wore beards to appease their bosses in the military and government offices, shaved or trimmed their beards in fear of being ambushed by angry youth. The Office to Foster Unity, together with all other pro-reform organisations and figures – including Khatami – expressed deep dismay over the actions of the police, Ansar-e Hezbollah, and the University Basij. Khatami, who was visiting the western city of Hamadan at the time of the Tehran University dormitory raid, said, 'I knew that following the case of the serial killings had a price,' explicitly linking the actions of the hardliners with the brutal methods adopted in killing and silencing intellectuals, methods that had caused public loathing.

Although most of the news about student demonstrations came from Tehran, there were demonstrations in the provinces, too. Such events occurred in Rasht, Yazd, Mashhad, Isfahan, Khorramabad, Hamadan, Shahrood, and Tabriz. Also, student unions in Bandar Abbas, Zanjan, Gorgan, Semnan, Yasouj, Maragheh, and Arak issued statements condemning police suppression of the initial events, the state news agency IRNA reported on 11 July.

At a demonstration on the campus of Tabriz University, scuffles broke out between students and the Basij Resistance Force. Muhammad Javad Farahangi, a Basiji theological student, was shot, and authorities later claimed they had arrested the culprit, a provocateur and member of the Iraqi-funded Mojahedin Khalq Organisation.

The Tabriz municipality said a number of other people were hurt and public buildings damaged. Between ten and fifteen people needed hospital treatment after the Tabriz fighting, the newspaper Arya reported on 12 July. Police entered Tabriz University on 11 and 12 July, and arrested over fifty students, *Arya* reported on 14 July.

In an interview with RFE/RL's Persian Service, a Tabriz student who requested anonymity said about 4,000 people attended the demonstration, and she estimated that 100 were injured in the scuffles. The authorities blamed the students for the outbreak of violence, but she rejected this. She said that the Basij attacked the students, and they just fought back.

Students in Tabriz demonstrated about the same issues as students in Tehran, the interviewee told RFE/RL. They wanted freedom of the media and the release of Heshmatollah Tabarzadi, editor-in-chief of *Hoviyyat-e Khish* weekly. She said the students also objected to the closure of the newspaper *Salam* by the Special Court for the Clergy. Tabriz University student Mahmood Ali Chehragani said that demonstrators in that city started at the university and marched about five kilometres. Along the way, offices and banks were attacked and government vehicles destroyed. The commotion ended only after negotiations reinforced by a massive security presence.

As the demonstrations continued and casualties mounted in the following days, concern grew that the situation was spinning out of control through the work of provocateurs (students blamed disguised hardliners, while the government blamed agents of foreign powers). On 11 July the Interior Ministry warned that unlicensed demonstrations would not be tolerated. University administrators warned students to be vigilant. The Office to Foster Unity warned that it did not endorse 'any extremist and unlawful moves,' and political groups affiliated with the 2nd of Khordad Movement (the date of Khatami's election) appealed for calm and cancelled a rally planned for 14 July. Khatami urged demonstrators to cooperate with the government.[16]

Ayatollah Khamenei addressed the nation in a 12 July speech. He condemned the 8 July attack: 'It is wrong regardless of the name under which it is done. It should be condemned.' While seeming to acknowledge that some may be unhappy with him, he said different opinions are permissible: 'We do not mind if there are different points of view and political differences.' He also said there should be 'limits to your political activities and political infighting. You should draw a red line.'

But Khamenei's other comments indicated a reluctance to address the causes behind the unrest. He warned, 'Watch out for the enemy ... Try to see the invisible hands; try to recognize those who are behind it.' He blamed the 'spy agencies of the world' and America specifically, which was met with chants of 'Death to America, Death to Britain, Death to Monafeqin [hypocrites] and Saddam, Death to Israel' and more chants of 'Death to America.'

Khatami also addressed the situation in an interview broadcast on 13 July. He promised to investigate the causes behind the student unrest, and said, 'We will try not to confront the violence with violence but with special and legal means.' Khatami noted that the 'issues raised, the slogans chanted ... are all meant to induce division and engender violence in society.'

Meanwhile, students were chanting 'Khatami, where are you? Your students have been killed,' Reuters reported on 14 July. In a letter to *Neshat*, a student wrote: 'They were looking for someone, they were looking for any traces of him. Yes, they were looking for Khatami, not that he would do anything about it, but simply that he would come and listen and see them cry.'

A unity council representing the students also condemned the violence, saying it only incriminated them. They also requested the dismissal of law enforcement chief Lotfian; transfer of law enforcement powers to the Interior Ministry; and dismissal of hard-line elements from security agencies. They also wanted open trials for those who ordered the initial attack; return of the corpses of dead students; an apology from the National Security Council; and a removal of the ban on *Salam*.

On 12 July Tehran was under a de facto martial law. Revolutionary Guards Corps and Basij militia were stationed in all major cities, backed by the police. Patrols were active on all crossroads and checkpoints were set up. That night there were more clashes between students, the Ansar-e Hezbollah, and police. Using tear gas and batons, the police emptied the university. Tens of people were injured and scores of them – many just passers by – were arrested. The Students' Unity Council accused the authorities of arresting over 1,400 people in Tehran.

By 14 July the tide had turned. Having regained full control of the cities, conservative figures called for demonstrations in support of Khamenei and to denounce the unrests. They mobilised the Basij, Revolutionary Guards and staunch hardliners to take part in the official rally that was held in Tehran and other major cities. Placards declaring 'Death to America' and 'Death to Israel' were abundant, as were those pledging allegiance to Khamenei. One remarkable fact was that among thousands of banners, posters and placards, none was in support of Khatami. Secretary of National Security Council Hassan Rowhani told the crowd that 'those involved in the last days' riots, destruction of public property, and attacks against the system will be tried and punished as *mohareb* (those at war with God, a term previously used for Mojahedin Khalq activists) and *mofsed-e fil-arz* (those spreading corruption on earth, a term chiefly coined for the officials of Pahlavi regime who were executed after the 1979 Revolution).' He went on to say that most of them were already under arrest. He also vowed vengeance against countries that supported the demonstrators, according to Reuters.

Meanwhile, Friday prayer leaders during their 16 July sermons blamed many sources – factionalism, newspapers, and the US – for the unrest. In Tehran Ayatollah Hassan Taheri-Khorramabadi said opportunists, oppositionists, and 'a group of people working for our foreign enemies' want to cause unrest. 'In Tehran in particular, they had planned a conspiracy and wanted to endanger the country's security.' He also condemned factionalism, because 'certain newspapers and journals exacerbate these disputes.' He ascribed America's actions to its reluctance to see 'a stable Islamic government anywhere in the world. It is afraid [that Iran] will become a model for other Muslims of the world. It is, therefore, striving to rise against this government by whatever means possible.'

Initially, state media's coverage of the events was non-existent. On 11 July the English-language daily *Iran News* editorialised about 'the deliberate indifference of the IRIB toward news coverage,' whereas information about the 8 July police assault on the university students was carried on the Islamic Republic News Agency wire. The English-language daily said if the state radio and television had reported the withdrawal of the Ministry of Intelligence and Security's complaint against *Salam*, the whole affair might have been avoided, or at least averted. Not only does this explain why people listen to foreign radio services, *Iran News* wrote, but it also explains how rumours can spread so easily.

Defence Minister Ali Shamkhani, in an interview broadcast by the state television on 13 July, accused foreign media of misrepresenting the events. He said, 'Headlines published by foreign press [and] the pictures broadcast by some foreign media' are 'signs of a well-coordinated move.' Therefore, 'we are going to end this much-favoured filmmaking session by the satanic global arrogance and Zionism, so as to prevent any further damage to the justice-seeking reputation of our students.' This meant that all scripts and video footage were reviewed by government censors before they could be transmitted, according to sources at CNN.

To block evidence of the violence, police rounded up photographers, the *New York Times* reported on 13 July. That day some of the worst violence occurred, with police, Basij Resistance Forces, and club-wielding thugs suppressing a student march. Reporters were not allowed to go to the scene or to take photographs, Rayshahri reported on 14 July, and only reporters from hard-line publications were allowed to take photos. Reporters were released only after having their notes and film confiscated. They were threatened and had to seek shelter in private homes. Yet, this was not always possible. While going home, an employee of *Neshat* newspaper was stopped by armed men. While searching him, according to *Neshat* on 14 July, they discovered papers with the logo from *Jame-eh* newspaper and accused him of being 'the correspondent of a mercenary newspaper.' They then destroyed his car. A photographer from *Kayhan* was shot in the leg and members of a German television crew were beaten up, according to the *Los Angeles Times*.

That same day, 13 July, state television repeatedly broadcast revolutionary songs and slogans. It exhorted viewers to attend government rallies on 14 July. Among the themes of the slogans were: 'maintain order and safeguard unity,' 'renewed allegiance,' and 'the enemy intends to catch the particular fish in muddy waters.' The Turkmen-language service of state radio, broadcasting from Gorgan, carried the following reports in its ten-minute newscast: people support the supreme leader; troublemakers caused disturbances in Tehran; CNN and other Western agencies are fabricating reports; and America and Israel support those who create unrest.

The Tehran newscast drew an even more explicit picture. After nine minutes of video and commentary about the damage and the funeral of a casualty in Tabriz, there was a three-minute piece about US, Israeli, and Mojahedin Khalq support for the demonstrations. Then ten minutes of Khatami saying the demonstrations harmed the system and some people were taking advantage of the situation, was followed by nine minutes of commentary condemning the BBC and US State Department spokesman James Rubin for their statements about the demonstrations.

On 14 July state radio and television broadcasts in Tehran carried a live relay of the government rally. Subsequent Tehran newscasts on all four channels were longer than usual due to coverage of the rally. Normal programming was interspersed with video footage of the rally. Programming in Mashhad had no local news. Instead, most of the newscast was dedicated to a statement from the supreme leader, Khatami's remarks on dealing with rebels, and the pro-government rally in Tehran. Later newscasts said the demonstrators condemned 'troublemakers' and 'corrupt groups,' while the leader of Pakistan's Jafari Shia group, said the unrest in Iran was led by the United States. State radio broadcasting in Turkmen from Gorgan carried Khamenei's message; Khatami's meeting with IRIB staff to discuss the unrest; coverage of the rallies; and repetition of the Security Council's warning to 'troublemakers.'

To make sure that public perception of the day's events was tightly controlled, the government shut down the mobile telephone service in Tehran. This also eliminated a means of communication for the demonstrators, *Tehran Times* reported on 18 July, and the conservative daily *Qods* claimed it was for security reasons. Muhammad Muhammadi Golpaigani, head of supreme leader's office, expressed his astonishment at the student protests: 'It was regretful that the majority of those arrested during the university dormitory event were under twenty years of age. This is a serious danger for our Revolution ... What have we done for the young generation?'

The student protests, also an outlet for popular expression of dissatisfaction with government policies in a wide range of areas, including the dire economic situation, the lack of opportunities for university graduates, restrictions on basic freedoms, and the slow pace of reform, were likened by commentators to the mass demonstrations in 1978 and 1979 that preceded the overthrow of the shah. Many opposition groups and analysts were in fact predicting an imminent overthrow of the regime. In doing so, they ignored three basic facts.

First, the spontaneous uprising by the students was a reaction to the closure of *Salam*, the newspaper that although promoted peaceful reforms, represented a part of the establishment and aimed at safeguarding the Islamic Republic through such reforms. Even the most vehement supporters of reform and the most ardent critics of the acts of Ansar-e Hezbollah had been asking for calm.

Second, even if some of the students were supposed to have broken up with the reform movement in general and Khatami as its leader in particular, they were outnumbered by pro-reform forces. In addition, there was no organising structure or leadership among them, let alone ideological bonds to boost the unrests into a public revolt.

Third, although enraged with the dormitory raid, the general public did not show much more than paying lip service to the student demonstrations. Sporadic riots and lootings could hardly have been taken as a mass movement. Through collective memory perhaps, the general mood of the society was against violent change and revolution. Frequent harassments by security forces and street thugs notwithstanding, the youth did not want to jeopardise its newly found personal liberties, however small those liberties may have seemed to be.

Following the unrest, hundreds of students remained in detention or were unaccounted for. The head of Tehran's Revolutionary Court stated on 11 September that four unnamed individuals had been sentenced to death in connection with the pro-democracy protests. The sentences were handed down in secret Revolutionary Court trials in which procedures fall far short of international fair trial standards. In an interview with the conservative daily *Jomhuri-ye Eslami*, Hojjatol-Eslam Gholamhossein Rahbarpour said two of the sentences had been confirmed by the Supreme Court and held out the possibility of further death sentences among the 'thousand arrested' during the protests.

To corroborate the conservatives' charge that the events of 8–13 July were backed by sources outside the country, the television started broadcasting heavily edited 'confessions' of two leaders of student organisations. On 19 July the Ministry of Intelligence and Security announced that student leader Manuchehr Muhammadi was behind the unrest. Muhammadi was arrested and beaten last July, and he was arrested again in May. Last autumn, Muhammadi visited America via Turkey through the assistance of a 'fugitive counterrevolutionary element.' He was arrested after returning from that trip, Muhammadi said in an interview printed by Rome's *La Republica* on 21 July. The Intelligence Ministry said the information leading to his most recent arrest was secured after 'the people were asked to demonstrate vigilance and to report any news on the chaos-mongers.'

In the television broadcast, Muhammadi looked tired and dishevelled. He said he had contacted nationalists, including the Nation of Iran Party (of the assassinated Forouhars) and the National Front. He also was in touch with Elaheh Amir-Entezam, the wife of Abbas Amir-Entezam, so his 'link with the outside world expanded.'

Other names, including that of Muhammadi's host when he visited Connecticut, were deleted. The announcer said the Islamic Union of Students and Graduates also was behind the unrest. That organisation's secretary-general, Heshmatollah Tabarzadi, is the editor of *Hoviyyat-e Khish* and is imprisoned. In another video clip, Muhammadi said: 'all these students believe that religion should be separate from politics.' He then said: 'The forces outside the country say that we must pick up arms to go forward by adopting a policy of violence to take over the government.'

On 22 July the 'confession' of Gholamreza Mohajerinezhad was broadcast. In a heavily edited mix of studio footage and a student rally, Mohajerinezhad described himself as deputy leader of the Nationalist Union of Students and a follower of the National Front. He admitted to, in a way, connections with both Muhammadi and Rezaei. While in Texas and Germany, Mohajerinezhad said, he met with Iranian exiles who urged armed struggle to create unrest and to overthrow the government. And they held demonstrations in May 'to create tension and strife so that it would be said that members of Hezbollah had done this.'

The US comments were mild compared to those of other governments. Turkish Prime Minister Bulent Ecevit said the students' actions were the natural reaction to a 'repressive regime.' Sweden, in an official 13 July letter to the Iranian embassy in Stockholm, said it hopes reformers emerge with greater influence in Iran because, 'it is with them that Stockholm intends to work.' Egyptian President Hosni Mubarak said he hoped for a victory of the moderate camp, *al-Ahram* reported on 14 July.

Be that as it may, President Bill Clinton was more cautious when he discussed Iran on 22 July. He said: 'Frankly, I'm reluctant to say anything for fear that it will be used in a way that's not helpful to the forces of openness and reform ... I just hope they find a way to work through all this, and I believe they will.'

Under much pressure from the reformist press, the trial of about twenty police officers, including Tehran police chief Farhad Nazari, started in February. From the outset it appeared that they were merely being used as scapegoats for higher-ranking individuals who gave the actual orders and who created the atmosphere in which such brutality and violence is considered an acceptable reaction to political expression. All but two of the accused were acquitted, while Commander Farhad Arjomandi and Private Orujali Badrzadeh were sentenced to two years in jail for breach of order and to 91 days in jail, plus a fine, for stealing an electric razor. Thirty-four students were to receive blood money from the public properties department. Reformers were unanimous in calling the trial a kangaroo court.

With the subsiding of consequences of the student unrests, the reformists concentrated their efforts to challenge their rivals in the upcoming Majles elections. The move, however, received a major blow when the Special Clerical Court, acting under direct supervision of the supreme leader, arrested and tried Abdollah Nouri. His newspaper *Khordad* had already been closed by the judiciary.

There had been little doubt that Abdollah Nouri would be found guilty, but hardly anyone expected the sentence to be so heavy. The outspoken and popular reformist cleric was sentenced to pay 5,000 dollars in fines, and went to Tehran's Evin prison directly from the Islamic court on 27 November to begin his five-year term without appeal.

Officially, Nouri was imprisoned for 'insulting Islamic sanctities, undermining the authority of the supreme leader, disturbing public opinion,' and a catalogue of other serious crimes. In actuality, the 50-year-old cleric was the latest victim in Iran's ongoing struggle between reformists and a conservative establishment uneasy with the newly found public freedoms. Reformists say that Nouri's indictment was a thinly veiled political move by the conservatives to dash his hopes of running in February's parliamentary elections.

'The charges levelled against me are baseless ... Iranian society feels that there is a connection between the indictment and my potential parliament candidacy,' Nouri said in an interview before his conviction.

During the trial for what he had published in his daily newspaper *Khordad*, the white-turbaned cleric not only rejected the legitimacy of the Special Clerical Court; he turned his defence statement into what one reformist daily called 'the manifesto of reformism in Iran.'

'The closure of six newspapers and the conviction of numerous figures implies a tactical success [for the conservatives],' the reformist daily *Aftab-e Emrooz* said. 'But the nation will not give its answer on the streets as the conservatives want but at the election ballots,' it added.

Behind the bars, Nouri became a best-selling author. In Iran's dormant book market where the average circulation of the books is around 3,000, *Hemlock of Reform* went to the seventh edition and sold more than 60,000 copies in less than a month, sweeping aside popular novels and thrillers.

Described as the 'manifesto of reformism in Iran' by Nouri's backers, the book included his defence statement at the Special Clerical Court. It touched upon nearly every subject hitherto considered taboo in Islamic Iran, ranging from the authorities of the supreme leader to women's dress code, and from resumption of ties with the United States to dealing with the Middle East peace process. 'The essence of my approach in this statement is reformism. I expect reforms to promote the legitimacy of political power in the Islamic republic,' he wrote in his introduction to the book.

> The leader in the Islamic Republic is essentially equal to all of the people and has no powers beyond what the constitution and the law have determined,' Nouri wrote. Elsewhere he described Iran's refusal to hold talks with the states as 'childish stubbornness' which is to the detriment of Iran's national interests. On the Middle East peace process, Nouri said that Iran's opposition stance 'brings no benefit but to introduce the Iranian nation as an advocate of terrorism.

University students in Tehran staged a calm demonstration in support of Nouri, calling for his release. But Ayatollah Khamenei said it was sad that 'some persons changed their course in a way that pleases the enemy. He did not mention Nouri by name. Nouri kept slamming the conservatives from behind bars, saying in a statement that he would not request an appeal because he did not recognise the court. 'The proceedings of the court were a reminder of the Inquisition ... condemning people because of their ideas,' he said in his statement.

Khatami's reaction to the imprisonment of his former minister and proponent of his 'political development project' has so far been constrained by the independence of the judiciary. 'We have been deprived of the capacities, experience and abilities of Mr Nouri,' Khatami said on 29 November. 'We must be extremely alert and avoid any behaviour that might increase tensions,' he added.

Overall, reformists saw Nouri's conviction as a two-pronged attack aimed to provoke reformists. 'The next step of the monopolists of power will be producing unrest and a vast suppression of the civil society. Any gathering will be turned into a turmoil by violent groups so that it would become possible to militarise the country and suppress the [reformist] front,' Akbar Ganji, wrote in his column in *Sobh-e Emrooz*.

As Khatami's minister of the interior, Nouri angered conservatives by freely granting protest permits to reformist student groups. As a result, Nouri was impeached by parliament in June 1998, whose slim conservative majority was a major obstacle to Khatami's reform efforts. Conservative efforts to discredit Nouri, however, have only enhanced his popularity.

Most analysts agreed that if Nouri were allowed to run in February's elections, he would handily defeat his opponents and even have a shot for the speakership.

The conviction was not the only setback for reformists. The same day Nouri was sentenced, another prominent reformist was sentenced to a three-year term. Mashallah Shamsolvaezin, a leading religious intellectual and editor of the banned *Neshat* daily, was also found guilty of 'insulting Islamic sanctities.'

Nouri's jailing, however, was not much help for the conservatives in the Majles elections, which ended with an overwhelming reformist triumph. Twenty-eight out of the thirty seats at stake in the capital have gone to reformers, as the former president Ali Akbar Hashemi Rafsanjani – who was the forerunner on the conservatives' lists – ranked no higher than 27th. As in Khatami's landslide victory in May 1997 – the symbolic democratic turning point in Iran's post-Revolution history – women and youngsters played a key role in the reformists' conquest of this key conservative stronghold. In the end, conservatives failed to attract these key constituencies despite the adoption of trendy election tactics.

One of the first questions that cropped up about the parliamentary election was whether or not Expediency Council chairman Rafsanjani would enter the race. Adding fuel to the fire were persistent rumours that the current speaker, Hojjatol-Eslam Ali Akbar Nateq-Nouri, would not stand in the election. Finally, a private member's bill in parliament made Rafsanjani an exception to the rule that a candidate must resign from government office three months before registering for the election.

Some observers believed that Rafsanjani would have a wide appeal because of his links with both of the rival clerical bodies, as well as being the mentor of Executives of Construction party that helped engineer Khatami's successful presidential campaign. However, both the first generation revolutionaries and the pro-democracy youngster spoke disparagingly about him. During a Khatami speech in December, students chanted: 'Political development is impossible with Rafsanjani!' The more radical figures of the reform movement, Abbas Abdi and Akbar Ganji in particular, had openly started to slander Rafsanjani, questioning his past policies. Among the long list of accusations thrown at him were the disastrous continuation of the war with Iraq in the 1980s, and turning a blind eye on the killings of dissidents during his presidency. Abdi was particularly pungent in criticising the man who was supposed to have ordered his imprisonment back in 1992. 'In the coming election,' he wrote in one of his venomous commentaries in *Sobh-e Emrooz* daily, 'the Iranian nation will show that it does not need a godfather.' The chasm that begun between Rafsanjani and reformers prior to the election, later turned into an unbridgeable gulf. Many analysts said afterwards that alienating Rafsanjani and pushing him to the right was perhaps the reform movement's biggest single mistake.

As before, the reformist press also played an important role in the election by raising many important issues that the state broadcast media tried to avoid. Hardliners had for months tried to silence reformist voices by imprisoning outspoken journalists and closing publications. Although several publications, including *Salam*, *Khordad*, *Adineh*, Fakour, *Hoviyyat-e Khish*, *Neshat*, and *Zan* were closed for offences such as questioning religious principles, the remaining reformist newspapers and journals openly criticised conservative policies. Also, new publications kept emerging, often using the same facilities and personnel of a just-closed publication.

18 February was another great day of excitement for the youth, who once again played a crucial role in deciding the outcome of the election, both by their own votes, as well as by persuading relatives and friends to vote. 69.25 percent, or 26.8 million, of Iran's 38.7 million voters cast ballots in the election. Even as the votes were being counted, it became clear that mostly conservative or independent candidates had lost to reformists identified with Khatami.

The outcome of the benchmark elections gave conservatives more cause to review their strategy. 'Religious thought and particularly the notion of a religious state should be revised ... Without understanding the generation gap, thinking of the future is looking into a distorted mirror. Political, social and cultural variables are much more important than this faction used to think in the past,' Entekhab wrote.

Muhammad Reza Khatami, a younger brother of the president, was the undisputed number-one winner, followed by other candidates of the coalition of some seventeen groups that supported the president's platform in the nationwide elections. Also included was Ali Reza Nouri, a brother of the jailed reformist cleric Abdollah Nouri. The state radio and television, controlled by the conservatives, responded by continuously playing patriotic hymns and thanking people for their participation at the polls – citing the event as a renewal of their commitment to the Islamic revolution and its ideals.

They also broadcast the remarks of the late revolutionary leader Ayatollah Ruhollah Ayatollah Khomeini, stressing that 'there are no winners or losers in the elections, because the goal of all candidates is to serve the people.' Supreme leader Ayatollah Ali Khamenei also thanked the nation in a message on 20 February, adding that it was a secondary issue which faction would win the elections.

Reformist press began joyous but cautious celebrations, trying not to hurt the feelings of the conservatives, particularly the hardliners, who could create problems after they lose another lever of power to the pro-reform movement.

The results of the sixth Majles elections were indicative of meaningful shifts in political equations as well as in prevailing social trends. For the first time after the Revolution, non-clerical deputies outnumbered clergymen by a drastic ratio: of the 290 red leather seats, only 35 were won by clerics.

The new parliament was also an exceptionally young one: more than 80 percent of all the elected deputies were aged between 41 and 45, some 60 percent between 36 and 40, and almost 20 percent under 35. Only 27 deputies were more than 56 years old. Many of the new deputies were graduate students of the Office to Foster Unity. Some 169 deputies were newcomers who had not been in the Majles in previous terms.

Reformist leaders obviously saw a pro-Khatami parliament as a natural continuation of the drive for democracy. 'All who have hindered Khatami's government in the past two and a half years should be most respectfully dismissed,' Saeed Hajjarian told a rally a fortnight before the election. 'The next Majles should be the locomotive of political development.' A fortnight after the election, a bullet was put into his mouth, targeting what many saw as the designer of that locomotive.

Assailants riding on 1000-cc motorbikes, which were only allowed to be used by security forces, shot Hajjarian in open daylight when he was entering the Tehran city council he chaired. He sank into a deep coma, of which he finally recovered, but was paralysed for life. The attempt enraged the nation. Conservative officials who had him under fire for more than two years now categorically condemned the incident. The intelligence minister announced that the perpetrators, now in detention, are 'rogue elements' with no factional affiliations. Reformists disagreed.

'These elements are part of an organised group relying on the levers of power to defeat reforms ... The agents of this group are active in military and security bodies,' said pro-reform journalist Emadeddin Baqi.

Reformists also expressed concern over ideological justification by high-ranking clergymen of extralegal violent actions. A particular target was Ayatollah Mesbah Yazdi who, from the Friday prayer podium, openly rejected reforms and democracy as anti-Islamic, saying that any Muslim was obliged to kill (without resorting to the law) those who 'violated sanctities.'

'The characteristic of the new wave of terrorism in Iran, which can be called "ideological terrorism" is that it kills the rivals with the notion of physically eliminating political and ideological apostates,' said an editorial at reformist daily said.

Thus the reform camp was facing major problems even before the new parliament convened in May, when it would have to live up to promises ranging from economic improvement to legal housecleaning. Some reformists said that the hard-line conservatives might try to prevent the opening of the Majles by resorting to acts of violence, insinuating that the opposition lacks competence to run the country. Others believed that the conservatives would block any reformist bill by using their dominance of the Guardian Council. Former judiciary chief and a member of the Council, Ayatollah Muhammad Yazdi, had already warned the new parliament that it could not pass any law it wished.

In April 2000, a number of leading Iranian reformist politicians and cultural figures attended an international conference on Iran in Berlin, which was also attended by banned, exiled political activists. This gave a golden opportunity to conservatives to portray the reformists as linked to hostile foreign powers. After a heavy media blitz by the state television – which ironically included footage of subversive opposition members stripping and dancing naked during the conference in protest to the reformists – many of the participants were prosecuted. Veteran nationalist-religious politician Ezzatollah Sahabi, prominent women's rights activist Mehrangiz Kar and publisher Shahla Lahiji were detained and interrogated for several weeks before being released on bail. A number of other participants in the Berlin conference were given long-term prison sentences.

Meanwhile the judiciary began to close down independent newspapers and magazines, and to imprison leading journalists and editors. Mashallah Shamsolvaezin, a pioneer of independent media and editor of a succession of banned titles, was imprisoned for thirty months in April on the grounds that an article he had published criticising the death penalty defamed Islam. In the same month, Akbar Ganji was imprisoned by the Tehran Press Court for defaming the security forces in articles he had written about official involvement in political killings and the attack on Saeed Hajjarian. The Press Court also sentenced publisher Latif Safari for two and a half years. The same day, eight daily and three weekly newspapers were ordered closed. Other prominent publishers or editors, some of whom were also politicians, were indicted for press offences or summoned to appear before the press court. In August, Ahmad Zeidabadi, Massoud Behnoud, Ebrahim Nabavi, all journalists for independent newspapers, were taken into detention without charge or explanation.

Ayatollah Khamenei, while endorsing 'the free flow of information,' openly condoned the action taken against the press accusing some unnamed titles of being 'bases of the enemy.' Following this lead, conservatives redoubled their attacks on reformists as agents of hostile alien forces, and the last remaining major independent daily, *Bahar*, was closed down in August. Ayatollah Jannati, a member of the Guardian Council, remarked that closing down the newspapers was 'the best thing the judiciary had done since the revolution.'

With the reformist press suppressed, conservatives were emboldened to tamper with the election results. In May, the Guardian Council nullified the results in eleven constituencies and cancelled 726,000 of the more than three million votes cast in the Tehran constituency, without explanation. For the clerical establishment, the most embarrassing outcome of the election was former president Rafsanjani's failure to gain enough votes to win a seat in the new Majles. Revised results several months later placed Rafsanjani higher in the poll but, rather than face humiliating criticism that the vote had been rigged, the powerful former president stood down from his seat.

When the new Majles convened in late May the reformists controlled some 150 of the 290 seats, but it was unclear whether or not the diverse factions of the reformist bloc would be able to operate as a unified voting group. Many reformists appeared chastened by the conservative backlash and anxious to reassure conservatives that change would not undermine the foundations of the state. Mehdi Karrubi, a cleric with a long history of senior government service, was elected speaker as a candidate acceptable to all factions.

The new parliament promised to amend the repressive press law passed in the closing months of the previous parliament. The law required applicants for new newspaper licenses to obtain prior approval from the judiciary, closing a previous loophole that had enabled banned newspapers to reopen days later under a new name. The law also facilitated the closure of newspapers on vaguely worded charges of 'insulting Islam' or 'undermining the religious foundation of the republic,' leaving the press court with wide discretion to censor titles of which it disapproved. Reformists drafted a new bill that would better protect press freedom but this was vehemently attacked by conservatives as un-Islamic and likely to spread corruption in society. On 6 August Ayatollah Khamenei ordered the parliament to drop its consideration of a new press law. This unprecedented intervention in the legislative process by the supreme leader was accepted by Speaker Mehdi Karrubi, averting open conflict between the parliament and the Guardian Council, which was anyway expected to veto the proposed new law.[17]

Other early actions by the new parliament indicated a pragmatic approach. New legislation to facilitate access by foreign investors to the Iranian market passed unanimously, indicating a shared recognition that the country's severe economic problems needed government attention. Reformist pledges to carry out public inquiries into the attack on student dormitories remained unfulfilled, however. On a positive note, a parliamentary commission carried out an investigation into prison conditions, visiting prisons in different parts of the country. The publication of the commission's findings, scheduled for mid-October, was delayed, reportedly because of their critical tone and exposure of torture.

Former detainees, arrested after the student disturbances in July 1999, informed Human Rights Watch that they were tortured and sexually abused while in prison in 1999 and early 2000. Ahmad Batebi, a student sentenced to thirteen years of imprisonment, wrote a letter to the head of the judiciary that was published in the international press, protesting beating and lashing that he had suffered while in detention.

Unfulfilled expectations were the cause of several clashes between demonstrators and hard-line conservative supporters and the security forces. On the anniversary of the student demonstrations of July 1999, students marched and were joined by other demonstrators expressing their frustration at poor economic conditions. The protesters in Tehran were beaten by Ansar-e Hezbollah, and forcibly dispersed.

Nevertheless, hard-line vigilantes were less active in the early part of the year, partly because the judiciary was more actively targeting reformists. On 14 April the supreme leader condoned 'legal-violence' against the 'bases of the enemy' and 'centres of corruption,' suggesting that the vigilantes should act only when the judiciary and the legal authorities were not doing enough to maintain order. His remarks at Friday prayers contained a barely veiled threat that citizen violence to protect Islam was justified if the state was failing in its obligation to protect the faith. As demonstrations of popular discontent mounted towards the end of the year, the vigilantes resumed their usual activities of assaulting reformists, breaking up demonstrations, and provoking disorder designed to discredit the reformist cause. In September, a group of vigilantes attacked a book exhibit in Isfahan, claiming that the titles showed disrespect for Islam. After the extreme vigilante violence of July 1999, Intelligence Minister Ali Younessi declared that such violence would no longer be permitted, but one year later he could only acknowledge that 'they have their own leadership network and do as they please.' The activities of the shadowy paramilitary supporters of conservatism, and the identities of the leaders behind the violence, had been favourite topics of the independent press. With suppression of this media, hardliners were able to intimidate political opponents free from the threat of public exposure.[18]

Amir Farshad Ebrahimi, a former member of Ansar-e Hezbollah vigilante, stated in a videotape that vigilantes had received payments from senior clerics in order to carry out attacks on reformist personalities and to disrupt public events. He was sentenced in October, after a closed trial, to two years of imprisonment for defamation of public officials. His lawyer, Shirin Ebadi – who won the Nobel Peace Prize in 2003 – and another lawyer, Mohsen Rohami, who had received a copy of the tape, were given suspended prison sentences and banned from practising law for five years. False allegations were made by the conservative press that a Human Rights Watch researcher had been involved in the production and dissemination of the tape, but no formal charges were made against her.

With less than a year before presidential elections, Iran's conservatives, who had lost a number of levers of power to pro-reform forces in the last three years, were still busy mobilising all the means at their disposal to prevent the re-election of President Muhammad Khatami.

Since Khatami's 1997 landslide victory on a platform of political and social reforms, hardly a month had passed without a fresh crisis that threatened to paralyse the moderate president's plans. Faced with repeated defeats in the municipal elections in 1998 and then in the parliamentary elections last year, the still-powerful conservatives were now targeting Khatami himself, as the unifying factor of some eighteen reformist groups whose stances were in some cases on opposite poles.

An influential conservative daily newspaper urged Khatami to refrain from registering as a candidate for the next presidential elections, reasoning that the moderate president should follow the model of Nelson Mandela and withdraw at the climax of popularity. It further warned that if Khatami failed to do so, alienation of public opinion would await him, just as with the former president Akbar Hashemi Rafsanjani, who did not even succeed in securing a seat at parliament.

The Islamic Iran Participation Front (IIPF), the major pro-Khatami political outfit that won the majority of parliamentary seats in February, retorted by saying that Khatami's popularity was higher than three years ago and announcing that its strategy would be his re-election with a higher number of votes than in 1997.

Although Khatami had kept silent amid the battle of words between the two rivalling factions, speculation was rife that he would definitely run as a candidate even if there were no other prominent reformist politician of his calibre enjoying public support. Nevertheless, a major concern for reformers was that his eventual candidacy might face stern opposition by the Guardian Council, but whether it would actually take the risk of rejecting a president chosen by 75 percent of the voters remained dubious.

Another initiative launched by the conservatives, was to 'jump on the bandwagon of reforms and change its course,' as a Tehran-based political analyst put it. 'After supreme leader Ayatollah Ali Khamenei expressed his support for "Islamic reforms", the conservatives have been trying to put on a reformist guise and put the public in confusion,' he said.

Once explicitly rejecting reforms as a cause of diluting revolutionary principles, weakening the pillars of Islam and playing into the hands of the enemies, prominent conservative figures were now stressing the need for reforms, adding that a competent centre should be set up to guide reforms. A conservative newspaper went so far as to suggest that the process of reforms should be put in the hands of the Expediency Council, chaired by Rafsanjani.

Pro-reform forces had already been suffering several serious blows after their victory in the parliamentary elections. Most of the reformist publications had been banned by the judiciary, publishers were frequently summoned to the court, and a number of prominent journalists were in jail.

By suspending the reformist newspapers, the conservatives aimed to block the channels of communication between the president and the youth, *Hayat-e Now*, one of the two surviving pro-reform dailies said in a commentary. 'They [the conservatives] are trying to cause disillusionment and passivity among the large number of the youth who support Khatami,' it added.

In reaction, the reformist camp adopted a new strategy that it labelled 'active calm,' emphasising a gradual development of reforms without provoking the conservatives to create a state of emergency and a possible consequent resort to violence.

Hamidreza Jalaeipour, a reformist publisher whose newspaper was banned, summarises the situation thus: 'The ultimate losers are not the reformists ... If the conservatives are determined to take the pressure to the limit, the reformists will simply step out and leave them alone with millions of dissident people.' This happened to be what actually happened less than four years later. Only the reformers did not 'walk away'; they were thrown out of the Majles.

By the end of the Iranian year (20 March 2001), reforms were facing a stalemate. The reformists had the municipal councils and the parliament in their grip, but real power was still in the hands of the conservatives, as effectively displayed by the banning of newspapers, imprisonment of journalists, students and political activists, the blocking of Majles motions by the Guardian Council and the supreme leader himself, as well as by harassment and terror. In the words of reformist Majles deputy Mohsen Armin, it was 'like playing chess with an ape'.

To make the matters worse, it was not clear if Khatami would stand as a candidate in the upcoming presidential elections, as he was in practice rendered powerless by the Velayat-e Faqih system. Khatami's position was far from enviable: with twenty million votes already behind him, he was the flag carrier of popular demands; at the same time, becoming the opposition was the last thing he would ever think of. His indecision was vividly reflected in his New Year's address to the nation on 21 March

2000, when he ended his remarks by a famous line from the great Iranian poet Hafiz: 'This chapter has come to a close, but the story continues'.

The chapter was not closed, however. Heavy lobbying eventually overcame Khatami's reluctance, and he registered for the presidential elections of June 2001. How he was encouraged to run again was not clear. There was almost no doubt that within the existing constitution the president was powerless. Even more, the parliament was also straitjacketed by the Guardian Council, which had rejected every single motion to improve human rights and democracy. Subversive opposition, beaming radio and television programmes into Iran, called him a deceiver, a puppet in the hands of the clerical regime.

However, for the majority of the voters, he still represented the only ray of hope. The reformists rallying around Khatami, and even the non-violent opposition abroad urged the people to take part in the elections so as to turn it into a referendum, once more showing what they did not want. It may have been a classical example of political naivety, as the ruling conservatives had shown during the past four years how much they cared about votes. Nevertheless, the ball was rolling again.

Khatami won well over twenty-one million votes with his nearest rival Ahmad Tavakkoli trailing way behind with about four million. Tavakkoli platform epitomised the conservatives' main – albeit apparent – criticism of Khatami and the majority of the Majles supporting him: that priority was given to useless notions such as 'political development' at the expense of a deteriorating economy which was the nation's chief concern.

In terms of sheer numbers, Khatami's re-election was surely a referendum. Despite economic dire straits plaguing the country, his promise of continuing with the reforms won him more votes than in his first election. But ironically, the conservatives raised the question why some twelve million eligible voters had stayed home rather than go to the polls. They reasoned that this showed a frustration with Khatami's reform policies. The reformists answered by asking why those twelve million had not voted for the conservatives or the 'independent candidates'.

But, as a foreign correspondent observed, 'Khatami has not been able to do anything significant for the masses. Most Iranians, especially among the younger generation, know that Mr Khatami's best promises will still fall short of their aspirations. They also know that he will not be able to deliver even on what little he does promise. So, from all considerations, the vast majority of Iranians seem to have voted for Mr Khatami because they abhor the alternative.

'The masses have sent a powerful message. The problem in our country is that there are too many people who cannot or will not read these messages', said a veteran analyst who did not wish to be named. The most significant phenomenon of this election was the surge on Friday afternoon when people suddenly realised what they would have to contend with if they did not send Mr Khatami back to the presidency.'[19]

As if in a concerted move to show what Khatami's true powers were, Ansar-e Hezbollah attacked a celebration by Khatami's supporters the day after he was re-elected, an attack during which the BBC correspondent was also injured. During an angry altercation, one of the Ansar-e Hezbollah militants dug his finger into John Simpson's eye, narrowly missing the pupil with his fingernail. Simpson reported afterwards:

> For President Muhammad Khatami, winning his second presidential election with 78 percent of the vote, humiliating his nine opponents, and gaining more votes than he received in 1997, may well turn out to be the easy part.
>
> The events of Saturday evening in central Tehran, after the result of Friday's election became clear, showed how difficult a path he now has to tread.
>
> A crowd of several hundred, mostly young people, gathered in a park close to the television station in Val-I-Asr Avenue to celebrate the victory of the man who has campaigned on moderation and on widening the degree of personal freedom in Iran.
>
> Within a couple of hours riot police were out in force to clear them out, and tear gas was used to disperse them.
>
> 'This must be the only country on earth,' commented a leading government official, 'where the police stop people celebrating the success of the government.'
>
> The trouble is, President Khatami has not yet succeeded in defeating the hard-line forces of the police, reinforced by an often violent and shadowy force known as 'The Soldiers of the

Party of God' whose members support Iran's religious leader, Ayatollah Khamenei, were determined to stop the pro-Khatami celebrations turning into an anti-conservative demonstration.

The [Ansar-e Hezbollah], who form an elite secret police, mingled with the crowds, taking names, filming them with video cameras and using strong-arm tactics against foreign journalists who had come to observe the celebration. Three camera crews, including one from the BBC, were forcibly arrested, threatened, and held for several hours.

President Khatami and his allies in government have so far shown themselves unable to control hard-line elements like this, which owe their allegiance to the earlier leaders of the Islamic Revolution.

In his second four-year term, he will have to control or disband groups like the Soldiers of the Party of God if the people who voted for him in such large numbers on Friday are not to lose their faith in him.

Greater personal freedom cannot be achieved while such organisations rule the streets.[20]

Reformist solution to the powerlessness of the president was a rather strange one, and almost a contradiction in terms. Khatami's government, now fully aware of the legal restrictions in the face of the powers of the supreme leader stipulated in the constitution, presented two bills to the Majles. The first bill aimed at doing away with the Guardian Council's authority to screen candidates for all elections in Iran. The second included more powers for the president. It was a strange solution, for although the majority of the Majles supported Khatami and would almost surely ratify the bills, the Guardian Council was the ultimate authority that could reject them. Predicting such an act, the reformists most probably assumed that in such a case the issue would be referred to the Expediency Council, and then, with the intervention of the supreme leader, the matter would somehow be resolved.

In practice, the Council left the double bills suspended in the air until the term of the pro-Khatami came to an end in 2004, and Khatami himself revoked them.

Meanwhile, Ayatollah Montazeri, still under house arrest, issued his memoirs on the Internet, directly attacking the position of supreme leader, arguing that the concentration of power in the hands of one man was contrary to Islamic principles. Protests about the continuing restrictions on Ayatollah Montazeri's liberty mounted throughout the year. In June, the ayatollah's children (with the exception of his jailed son) circulated a letter calling for the lifting of these restrictions, and 126 out of 290 members of the Majles signed a similar statement. Khatami several times publicly criticised the stifling of dissent, including closures of newspapers and magazines, and the imprisonment of political dissidents, but he appeared to be unable or unwilling to remedy these problems. In a speech marking the Islamic Revolution's twenty-second anniversary, he warned: 'those who claim a monopoly on Islam and the Revolution, those with narrow and dark views, are setting themselves against the people.' He also complained repeatedly that he lacked the power to carry out his obligation as president to uphold the constitution. But he continued to shy away from open confrontation with his opponents and made no discernible progress in implementing his promised reforms. Increasingly, through his statements, he appeared to represent more of a safety valve for public frustration than an agent of tangible change.[21]

The following two years saw a continuous decline of the reformist cause and the fall of Khatami's popularity. The first big shock came in March 2003, when the elections for municipal councils registered the lowest relative voter turnout in the history of the Islamic republic, enabling conservative candidates to dominate the councils with a minimum number of votes. And less than a year after that, the last nail was put in the coffin of the 'state reformers', when the conservatives conquered the Majles.

The Majles elections of February 2004 were highlighted by vast disqualification of reformist candidates throughout the country by the Guardian Council, including tens of parliament deputies.

For three weeks, deputies in parliament staged a sit-in after the Guardians Council barred the reformist candidates, many vowing now to boycott the elections. More than 100 deputies resigned from parliament in protest to the disqualifications. However, such moves proved to be too little too late. Despite massive media coverage of the protest, the public support that the reformists were anticipating never came. Ayatollah Khamenei openly threatened the deputies, saying that any resignations were contrary both to the law and to Islamic principles and deserved serious punishment because they represented a disruption of the election process.

Khatami – who had previously vowed to have the elections held only if they were competitive, free and fair – backed off and said that his government would organise the polls at the set date after all. Major reformist political groups – with the exception of the League of Militant Clerics – as well as several hundreds pro-reform students called for a boycott of the elections. The students called on Khatami to resign, saying he had been indecisive and had backed down under conservative pressure. The elections were a textbook conservative victory: they were held on time, producing the desired results, and the boycott failed despite a rather low turnout, discrediting the reformist even more.

In Iran's major cities, voter turnout was only about 30 percent, and reformists claimed that about 15 percent of those votes were actually blank. People on the street are generally reacting with indifference to the conservative victory, but observers warn the situation could change.

Iranian 2003 Nobel Peace laureate Shirin Ebadi, speaking at a session of the European Parliament in February 2004, criticised the elections and warned that if the new leadership does not respect the wishes of the people, the patience of Iran's young people could run out.

Gholamali Hadad Adel, head of the Abadgaran party which was loosely put together to represent a 'modern' face of the conservatives, won almost all of the seats representing the capital, Tehran. He told reporters that the new majority's main focus would be on economic reform, and that his party would respect civil rights. He added that the new Parliament would support reformist President Muhammad Khatami until the end of his second and final term in June 2005.

The parliamentary elections were widely criticised in the West as being flawed, particularly drawing sharp criticism from the European Union, which had advocated a policy of constructive engagement with Tehran.

By this time, it was generally agreed that the reform movement had come to a close, a notion put forward by the likes of Akbar Ganji and Mohsen Sazgara. Saeed Hajjarian, the so-called theoretician of the reform movement, said, 'Reforms are dead; Long live reforms'. By this, Hajjarian and his fellow-thinkers insisted on a revision of reformist strategy and the forming of a legal opposition within the framework of the current constitution.

By contrast, others suggested that a constitution based on the virtually unlimited powers of Velayat-e Faqih left no leeway for a move for democracy. Jailed academic Hashem Aghajari warned that the reformist movement had now reached a dead end and that passive resistance was the only option.

'Organising an un-free election is an end point for reforms within the regime,' wrote Aghajari from his cell in Hamadan prison, where he was sentenced to death for apostasy in 2002 after he questioned the Shia clergy's right to rule. In an incendiary speech, Aghajari had called for a religious Protestantism of Shiism, espoused a major structural shake-up in Iran's religion of state, and asserted that Muslims were not 'monkeys' and 'should not blindly follow' religious leaders.

'We are witnessing a comical repetition of history: in a very short period of time, the democratic face of the Iranian constitution is going to be turned into an autocratic face,' he wrote. Like Ganji and Sazgara, but unlike some other reformist figures, Aghajari saw the only way out a non-violent, civil resistance: 'The current generation should be given the right to choose their own structure of government and constitution. The nation must say "No" to the totalitarians with its passive resistance.'

Aghajari went on to lash out at Khatami. 'Alongside this comical repetition of history we are also witnessing a tragedy: the tragedy of Khatami. During the six years that have elapsed for the reformist government and the four years of the reformist parliament, because of a lack of will and courage great opportunities were missed.' Khatami, he wrote, 'has reached a point where people are disappointed in him.'[22]

Clearly at stake was now the very survival of the theocracy in the long run. Sadeq Zibakalam said, 'I think the future of the Islamic Republic of Iran is tied to the outcome of this struggle. If the hardliners, if the ideologically oriented conservatives, take the leadership of the conservatives, then I don't see any bright future for the Islamic Republic. If, however, the more educated, the more pragmatic, the more moderate conservatives can manage to take control of the country's economy and government in their own hands and prevent hardliners from decision-making, then I think there are some lights at the end of the tunnel for the future of the Islamic Republic.'[23]

Ahmad Sadri, from the department of sociology at Lake Forest College, Illinois, wrote in 2002: 'The Iranian reform movement is about to molt out of the hardened, prudent and gradualist skin of the Khatami years. The discarded old casing already belongs to the historians. The young generations of Iranians are taking bets on the wing span and bright colours of the new, post-Khatami Reform.'[24]

In May 2004, Khatami admitted that there were 'signs of despotism' in the Islamic republic, as he countered criticism in a meeting with young people, in which he was given a tough grilling in a meeting to mark national youth day. 'I know that what you are saying to me now you cannot say anywhere else, because you would pay dearly and have already paid dearly, and that there are many signs of despotism in our society,' he said.

Shortly after the conservatives dominated the Majles, and about a year before his second term ran out, Khatami issued a 'Letter for Tomorrow', addressed to the nation, and 'all my beloved children, whose kindness and fury are both precious to me'. Khatami stressed that no group of people can choose its future by ignoring its past while the future of every group depends upon its alertness and determination.

Reminding that Iran's past was filled with despotism, and that 'this despotism has at times even been justified through philosophy and religion', he recounted the 'historic demand of the nation in the past three decades for the fulfilment of freedom, independence and progress.'

Praising Ayatollah Khomeini as the 'epitome of the nation's dignity and the harbinger of freedom and political independence', he criticised those who had tried to 'promote traditional interpretations of religiosity in the name of the imam and hence close their minds to all other interpretations.'

As a result of such an attitude, he added, 'Some of the people's legitimate demands have not been fulfilled. This especially applies to the demands of the youth and the intellectuals ... The point at stake is rather that we identify the obstacles to establishment of democracy.'

With the de facto end of the reform movement, more and more reformists started breaking away from the notion of 'reforms from above' and calling for a referendum. Proponents of a referendum, however, fell into two major categories. Those who believe that the religious rule can ultimately be modified, called for a referendum to amend the constitution. Others pressed on a referendum under the supervision of international bodies such as the United Nations, so that the nation could actually choose the form of the regime it wants to rule the country.

No one doubted that a chapter was closed: but there were different interpretations as to what the reform movement really was. Was it a plot devised by the theocracy to prolong its life in the face of rising demands of the young generations? Was it a trap the nation fell into? Was it a struggle between two factions of the establishment over a bigger share of the power-cake? Or was it a genuine pro-democracy movement at the grassroots level?

Regardless of those questions, or perhaps in response to them, one cannot deny that the so-called Tehran Spring led to deep changes in Iranian society. In the words of veteran journalist Massoud Behnoud,

> What happened in the past seven years opened the tongues and minds. Today, nothing is hidden, particularly from the youth and the students. The cracks and chasms are visible ... In order not to face another big defeat, the right faction knows that it must play its part in a way not to let the gap between the system and people be revealed ... They have to refrain from treating people harshly ...
>
> Although not said in many words, [the conservatives] have more or less submitted, or are being prepared to submit to the requirements of modern life – except to any form of freedom. It is because on the second of Khordad, people showed that they are aware of the power of voting and not voting. From here on, it is up to people to show if the majority of them demand freedom and a civil society.[25]

Behnoud believed that the reform movement accomplished what was within its capacities:

> People who voted [for Khatami] on that day should be proud of themselves ... With the message they sent, even the most hard-line and die-hard figures of the state have realised that they have to give concessions to people if they want to survive ...

Yet another surprise was in store. In June 2005, voters raised to the presidential chair an angry young man of the US embassy takeover generation who, in almost every aspect, was Khatami's opposite. A president whose key campaign slogan was 'I'm a dustman of the nation.' A man who called his election 'the second revolution'.

TEN

The Rorschach Test

Ours is a lost generation, it may be, but it is more blameless than those earlier generations.

Franz Kafka, *Investigations of a Dog*

Religious democracy is the essence of the Islamic system.

Ayatollah Ali Khamenei, May 2005

O, Mighty Ayatollah! The second of Khordad did not shake the building, it surprisingly and astonishingly revealed a huge crack which warned you of a bad earthquake that was on the way, and that you should promptly do something to repair your house. Instead of repairing it, however, you arrested and imprisoned engineers who were among your own associates and were reminding you of that large crack. You ordered a few navvies to cover up the crack ...

The walls of your regime are full of cracks. The foundation has been severely damaged. An earthquake is on the way, a dreadful, overwhelming earthquake ... The building will collapse, and if you ask why, you will be told that because you turned a blind eye on the cracks ...

From the F. M. Sokhan Persian weblog, May 2004

On 17 June 2005 Mahmoud Ahmadinejad appeared in a south Tehran polling station to cast his ballot before the cameras of dozens of domestic and foreign reporters. The underdog presidential hopeful was dressed in his usual uniform of oversize spring jacket, his shirt's top button undone and his thin untrimmed beard combed in the best tradition of the first-generation revolutionaries. Having cast his vote, he faced the cameras with a wide grin. One of the Iranian reporters asked him to wave his hand for the camera. 'Hands of a president are not for waving,' Ahmadinejad said. 'They are supposed to work for the people.'

Such populist displays of humility were reminiscent of an era that many Iranians thought long gone. That was what made the shock of Ahmadinejad's eventual election as president all the more incomprehensible for those who tend to take developments in Iran at face value. To them, Ahmadinejad's victory simply meant a return to the early 1980s. As a matter of fact, in the run-up to the elections, his supporters compared him to former president Muhammad Ali Rajaei, whose short tenure came to an abrupt end in August 1981 when a bomb blew up the presidential office in Tehran. Rajaei, a peddler for some time before the 1979 Revolution, took pride in leading a simple and down-to-earth life. Pictures showed him kissing poor villagers, while TV footage of his private life showed him sitting on the floor, having a simple traditional meal with his family. In his campaign, Ahmadinejad, son of a metal worker, drew heavily on Rajaei's image: going into poor districts and towns and sitting on the floor having bread and cheese with sugared tea for breakfast.

This apparent humility, however, did not detract from the revolutionary zeal of either of the two presidents. Shortly before the Islamic Republic's bloody crackdown on opposition groups in 1981, Rajaei said in a televised message, 'I am just a little soldier of the people. However, it doesn't mean I cannot deal with a handful of demonstrators and journalists.' Similarly, Ahmadinejad called himself 'a dustman of the people', at the same time stressing that Iran would not abandon its nuclear programme, at any price. Rajaei's widow, now a reformist, protested and warned Ahmadinejad's supporters not to use 'the martyr's name for propaganda purposes'. For the majority of Iranians, born after Rajaei's death, the debate had little meaning.

Shortly after becoming mayor of Tehran in April 2003, Ahmadinejad imposed a system in his office building of segregated lifts for men and women. He shut down popular fast-food restaurants and converted several cultural centres into prayer halls. He banned posters of England and international football star David Beckham from appearing on advertising billboards. He also proposed that some of the 'martyrs' of the Iran-Iraq war be buried in several of Tehran's main squares. In an interview on state television before the elections, Ahmadinejad said Iran was the target of a destructive Western cultural onslaught, which intended to undermine the self-confidence of Iranian managers and influence the young.

Taking a populist stand on domestic issues, Ahmadinejad referred to the problems of the underclass, declaring that any solution to the unemployment problem required financial support from the state, land distribution to farmers, and the promotion of small workshops. He said the gap between rich and poor was increasing, and added that the state should employ people directly, rather than using contractors, and state employees should receive housing and good wages. He called for the use of one percent of the state budget to create a Young People's Fund that would, among other things, create jobs.

He did not seem friendly towards the United States. 'America's unilateral move to sever its ties with the Islamic Republic was aimed at destroying the Islamic Revolution,' he said on his website. 'And it is for the same reason that America is trying to re-establish relations with Iran.' He said Iran should resume relations with the United States only after careful consideration of its interests. No part of Ahmadinejad's rhetoric offered anything fresh for the mostly disillusioned public, and he had become the subject of several jokes even before the elections. He was generally considered an outsider with no chance of even challenging other candidates.

As 17 June approached, there seemed a sense of almost total indifference in society; the same indifference that had handed easy victories to the conservatives, albeit with low turnouts, in the municipal council and parliamentary elections in 2003 and 2004. It was almost taken for granted that the ruling conservatives would one way or another take the final step in unifying the ruling system, correcting the error they had made by allowing Khatami to run for presidency back in 1997. Major student organisations boycotted the elections, and a number of prominent dissidents were calling for an internationally observed referendum on the future of the political system. But ruling political factions were in commotion. With the reforms proclaimed 'dead' almost by everyone, the reformists were desperately trying to promote their candidate Mostafa Moin, Khatami's former higher education minister who had resigned under pressure from conservatives. Moin's lack of charisma, however, did not provide the conservatives with much relief, as they were facing an in-house dilemma: despite much lobbying, none of the four conservative hopefuls showed any willingness to resign in favour of others, with the obvious result that conservative votes would be worryingly fragmented. To make matters worse for both camps, on the very last day of candidates' registration, Rafsanjani announced that he would enter the race, to 'rescue the country'.

For months Rafsanjani had been transmitting contradictory signals about his possible candidacy. He seemed to be testing the weight of other hopefuls as well as tantalising would-be voters, so that he would finally emerge as the only firewall between the people and the ruling conservatives' drive to capture all the branches of government. He was also seeking to eradicate the memories of his humiliating defeat in the Majles elections some five years before. But once more the Guardian Council changed the equation, when, on 22 May it disqualified Mostafa Moin and more than a thousand other candidates, including its own former member Muhammad Reza Zavarei, leaving four conservatives, Rafsanjani and former Majles speaker Mehdi Karrubi.

The disqualification of Moin prompted anger among reformists, who called it illegal. Moin's party the Islamic Iran Participation Front (IIPF) warned that the move would turn the vote into 'a sham' and suggested it would not participate in the election. Some of its members called for an election boycott. Some 100–150 students at Tehran University protested the disqualification of Moin and chanted slogans against the Guardian Council. Shortly afterwards Ayatollah Khamenei specifically called on the Guardian Council to review its disqualification of the two reformist candidates, namely Moin and Vice President Mohsen Mehralizadeh who had been running as an independent. 'It is desired that all people in the country from different political interests have the opportunity to take part in the big test of the elections,' Khamenei said in his letter. Less than twenty-four hours later, the head of the Guardian Council announced the decision to reinstate Moin and Mehralizadeh. Some said Khamenei's request to the Guardian Council was an attempt to prevent the spread of protests in the country. Others held that the letter showed his concern about a low turnout in the upcoming ballot.

Still others suggested that it was intended by Khamenei to take votes from Rafsanjani.

Thus it seemed that the main rivalry would be between Rafsanjani and Moin. In their campaigns, both candidates reached out to the youth; both made statements challenging the legitimacy of the Islamic Republic and its current leadership; both even called for new limits on the power of Khamenei and his colleagues in the Guardian Council – a reform pledge that Khatami never, not even once, made. To varying degrees, both candidates also claimed the mantle of democracy and promised political reform. Although outsiders did not interpret this rhetoric of reform as a sign that either candidate (especially Rafsanjani) was sincere in his commitment to change, or able to carry out such commitment, it was regarded as a genuine challenge to the supreme leader and his autocratic hold on power. Furthermore, both Moin and Rafsanjani promised to improve relations with the United States, another affront to Khamenei. The Rafsanjani camp was even telling its supporters that statements by the Bush administration, exhibiting less militancy toward Iran, were de facto indications of America's approval of his candidacy. For everyone except the extreme right, it had become clear that normalising relations with the United States was popular enough to be a campaign promise.

But as election results started coming out, supporters of reform panicked. Exit polls showed that Rafsanjani narrowly led not Moin, but the least likely conservative challenger, Ahmadinejad. None of the candidates secured the minimum of 50 percent-plus of the votes that are required to win outright. Rafsanjani secured more than about 21 percent, while Ahmadinejad got about 19.5 percent of the votes.

Closely following Ahmadinejad came former Majles speaker Karrubi with a little more than 5 million votes, former national police chief Muhammad Baqer Qalibaf and then Moin, with about 4 million votes each. Trailing far behind were former state radio and television chief Ali Larijani with 1.7 million votes, and Vice-President for Physical Training Mohsen Mehralizadeh with 1.2 million. According to the Election Headquarters on 18 June, the turnout was around 63 percent. This turnout equalled that of the 2001 election and surpassed those of the 1985, 1989, and 1993 elections.

As soon as the surprise results of the 17 June elections were announced, Karrubi and other candidates immediately raised concerns about ballot-fraud and vote-rigging. In an unprecedented, strongly-worded letter to the supreme leader, Karrubi claimed the Revolutionary Guards and Basij forces had used money for a vote-buying scheme. He also alleged the groups had campaigned illegally on behalf of one of the candidates, whom he did not name. A Revolutionary Guard spokesman rejected the charges and said that Karrubi, who finished third, should not blame others for 'his failure in the elections'.

In the letter, Karrubi also called on Khamenei to stop what he claimed was illegal intervention on the part of the Revolutionary Guards and the Guardian Council. In a gesture of utter dismay, the former Majles speaker submitted his resignation from the Expediency Council, and announced that he intended to set up a party of his own.

Karrubi also accused the Guardian Council of supporting Ahmadinejad. 'I had one hour's sleep last night. And when I woke up to check the results again, I saw that the chairman of the Guardian Council was making comments about the results,' Karrubi said. 'I contacted the election commission at the Interior Ministry and was told that it appeared that Mr Rafsanjani was in the lead, and that I was in second place. But suddenly the situation changed. I contacted Mr Khatami and he said he was on his way to the Interior Ministry and would check.'

On the same day, Tehran's hard-line prosecutor blocked publication of the newspaper *Eqbal*, because it had printed Karrubi's letter, according to *Eqbal*'s editor-in-chief. Two other newspapers, *Aftab-e Yazd* and *Etemad*, were also shut down for the same reason. Karrubi's letter was published on several Iranian websites. Karrubi's concerns were also echoed by Moin, who finished in fifth place. Moin, in a statement on 19 June, accused military forces of working together with political organizations to promote a particular candidate and rig the elections.

Amir Mohseni, the deputy head of Rafsanjani's campaign in Tehran, also expressed doubt over Ahmadinejad's election results. 'We are suspicious. We feel that he was not so popular as to gain this number of votes,' he said. Rafsanjani called on Iranians to use the run-off to vote against 'extremists' whom he said had 'tarnished' the poll.

According to Abbas Milani, to bring the voters out, the regime also started a campaign of rumours, threatening dire consequences for those who did not vote. 'That students will not be able to get their grades and citizens their passports are among the less ominous of the threats. This is significant because powerful, stable, autocratic regimes do not worry about low voter turnouts,' he said.[1]

'For an election that was supposed to be a non-event for those committed to democratic change in Iran, these developments are encouraging. Contrary to the claims of the regime and its apologists, the current clerical despotism is far from stable. Unlike recent votes in Ukraine or Georgia, this election will not bring down autocracy. But it may sow the seeds of discord within Iran's dictatorship and lead to a genuine democratic breakthrough sooner than most think,' Milani added.

During a press conference on 18 June, Ahmadinejad said he was running as an independent and did not have the support of any political parties or groups. He said he, for one, was not surprised by his successful finish. 'For me, it was not a big surprise. I know the culture of Iranians,' he said. 'I know how great the people of this country are. And I know that I have developed good relations with the people.' But many still questioned his second-place finish in the vote.

Muhammad Sadeq Javadi Hessar, a pro-reform journalist in Mashhad, said it was highly unlikely that a relatively unknown candidate could have received nearly one-fifth of the vote. 'If in Tehran if we had about two million participants, it means about 25 percent of the eligible population voted,' Javadi Hessar said. 'From this 25 percent, it is impossible that about 700,000 people voted for him. I think there is a problem, and Mr Karrubi has also pointed to it. This behaviour is not at all natural. Mr Ahmadinejad could not have gained so many votes unless there was some interference that disrupted the normal election process.'

Mashallah Shamsolvaezin, a prominent journalist and the spokesman of the Tehran-based Society for Defence of Press Freedom, said the government should investigate the rigging allegations. 'All the polls showed that between 40–45 percent of the eligible voters would participate in the elections. What we got was 15–20 percent higher than that. This indicates that something happened with the ballot boxes. I think Khatami's government – even though it was not able to fulfil many of its promises in the last eight years – should fulfil its promise of being trustworthy in safeguarding people's votes. It should inform the public about people's real votes,' Shamsolvaezin said.

Notwithstanding all complaints about possible fraud and vote-rigging, the Guardian Council confirmed the results of the elections. For the first time, presidential elections in Iran were headed for a second round. And for the first time, one of the founders, custodians and figureheads of the Islamic Republic was to compete against a second-generation revolutionary. Rafsanjani had to fend off a contender who promised to revive the principles of the revolution that the 70-year-old cleric himself had cherished and fostered.

Some of the contrasts between Ahmadinejad and his rival were borne out in a television programme on 19 June. Ahmadinejad's representative took a swipe at the children of the wealthy, saying that although the names had changed, the rule of the Thousand Families (a term originally used to refer to the pre-Revolutionary aristocracy, but widely used for the ruling clerics also) continued. He promised that Ahmadinejad's cabinet would include young people. When Hashemi-Rafsanjani's representative said the country needed evolution rather than another revolution, Ahmadinejad's representative retorted that the country's current management had grown rigid and unresponsive and a revolution was necessary. The two also argued about Basij's involvement in the election, and Hashemi-Rafsanjani's representative said the Basij must not intervene in politics.

A 22 June editorial in one of the few surviving reformist dailies called Rafsanjani a 'shield against extremism' and urged him to 'respond positively' to his new coalition of supporters. Iranians – and Rafsanjani – must be considering the irony in this unexpected turn of affairs, an analyst said. 'But as reformers who started their political lives as revolutionaries have shown, politicians can change from left-wing radicals to moderates or even dissidents in response to changing times, as too may Rafsanjani,' he added. The irony was particularly excruciating for reformists who had subjected Rafsanjani to fierce attack not only back in 2000, but even until a few days before, when they still had high hopes of Moin's victory. In its websites and publications, IIPF leaders were at pains to persuade their supporters to vote for Rafsanjani, saying that it was the only way to stop 'fascism' taking over Iran. Many political groups and figures, as well as intellectuals and artists, joined forces to prevent the election of Ahmadinejad, whose supporters had already proved to be organised as well as determined. Candidates who lost in the first round moved to Rafsanjani's side. They included Karrubi, who initially criticised Rafsanjani's candidacy and blamed him for many of Iran's existing problems, but also Ali Larijani, who was often described as 'close' to the supreme leader. Moin also said that he would vote for Rafsanjani.

Rafsanjani even managed to wrench the support of some dissidents who have known prison and harassment in past years. Emadeddin Baqi, a writer jailed for articles he wrote about the murder of dissidents in the 1990s – during and shortly after the Rafsanjani presidencies – said that as a 'human rights activist, I am sounding the alarm bell'. Reformers and some of the men of reason in the right-wing faction must unite so the candidate opposed to Hashemi is not elected, he added. Another dissident, Ezzatollah Sahabi, said, 'All people and groups, even those who boycotted the polls, must support Rafsanjani.' As 24 June approached, the date of the unprecedented second round, the list of his supporters kept growing: former parliament members, moderate conservatives, and prominent representatives of the Chaldean and Assyrian Christian minorities. The popularity that eluded Rafsanjani but was present in the eight-year presidency of Muhammad Khatami – especially evident when Rafsanjani failed to win a seat in the 2001 parliamentary elections – seemed suddenly to have been thrust upon him.

Rafsanjani, seemingly elated, rose to these calls and the perceived urgency of a victory. Usually noncommittal on controversial issues, he deplored in a 20 June statement the 'shocking instances of abuse [against candidates] and unjust, organized interventions' on polling day. The complaints of 'my brother' Karrubi must be addressed, Rafsanjani said. More vigorously, he told students from Tehran University on 21 June that he would use 'all means' to prevent the Guardian Council from trying to change votes in the next round. 'If the system tries to act above the law, it will face problems,' he said. He added that the present conditions require 'an open atmosphere where people are not afraid to express what is on their mind.' In his statement, Rafsanjani mentioned 'safeguarding political and social liberties, and attention to women's rights', as items on his presidential agenda. A day later, Rafsanjani echoed Khatami's calls for the rule of law, and said all people in Iran, including students and journalists, must respect the law. The law, he added, 'may not be good, and what is legal today may become a better law, but ... the way is to act lawfully.' He cautioned students that 'if anyone breaks the law, they cannot expect' not to be prosecuted, whether the offences are 'political or not', the daily added.

Rafsanjani promised not to let 'parallel bodies' interfere in state security work, and approved of the 'present methods' of the Intelligence Ministry, which the Khatami government said had been purged of lawless agents who were accused of killing dissident Iranians in the 1990s. 'I will not let them interfere in the Intelligence Ministry's work,' declared Rafsanjani. The reforms that he claimed to have initiated, and Khatami to have pursued, 'must move forward and nobody wishes to oppose that'. Rafsanjani appeared to reach the limits of his democratic potential when he said he would oppose unjust imprisonments, and students shouted out the name of Akbar Ganji, jailed for critical writings not unrelated to Rafsanjani's political past. Ganji, he said, 'is also an instance that must be examined', but he remained silent when a student suggested he should, as candidate Moin had at an earlier stage, present parliament with a general amnesty bill if elected.

Despite relying heavily on the youth to provide votes, perhaps in a repetition of Khatami's 1997 landslide, needed by Rafsanjani, young people showed little – if any – willingness to do so. After all, it was less than one week that, in the words of a young Tehrani boy, 'Rafsanjani's dirty clothes have been hung in public'. For sure, in the run-up for the first round, candidates from different factions had, more than anything else, reminded the electorate that Rafsanjani could not be trusted. Candidates from political affiliations poles apart had accused him of a catalogue of wrongdoings, from financial corruption to the brutal silencing of his opponents. And anyway, many youngsters identified him simply as one of the leaders of the regime.

The night before the run-off, I asked Mehran, a 20-year-old jobless boy in Tehran, if he was going to vote for Rafsanjani.

'You got to be kidding,' he replied in an offhand way. 'He's the laughing stock of us all.'

'But what about Ahmadinejad? Aren't you scared of him?'

'He's even more laughable,' he said, and told me the latest rude joke circulating in Tehran about the would-be president. 'The president's just a nothing in this country. Have you forgotten Khatami?'

I remembered Mehran telling me that he had voted in the first round, and I asked him why.

'I just made a bet on fifty thousand toomans for nothing,' he giggled. He was referring to Karrubi's election campaign, in which he had promised to give the equivalent of 50 dollars to every Iranian if he won.

Meanwhile, reformists kept repeating that an Ahmadinejad victory would bring a Taliban-style rule to Iran. Jalal Jalalizadeh, an Iranian Kurd and a former Majles deputy, said an Ahmadinejad win would deal a blow to freedom of expression. 'The people of Iran have many economic problems, but an open political atmosphere – for criticism and also for cultural activities – is also important today. Iranian people, including Kurds, need an open atmosphere in which to voice their criticism of the regime. I think an Ahmadinejad victory will stifle that atmosphere for all people, especially for minorities,' Jalalizadeh said.

Ahmadinejad's supporters dismissed accusations of the rival camp, saying that his presidency would not put civil liberties at risk. Ahmadinejad said that 'real freedom' could only be found within the parameters of Iran's Islamic establishment.

Muhammad Hossein Jaafarian, a conservative columnist, said Ahmadinejad's opponents were waging a campaign to tarnish his image. 'This image by the opponents of Mr Ahmadinejad is very unfair. They have become so terrified, and all without reason. I feel that [the reformists] want to prevent their rival from taking power at any price. It does not mean that [Ahmadinejad] will follow policies that might cause limitations. From what we have seen, he has an open view on cultural issues. It is not as [critics] say,' Jaafarian said.

Ahmadinejad said that if he won the run-off election, he would do his best to serve the poor, farmers, and people in rural areas. Ahmadinejad's backers played the religion card as well. Senior conservative cleric Muhammad Taqi Mesbah Yazdi quoted a 'man of God' who had dreamed of the twelfth Shi'i imam as ordering him to vote for Ahmadinejad, adding that the man had not even heard the name of the presidential candidate before.

As the heated debates went on between the two contenders, proponents of a boycott reasoned that Iran was already in the grip of a religious despotism, and at the end of the day it did not matter who won the elections because, they said, Khatami's tenure had showed that the president had no powers in a system ruled by a supreme leader. Some went so far as to say the whole thing was a scenario written by the regime to make people go to the polls and thus gain legitimacy.

Hardly could any of the vox pops conducted by the press indicate that the conservatives stood a chance of beating Rafsanjani. 'We are tired of disputes, arguments, violence, and instability, and we want someone who can establish stability – that is to say, economic, social, political, and cultural, stability,' a prospective voter in Tabriz told Iran daily on 23 June. A Tabriz student promised to back the candidate who could resist efforts to weaken the country's student movement, while another called for a president who would not waste state resources. 'Our society needs economic development, and economic development, in turn, cannot materialize without 'stability', a Tabriz bazaar merchant told the daily.

Just before the run-off, many observers drew analogies with the 2002 presidential elections in France, when Jean-Marie Le Pen obtained nearly 17 percent of the votes in the first round of voting. This was enough to qualify him for the second round, as a result of the scattering of votes among fifteen other candidates. This was a major political event, both nationally and internationally, as it was the first time an extreme right-wing candidate had qualified for the second round of the French presidential elections. There was a widespread stirring of national public opinion, and more than one million people in France took part in street rallies, in an expression of fierce opposition to Le Pen's ideas. Le Pen was then soundly defeated in the second round when incumbent president Jaques Chirac obtained 82 percent of the votes. This gave ample reason to many reformists to suggest that the Chirac-Le Pen showdown was being replayed in Iran. It wasn't.

Even Ahmadinejad's supporters watched in disbelief as he won 62 percent of votes, defying predictions of a close race and humiliating Rafsanjani, whose backers had said before the result that an Ahmadinejad victory would signal voting fraud. According to official results, some twenty-two million people voted in the run-off poll – a turnout of 60 percent, down from 63 percent in the first round a week earlier. Khamenei called the election result an 'enormous humiliation' for the US. Once again the Iranian people showed, he said, 'your greatness to the people of the world, and your power to your bitter and malicious enemies.' He also banned both camps from celebrating or protesting, and urged people to keep off the streets.

As with the first round, fingers of accusation were immediately pointed at the Revolutionary Guards and Basij for vote-rigging and electoral manipulation. Some untoward incidents on election day invited questions about the final result. On election day, security personnel arrested an Interior Ministry official who was trying to inspect a polling station, and in northern Tehran members of the semi-official hard-line unit, Promoting Virtue and Prohibiting Vice, prevented people from voting. The interference got so bad that the Interior Ministry tried unsuccessfully to close some polling stations. Interior Ministry spokesman Jahanbakhsh Khanjani said, 'Reporting of violations of the Election Law at such a broad level is quite unprecedented and according to the latest reports the violations are no longer limited to trivial illegal affairs.' After his release from police custody, Interior Ministry director of parliamentary affairs Ali Mirbaqeri said he witnessed Guardian Council interference at all the polling stations he visited. 'The monitors of the Guardian Council were not only filling out the tariffs and controlling the voters' IDs, but also constantly issuing orders to everyone,' he said. Mirbaqeri said council officials confined him to a room for two hours and then turned him over to the police, who held him for another two hours.

Amid rumours that his brother, a former vice-president, had suffered a heart attack, a somber Rafsanjani congratulated his rival on 25 June, but he too referred to foul play by his opponents and noted the pointlessness of complaining to the body charged with supervising elections, the Guardian Council. 'I do not intend to take my complaint about the elections to those arbitrators who have proved that they do not want to, or cannot, do anything,' he said. 'I only seek my right in the court of divine justice ...' His rivals, Rafsanjani noted, 'have interfered in the elections by utilizing the facilities of the [Islamic] system in an organized and illegitimate manner', in a clear allusion to the military.

According to Abbas Milani, Ahmadinejad's victory was masterminded by Supreme Leader Ayatollah Khamenei, and a cabal of conservative clerics and Revolutionary Guards. 'According to three of Mr Ahmadinejad's opponents, members of the Revolutionary Guards and the Basij militia, who together number in the millions, were told whom to vote for and to bring up to ten family members along with them to the polls. The same sources allege that millions of dollars from public coffers were distributed among militia members in order to bring out the hard-line vote,' Milani said.[2]

In his analysis of the election results, William A. Samii suggested that something was amiss in the Ahmadinejad victory:

> There were 46,786,418 eligible voters, and 27,959,253 of them voted on 24 June, for a total turnout of almost 60 percent. The previous week, 29,439,982 people voted, for a turnout of almost 63 percent.
>
> In the second round of the election, Ahmadinejad received 17,248,782 votes, while in the first round he got 5,710,354 votes. How did he gather an additional 11.5 million votes in one week? Even if voter participation remained the same, and if Ahmadinejad received the 5,815,352 votes that went to the other hard-line candidates in the first round – Ali Larijani and Muhammad Baqer Qalibaf – that would only amount to 11,525,706. It defies logic that under circumstances where there were fewer people voting, support for Ahmadinejad almost tripled.
>
> Rafsanjani received 10,046,701 votes on 24 June, while he got 6,159,453 votes the previous week. Obviously, not all Iranians who backed reformist candidates in the first round (Mehdi Karrubi, Mohsen Mehralizadeh, and Mostafa Moin) backed Hashemi-Rafsanjani, or he would have received their 10,409,943 votes, for a total of 16,569,396. This would indicate that approximately 6 million voters stayed home, yet according to the official turnout figures, there were only 1.5 million fewer voters on 24 June.
>
> In the second round of the election, 663,770 ballots were spoiled (approximately 2 percent), compared to 1,221,940 spoiled ballots the previous week (approximately 4 percent). Apparently, people were much more careful and wanted to be sure their votes counted.[3]

Samii, however, added that although this kind of quantitative analysis is useful, in the Iranian case it has serious limitations. 'The greatest shortcoming is that the Iranian government does not give access to independent foreign observers. They cannot visit polling places to observe voter behaviour, and there is no telling what happens to the ballot boxes when they are transferred from the polling station to the counting area. One is therefore dependent on whatever figures the regime chooses to provide, and in the absence of direct evidence to the contrary, it is purely speculative to say there was fraud.'

Iran's regime, he argued, is less concerned with the outcome of the election than it is with the fact that it holds them on a fairly regular basis. Thus, it can claim public support and therefore legitimacy. 'As the case of Khatami shows, furthermore, powerful unelected institutions can counter elected officials when their interests are threatened or when it appears that the system will be undermined. As a former member of the Revolutionary Guards, Ahmadinejad's victory is representative of the rightward drift that started a few years ago. But the Revolutionary Guards were quick to remind Ahmadinejad that there are limits to how far he can go. In a 25 June statement it told him to stay true to his campaign promises. This could be a reminder that he is indebted to the Guards for his victory and should not threaten its economic interests, or it could be a reminder that the corps has a constitutionally defined political role.'

Politicians all along the factional spectrum, opposition figures, and analysts were at pains to understand the reasons behind, and the implications of, Ahmadinejad's surprise victory. His election became a Rorschach test for observers. Some compared it to the 2004 presidential elections in the US, whereas others attributed the results to the lack of a charismatic figure among the candidates. Revisionism, populism and even national masochism were other reasons suggested to explain Ahmadinejad's victory. Apart from fraud, which the opposition said was the main cause of the shocking results, many analysts pointed fingers at the growing economic dire straits of a large part of the Iranian population, regarding Ahmadinejad as a sort of Iranian Robin Hood. A BBC correspondent said it was 'Ahmadinejad's appeal to the poor that seems to be the secret to his success. Despite Iran's huge oil wealth the country has high unemployment and a big gap between rich and poor'.

Some reformers went to extremes in trying to explain their defeat. Amir Hossein Barmaki, a middle-class Tehrani who later worked for the United Nations in the city, said that the chief mistake of the reformers was that they did nothing for the veterans when they came to power after the war. 'These boys from the poor districts came home, having saved the country, and we did nothing for them. There were some who were dying of Saddam's poison gas attacks who didn't even get a pension.'

Khatami's victory in 1997 carried many reformers away, leading them to believe that democracy was round the next corner. Now Ahmadinejad's shock election seems to have caused the reformers to mix fact and fiction in their attempts to conduct a ruthless soul-searching. 'There was worse,' Barmaki said. 'None of us actually went to the war. All the middle class went abroad or stayed in university. We sent the poor instead. We could even buy our way out of military service. It is our shame.'

Samii holds that the victory of Ahmedinaejad represents the ascendance of the country's second post-Revolution generation, and the return of the common man to the country's politics. 'The 48-year-old Ahmadinejad's victory represents the ascendance of the Islamic Revolution's second generation, and Rafsanjani's loss represents the twilight of the first generation. The Iran-Iraq war shaped the second generation, while opposition to the monarchy and trying to establish an Islamic state shaped the first one. Ahmadinejad's generation sacrificed a great deal in the war, and now it wants something in return. It worked up to this election victory slowly and subtly, emerging from nowhere to win the 2003 municipal-council elections and then building on that to win the 2004 parliamentary elections.

'Ahmadinejad's victory also represents the return of the common man to Iranian politics. Parties in post-Revolutionary Iran are elite institutions, and at election time they only present voters with a list of recommended candidates. The reformist parties and the 2nd of Khordad Front promoted important issues – civil society, press freedom, and dialogue – but they forgot about the basics – employment, a living wage, and shelter. Ahmadinejad therefore stressed the themes that resonated – such as job creation when there is double-digit unemployment, and the elimination of corruption. Although some people may worry about Ahmadinejad's conservative stance on cultural and social issues, that is probably irrelevant to the average citizen.'[4]

Michael Ignatieff echoed a similar view. 'Ahmadinejad had capitalized not only on his war service but also on gathering disillusion with the failure of the reformers – nominally in power since the election of

President Muhammad Khatami in 1997 – to address popular grievances relating to jobs, housing, transport and, above all, the growing class divide,' he says. 'In leafy north Tehran, reformers were talking about human rights and democracy, while in dusty south Tehran, the poor were struggling to hold onto jobs in an economy in which unemployment was officially 15 percent and probably twice that. For the reformers, the victory brought home how out of touch with ordinary Iranians many of them had become.'[5]

Pro-reform journalist Muhammad Javad Rooh also believes that it was the 'marginalised ones' that determined the fate of the elections. 'Those who voted for Ahmadinejad were those who saw themselves as victims of a development plan that started with the eight-year reconstruction [Rafsanjani's tenure] and followed by the reformist government [of Khatami].'[6]

Although there is some truth in such arguments, they suffer from a basic flaw. In 1997, and then again in 2001, Iran's economic outlook or the economic situation of the average citizen was not significantly better than that in 2005. It was quite possibly worse. Yet an overwhelming majority of people voted for Khatami, the candidate whose platform was least characterised by economic plans and promises. Those who voted for Khatami included peasants, workers, the jobless and the shantytown dwellers, as well as intellectuals and uptown kids. It is true that in the absence of political parties with clearly defined goals and strategies, Iranians are exposed to all sorts of demagogic propaganda by false messiahs and saviours, but it would be misleading to reduce a sophisticated equation to a basic linear economic assumption.

A fundamentally different, but still unconvincing, interpretation was suggested by religious-nationalist analyst Ahmad Zaidabadi. He maintained that after eight years of witnessing their elected president and parliament being paralysed by unelected bodies, this time people voted for someone who was close to the real core of political power, so that power and responsibility would finally be united. Once people found out that Khatami had only responsibilities but no power, even after the Majles was dominated by his supporters, Zaidabadi argues, they were convinced that in Iran's political system, true power lies in the hands of those who have no responsibility at all. 'People instinctively realised that power and responsibility should be integrated ... and then if no result was borne even then, everything would be transparent and those responsible for the problems would be clearly recognised.[7]

'During the past eight years, people failed to give power to those they had already given responsibility. But couldn't they give responsibility to those who had power? Yes, they could, and that's exactly what they did,' Zaidabadi said.

Overlooking the fact that it attributes an unthinkable degree of collective genius to Iranians, Zaidabadi's theory helps explain pieces of the puzzle, if not the whole picture. On the eve of the run-off elections, I spoke to Vida, a 26-year-old girl from a lower middle-class family. I knew that her cleric-skeptical parents, both civil servants, had never taken part in any elections after the 1979 Revolution, and that she had voted only once – for Khatami in 1997. I was surprised to learn that all three were going to vote for Ahmadinejad, and I asked why. 'Because he represents what the Islamic Republic really is. We're sick of this hole-and-corner way of the past eight years. We want the world to know whom they're dealing with. We no more want to be deceived by an ostensibly humane face of a regime that's giving us hell,' she said.

Tehran university professor Sadeq Zibakalam confirmed that there was such a tendency among the largely disenfranchised students. 'There's a significant division among students,' he said. 'There are those who believe that the [ruling] system is beyond reforms. They have boycotted the elections. And there are those who are going to vote for Ahmadinejad, ironically for the same reason. They say that if the regime became monolithic, its downfall would be accelerated.'

But could this argument justify Ahmadinejad's more than eleven million extra votes in the run-off – if one accepts the official results, that is? As I mentioned in chapter nine, the lack of reliable official statistics or opinion polls in Iran means, one has to resort to other barometers to gauge the social undercurrents. On 8 June, less than ten days before the presidential elections, Iran's national football team beat Bahrain in Tehran's Azadi stadium, securing a place in the 2006 World Cup in Germany. Streets in all cities and towns across the country – from affluent north Tehran to working-class neighbourhoods in Ahvaz – were immediately flooded with millions of cheering fans who openly ridiculed restrictions imposed on them by Ahmadinejad's fellow thinkers. Thousands of young women brazenly flouted the dress code, taking off their mandatory headscarves, waving them in the air and dancing with young men. As a foreign correspondent observed, once more, football served as a vehicle for reform in the Islamic republic. 'Who cares about the elections?' laughed one young woman draped in the red, white and green Iranian flag. 'We're going to the World Cup!'[8]

This of course does not mean that traditional beliefs, Islamic fanaticism or economic poverty do not play roles in the public's voting behaviour, but it may help decipher the seemingly enigmatic discrepancy between such manifestations of discontent and the election of a hard-line president. For those more familiar with the dynamics of Iranian society, there is no enigma at all. As Abbas Milani said, contrary to the common perception, the June 2005 election was not so much a sign of the Iranian system's strength as of its weakness. 'The presidential election, in his view, is only the most recent example of the tactical wisdom and strategic foolishness of Iran's ruling clerics. All the reformist candidates, particularly Rafsanjani, as well as the approximately 70 percent of the electorate who voted for reformists or boycotted the election, sought above all to limit Ayatollah Khamenei's increasing despotism.'[9]

If the officially published results are true, they are indicative of a number of major trends in Iran. First, the plethora of different factions and tendencies that come under the broad definition of 'conservatives' has a popular basis of about 10 percent. This assumption obviously disregards the military who were *ordered* to vote for Ahmadinejad, or the illiterate who were *told* whom to vote for, or those who voted out of fear of losing their jobs or facing other problems. It also discounts those who allegedly voted for him to accelerate an ultimate showdown between the people and the regime. Second, despite being an obvious minority, the conservatives have considerable organisational powers, thanks to their control over the armed forces, the judiciary and the mass media. This, of course, is bound to change as they take over all the levers of power, and consequently rifts begin to emerge as they begin to fight for power among themselves. Third, as demonstrated earlier in the municipal and parliamentary elections of 2003 and 2004, the younger generations and middle classes that brought Khatami to power in 1997 have lost hope and trust in intra-state reformers, and are no more willing to turn to them even when their already limited liberties seem to be at stake. Following the failure of Khatami's reforms, they are disorganised and confused. And last but not least, the majority of people are finished with the Islamic Republic as a whole – not only the supreme leader, but any representative of the first or second generation – be they leftist; centrist or conservative revolutionaries; pragmatic or fundamentalist; hard-line or moderate; clerics or laymen.

In the words of Abbas Milani, Ayatollah Khamenei and his allies turned a blind eye on the meaning of the June 2005 elections and instead made a grab for absolute power. 'In the process they may have unwittingly opened the door for democracy – because their hardball tactics have created the most serious rift in the ranks of ruling mullahs since the inception of the Islamic Republic. The experience of emerging democracies elsewhere has shown that dissension within ruling circles has often presaged the fall of authoritarianism.'[10]

As for Ahmadinejad's promised revolutionary economic policies, Ignatieff has said that they sound like the Islamic Marxism that has passed for economic theory in Iran since the Revolution: don't depend on foreigners; keep the economy in state hands, otherwise foreign capitalists will get control of it; restrain the financial sector, because a free financial sector will cause the economy to melt down.

'With oil at about 60 dollars a barrel,' he said, 'there is little likelihood that the regime will be forced to open up and reform the economy. But unless it does, there won't be much democracy or progress for the poor. One human-rights truth, universally acknowledged, is that oil is an obstacle to democracy in every developing society. When a government can get what it needs out of oil derricks and ceases to derive its revenue from taxes, it loses any incentive to respond to the people. Theocracy in Iran is built on oil and will endure as long as the oil price holds up.'[11]

Milani disagreed. 'Instead of finding a sound strategic solution to Iran's economic woes,' he said, 'Ayatollah Khamenei and his allies have trotted out the old populist slogans of revolutionary justice, economic autarky and pseudosocialism. When that formula fails, as it did in the 1980's even with the charisma of Ayatollah Ruhollah Khomeini to help it along, the mullahs will be denied their last bastion of support among the country's poor, whose piety and deprivation they have long exploited. In the short term, the right wing has scored a major victory. In the long run, they have helped bring Iran one step closer to democracy.'[12]

ELEVEN

Childhood's End

What right has the nation of fifty years ago to determine the fate of the nations to come after them? Each nation holds its destiny in its own hands ... Are our fathers supposed to be our guardians?
Ayatollah Ruhollah Khomeini, 1978

We will wear your white feathers,
We will carry your white flags,
We will swear we have no nation,
But we're proud to own our hearts.
Marillion, *Misplaced Childhood*

Though it cannot be much comfort to those who have to live, here and now, under public and private tyrannies, I came away from a night in Isfahan believing that Persian pleasure, in the long run, would outlast Shi'i puritanism.
Michael Ignatieff, 2005

In the scorching heat of August, pavements of Vali-e Asr Avenue, lined with magnificent plane trees, were suddenly overrun by a stampede of thousands of people, mostly young men and women who were dashing into side streets. Boutique owners and attendants were hurriedly closing their shops. Young girls were busy pulling their headscarves forward to cover coiffeurs of blond-dyed hair or wiping deep purple coloured lipstick off their lips. Shouts and screams echoed through the summer dusk. 'Moral Police' had stormed Vali-e Asr, aided and abetted by

Ansar-e Hezbollah thugs. Under the watchful gaze of officers in olive-coloured uniforms, female police agents clad in black chadors stopped young women, barking at them, questioning them and dragging the more defiant ones towards buses waiting in line. Members of Ansar-e Hezbollah were busy chanting 'Marg bar Badhejab' (death to those with improper hejab), breaking with stones the windows of shops displaying lingerie or short robes, and beating up whomever happened to be in their way. Pedestrians were looking on in desperation.

Next to a florists' shop, one of the 'sisters' had cornered a young woman wearing a tight sky-blue tunic, tight jean pants, high-heel white sandals and a pink triangular headscarf.

'Aren't you ashamed of the martyrs' families?' the sister snarled.

'What have I done?' The young girl retorted.

'Quiet! Take this!' She handed a paper tissue to the girl. 'Wipe it off. Now!'

The girl started wiping the make-up off her face. A mixture of black mascara and tears had smeared her cheeks. 'Ok, ok, whatever you say. Just don't take me away. My parents will have a heart attack.'

'Quiet! Just get into the bus!'

'No, please no. See, I've wiped all my make-up!'

'How about these?' The sister angrily pointed at the young girl's fingernails and toenails that were painted the colour of oxblood. 'Will you get into the bus quietly or shall I call the brothers?' And with the help of another sister, she finally forced the sobbing girl into the bus.

Other young women were not as meek, though. A girl in a short orange coat and a colourful floral scarf was screaming at the sisters who were trying to yank her towards a bus. 'Let go of me! Go get back the lands you lost to Iraq if you're so brave! Go get those thieves who plunder the country if you dare! Let go of me!'

The arrested girls are usually released a few hours later, with or without having paid a fine, but having suffered much humiliation. According to the law, appearing in public without proper hejab can be punishable by imprisonment of up to two months. This, however, happens very seldom, if at all, perhaps for the simple reason that prisons are not able to accommodate millions of such 'offenders'.

Every summer, the streets of Tehran and other large cities turn into battlefields of sorts. A battle that, unlike its appearance, in essence bears a close resemblance to a Crusade: zealous believers trying to reclaim the 'holy land' from the 'infidel'. Only in this case, it is the minds of the young people that the zealous try to conquer. And although Iran's ruling theocracy has so far succeeded in suppressing its political foes, this is one protracted battle in which it has failed to triumph. The 'hejab wars' are but one of the manifestations of the clash between tradition and modernity that has dominated Iran in the past century or so.

Back in 1989, during a live radio vox pop, the reporter asked a young girl a stereotype question. 'How do you think Fatemeh (Fatima) can be a role model for our women?' he asked, referring to the daughter of the Prophet Muhammad, who is regarded by the Shias as one of the fourteen infallible ones besides the Prophet himself and the twelve imams. In an anti-cliché surprise, the young woman said that although she held Fatemeh in high esteem, she did not think that modern Iranian women could pick her as a role model. She went on to say that in her opinion, Oshin, the self-made businesswoman protagonist of a popular Japanese TV series, would suit better to the needs of today's women. Ayatollah Khomeini was quick to issue a death sentence for the interviewee and order the dismissal of the producers of that radio programme. The first sentence was never carried out, however, because the interviewee could not be identified.

Once the uproar was over in Vali-e Asr, I approached Mehrnoush, a young woman who had managed to evade the storming moral police. She had freshened up her make-up and was now joined by her boyfriend Kasra. He had longish curly black hair and he was wearing a black Iron Maiden T-shirt, black jean pants and Timberland boots. They seemed relieved and furious at the same time.

'Dirty-minded dogs! They've taken away everything from us, and they don't seem to get enough of that!' Mehrnoush said.

Kasra was trying to calm her down: 'Easy now, cheer up. This is not new to any of us. We've got a party to go to. Cheer up! Don't think about the blockheads! They won't be around for much longer.'

Which was true, although his remark was meant to encompass the entire Islamic system and not solely the police. An hour later, with the moral police and the Ansar-e Hezbollah no more around, Vali-e Asr was once again a public catwalk crowded by flamboyant boys and girls.

As the long hot season – beginning as early as late April and going on until late September in many parts of Iran – approaches, hard-line authorities start issuing stern warnings against women who flout the strict Islamic dress codes. In May 2005, Tehran police chief Saeed Zarei said that his forces would 'deal with street mannequins'. Asked by reporters what he meant by 'street mannequins', he said, '[Those who wear] short pants that sometimes don't cover more than a little under the knee, and headscarves that can't be called headscarves. They threaten the moral security of the society; they are obvious manifestation of corruption.'[1] But the hard-line authorities have been increasingly losing control and have often found it difficult – if not impossible – to enforce such measures in the past.

A favourite slogan of the conservatives, written in beautiful *nasta'liq* script on many walls throughout Iran, reads, 'A woman is like a pearl, and the hejab is like the protecting shell.' In 2004, boutiques were banned from putting lingerie, as well as 'short and indecent' clothes, in their windows, or using mannequins inside the shops. The true reason for the conservative-minded behind the ban – never expressed openly – is that such items provoke men's sexual desire. But the pearls seem to be growing increasingly sick of the shells.

Notwithstanding the frequent crackdowns, the situation goes back to where it was shortly afterwards: bustling streets, squares, parks and shopping centres of large cities are swarmed with women wearing heavy make-up, gowns that grow ever tighter, brighter, shorter and thinner and headscarves that grow ever smaller and more colourful. In the face of repeated laments by traditionalist clerics, more pragmatic authorities hope that turning a blind eye on such minor acts of defiance will relieve pressure for major change.

Police officer Rahman Mahmoudi says that the way some young Iranian women dress makes him feel they have got miles away from the characteristics of an 'original Iranian woman'. 'Wearing heavy, insulting make-up, leaving the buttons of their gowns open, wearing summer sandals without socks and short pants that clearly show the ankles are all signs of promiscusity,' Mahmoudi told SYNA news agency in 2005.[2]

Nevertheless, such harsh language of the authorities begin to soften whenever elections time approaches and the conservative politicians try to win the potentially multi-million-strong votes of the youth, or at least not to lose the votes of their parents. In the few months preceding the June 2005 presidential elections, even the most hard-line candidates chose not to directly address the personal appearance issue. Tehran's hard-line mayor Mahmoud Ahmadinejad said that the Islamic Republic had not imposed the hejab on women, and that Iranian women chose the Islamic dress code of their own free will. Former police chief Muhammad Baqer Qalibaf – whose forces had been actively involved in cracking down on young girls – said that he was against using force in dealing with women who did not fully observe the hejab. And clergyman Mehdi Karrubi, former Majles Speaker, said that he was against 'some imposing approaches under the title of fighting improper hejab'. He was quick to add, however, that he believed 'most Iranian youth did not have a problem with the essence of the hejab'. Ironically, in Karrubi's website, a letter from a 17-year-old girl was published, in which she bitterly complained about the imposed dress code. 'If you mean what you say,' she wrote to Karrubi, 'Let there be a referendum on the issue to see how many girls do want to observe the hejab.'

In the run-up to the presidential elections in June 2005, several candidates went to far lengths to convince the young population that they understood them and cared for them. As a commander in the Revolutionary Guards and later police chief, Qalibaf used to sport the trademark appearance and outfit of all devoted revolutionaries: long beard, shabby clothes and pistol holster. Once an election hopeful, he went through a metamorphosis, trimming his beard and wearing designer suits and latest fashion sunglasses. Former higher education minister and reformist candidate Mostafa Moin appointed a woman – former Majles deputy Elaheh Koolaei – as his spokesperson. Koolaei then appeared in her first press conference not only without a chador, but wearing a colourful headscarf. And Rafsanjani's campaign was highlighted by a 'carnival' of young boys and girls in blue jeans riding fancy cars and brandishing headbands with his name on them in Latin letters. In the words of satirist Ebrahim Nabavi, 'we have succeeded in imposing other ways of thinking on the regime. It would suffice to take a look at the election campaigns to see how far we have succeeded.'[3]

Although the hejab wars have been a constant feature of the past two decades, not all the youth are openly defiant to the Islamic codes of appearance. There are still many young girls, particularly in smaller towns and cities, that choose to wear the chador in public; many boys who dress in the bland, traditionally religious uniform of plain shirts and trousers. However, as it becomes more and more difficult to forestall youngsters' exposure to what is happening beyond Iran's borders, this is undergoing a rapid change, even among strict traditional religious families. Parissa, a 16-year-old high-school student whose parents have brought her up wearing the chador since the age of nine, told me how every day in her life was a constant show.

'On my way to school, as soon as I get far enough from home, I turn into a back alley. I carefully fold my black chador and stuff it in my schoolbag. I daub my cheeks with some rouge that I have stacked away in my bag, and then I walk towards the school. At a safe distance from the school, I wipe off the rouge and put on the chador again.'

Being a relative of mine, she confided in me that she sometimes saw a young boy and that they walked a short distance holding hands.

'Do you call up each other?' I asked.

'Why, of course not. My parents have their eyes and ears glued to the telephone!'

'So how do you communicate?'

'Why, of course through the web. Whenever I'm allowed to log on to the web for some research work, he comes into the same chat-room as I do.'

'And do you ever see each other except on the way to the school?'

'Sometimes. Particularly during Moharram ceremonies.'

Although public mood seems subdued and somber during this most sacred month in the lunar Shi'i calendar, the Moharram mourning period provides an exceptional opportunity for young boys and girls to flirt without fear of being harassed or persecuted, and away from the gaze of parents. The youth have practically transformed the nationwide traditional ceremonies marking the martyrdom of the third Imam Hossein. In 2005, in parts of Tehran the Ashura ceremonies turned into what conservatives described as 'indecent displays'. Failure to stamp out such affront against the holiest mourning day in Shiism, some hard-line newspaper commentators said, would force pious citizens to take matters into their own hands. 'Let the officials realize that the heroic and passionate people of Iran can easily deal with a handful of hoodlums and promiscuous elements that ridicule our sanctities,' the conservative *Jomhuri-ye Eslami* daily said in an editorial.

The main focus of hard-line anger was a gathering of several hundred youngsters at Mohseni Square in affluent northern Tehran on the night of Ashura. 'In the sunset of Ashura, women and girls in tight clothes and transparent scarves and guys dressed in Western fashion lit candles while laughing their hearts out,' said the *Ya Lesarat* weekly, mouthpiece of the feared Ansar-e Hezbollah hard-line vigilante group, members of whom later dispersed the crowds. Other newspapers printed pictures from the Mohseni Square gathering, focusing on young girls wearing make-up, laughing and mingling freely with the opposite sex.[4]

'In this disgraceful event which was like a large street party, women and girls ... as well as boys ... mocked Muslims' beliefs and sanctities in the most shameless manner,' *Jomhuri-ye Eslami* said.

'Some long-haired guys would openly cuddle girls creating awful and immoral scenes. Fast, provoking music ... nearby gave the street party more steam,' it added. Instead of beating their chests or flagellating themselves with metal chains in bouts of sorrowful frenzy, boys in Mohseni Square, dressed in latest Western fashion black outfits, were holding candles, which they passed to girls with loud make-up and equally fashionable black dresses.

Tehran residents say the Mohseni Square Ashura gathering has swelled in size over recent years, attracting growing numbers from the generally more affluent parts of the city. But political analysts said the trend observed at Mohseni Square was in evidence, to a lesser extent, elsewhere. 'In general, religious events like Ashura have become a way for young people to interact freely in public,' said one analyst who follows religious affairs closely. 'The religious side of it is much less important to them than the social aspect,' the analyst, who declined to be named, added.[5]

Mohsen Kadivar, a mid-ranking cleric and philosophy lecturer whose views landed him in prison a few years back, told Reuters that young people in secular Turkey were more interested in religion than those in Iran. 'This shows that religion is voluntary. Forcing it on society has the opposite effect,' he said.

Traditionally marked by a deep sense of gloom and sorrow that was manifested by mourners weeping for what had happened to Imam Hossein in the Karbala desert, Moharram acquired a political meaning and played a vital part in the demonstrations that led to the ousting of the shah in 1979. In fact, in one of his famous remarks after the Revolution, Ayatollah Khomeini had said, 'Whatever we have today is owing to all this weeping ... we are a nation of political weeping.' In recent years, however, the Moharram mourning – which tends to incorporate a constantly diminishing amount of weeping – has posed a new political menace for a system that once relied heavily upon emotional teardrops. The fact that ceremonies of the mourning period of Moharram are widely held in every point of every town and village in Iran makes it all the more difficult for the authorities to control them.

Every year, Sattar Khan Aveneu in west Tehran is the meeting place of tens of thousands of mourners during the ten sacred evenings of Moharram, culminating in Ashura, the day when Imam Hossein and his 72 loyal companions were brutally slain. Huge black sheets of cloth, decorated with calligraphies on the margins with religious poetry, enshroud the walls, and black flags fly over almost every building. Large makeshift tents are erected to host mourning men after they come to the end of their procession. Gigantic rice pots boil on log fire. Sheep and cows and sometimes camels are slaughtered to make stew for the mourners. With the falling of dusk, people begin to swarm the streets, seemingly more in a picnic spirit that willing to shed tears. While processions go on to the beat of drums and cymbals, thousands of boys and girls freely mix and flirt, sometimes until dawn.

Leaning against a parked car on Sattar Khan Avenue with a couple of his friends, Bahman told me what the ceremony meant to him. 'It's the only entertainment that we can have on these days. And it's the only occasion we can stay out late without our parents giving us a hard time.' He looked eighteen, he was wearing a black skull-and-crossbones-marked Metallica sweater and black leather pants. He sported a black headband, ostensibly a token of mourning, framing his handsome features and accentuating his wide black eyes. His mouth slightly smelt of alcohol.

'Have you been drinking?' I asked.

He grinned and pulled a face to his friends. 'Only sherbet,' he said.

A young girl in a fine ebony gown, open in front and showing her slender build in blue jeans and a black top, approached us. 'They're busy with my uncle's family,' she said, probably referring to his parents. 'Let's go for a ride.' Bahman leapt onto the saddle of a small motorbike and the girl sat behind him. He started the engine and zoomed away amid cheering sounds of the other boys.

But there are also people among the youth who despise the way the mourning ceremonies have transformed. In a grocer's shop down the road, a young man in black shirt was standing behind the counter, shaking his head. 'Everything's become a farce. They no more respect anyone, even Imam Hossein,' he said.

I asked him why he thought that had happened. 'Loss of belief,' he said. 'When I was a kid, during Moharram we felt so close to God. They seem to believe in nothing any more these days.' And then he fell silent again.

Half an hour later I ran into Bahman again. One of his friends was gone, so was the motorbike. I asked him if Ashura had any religious meaning for him. 'Sure', he said. 'Of course I love Imam Hossein. But I don't think he was the kind of person *they* try to portray. He loved freedom. So do I. Times have changed from 1,400 years ago. So has the meaning of freedom.'

With a young couple riding on it, the motorbike appeared again, made an abrupt semicircle and stopped. The girl vanished into the crowd. 'It's a kind of outdoor party,' the boy said. 'You know how tricky indoor parties can be.'

Which was more or less true. In Iran, organising a party, which invariably means a dance party, is sometimes the equivalent of a clandestine operation. For young people who live with their parents, the first question is to obtain their consent and reassure them that no evil act, such as using drugs, would be included. The next question involves location and acoustics: how and where to hold the party so that the sound of music would not attract the attention of neighbours or passersby. Then comes the problem of logistics: how to get the booze – for middle and lower-class youth, home-made Armenian vodka (coming in one-gallon plastic containers), and for the well-off, foreign-made drinks smuggled mostly from neighbouring countries, ranging from Turkish beer to canned Ukrainian vodka to French cognac to Scotch whisky and gin. In some parties, the supply of prohibited material extends to marijuana, opium and designer drugs. Last but not least is the worst-case scenario: how to negotiate your way out to safety if the police or the Basij storm in. None of these complications mean that the youth will have second thoughts about holding parties. BBC's Pooneh Ghoddoossi gave accounts of a Tehran party she attended in 2004:

> On a recent trip home to Tehran I was invited to a birthday party. When I arrived I found the 70 or so guests wearing fancy dress and dancing to the latest Western pop music.
>
> The partygoers were all young and from well-to-do families. One was dressed as Tarzan, another as a pilot from the film *Top Gun*.
>
> Assorted 'ayatollahs' and 'mullahs' were whirling drunkenly under the strobe lights. A girl in a black chador flung it off to reveal a skin-tight Cat Woman costume underneath.
>
> In the middle of the fray, a waiter with a bow tie was trying to manoeuvre through the crowd, balancing a tray filled with glasses of wine, gin, vodka and whisky.
>
> The partygoers seemed not just to be defying the authorities, but actively poking fun at them ...
>
> The Tehran fancy dress party was taking place against a background of one of the worst political crises in Iran in the past twenty years.
>
> The hardliners had just banned hundreds of reformist MPs from taking part in the forthcoming parliamentary election. I asked one partygoer what he thought about it all.
>
> 'Actually I'm more interested in trying to remember the words to Eminem's latest song,' he said, and launched into an impromptu version of 'Lose Yourself'.
>
> At that moment there was a knock on the door. It was the Revolutionary Guards, wanting to know why there were so many cars in the street.
>
> I was terrified, but needn't have worried. One of the party guests, dressed as a mullah, told them it was a religious gathering and slipped them some money to leave us alone.[6]

In recent years, the 'party blackmail', usually termed 'coordination' in a mockery of revolutionary lexicon, has become a constant feature of joyous gatherings in Iran where loud music is played, men and women mix and dance, and the Islamic dress code is not observed. A few years

ago I went to the wedding party of the daughter of a colleague. By
Iranian standards, it was a very conservative party. The party was held in
the parking lot in the basement of an apartment block in central Tehran.
A trio of young men was playing Los Angeles-made Persian pop music.
Men and women of every age were dancing with the newlywed couple.
Guests who desired to drink alcohol would have to go to a storage room
at the far end of the garden, have a slug of vodka and come back to the
parking lot. The dance was in full swing when suddenly the band stopped
playing, the dancers sat down and women reached for their headscarves.
There was a general sense of commotion and suspense. I went out of the
parking lot and climbed the stairs to the front door, where the bride's
father was speaking to the commander of a police squad that had arrived
in Nissan Patrol SUVs.

'It's my daughter's wedding,' my colleague said. It's a family gathering.
I've already made coordination with the brothers.'

'Those brothers were from a different station probably,' the bearded
officer said. 'No coordination has been made with *us*.'

'Sorry, I didn't know you were also in charge of this neighbourhood.
Wait a second here please. No need to come in. It's only a family
gathering. I'll be back presently.'

When he came back, two men, each carrying a large tin pot filled
with saffron rice and chicken shish kebab were accompanying him.
'Your forces must be hungry. Please help yourself.' And while the men
were handing the pots to the officer's subordinates, my friend stealthily
slipped a wad of banknotes into his pocket.

'I wish you and your family a happy life,' the officer said. 'Please
convey my congratulations to the young couple. But make sure to keep
down the music volume.'

Money does not always talk, however. When it is the paramilitary volun-
teer Basijis that raid a party, the story usually ends in custody, court, fines,
and sometimes lashes. Things get more complicated if the party involves
the use of drugs. Increasing numbers of Iranian youngsters are getting
familiar with designer drugs such as Ecstasy and Ice, which are smuggled
chiefly from Thailand and Malaysia. Although not usually used in parties,
heroin is the most readily available drug. Neighboring Afghanistan is one
of the world's largest producers of opium. A daily fix of heroin in Tehran
costs only about 7,000 toomans, the equivalent of 7 dollars.

Some experts say that drug abuse among Iranian youth is getting out of hand. 'I have lost my hope', says retired social worker Naser Alikhani. 'Drug abuse is going wild and out of control. Honestly speaking, I do not think we can do anything to fight the increasing number of addicts in Iran.'[7]

The use of drugs has traditionally been tolerated within Persian society, particularly the consumption of hashish and opium by men of middle-age and older. Today, however, drug use is no longer the 'old people's bad habit,' as Muhammad Ali Zam says. 'The pattern of the drug abuse has changed, and most of the addicts are young.'

In the government's view, reiterated regularly by the state-run radio, television and print media, this shift has been caused by several factors: Iran's proximity to Afghanistan, which produces most of the world's supply of opium, the source of heroin; parental permissiveness; youth idleness; and family conflict. Government officials also blame the influences of Western culture, including the Internet, where they say hallucinogenic drugs are readily available. According to police, increased opium production in neighbouring Afghanistan is the single greatest factor fuelling drug abuse.

Addicts trying to kick their habit are also critical of the government's approach to treating drug abuse, but for other reasons. They believe officials provide insufficient support. At Aftab (Sunshine) Society, a non-profit clinic founded by President Muhammad Khatami's office a year ago, Haddad Eatemadi complained, 'They have only seventeen beds here in the clinic to hospitalise addicts. You see, we need millions of beds.' The 30-year-old user, who, at his wife's urging is trying to quit using opium, also criticised the government for ending its subsidy of detoxification medicine, a move that has increased the financial burden on him and other addicts.[8]

Drug addicts are increasingly turning to one another for assistance. In the basement of the Aftab Society, hundreds of drug addicts gather everyday at 7 pm to talk about their struggle to give up drugs. These free chats are guided by former addicts.[9]

Although drug addiction is particularly targeting young men, the number of female drug users is said to be growing. Iranian newspapers estimate that there are currently about 300,000 women working the streets. Many are runaways who have fled abusive families. Others sell their bodies out of simple poverty.

A documentary made by an Iranian-born director in 2004 has brought the issue under the spotlight. *Prostitution Behind the Veil* follows the lives of two young friends – Minna and Fariba – who have turned to prostitution to make a living. Nahid Persson spent more than a year filming the daily lives of the film's two young mothers, who are raising their children alone and supporting heroin addictions through prostitution.[10]

Persson, who left Iran for Sweden two decades ago, says she met and befriended Fariba and Minna while filming a fortune-teller in Tehran about two years ago. She says the women were happy that someone was interested in their plight. Once filming began, Persson says she was herself at risk filming in Iran – where prostitution is illegal and adulterers can face the death penalty.

Persson says that the two women asked her on several occasions to go with them when they were going to meet some of their regular customers, because they were from a police station. She adds that most of Fariba and Minna's customers complied with Islamic law through temporary marriages of convenience called *sighehs*.

The filmmaker says both women acquired their heroin addictions through drug-addicted husbands, and that they turned to prostitution out of distress and desperation. To the dismay of authorities in the Islamic Republic, the number of prostitutes has grown in recent years. Iranian authorities have warned that without adequate support and an improvement in living conditions, the ranks of those who are officially labelled 'street women' could increase.[11]

While the reformists in the government have come to view prostitution as a rising social problem that requires sociological solutions, some hardliners prescribe harsh methods to eradicate what is regarded as a 'stain of shame' from the face of the Islamic Republic. In her speech in the Majles in 2004, female deputy Eshrat Shaieq said, 'There are no laws specifically designed to deal with "street-walkers", and if we execute ten of them, we will have dealt with the problem once and for all.' She went on to say that single women were worth nothing and in many cultures single women were shunned from society. 'Our culture respects women; it is the women themselves who have no self-respect,' Shayeq said.[12]

Prostitution may seem the ultimate form of selling one's body out of distress and desperation. It is not. Young people are sometimes forced to go to unimaginable extremes to make ends meet, such as selling body organs by advertising in newspapers. A 24-year-old electrical engineering student who advertised in *Hamshahri* daily newspaper in 2004 to sell his kidney said in an interview that he wanted to tackle his financial problems.

> I have tried everything ... well, not really everything. I was working in the Bazaar, but I suddenly went bankrupt. I have sold my car, but I still need more money. I have too much debt. Someone borrowed from me and never paid back. I'm not in a good family situation, I can't cope with this. It's some time that I've been engaged to a girl. My fiancé's family agreed to our engagement considering my financial situation at that time. Now that I'm plighted with this situation, they won't understand.

Asked how much he was asking for his kidney, the young man said, 'No fix price; I told the recipients that we'd talk about the price when we were ready for transplant. I don't think that it's nice to call it 'price' – it's a donation, and one would pay whatever he or she can pay.

According to the head of Iran's Kidney Diseases Foundation, every year 1,500 to 1,700 transplants take place in the country, 98 percent of which is based on 'transactions' and only 2 percent involves humanitarian donation. Kidneys are for sale, and donors usually sell their kidneys out of poverty. The government has set the price of each kidney at about 1,000 dollars, but most of the people in need of transplants cannot afford to buy the required kidneys, partly because many of the 'kidney sellers' ask for 4,000 to 10,000 dollars.[13]

Iran's Kidney Foundation has announced that kidney donors should be between 22 and 34 years old. The government pays about 1,000 dollars to donors as a 'humanitarian award'. The head of Iran's Kidney Foundation believes that paying this award helps create a lucrative black market for 'dealers'.[14]

Kidney dealers usually receive about 2,000 dollars for fees and in return provide the patients with a list of people whose blood and tissue type match those of the patient. The more healthy a kidney is, the higher its price.

Since the victory of the Islamic Revolution, which, among other lofty ideals, promised to release the deprived masses of the burden of poverty, the issue of class gap has been overshadowed by the general demand for personal liberties. This, however, does not mean that such gap has not widened under the clerical rule. While some university students resort to selling their kidneys to subsist, affluent youth can afford almost every luxury that can – or cannot – be enjoyed in the Islamic Republic, from in-house sauna and Jacuzzi to scuba diving and skiing. Iran's snowcapped Alborz and Zagros Mountains boast some of the best ski slopes in the world. Developed for the high society under the shah, a ski lover himself, ski resorts near Tehran are today the meeting place of youth from families some of which have rocketed to overnight wealth thanks to a corrupt economy.

Dizin is perhaps Iran's most famous ski resort. In the heart of the towering Alborz mountains and covered with fresh snow sometimes until July, it was developed under the personal attention of the shah, a ski buff whose favourite resort after Dizin was St Moritz in Switzerland.

On weekends, Dizin represents the very epitome of what the Islamic Republic's founders most despised. Young men and women from wealthy families in state-of-the-art ski outfits and sunglasses mixing freely, laughing loudly and having fun. Despite the fact that alcohol is forbidden in Dizin, as in any other place in Iran, many skiers candidly bring in their booze and share it not too secretly. A female skier told ABC News that it is nice to be able to go to the resort and have a little bit more relaxation. 'That's part of the reason that we come,' she said. 'Partly to ski and partly to just have a good time breathing.'[15]

The relaxation could not happen without the knowledge of the country's hard-line religious leaders. Many at the resort told ABC News that they privately believe the government is trying to distract them from continuing restrictions on political reform. 'I think that they're well aware of it,' a male skier said. 'It's been awarded by them and there's reasons behind it.' It wasn't always so. Just after Iran's Islamic Revolution in 1979, many ski resorts were closed. Skiing was believed to be un-Islamic. When they reopened in the 1990s, skiers had to follow strict Islamic rules on the slopes.

The young Iranians who go to Dizin belong to a very select group. Skiing is expensive. And the relative freedom allowed at the resort is available almost exclusively to the wealthy. 'This place, the people come here to have fun, just to be free,' one skier said, 'and they don't want to hurt nobody, and they don't want to be hurt.'[16]

The oasis of Dizin – operated by Bonyad-e Mostaz'afan (literally the Foundation for the Disinherited) – seems to be a world out of the Islamic Republic. So does Kish Island in the Persian Gulf, where there remains no more than a crust of the strict rules implemented by the authorities. Just like Dizin, the picturesque coral island was a favourite resort of the shah. With less than 90,000 square metres of area and less than 16, 000 native residents, Kish island boasted in the 1970s one of a handful of airports where the Concorde landed, bringing in the Royal Family's distinguished guests from Europe to bask in the soothing semitropical wintertime sunshine by the limpid turquoise waters. Left in isolation after the Revolution as a particular symbol of the excesses of the shah, the Islamic rulers began pondering the island's potential as a free trade-zone. After years of trial and error, Kish island has now for many people become a shopping hub as well as a refuge from the restrictions of the mainland. Hejab is almost non-existent, live pop music is played in cafes and restaurants, alcohol and opium are much more easily accessible, and no-one stops couples on the beach or in the malls and coffee shops to inquire if they are relatives. Beaches are still segregated for the sexes, though. A few years ago in Kish, a travel agent told me about a new solution that young women and men had came up with to meet each other: they would book separate tours to Kish, but once they were on the island they would cautiously visit each other's bungalows.

For most of the Iranian youngsters who cannot afford the luxury of having fun in places such as Dizin or Kish, the internet opens a gateway to the outside world. In 2004, there were nearly 5 million Internet users in Iran, compared to 250,000 just four years before. Blogging has had an exponential growth, and Persian is currently the third most commonly used language on the Internet, after English and Chinese. However, Cyberspace has not been spared the crackdown of the hard-line conservatives. In 2004 several Iranian online journalists and web technicians were arrested. After months in solitary confinements, several of the web journalists went 'confessing' on TV, saying they were brainwashed by 'foreigners and counter-revolutionaries' into writing articles critical of Iran's Islamic Republic. Reporters Without Borders and Human Rights Watch, however, said the confessions were extracted under extreme duress from Iran's hard-line judiciary. The wave of arrests began early last fall. Shahram Rafizadeh, cultural editor of the daily *Etemad*, was arrested on 7 September. A day later, Hanif Mazrui, who wrote for several reformist newspapers and is the son of a former reformist Majles deputy, was also arrested. In all, seven Internet journalists were thrown behind bars. All had written articles critical of the establishment. Including non-journalists such as technicians, some twenty people were arrested in connection with independent or reformist websites, many of which have been blocked.

After being released on bail, a number of them published open letters expressing repentance and saying they had been 'treated well' in prison. But the case took an unexpected turn when some of the freed bloggers met judiciary chief Ayatollah Mahmoud Hashemi Shahroudi and told him the truth about the treatment they had received in prison. In April 2005, a judiciary spokesman announced that all but four of the arrested had been acquitted of their charges. He added that in some cases, the arrested had been treated 'in unlawful ways'. Ali Mazrui subsequently published an open letter, saying that the arrested had been subject to extreme psychological pressure and intimidation and forced to confess to baseless accusations.

In the words of Afshin Molavi, it is increasingly apparent that Iran's young are turning out a preachy government for an alternative world of personal web logs, private parties, movies, study, and dreams of emigrating to the West. While young Iranians of an earlier generation once revered Che Guevara and romanticized guerrilla movements, students on today's college campuses tend to shun politics and embrace practical goals such as getting a job or admission into a foreign graduate school. Some 150,000 Iranian professionals leave the country each year – one of the highest rates of brain drain in the Middle East.

'Iran today is at a turning point,' Molavi says. 'Either the Islamic Revolution must mellow and embrace political change, or face a reckoning down the road when hard-line clerics come into conflict with the secular, democratic ideals of the younger generation.'

'Of course, Iranians who feel that they were let down by the Khatami regime feel discouraged,' wrote Bernard Hourcade of the *Le*

Monde Diplomatique in 2004. 'Yet fundamental achievements must not be overlooked. During his two terms in office Khatami and his supporters have allowed new generations that had grown up with the Islamic Republic to learn about political debate and establish a balance of power at local level. This has been a difficult struggle, especially for women, but it has succeeded because the Khatami government has checked repression and developed the constitutional state.

'There is still a long way to go, but this period has enabled the ideas of republicanism, democracy and freedom of thought to become widely established in political and social practice, particularly in the provinces. The conditions are present for major change that will reposition political Islam.'

Hourcade observed that Iran is a country in which people debate, talk, express their views and protest, notwithstanding repression. 'Despite its best efforts,' he wrote, 'the theocracy that controls the justice system and police force is no longer able to control access to information or prevent demands being voiced. So repressive acts intended to make an example of people, especially journalists, may be increasingly violent and systematic, but they are also forcefully and effectively condemned, sometimes by members of the government.'[17]

Analysts have been quick to notice the change in the attitude of the Iranian youth. In the words of Jahangir Amuzegar, the government-encouraged baby boom of the early 1980s has now spawned a new generation, the Third Force, which sees neither the fundamentalists' concept of Velayat-e faqih nor Khatami's 'Islamic democracy' as the answer to Iran's current predicament.

'This highly politicised generation', writes Amuzegar, 'has no recollection of the 1979 Revolution and no particular reverence for the eight-year "holy war" between Iran and Iraq. Rather, they focus on their frustrated ambitions for a better future. This group includes almost everyone who is not in power and a few who are, representing a wide swath of Iranian society. The common bond among these disparate groups is their disenchantment with the revolution and its aftermath and their distrust of the clerics' ability to cope with Iran's many problems. The Third Force, although still lacking resolute leadership and a specific platform, is united by a common goal of an independent, free, and prosperous Iran blessed by the rule of law. Indeed, some members have proposed a new constitution separating mosque and state, to be established by an internationally observed referendum.'[18]

Along similar lines, many political analysts maintain that the confrontation between the reform movement and the conservative establishment that has dominated Iranian politics since Khatami's election in 1997 has reached a watershed. Mahan Abedin writes, 'The refusal of hard-line clerics who control the commanding heights of government to allow further reforms, coupled with President Mohammed Khatami's reluctance to confront the clerical establishment, has led some to predict the rise of a 'third force' in Iranian politics – the disaffected public, particularly the youth – and the eventual demise of the regime.'[19]

'One problem with this type of analysis,' Abedin adds, 'is that it ignores the essentially elitist nature of the reform movement and exaggerates grassroots pressures for reforms. This so-called 'third force' is too amorphous and fractured to buttress even the broadest reform coalition.'[20]

Besides being disorganised, certainly a lack of 'ideology' characterizes the younger generation of Iranians. In the words of Akbar Ganji, 'There is a drastic difference between the generation of 1970s and that of 1980s. More than half of the country's population was born after the 1979 Revolution. Their discourse and lifestyle is much different from the generation of the Revolution.'[21]

After Iraq invaded Iran in 1980, the founder of the Islamic republic, Ayatollah Khomeini, called on families to produce children for the defence of Islam and the Revolution. But, according to *The Guardian*'s Dan de Luce, 'instead of being disciples of the cause, the generation now coming of age poses a daunting challenge to the survival of his theocracy.'

'Unable to contain the vast youth population,' he wrote, 'the Iranian establishment has been forced to grant a limited degree of social freedom, allowing couples to hold hands on the street, spicing up programming on state television and permitting concerts and billiard halls ... The leadership hopes to follow China's example, easing social and economic restrictions while holding on firmly to power.'[22]

What most of the foreigners visiting Iran immediately notice is the 'fun seeking' tendency among large parts of the young generation.

'In the ski resorts, life is more free than the socially restricted cities, drawing criticism from conservative parts of the establishment,' wrote Angus McDowall of *The Independent*. 'Shemshak, the main resort town a 90-minute drive from Tehran, is known for illegal parties, where young men and women mix without supervision, drink alcohol and use drugs.

'Shemshak is as far from the traditional image of Iran as you can get. Girls wear hats and ski jackets instead of the regulation scarves and long manteaus. The resort appears a declared area of truce in the public morality battle being waged between the young and the conservative elements in Iran. Here, the talk is of foreign holidays, parties and expensive clothes.'[23]

Joyce Davis of *Mercury News* also saw a similar trend in Iran, writing that even young Iranians who care little about politics were rebelling against the society whose architect was Ayatollah Khomeini.

'Instead, many Iranian youth are intent these days on having fun,' she wrote. 'And their increasing defiance may represent the most potent challenge to one of the world's strictest Islamic societies.

'Two decades after their parents revolted against the excesses of the then-ruling shah's pageants and palaces, more young people in Iran are risking jail, fines and official beatings for things American youth take for granted: wearing make-up, slow dancing at a party and holding hands on a date.'[24]

Many statesmen of the Islamic Republic have in recent years come to acknowledge that the main concern of the youth is changing their lives and not conquering power. They oppose the theocracy because their quest for personal experience is blocked by its imposed restrictions. And since the reformists represented a more relaxed social atmosphere, they voted for Khatami and his fellow thinkers in 1997 and 1999. This, of course, applies to those who actually did take part in elections. Others found elections just a useless charade, with no practical impact on their lives, except that their votes might be used as a weapon for more repression.

Obvious as this may seem today, such a suggestion would have caused much uproar within both factions of the government until quite recently, for they both have embraced 'piety' as a central value. When Christiane Amanpour's 'Revolutionary Journey' – a programme that included footage of a private party in Tehran – was aired on CNN in 1999, both conservatives and reformists were furious.

'She unknowingly pictured Iran's reformist campaigns and struggles as a movement aspiring to reach such base and mundane goals as allowing the Iranians to hold parties in which boys and girls could mingle and dance and enabling the women to bare their heads and show their tresses,' wrote pro-reform journalist Dariush Sajjadi.

'Even though Amanpour's documentary chronicles a part of the reality permeating Iran today, it mistakenly takes this slice of the reality to represent the entirety of Iran's reformist movement.

'This is while the reformists have been the standard bearers of a relentless struggle against the conservatives to enshrine sublime ideals such as setting up a civil society, providing citizenry rights, fostering freedom of expression and thought, and promoting reason, realism, and divine reading and interpretation of religion,' he added.[25]

Such imaginary distinction between the 'carnal' and the 'sublime', the supposed contradiction between the 'sacred' and the 'profane' has long prevented an objective analysis of the social trends in Iran.

Ganji, one of the most daring of such 'standard bearers of reform', wrote from his prison cell in 2002 that although there is talk of an 'identity crisis' among the youth, the plain truth is that the young generation does not possess a unified identity; it welcomes diverse lifestyles. 'Jalal Al-e Ahmad or Dr Shariati are no longer their heroes; essentially their heroes are not political figures or ideologues at all ... The new generation knows movie stars, pop stars, sportsmen and Western thinkers much better than its own cultural and religious heritage ... The moral criteria of previous generations have crumbled, without being replaced by a new morality.'[26]

While the major gap in the political arena is one between autocracy and repression on the one hand and freedom and democracy on the other, for the young generation the chief demand is social liberties, Ganji said. Western music and films are more attractive to the youth than all political confrontations.

That is a point stressed by the proponents of an international referendum, in contrast to those who suggest changing the current constitution. The Islamic government vastly intervenes in most social and cultural activities, and even personal life, imposing all sorts of restrictions on people. State reformers seek to limit the political powers of the Velayat-e Faqih in the constitution, but they fail to propose a concrete idea of the state's relationship with social and cultural activities. A minimal state could no longer assume the function of exerting the Sharia, and thus, for instance, could no more intervene in such issues as making the Islamic dress code compulsory. In such a case, in Ganji's words, 'the jurisprudential dimensions of the Islamic Republic would be eliminated. And since the state will no more have the duty of implementing the Sharia, there would no more be any need for jurisprudents and Velayat-e Faqih.'

In *The Last Great Revolution* Ray Takeyh wrote that in the near future, Iran was unlikely to witness either revolutions or dramatic democratic breakthroughs. The appeal of the reform movement was in its promise to an economically hard-pressed and socially restive population that change was possible within the confines of the system. Indeed, one of the strengths of the Islamic Republic had been its accommodation of some of the demands of its constituents. Yet, the deepening economic crisis and the growing cultural demands of Iranian youths have outstripped the system's ability to be responsive. It is not apparent whether Iran's reformers will be able to make slow but consistent progress in translating their overwhelming popular support into liberalization of the theocracy.

> Should the hardliners succeed in completely obstructing reform, Iran may not see a revolution similar to the 1979 mass uprising, but rather a state that increasingly resembles the Soviet Union of the 1970s. As with the Soviet Union, Iran's hard-line clerics are poised to create a stagnant bureaucratic state infected with mass corruption, idly cloaking itself in stale revolutionary rhetoric of martyrdom and sacrifice that inspires no one. In such a situation, the electoral process will cease to be the venue for expression of popular will, as many will largely abandon the political arena. The alarming rise in drug addiction is an ominous indication of a young generation that is becoming not only disengaged from politics, but also disillusioned about life in the Islamic Republic. As such, Iran's dangerous impasse is threatening to produce a lost generation of Iranians in addition to extinguishing a once bold reform movement.[27]

It has been said by many Iranian historians that Iran's soil is not fit for reformist leaders, and that the errant iconoclasts of reformist and innovative thought are quickly killed or overthrown by a patriarchal, tribal, traditional culture that fails to appreciate their efforts. But 25 centuries of absolute and often despotic rule in Iran have bred a traditional, anti-authoritarian, and sometimes cynical political culture. With governments to be feared, the Iranian everyman would inevitably view politics as a dangerous game played by elites. In this light, it would seem to be asking too much of the Iranian youth to turn its back on its day-to-day life and embark on a spontaneous struggle for a cause that at best is ambiguous.

As Homa Katouzian has said, in Iran, both before and after Islam, the ruler was thought to be God's vicegerent on earth and, unlike Europe, his legitimacy was not dependent on the law of primogeniture.

> Thus he was not bound by any written or unwritten law or tradition and could take decisions up to the utmost of his God's Grace and somehow fall from power if he ruled unjustly, but there was no test either for possessing the grace or for losing it except by virtue of holding power or being overthrown. There were thus no rules for succession and rebels could and did claim legitimacy once they were successful. The position both justified and was justified by arbitrary rule, where long-term functional social classes did not exist and history became a series of connected short terms, a sociological phenomenon which still persists in Iranian society ...
>
> Absence of established rules and procedures for determining legitimacy and succession, and non-existence of aristocratic and other ruling classes which acted as the state's social base, were the chief causes of the insecurity of the position and the lives of rulers, princes of the blood, chief ministers and other high officials, since the latter's successful coups or rebellions would have been sufficient for the ruler to lose his power (usually together with his life) and be replaced by the leader of the coup or rebellion.
>
> 'These features were important aspects of the 'lack of continuity' observed in Iranian society, which, despite its long history, turned it into a 'short-term society' and its history into a series of 'connected short periods.'[28]

However, as Bernard Hourcade has noted, like most young people worldwide, young Iranians want to be part of a consumer society and have access to international culture, but they are also politicised. 'They know that having the right to vote at the age of fifteen empowers them. These children of Ayatollah Khomeini are not yet old enough to take power, but they have been well educated during the Khatami years and will continue to be so for the next five years. They can sharpen their ideas and translate them into political terms, to replace the apolitical, technocratic or Islamic elites clinging to power. That kind of transfer of power does not require a revolution; but it will still not be smooth.'[29]

In 1999, Ayatollah Abolqassem Khazali, an ultra-traditionalist cleric and at that time a member of the Guardian Council, said that the clergy's duty was 'to prevent young people from becoming preys to hell fire'. Shortly afterwards, I attended a Nowruz party in the house of a relative of mine named Hassan. Since Hassan was an employee at a 'revolutionary organisation', he kept a permanent beard. His wife, Fereshteh, however, did not observe the hejab other than in public. Nor did his daughter. They all prayed five times a day and fasted in Ramadan, though. On that day, more than a dozen family members had gathered to celebrate Nowruz. All had gathered round the TV set, which showed a performance of the Lambada dance via the VCR. Some of the men were drinking vodka. Soon after dinner, Los Angeles-made Persian pop music was played on the stereo, and most of the young, together with Hassan, Fereshteh, and their teenage daughter, started dancing. After the party was over, Hassan and his family dutifully said their prayers. Hassan told me: 'They want to drag us to heaven by chains. I don't want to go to their heaven. I'd rather to go to my own hell.'

Just after Ahmadinejad's election as Iran's new president in June 2005, a professor of human rights at the Kennedy School of Government at Harvard University visited Iran. He observed that in Persian culture, the taste for pleasure runs deep. 'Just think of the music-making, dancing and the costumed beauty of the men and women in classical Persian miniatures. During the Revolution, many of these Persian treasures were hacked off the walls of mosques and palaces by Shi'i zealots,' Michael Ignatieff wrote.[30]

Thankfully, Persian pleasure remains stubbornly alive. When I

flew south from Tehran to Isfahan, the astounding capital of the
Safavid shahs of the 17th century, I spent one night wandering
along the exquisitely lighted vaulted bridges, watching men, not
necessarily gay, stroll hand in hand, singing to each other and
dancing beneath the arches, while families picnicked on the grass
by the banks of the river and men and women passed a water pipe
around. Though it cannot be much comfort to those who have
to live, here and now, under public and private tyrannies, I came
away from a night in Isfahan believing that Persian pleasure, in
the long run, would outlast Shi'i puritanism.

Today's young generation, the so-called 'third force', seems to have
developed, undoubtedly as a result of official indoctrination as well as
owing to enjoying access to an up-to-date picture of the outside world,
features that may promise the final breaking of that closed orbit of the
past hundred years some time in the future. They do not subscribe to
any ideological dogma. They have lost faith in heroes. They have come
to despise violence. They value human life and its pleasures. They want
change, but not at any cost.

Childish as it may seem, they might as well be heading for childhood's
end.

Notes

Chapter 1

1. Dan De Luce, 'Anger Grows Among Children of Iran's 25-year-old Revolution', *The Guardian*, 9 February 2004.
2. Ben Barber, 'Shutting Down the Tehran Spring', *Salon.com*, 11 January, 2001.
3. Joyce M. Davis, 'Modern Teens Rebel Against Strict Society', *Mercury News*, winter 1999.
4. Angus McDowall, 'Drink, Drugs and Sex on the Slopes: the Secret World of Iranian Youth', *The Independent*, 8 May 2004.
5. Davar Sheikhavandi, interview with the author, 17 March 2001.
6. Sadeq Zibakalam, interview with the author, 10 May 2004.
7. Iran-Demographic Characteristics of Adolescents, UNESCO, 2000.
8. Ibid.
9. Nima Rashedan, interview with the author, 5 May 2004.
10. Ali Rabii, cited by Bill Samii, *RF/RL Iran Report*, 25 January 1999.
11. Sadeq Zibakalam, interview with the author, 10 May 2004.
12. Mohammad Qaed, interview with the author, 24 January 1999.
13. Reza Pahlavi, *Winds of Change*, Regnery Publishing, Washington DC, 2002, p. 41.
14. Ahmad Batebi, Letter to the Judiciary, 23 March 2000, translated by SMCCDI, Campaign to Free Iranian Students.
15. Iran-Demographic Characteristics of Adolescents, UNESCO, 2000.
16. Mohammad Qaed, interview with the author, 24 January 1999.
17. Sadeq Zibakalam, interview with the author, 10 May 2004.

Chapter 2

1. Omid Memarian, 'Javanan va Shiftegi-zodayi az Ghodrat' ('The Youth and Demystification of Power'), *Sharq*, 12 May 2004.
2. Elaine Sciolino, 'The Post-Khomeini Generation', *New York Times*, 1 November 1998.
3. *Salnameh-ye Amari-ye Keshvar* (*The Country's Statistical Yearbook*), Statistical Centre of Iran, 1997.
4. Ali Rashidi, interview with RFE/RL, May 2004.

5. *Salnameh-ye Amari-ye Keshvar* (*The Country's Statistical Yearbook*), Statistical Centre of Iran, 1997.
6. Nicholas D. Christof, 'Those Friendly Iranians', *New York Times*, 6 May 2004.
7. 'Enemies of the Internet', Reporters Sans Frontiers, 2004.
8. Ibid.
9. Ibid.
10. Muhammad Mehdi Gouya, interview with RFE/RL, April 2004.
11. Arash Alaei, interview with RFE/RL, April 2004.

Chapter 3
1. Ervand Abrahamian, *The Iranian Mojahedin*, Yale University Press, New Haven and London, 1989, p. 27.
2. Satyananda J. Gabriel, 'Class Analysis of the Iranian Revolution of 1979', edited by Gibson-Graham, Resnick, and Wolff, Duke University Press, 2001.
3. *Iran, A Country Study*, Federal Research Division, US Library of Congress.
4. 'Ayatollah Khomeini, Historic Personalities', Iran Chamber Society.
5. Ibid.
6. Ibid.
7. Ibid.
8. *Khaterat-e Alam* (*Alam Memoirs*), Ketab Sara Publishers, Tehran, p. 211.
9. *Iran, A Country Study*, Federal Research Division, US Library of Congress.
10. Ibid.
11. Ayatollah Ruhollah Mousavi Khomeini, *Hokumat-e Eslami: Velayat-e Faqih*, Tehran, 1970.
12. Mohsen Sazgara, interview with Deutsche Welle, cited by Peiknet, 14 March 2004.
13. Ibid.
14. *Iran, A Country Study*, Federal Research Division, US Library of Congress.
15. Ibid.
16. Ibid.
17. 'Dastan-e Enqelab, Part 1: Ayatollah Khomeini Returns', BBC Persian Service, February 2003.
18. Ibid.
19. Akbar Ganji, 'Manifest-e Jomhurikhahi' ('Manifesto of Republicanism'), Evin Prison, Tehran, April 2002, cited by Mihan.net.
20. Ibid.
21. *Iran, A Country Study*, Federal Research Division, US Library of Congress.
22. Ibid.
23. 'Dastan-e Enqelab, Part 1: Ayatollah Khomeini Returns', BBC Persian Service, February 2003.
24. Ibid.
25. Ibid.

Chapter 4
1. *Presbyterian Heritage*, Fall 2002, vol. 15, no. 3.

2. *Iran, A Country Study*, Federal Research Division, US Library of Congress.
3. Ahmad Salamatian, interview with RFE/RL, November 2003.
4. *Iran, A Country Study*, Federal Research Division, US Library of Congress.
5. Homa Katouzain, interview with RFE/RL, November 2003.
6. Shojaeddin Shafa, interview with RFE/RL, December 2003.
7. Mashallah Ajudani, interview with RFE/RL, December 2003.
8. Ali Behzadi, *Shebh-e Khaterat (Quasi-Memoirs)*, Zarrin Publishers, Tehran, 1997, p. 358.
9. Shojaeddin Shafa, interview with RFE/RL, December 2003.

Chapter 5
1. *Iran, A Country Study*, Federal Research Division, US Library of Congress.
2. Ahmad Salamatian, interview with RFE/RL, November 2003.
3. *Iran, A Country Study*, Federal Research Division, US Library of Congress.
4. Ali Behzadi, *Shebh-e Khaterat (Quasi-Memoirs)*, Zarrin Publishers, Tehran, 1997, p. 584.
5. Ibid, p. 452.
6. Ibid.
7. Homa Katouzian, *The Political Economy of Modern Iran, 1926–1979*, New York University Press, 1981, p. 181.
8. 'The Secret CIA History of the Iran Coup, 1953', National Security Archive Electronic Briefing Book no. 28, edited by Malcolm Byrne, updated 29 November 2000.
9. Ibid.
10. James Bill, 'United States and Iran: the Role of the Special Envoy', cited by Boardman Room of the Middle East Institute, 20 February 2004.
11. *Iran, A Country Study*, Federal Research Division, US Library of Congress.
12. Ibid.
13. Ibid.
14. Ibid.
15. Ervand Abrahamian, *The Iranian Mojahedin*, Yale University Press, New Haven and London, 1989, p. 112.
16. Ibid.
17. Saeed Hana'ee Kashani, interview with *RFE/RL*, 16 December 2003.
18. James Bill, 'United States and Iran: the Role of the Special Envoy', cited by Boardman Room of the Middle East Institute, 20 February 2004.
19. Shojaeddin Shafa, interview with RFE/RL, December 2003.
20. Reza Pahlavi, *Winds of Change*, Regnery Publishing, Washington DC, 2002, p. 11.

Chapter 6
1. Morteza Avini, cited by Shabakeh Khabar Daneshjui website.
2. *Iran, A Country Study*, Federal Research Division, US Library of Congress.
3. Ibid.
4. Ibid.

5. Robert C. Ode, 'Excerpts from an Iran Hostage's Diary', Jimmy Carter Library website.

6. Muhammad Quchani, *Nazziabadiha*, cited by Emadeddin Baqi, 28 December 2002.

7. Scott MacLeod and Azadeh Moaveni, 'Confronting the Dark Past', Time Europe Web Exclusive, 10 July 2000.

8. 'Changes in Iran, through the Eyes of a Hostage Taker', *Christian Science Monitor*, 10 February 1999.

Chapter 7

1. 'Changes in Iran, through the Eyes of a Hostage Taker', *Christian Science Monitor*, 10 February 1999.

2. Moojan Momen, *An Introduction to Shi'i Islam: The History and Doctrines of Twelver Shi'ism*, Yale University Press, New Haven and London, 1985.

3. *Iran, A Country Study*, Federal Research Division, US Library of Congress.

4. 'Enqelab-e Farhangi', Islamic Republic of Iran Broadcasting World Service.

5. Muhammad Maleki, 'Dosad Gofteh Chon Nim Kerdar Nist', cited by Gooya News, 2 May 2004.

6. Ibid.

7. Ervand Abrahamian, *The Iranian Mojahedin*, Yale University Press, New Haven and London, 1989, p.218.

8. Ibid.

9. Akbar Hashemi Rafsanjani, *Obour az Bohran* (*Passing the Crisis*), Tehran, 1998, pp. 163–6.

10. Ibid.

11. Muhammad Maleki, 'Dosad Gofteh Chon Nim Kerdar Nist', cited by *Gooya News*, 2 May 2004.

12. *Iran, A Country Study*, Federal Research Division, US Library of Congress.

13. 'Imam Khomeini's Life', Islamic Republic of Iran Broadcasting World Service.

14. Ibid.

15. A.Singleton, *Saddam's Private Army*, Iran Payvand Association, 2003, pp.112–3.

16. Ayatollah Hosseinali Montazeri, *Memoirs*, 2000.

17. Ibid.

18. Ibid.

19. Mr Hossein Mokhtar's Testimony, Mission for the Establishment of Human Rights in Iran, 1 September 2002.

20. 'The Final Years of Imam Khomeini's Life and the Sorrowful Events', IRIB World Service.

21. Ibid.

22. Ibib.

23. Ayatollah Hosseinali Montazeri, *Memoirs*, 2000.

24. Daniel Pipes, World and I, Daniel Pipes website, August 1989.

1. Lars Haugom, 'Towards Secularisation? Developments in the Islamic Republic of Iran after Khomeini', The Fourth Nordic Conference on Middle Eastern Studies: The Middle East in Globalising World, Oslo, 13–16 August 1998.

2. Anoushiravan Ehteshami, *After Khomeini: The Iranian Second Republic*, Routledge, 1995, p.146.

3. Jahangir Amuzegar , 'Iran's Economy and the US Sanctions', *The Middle East Journal*, Spring 1997, vol. 51, issue 2, pp. 185–99.

4. 'Rafsanjanis Are Iran's Power Brokers for Investors', Bloomberg News Feature, 21 April 2004.

5. Faezeh Hashemi, interview with the Asahi Shimbun, 6 February 1997, cited by zan.org.

6. Overview of Human Rights Developments in Iran, Human Rights Watch, 1997.

7. Ibid.

8. Jahangir Amuzegar , 'Iran's Economy and the US Sanctions', *The Middle East Journal*, Spring 1997, vol. 51, issue 2, pp. 185–99.

9. 'Rafsanjanis Are Iran's Power Brokers for Investors', Bloomberg News Feature, 21 April 2004.

10. Dariush Sajjadi, 'The Essence of the Power Mafia', 5 October 2000.

11. Ibid.

12. 'Overview of Human Rights Developments in Iran', Human Rights Watch, 1997.

13. Dariush Sajjadi, Ibid.

14. Robert Fisk, 'Murder by Decree', *The Independent*, 8 March 2000.

Chapter 9

1. Morteza Haji, interview with baztab.com, May 2004.

2. Ibid.

3. 'Tehran Spring', *The Nation*, 16 June 1997.

4. Mohsen Sazgara, interview with Deutsche Welle, cited by Peiknet, 14 March 2004.

5. Mahan Abedin, 'The Origins of Iran's Reformist Elite', *Middle East Intelligence Bulletin*, vol. 5, no. 4, April 2003.

6. Ibid.

7. Dariush Sajjadi, 'Middle East Insight', January 2000.

8. Nima Rashedan, interview with the author, 5 May 2004.

9. Ali Shakuri Rad, interview with rouydad.com, May 2004.

10. Scott Peterson, 'Ecstasy in Iran, Agony for the Clerics', *The Christian Science Monitor*, 5 December 1997.

11. 'Wrestling a Route to Peace', *Search for Common Ground*, February 1998.

12. Nahid Mousavi, 'A Review of the Serial Murders', *Zanan (Women)* Monthly, December 1999.

13. Ibid.

14. Akbar Ganji, 'Tarikkhaneh-ye Ashbah' ('The Dungeon of the Ghosts'), *Tarh-e Now*, Tehran, 1999, p. 394.

15. William A. Samii, *RFE/RL Iran Report*, September 27, 1999.
16. Ibid.
17. Overview of Human Rights Developments in Iran, *Human Rights Watch*, 1999.
18. Ibid.
19. 'Khatami's Huge Victory Stumps Rivals', *The Hindu Times*, 11 June 2001.
20. 'Khatami Victory Soured by Vigilantes', John Simpson, BBC, 10 June 2001.
21. Overview of Human Rights Developments in Iran, *Human Rights Watch*, 2001.
22. Hashem Aghajari, cited by Rouydad.com, May 2004.
23. Sadeq Zibakalam, interview with RFE/RL, May 2004.
24. Ahmad Sadri, 'The Iranian Reform Movement: On the Road to Success', MideastWeb, 16 December 2002.
25. Massoud Behnoud, 'Dovvom-e Khordad-e Sard' ('The Cold End of Khordad'), Gooya.com, 22 May 2004.

Chapter 10
1. Abbas Milani, 'Cracks in the Land of the Ayatollahs', *International Herald Tribune*, 17 June 2005.
2. Ibid.
3. William A. Samii, 'Iran: Do The Presidential Vote Numbers Really Add Up?', *RFE/RL Iran Report*, June 2005; William A. Samii, 'Iran: A New Paradigm and a New Math', *RFE/RL Iran Report*, July 2005.
4. William A. Samii, 'Iran: A New Paradigm and a New Math', *RFE/RL Iran Report*, July 2005.
5. Michael Ignatieff, 'Iranian Lessons', *New York Times Magazine*, 17 July 2005.
6. Muhammad Javad Rooh, 'Forsati Baraye Democracy' ('An Opportunity for Democracy'), *Rooydad*, 27 July 2005.
7. Ahmad Zaidabadi, 'Entekhab-e Iranian; Erja-e Mas'ouliyyat beh Saheban-e Ghodrat' ('The Choice of Iranians; Referring Responsibility to the Holders of Power'), *Emrouz*, 1 July 2005.
8. Michael Theodoulou, 'Iranian Women Gatecrash Team's World Cup Party', *New Scotsman*, 10 June 2005.
9. Abbas Milani, 'The Silver Lining in Iran', *International Herald Tribune*, 30 June 2005.
10. Ibid.
11. Michael Ignatieff, 'Iranian Lessons', *New York Times Magazine*, 17 July 2005.
12. Abbas Milani, 'The Silver Lining in Iran', *International Herald Tribune*, 30 June 2005.

Chapter 11
1. *Eqbal* daily newspaper, 29 May 2005.
2. SYNA News Agency, 29 May 2005.
3. Ebrahim Nabavi, 'Khatami, Ashkha va Labkhandha', cited by *Gooya News*, 23 May 2005.
4. Paul Hughes, 'Flirting Youths Outrage Iranian Hardliners', Reuters, 28 February 2005.

5. Ibid.
6. Pooneh Qoddoosi, 'Postcards from Iran: Tehran Party', BBC News, 13 February 13, 2004.
7. Ramin Mostaghim, 'Drug Abuse Among Youth Getting "Out of Control"', *IPS*, 25 June 2004.
8. Ibid.
9. Ibid.
10. Golnaz Esfandiari, 'Documentary Exposes Hidden Side of Iranian Society', *RFE/RL*, 25 March 2005.
11. Ibid.
12. Gooya News, 20 November 2004.
13. Farin Assemi, 'Sale of Kidneys in Iran', cited by *Reflex weekly*, 26 May 2005.
14. Ibid.
15. Jim Scuitto, 'Breathing Freely in Iran', ABC NEWS, 29 February 2004.
16. Ibid.
17. Bernard Hourcade, 'Iran: A Spring of Change', *Le Monde Diplomatique*, February 2004.
18. Jahangir Amuzegar, 'Iran's Crumbling Revolution', *Foreign Affairs*, January/February 2003.
19. Mahan Abedin, 'The Origins of Iran's Reformist Elite', *Middle East Intelligence Bulletin*, volume 5, no. 4, April 2003.
20. Ibid.
21. Akbar Ganji, 'Manifest-e Jomhurikhahi' ('Manifesto of Republicanism'), Evin Prison, Tehran, April 2002, cited by Mihan.net.
22. Dan De Luce, 'Anger Grows Among Children of Iran's 25-year-old Revolution', *The Guardian*, 9 February 2004.
23. Angus McDowall, 'Drink, Drugs and Sex on the Slopes: The Secret World of Iranian Youth', *The Independent*, 8 May 2004.
24. Joyce M. Davis, 'Modern Teens Rebel Against Strict Society', *Mercury News*, winter 1999.
25. Dariush Sajjadi, 'Illusion', 1 March 2000.
26. Akbar Ganji, 'Manifest-e Jomhurikhahi' ('Manifesto of Republicanism'), Evin Prison, Tehran, April 2002, cited by Mihan.net.
27. Ray Takeyh, 'Iran as Part of the Axis of Evil: Reforms Stagnate', (Part 1), *Policywatch*, 4 February 2002.
28. Homa Katouzian, 'Legitimacy and Succession in Iranian History', *Comparative Studies of South Asia, Africa and the Middle East*, 23:1 & 2, 2003.
29. Bernard Hourcade, 'Iran: A Spring of Change', *Le Monde Diplomatique*, February 2004.
30. Michael Ignatieff, 'Iranian Lessons', *New York Times Magazine*, 17 July 2005.

Select Bibliography

Abedin, Mahan. 'The Origins of Iran'sRreformist Elite', *Middle East Intelligence Bulletin*, volume 5, No. 4, Philadelphia, April 2003.

Abrahamian, Ervand. *Iran Between Two Revolutions,* Princeton University Press, Princeton, 1982.

Abrahamian, Ervand. *The Iranian Mojahedin*, Yale University Press, New Haven and London, 1989.

Alam, Amir Assadollah. *Khaterat-e Alam* (Alam's Memoirs), Ketab Sara Publishers, Tehran, 1999.

Amuzegar, Jahangir. *Iran's economy and the US sanctions*, The Middle East Journal, Washington, DC, Spring 1997.

Amuzegar, Jahangir. 'Iran's Crumbling Revolution', *Foreign Affairs*, New York, January/February 2003.

Barber, Ben. *Shutting down the Tehran Spring*, www.salon.com, 11 January 2001.

Behzadi, Ali. *Shebh-e Khaterat* (Quasi-Memoirs), Zarrin Publishers, Tehran, 1997.

Behnoud, Massoud. *Dovvom-e Khordad-e Sard*, (The Cold 2nd of Khordad), www.gooya.com, 22 May 2004.

Byrne, Malcolm (ed.). *The Secret CIA History of the Iran Coup, 1953*, National Security Archive Electronic Briefing Book No. 28, updated 29 November 2000.

Ehteshami, Anoushiravan. *After Khomeini: The Iranian Second Republic*, Routledge, Oxford, 1995.

Fuller, Graham E. *The 'Center of the Universe': The Geopolitics of Iran*, Rand Corporation Research Study, Westview, Philadelphia, 1991.

Ganji, Akbar. *Manifest-e Jomhurikhahi* (Manifesto of Republicanism), Tehran, April 2002.

Ganji, Akbar. *Tarikkhaneh-ye Ashbah* (The Dungeon of the Ghosts), Tarh-e Now, Tehran.

Gabriel, Satyananda J. *Class Analysis of the Iranian Revolution of 1979*, edited by Gibson-Graham, Resnick, and Wolff, Duke University Press, Durham, NC, 2001.

Hashemi Rafsanjani, Akbar *Obour az Bohran* (Passing the Crisis), Dafter-e Nashr-e Ma'aref-e Enghelab, Tehran, 1998.

Haugom, Lars. *Towards Secularisation? Developments in the Islamic Republic of Iran after Khomeini,* The Fourth Nordic Conference on Middle Eastern Studies: The Middle East in Globalising World, Oslo, 13–16 August 1998.

Human Rights Watch, *Overview of Human Rights Developments in Iran*, Human Rights Watch, New York, 1999.

Katouzian, Homa. 'Legitimacy and Succession in Iranian History', *Comparative Studies of South Asia*, Africa and the Middle East, Toronto, 2003.

Katouzian, Homa. *The Political Economy of Modern Iran: Despotism and Pseudo-Modernism, 1926–1979,* New York University Press, New York, 1981.

Kaviani, Hamid. *Dar Jostojoo-ye Mahfel-e Jenayatkaran* (In Search of the Murderers' Circle), Negah-e Emrooz, Tehran, 1999.

Khomeini, Ayatollah Ruhollah Mousavi. *Hokumat-e Eslami: Velayat-e Faqih* (The Islamic State: Governance of the jurisprudent), Tehran, 1970.

Lambton, Ann. A. K. S. *Qajar Persia: Eleven Studies,* University of Texas Press, Austin, 1988.

Metz, Helen Chapin (ed.). *Iran: A Country Study,* Washington: GPO for the Library of Congress, 1987.

Moaveni, Azadeh. *Lipstick Jihad: A Memoir of Growing Up Iranian in America and American in Iran,* PublicAffairs, New York, 2005.

Moin, Baqer. *Khomeini: Life of the Ayatollah*, St. Martin's Press, New York, 1991.

Molavi, Afshin. *Persian Pilgrimages: Journeys Across Iran,* W. W. Norton & Company, New York, 2002.

Momen, Moojan. *An Introduction to Shi'i Islam: The History and Doctrines of Twelver Shi'ism,* Yale University Press, New Haven and London, 1985.

Montazeri, Ayatollah Hosseinali. *Khaterat-e Ayatollah Montazeri* (Ayatollah Montazeri's Memoirs), www.montazeri.org, 2000.

Nouri, Abdollah. *Showkaran-e Eslah* (Hemlock of Reforms), Tarh-e Now, Tehran, 1999.

Ode, Robert C. *An Iran Hostage's Diary*, carter.library@nara.gov

Pahlavi, Reza. *Winds of Change,* Regnecy Publishing, Washington, DC, 2002.

Reporters Sans Frontières. *Enemies of the Internet*, Reporters Sans Frontières, Paris, 2004.

Rooh, Mohammad Javad. *Forsati Baraye Democracy* (An Opportunity for Democracy), www.rooydad.com, 27 July 2005.

Sajjadi, Dariush. *Mahiyyat-e Mafia-ye Ghodrat* (The Essence of the Power Mafia), www.geocities.com/dariushsajjadi, 5 October 2000 .

Samii, William A. 'Iran: Do The Presidential Vote Numbers Really Add Up?', *RFE/RL Iran Report*, June 2005.

Samii, William A. 'Iran: A New Paradigm and a New Math', *RFE/RL Iran Report*, July 2005.

Shawcross, William. *The Shah's Last Ride*, Touchstone, New York, 1988.

Singleton, A. *Saddam's Private Army: How Rajavi Changed Iran's Mojahedin from Armed Revolutionaries to an Armed Cult,* Iran Payvand Association, 2003.

Statistical Centre of Iran. *Salnameh-ye Amari-ye Keshvar* (The Country's Statistical Yearbook), Publications of Statisticasl Centre of Iran, Tehran, 2000.

Verhoeven, J. *Wrestling a Route to Peace,* Search for Common Ground, Washington DC, 1998.

Wright, Robin. *The Last Great Revolution: Turmoil and Transformation in Iran*, Random House, New York, 2000.

Zaidabadi, Ahmad. *Entekhab-e Iranian; Erja-e Mas'ouliyyat beh Saheban-e Ghodrat* (The Choice of Iranians; Referring Responsibility to the Holders of Power), www.emrouz.com, 1 July 2005.

Index